HIP SUBLIME

BEAT WRITERS AND THE CLASSICAL TRADITION

EDITED BY

SHEILA MURNAGHAN AND RALPH M. ROSEN

THE OHIO STATE UNIVERSITY PRESS
COLUMBUS

Library of Congress Cataloging-in-Publication Data

Names: Murnaghan, Sheila, 1951– editor. | Rosen, Ralph Mark, editor.

Title: Hip sublime : Beat writers and the classical tradition / edited by Sheila Murnaghan and Ralph M. Rosen.

Other titles: Classical memories/modern identities.

Description: Columbus : The Ohio State University Press, [2018] | Series: Classical memories/modern identities | Includes bibliographical references and index.

Identifiers: LCCN 2017052242 | ISBN 9780814213551 (cloth ; alk. paper) | ISBN 0814213553 (cloth ; alk. paper)

Subjects: LCSH: Beat generation. | Authors, American—20th century. | American literature—20th century—History and criticism. | Classical literature—Influence.

Classification: LCC PS228.B6 H57 2018 | DDC 810.9/0054—dc23

Cover design by Christian Fuenfhausen
Text design by Juliet Williams
Type set in Adobe Minion Pro and Futura

For Alisdair Gibson

CONTENTS

Acknowledgments vii

INTRODUCTION
Stephen Dickey, Sheila Murnaghan, and Ralph M. Rosen 1

CHAPTER 1 Beats Visiting Hell: *Katabasis* in Beat Literature
Stephen Dickey 15

CHAPTER 2 "Thalatta, Thalatta!": Xenophon, Joyce, and Kerouac
Christopher Gair 38

CHAPTER 3 "The Final Fix" and "The Transcendent Kingdom": The Quest in the Early Work of William S. Burroughs
Loni Reynolds 55

CHAPTER 4 The Invention of Sincerity: Allen Ginsberg and the Philology of the Margins
Matthew Pfaff 73

CHAPTER 5 Radical Brothers-in-Arms: Gaius and Hank at the Racetrack
Marguerite Johnson 97

CHAPTER 6 Riffing on Catullus: Robert Creeley's Poetics of Adultery
Nick Selby 116

CHAPTER 7 Sappho Comes to the Lower East Side: Ed Sanders, the Sixties Avant-Garde, and Fictions of Sappho
Jennie Skerl 138

CHAPTER 8 Robert Duncan and Pindar's Dance
Victoria Moul 160

CHAPTER 9 Kenneth Rexroth: Greek Anthologist
Gideon Nisbet 184

CHAPTER 10 Philip Whalen and the Classics: "A Walking Grove of Trees"
Jane Falk 210

CHAPTER 11 Troubling Classical and Buddhist Traditions in Diane di Prima's *Loba*
Nancy M. Grace and Tony Trigilio 226

CHAPTER 12 Towards a Post-Beat Poetics: Charles Olson's Localism and the Second Sophistic
Richard Fletcher 252

AFTERWORD "Standing at a Juncture of Planes"
Nancy M. Grace and Jennie Skerl 271

List of Contributors 277

Index 281

ACKNOWLEDGMENTS

This volume, which brings together for the first time classicists and specialists on writers of the Beat generation, is the result of several years of cross-disciplinary discussion and collaboration, and the editors are grateful to the many friends and colleagues who helped to make it possible. The project was originally the brainchild of Alisdair Gibson of the University of St Andrews, and we are pleased to acknowledge our debt to his vision and inspiration by dedicating the volume to him. For various forms of support, encouragement, and intellectual stimulation, we thank, in addition to our distinguished contributors, Kevin Batton, Netta Berlin, Renee Campbell, Michael Coyle, Cynthia Damon, Jim English, Al Filreis, William Lawlor, Jo Park, Bob Perelman, Jaap van der Bent, and Emily Wilson. Our work was generously funded by several Penn entities, the Department of Classical Studies, the Dean's Research Fund of the School of Arts and Sciences, the Provost's University Research Fund, and the Center for Ancient Studies, and additionally by the School of Classics of the University of St Andrews.

We are fortunate that, in our efforts to shape and frame the volume, we could draw on the expertise of Stephen Dickey, whose insights and deep knowledge enriched our introduction, and of Nancy Grace and Jennie Skerl, two leading Beat scholars whose splendid afterword considers our assorted essays from the perspective of Beat Studies. Throughout the process we have benefited from the advice and encouragement of our editors at The Ohio State University Press, Eugene O'Connor and Kristen Elias Rowley; from the support of the Series Editors, Paul Allen Miller and Richard H. Armstrong; and from the many valuable comments and suggestions of Dennis Trout and the press's other referee.

Credits

"the love poems of Catullus" from SIFTING THROUGH THE MADNESS FOR THE WORD, THE LINE, THE WAY: NEW POEMS by Charles Bukowski and edited by John Martin. Copyright ©2003 by Linda Lee Bukowski. Reprinted by Permission of HarperCollins Publishers.

Quotations from the works of Ed Sanders, reprinted by permission of the author.

"red up and down" from LOVE IS A DOG FROM HELL: POEMS 1974–1977 by Charles Bukowski. Copyright ©1977 by Charles Bukowski. Reprinted by Permission of HarperCollins Publishers.

Robert Creeley, "Stomping with Catullus," "The Whip," and "The Rain," from *The Collected Poems of Robert Creeley 1945–1975*. Copyright ©1962, 1979 by Robert Creeley. Reprinted with the permission of The Permissions Company, Inc., on behalf of the estate of Robert Creeley.

"A Poem Beginning with a Line by Pindar" by Robert Duncan, from THE OPENING OF THE FIELD. Copyright ©1960 by Robert Duncan. Reprinted by permission of New Directions Publishing Corp.

"Poetry, a Natural Thing" by Robert Duncan, from THE OPENING OF THE FIELD. Copyright ©1960 by Robert Duncan. Reprinted by permission of New Directions Publishing Corp.

"Under Ground" by Robert Duncan, from THE OPENING OF THE FIELD. Copyright ©1960 by Robert Duncan. Reprinted by permission of New Directions Publishing Corp.

"An Interlude" by Robert Duncan, from THE OPENING OF THE FIELD. Copyright ©1960 by Robert Duncan. Reprinted by permission of New Directions Publishing Corp.

"The Question" by Robert Duncan, from THE OPENING OF THE FIELD. Copyright ©1960 by Robert Duncan. Reprinted by permission of New Directions Publishing Corp.

"Such is the Sickness of Many a Good Thing" by Robert Duncan, from BENDING THE BOW. Copyright ©1968 by Robert Duncan. Reprinted by permission of New Directions Publishing Corp.

"At the Loom—Passages 2" by Robert Duncan, from BENDING THE BOW. Copyright ©1968 by Robert Duncan. Reprinted by permission of New Directions Publishing Corp.

"Bending the Bow" by Robert Duncan, from BENDING THE BOW. Copyright ©1968 by Robert Duncan. Reprinted by permission of New Directions Publishing Corp.

"Let Him Drink from the Fountain" by Robert Duncan, from GROUND WORK: BEFORE THE WAR. Copyright ©1968, 1969, 1970, 1971, 1972,

1974, 1975, 1976, 1977, 1978, 1979, 1980, 1981, 1982, 1983, 1984, 1985, 1987, 1988 by Robert Duncan. Reprinted by permission of New Directions Publishing Corp.

"A Set of Romantic Hymns" by Robert Duncan, from ROOTS AND BRANCHES. Copyright ©1964 by Robert Duncan. Reprinted by permission of New Directions Publishing Corp.

Excerpts from "Duncan" from BOSS CUPID by Thom Gunn. Copyright ©2000 by Thom Gunn. Reprinted by Permission of Farrar, Straus and Giroux.

Poems from the Greek Anthology: Translated by Kenneth Rexroth. Copyright ©1962, 1999 by the University of Michigan. Reprinted by permission of the University of Michigan Press.

"The Slop Barrel," "Since You Ask Me," "Treading More Water," "Translation of a Lost Play by MM," "Gradus ad Parnassum," "To My Muse," "M," "Hymnus ad Patrem Sinensis," "Sourdough Mountain Lookout," "With Compliments to EH," "The Education Continues Along," "The Greeks," "The Best of It," "Minor Moralia," "Scenes of Life at the Capital" by Philip Whalen. Reprinted by courtesy of the Estate of Philip Whalen.

Charles Olson at Goddard College, April 12–14, 1962. Copyright ©2011 by Kyle Schlesinger. Reprinted by permission of Kyle Schlesinger.

"A Later Note on Letter # 15" by Charles Olson, from THE MAXIMUS POEMS. Works by Charles Olson published during his lifetime are held in copyright by the Estate of Charles Olson. Used with permission.

"The Kingfishers" by Charles Olson, from THE COLLECTED POEMS OF CHARLES OLSON. Copyright ©1987 by the Estate of Charles Olson. Reprinted by Permission of the University of California Press.

"Letter to Elaine Feinstein" by Charles Olson, from COLLECTED PROSE OF CHARLES OLSON. Copyright ©1987 by the Estate of Charles Olson. Reprinted by Permission of the University of California Press.

INTRODUCTION

STEPHEN DICKEY,
SHEILA MURNAGHAN,
AND RALPH M. ROSEN

This collection of essays explores for the first time a rich, often paradoxical confluence of literary traditions in twentieth-century America: the intersections between Beat writers of the post–World War II decades and the classical tradition. Beat writers—or "the Beats" as they are sometimes loosely called—hardly constitute a group with a monolithic aesthetic or literary agenda, yet all of them were responding to the same nexus of cultural forces. In the wake of World War II, values were being vigorously challenged in every sphere. Throughout the arts, the burdens of older forms and generic constraints gave way, sometimes quite abruptly, to modes that stressed instead the "nowness" of the present moment and a future that didn't need a past except as something not to repeat. At the same time, the Beats were inescapably formed by their own education and inspired by writers across a long Western, and increasingly Eastern, tradition. What is more, in their continual attempt to transcend what they perceived as the commercialism, superficiality, and overall precariousness of life in the post–World War II era, they were often reaching for exactly the kind of stability and continuity that they thought they were casting off.

In such moments, it was classical authors who provided, on the one hand, a discourse of sublimity to help some Beats articulate their desire for a purity of experience, and, on the other, a venerable literary tradition that attracted them precisely because of its uncanny ability to be as "hip" as it was "square."[1]

1. Such a paradox, for example, underlies the description of the poet Allen Ginsberg (as the character Alvah Goldbook) as a "hornrimmed intellectual hepcat with wild black hair" in

Cross-country Odyssean journeys, a timeless sublime in the landscape of the American West, hipster lotus-eaters in smoky jazz clubs and bohemian cafés, underworld descents into urban infernos, or exhilarating experiments in Catullan erotics—these are just a few of the classically infused topoi that surfaced in the work of many Beats, shaping a generation of writers who saw themselves as pioneers in a quest for spiritual and aesthetic freedom within a world of conventionality and pragmatism. While the Beats' debt to romanticism, in both its English and American forms, has been well established by literary scholars, their debts to classicism have not—a striking critical imbalance that this collection seeks to correct.

A few of these authors—notably Jack Kerouac, Allen Ginsberg, Gregory Corso, and William S. Burroughs—have by now attained canonical status and are generally taken as defining the Beat movement. But these figures hardly tell the whole story of a "migratory . . . international avant-garde" (Grace and Skerl 2012, 1), "a loosely affiliated arts community . . . encompass[ing] two or three generations of writers, artists, activists, and non-conformists" (Skerl 2004, 2).[2] This collection aims to show the impact of classical literature and myth on a broad range of mid-century experimentalists. The most famous Beats, including Kerouac, Ginsberg, Burroughs, and Philip Whalen, are discussed alongside less well-known but important figures such as Robert Duncan, Ed Sanders, and Kenneth Rexroth. Attention is also paid to writers who did not identify themselves straightforwardly as Beats but were allied through a similar sensibility—such as Charles Bukowski and Robert Creeley—or were themselves influenced by the Beats—such as Charles Olson, a self-described "post-Beat" writer whose compositional theories and practices were, in turn, influential upon the Beats. An essay on Diane di Prima addresses the often-overlooked role of women writers among the Beats.

Our aim is to counter prevailing misconceptions about the Beats through a fuller and more nuanced account of the movement. The literary-historical narrative constructed around the most widely recognized Beats has, until quite recently at least, been misleadingly one-dimensional, and often more concerned with the glamorously self-destructive features of their lives than with analysis of their work. Even as the generation passes, and more and more archival material such as letters, drafts, and unpublished manuscripts

---

Jack Kerouac's *The Dharma Bums* (1958, 11), in a scene that describes the famous reading at the 6 Gallery in San Francisco in 1955 where Ginsberg first publicly presented "Howl." The narrator of that passage, Ray Smith, also singles out other poets at the reading for their "square" demeanor in a hip setting. See chapter 9 below for more on this event, which was to become a foundational moment in Beat mythology.

2. For more on the problem of defining the Beats, see the afterword to this volume.

becomes accessible, the conceptualization of the Beats in our own era remains coalesced around post-1960s aesthetics and tends to stress the manic, freewheeling side of their work to the exclusion of their achievements as practitioners of a disciplined craft in dialogue with past traditions.

Ginsberg, in particular, did his part to encourage such an approach, evolving along with the culture of the 1960s from 1940s hipster to psychedelic guru of "peace and love." The "beat-itude" Kerouac had once craved and romanticized came to seem, by the time of his death in 1969, naïve and adolescent next to Burroughs's rigorously avant-garde satirical program, Gregory Corso's intuitively surrealist syncretism, and Ginsberg's peculiar blend of quasi-mystical "orientalism" with a leftist politics of liberation. Missing from this account, moreover, is an entire array of important figures who never became celebrities, but who fill out the complex picture of this vibrant movement—modernists like Kenneth Rexroth who immediately preceded and overlapped with the Beats, shaping the Beat sensibility with a similar cry to "make it new," and the generation of writers who came of age after World War II and made their mark in the 1960s as a kind of second wave of Beat—Gary Snyder, Ed Sanders, and Michael McClure, for example. Added to the mix are the academics at Columbia in the 1940s who brought to the restless, impressionable minds of Ginsberg, Kerouac, and the rest of their literary coterie a sense of literary tradition and form, which those writers absorbed even as they bristled against it.

That bristling looms large in any construction of the Beats' legacy, as when the social activist Abbie Hoffman summed up the appeal of the Beats to younger writers like himself through a sweeping denunciation of canonical figures from the ancient tragedians to Robert Frost: "Who gives a fuck which ancient Greek stabbed which ancient Greek in the back, or how many poems do you want to hear about 'I'm walking along a country road, staring at a wall'?"[3] But a closer look at the Beats' own writing reveals that they were just as likely to see the ancient past as offering a telling contrast to the sordid present. In "Call For Aga-Memnon," a 1948 poem by John Clellon Holmes, author of influential early definitions of the Beat movement, the speaker asks, "Where is the era's truly tragic man / who understood why he was ground to dust, / and knew the Furies' ague while he ran?" (1–3). For Holmes, in post–World War II America, "No man seeks to avoid his curse: / none are compelled except in morbid mental grooves / no Athens ran in" (7–9). Dismissals like Hoffman's are countered by a readiness to draw upon classical culture, whether simply to take the measure of the modern world or to reinvigorate it,

3. In an interview filmed in 1982 during the ten-day "On the Road" Conference in Boulder, Colorado, which celebrated the first quarter century of Kerouac's novel.

as examples drawn from two central figures of the Beat generation will illustrate. In the case of Gregory Corso, a career-long fascination with the origins of Western culture shows how fully engaged the Beats could be with the classical past. In the case of Lawrence Ferlinghetti, a single poem demonstrates the allusive complexity that can result from an appropriation of classical material that is inevitably mediated by other literary periods, chiefly romanticism and modernism.

Gregory Corso—honored by Ginsberg as "great Orpheus of these States" (1985, 17)—is probably the most frequent and explicit of all the Beats in his references to classical lore, whether despite or because of the fact that he was the least formally educated. His reading of classical texts began at New York's Clinton State Prison and continued when he moved to Cambridge, where he illicitly audited courses at Harvard and spent hours in the Widener Reading Room. Much later, as a teacher at the Naropa Institute summer session of 1977, Corso included *Gilgamesh* on his syllabus, explaining: "*Gilgamesh* was the first thing written down. You know why it's important to me? Because I like to go back to the sources" (quoted in Olson 2002, 75).

Eclectic to the point of surrealism, Corso's verse has frequent recourse to classical allusion, especially in his earlier volumes (published between 1958 and 1962) and often in the service of establishing a temporal and rhetorical continuum between ancient and modern. In his second collection, *Gasoline* (1958), among references to Neptune, Pan, Penthesilea, and Mimnermus, Corso begins to treat the classical past as something more than a repository of fragmentary allusions, like scattered stones at the site of an ancient temple. "In the Fleeting Hand of Time" presents the poet reflecting upon his birth not as a beginning but as a time of decision:

> Born March 26 1930 I am led 100 mph o'er the vast market of choice
> what to choose? what to choose?
> O — — — and I leave my orange room of myth
> no chance to lock away my toys of Zeus
> I choose the room of Bleecker Street
> A baby mother stuffs my mouth with a pale Milanese breast
> I suck I struggle I cry O Olympian mother
> unfamiliar this breast to me. . . .
> (17–24)

Unlike Wordsworth's newborn who forgets what he has known, the infant Corso comes into the world trailing clouds of Greek mythology which, inevitably, begin to fade when "Time leads [him] into conditional life" (41) and thus "profanely I shed my Hermean wings. . . . I discard my lyre of Orphic futility (29, 34)."[4]

In several poems from *The Happy Birthday of Death* (1960), however, the allusions thicken into a portrait of the artist as a young classicist who studiously recovers that lost birthright. In "Clown," for example, the poet welcomes a new season:

> Spring!
> Good to go to the East River
> and sit before Brooklyn
>   with fresh knowledge of Hesiod on farming;
> good to be intent on Alcman's *Maiden Song*;
> sit good for hours re-learning
>   the craft of classical verse —
> Welcome Epinikian ode!
> (6.21–28)

And in one of Corso's best-known poems, "Marriage," the prospective bridegroom imagines future collisions between bourgeois familial expectations and his private, antiquarian, and decidedly idiosyncratic sensibility:

> Yet if I should get married and it's Connecticut and snow
> and she gives birth to a child and I am sleepless, worn,
> up for nights, head bowed against a quiet window, the past behind me,
> finding myself in the most common of situations a trembling man
> knowledged with responsibility not twig-smear nor Roman coin soup—
> O what would that be like!
> Surely I'd give it for a nipple a rubber Tacitus
> For a rattle a bag of broken Bach records
> Tack Della Francesca all over its crib
> Sew the Greek alphabet on its bib
> And build for its playpen a roofless Parthenon
> (68–78)

The second part of this stanza stands out not just because it emulates traditional "square" poetic typography by capitalizing every line, nor for its pro-

4. The consistency of Corso's reliance on this vocabulary of ancient myth is apparent when he revisits an image from this poem in "Return," from his later volume *Herald of the Autochthonic Spirit* (1981): "The days of my poems/were unlimited joys / of blue Phoenician sails / and Zeusian toys" (1–4).

phetic mockery of future Baby Einstein fads, but because it playfully envisions the Beat artist—or perhaps any artist—as the inheritor of diverse aesthetic traditions, traditions he will hand on to his offspring, genetic or artistic. (It may also record the first pacifier pun in literature: reading Tacitus may not, realistically, calm a squalling child, but what better name to encourage silence?)

Questions of modernity's claim on the classical arise for the artist as well as the parent. "Is it for me to wipe my dirty pickle hands on the plektron?" (107) asks Corso in "Greece," a poem from 1960 responding, in part, to his recent travels in that country. The question is not merely rhetorical, and the poem continues to worry the matter of influence and originality, of the urgent "nowness" of then versus the immediate historical moment of the speaker—

Is this my song? Do I forget my New York City subway
    and rooftop sleep
But the sight of ecru-shredded Nike coiled in moonmarbled
    snow
her rippling gown her ever-loosened sandal seen
    in my 17th year
is more to me than the sight of the subways hurtling
against the rooftops or the sad meaning of Times Square
(Corso 1962, 112–19)

—before concluding with an assertion that the poet's chief obligation to the past is to carry it onward. Clearly, though, there is tension as well as continuity between past and present, and Corso's poems articulate an ambivalence toward antiquity that declares its obsolescence even as it admits its influence:[5]

Hear me hear
        the once Grecian
Grecian no more
        charged with rusty minutest liberty
          kingdoms dust at her victory
I've new delight—and eternally toward delight
        I've a possession to assume
          to bestow
(223–30)

5. For an obverse instance of Beat ambivalence to the usefulness of classical models, or more generally of the modern inferiority complex before ancient art, consider Kerouac's unpublished "Reflections on *Ulysses* of James Joyce," which concludes that Joyce's use of Homer's *Odyssey* shows a kind of authorial weakness. Joyce "is not quite sure of the nobility of his theme" or, indeed, "of the nobility of Ireland and Irishm[e]n" (quoted in Gewirtz, 2007, 28–29). Unlike Corso, Kerouac asks, in effect, why Joyce should even want to use a *plektron*.

But to assume a possession is, in the end, to bestow it again—just as not locking away the toys of Zeus means that others, too, can play with them—and the essays in this volume make clear how thoroughly the Beats absorbed the Classics in ways large and small, respectful of their mutual distance but eager to converse informally, thereby transforming the legacy they claimed.[6]

"Sailing thru the straits of Demos" are the opening words of the second poem of Lawrence Ferlinghetti's best-known collection, *A Coney Island of the Mind* (1958), a volume direct and plentiful in its references to canonical writers and artists. As the poem quickly makes clear, the straits of Demos are not Greek waterways but rather the American people, through whom the poem takes an Odyssean journey while satirically reconfiguring epic motifs into some of the more vulgar and ridiculous features of U.S. political conventions and campaigns. Upon the promise of "Free Elections" (25), however, the last third of the poem acquires a darker, more nuanced tone:

> So that
> we set up mast and sail
> on that swart ship once more
> and so set forth once more
> forth upon the gobbly sea
> loaded with liberated vestal virgins
> and discus throwers reading Walden
> but
> shortly after reaching
> the strange suburban shores
> of that great American
> demi-democracy
> looked at each other
> with a mild surprise
> silent upon a peak
> in Darien
>
> (26–41)

This passage begins with the last two words of Ezra Pound's *Canto 1* ([1925] 1973)—"So that"—before returning to its first lines:

6. In a parallel instance, Corso twice mentions having written "a play, my first, about 12 pages, *Sarpedon*, 1954, in verse" before summing up the complex ratio of debt and innovation that is in a general way the theme of this volume of essays. The play, writes Corso to his publisher James Laughlin, is "an attempt to replicate Euripides, though the whole shot be an original." See Morgan 2003, 405.

And then went down to the ship,
Set keel to breakers, forth on the godly sea, and
We set up mast and sail on that swart ship[7]

Ferlinghetti's rearrangement of these phrases advertises rather than conceals the debt to Pound, even as he adds the crucial, and now explicitly self-referential phrase "once more," and again "once more," to leave no doubt about the repetition compulsion of his own poem. Yet as *Canto 1* will reveal at its conclusion, it too is an act of iteration via Pound's rendering of Andreas Divus's 1538 Latin translation of Homer's *Odyssey.* Ferlinghetti has repeated the gesture "once more," while indeed compounding the debt as he steers the poem to its allusive anticlimax where "we" the people

looked at each other
with a mild surprise
silent upon a peak
in Darien

Just as the absurd "gobbly" jests with Pound's "godly" sea, so, more subtly, these lines recast the end of a poem by John Keats in which the poet describes a moment of literary epiphany in heroic terms:

Then felt I like some watcher of the skies
When a new planet swims into his ken;
Or like stout Cortez when with eagle eyes
He star'd at the Pacific—and all his men
Look'd at each other with a wild surmise—
Silent, upon a peak in Darien.
(9–14)

This passage, of course, is the sestet concluding Keats's sonnet, "On First Looking into Chapman's Homer" (1816), celebrating the sense of discovery granted him by George Chapman's translations (first published incrementally over the years 1598–1616). The local effects gained by Ferlinghetti's transformation of "wild surmise" into "mild surprise"—and the implication that "Darien" is no longer Darién, a province in Panama, but an unaccented town in Connecticut (the bland terrain of Corso's projected marriage)—serve his poem's wry diminuendo. But the deeper effect occurs within the literary subplot of the

7. "So that" is itself an allusion to Browning's "Sordello," a major influence on the following Cantos.

poem, where the complex play of Homeric allusion warps and twists through endless translations and echoes. Ferlinghetti quotes Pound translating Divus translating Homer, then summons Keats to witness Chapman's Englishing of the epic poet.

All roads, all voyages, lead to Homer, evidently. The recursive pattern of epic references in Ferlinghetti's mock-epic poem epitomizes the Beats' appropriation of a usable classical past—one that cannot be, and could never have been, reached directly but only grasped at through a series of precedent acts of allusion and response that chart a course back through other vernacular transformations and new world explorations. Fittingly for this metapoetic theme, the nautical preparations quoted from Homer are those of Odysseus when preparing for his journey to the underworld (*Od.* 11.1–3). If epic heroes speak with the dead, perhaps it is fair to say that allusions do as well, speaking not just with the dead, but for and as the dead. And although the political satire of "Sailing thru the straits of Demos" is broad and obvious, the Attic made antic, the end of the poem turns to a subtler and sharper purpose, for if we follow the thread of Homeric allusion to its logical end, the satire is indeed deadly: "the strange suburban shores" of America are nothing other than entrances to the Underworld.

As they investigate further encounters between Beat writers and the classics, the essays that follow sketch out a vision of antiquity in which the classical past emerges as an alternative—sometimes inspiring, sometimes dispiriting—to a debased present and as the home of an eclectic array of proto-Beat soul mates. This past is accessed, not only through the canonical authors of the Great Books curriculum, but through assorted intermediaries, including Walt Whitman, James Joyce, and H.D.,[8] and Western classical traditions are frequently combined with those of the East—a synthesis that the Beats were instrumental in promoting.

The combined influence of the Great Books tradition and the Beats' more immediate literary precursors—authors who had integrated aspects of the classical canon into their own modernist projects—left its mark even where overt references to classical sources, such as we have seen in the poems of Corso and Ferlinghetti, are absent. As Christopher Gair observes in his discussion of Kerouac's debt to Xenophon via Joyce, more mediated references, "filtered through at least one other narrative" are "significant as a kind of classical unconscious that highlights important formal continuities across Western literature" (42). Burroughs, for example, as Reynolds discusses in her chapter on his early novels, shows little interest in directly engaging with Clas-

8. On the integral role of intermediaries in classical reception, see Martindale 2013, 172.

sical authors, yet his plots follow archetypal quest patterns that have become indelibly associated in Western culture with the Homeric *Odyssey.*

As Nancy Grace and Jennie Skerl point out in their afterword to this volume, a number of Beat writers were drawn to the "mythical method" exemplified by Joyce's *Ulysses.* Dorothy Van Ghent's observation in a seminal 1959 article that the Beats could claim a "myth" that followed "authentic archaic lines" gets at this looser, but no less powerful, form of classicism.[9] And Richard Fletcher's account of how Charles Olson identified a significant precursor in Maximus of Tyre, an author whose actual work he found boring and difficult to read, is a reminder that classical influence takes many forms. A modern writer may be responding to ancient figures and cultural practices, or to a broad conception of the classical, rather than to a particular ancient text. In the variety and eclecticism of their dealings with antiquity, as well as in their resistance to the idea of an elite, authoritative cultural standard, the Beats anticipate the critical concerns that have made "The Classical Tradition" an increasingly contested term among classicists—no longer viewed as straightforward and self-evident and now often replaced by "Classical Reception."[10]

As we have seen with Ferlinghetti, Homeric epic, and especially the *Odyssey,* was a primary source of inspiration, not only for its mythic motifs of exile, uncharted travel, and descent to the underworld but also as a model for new forms of compositional freedom. The twentieth-century discovery of Homer as an oral poet made him an apt prototype for the modern bard who seeks to speak with spontaneity and performative immediacy. We can perhaps see the unbroken speech of the ancient poet behind the continuous scroll on which Kerouac typed *On the Road.* Ginsberg's complementary adages—"First thought best thought" (from Kerouac) and "Mind is shapely, Art is shapely" (*Cosmopolitan Greetings*)—together suggest that such spontaneity is both genuine and always conditioned by practice, by the artist's absorption of past models and forms that have shaped the newly creative mind.[11]

---

9. See Dickey's essay, chapter 1, 15–18, for further discussion of Van Ghent's essay outlining the Beats' particular version of the mythical hero—at once idiosyncratic, universal, and firmly embedded in the Western tradition.

10. On the stakes involved in the choice of "Classical Reception" over "Classical Tradition," see Hardwick 2003, 1–11; on the ongoing utility of the term "tradition," see Budelmann and Haubold 2010.

11. Burroughs's Dadaesque experiments with cut-ups and fold-ins could be said to furnish a textual parallel to this creative process, as he recycles and modifies preexisting materials, juxtaposing inherited images, recordings, and words to "make it new," if only phenomenologically, for the reader, now jarred out of stock responses into a fresh awareness of the textual artifact as something simultaneously derivative and original.

The first three essays in the volume trace the Beats' redirection of the epic journey across mid-twentieth-century landscapes. Stephen Dickey ("Beats Visiting Hell: *Katabasis* in Beat Literature") shows how the Beats drew upon the already allusive tradition of epic journeys to and from the dead by such heroes as Odysseus, Aeneas, and Dante the Pilgrim to dramatize their own relationships with their literary predecessors. Examples include Allen Ginsberg's "Howl," which maps its tour of postwar America upon a Dantean cosmos, and "A Supermarket in California," which elegiacally revises the geography of the classical underworld as it depicts Ginsberg's encounter with the shade of Whitman. Jack Kerouac's very titles *Orpheus Emerged* and *The Subterraneans* imply katabatic themes, especially as the latter tells its "history of the hip or beat . . . or subterranean generation," whose members leave their apartments on Heavenly Lane to see films like Kurosawa's *The Lower Depths* before drinking at Dante's Bar. Dickey argues that these katabatic motifs were ultimately figured by Beat writers as moments of literary renewal and inspiration.

Christopher Gair ("'Thalatta, Thalatta!': Xenophon, Joyce and Kerouac") pursues a different epic genealogy to a bleaker conclusion. He takes Kerouac's invocation in *Doctor Sax* of the famous cry "Thalatta, Thalatta!" from Xenophon's *Anabasis* as a focal point for defining Kerouac's "Greek Beat aesthetic"—a vision that blends the epic journeying and revolutionary philhellenism associated with both Xenophon and modern Greek history with the modernist outlook of Joyce, whose quotation of the phrase in the opening pages of *Ulysses* was most likely Kerouac's source. Gair shows how, over the course of Kerouac's career, the sea itself evolves from the end point of a liberating journey in *On the Road* to the corrupted milieu of a jaded and alienated protagonist in *Big Sur.*

Loni Reynolds ("'The Final Fix' and 'The Transcendent Kingdom Boon': The Quest in the Early Work of William S. Burroughs") identifies the epic journey, not as a set of specific allusions, but as a governing paradigm in Burroughs's early works (*Junky, Queer, The Yage Letters,* and *Naked Lunch*), where archetypes of myth and quest coexist with transgressive, avant-garde themes. Burroughs's surprising debt to traditional sources—inexplicit or unconscious as it often was—grounds his experimental style in a sturdy framework, even as he deviates from and reshapes this trope to question whether the classical goals of unity and fulfilment can be found within the fragmentation of the modern world.

The next group of essays explores the Beats' attraction to a very different classical source, the poetry of Catullus, with its transgressive sexual content, satiric bite, and autobiographical stance. As Matthew Pfaff ("The Invention of

Sincerity: Allen Ginsberg and the Philology of the Margins") shows, it was by engaging with Catullus's work that Allen Ginsberg was able to counter and critique what he saw as the co-optation of the classics by a cultural mainstream that was essentialist and fundamentally straight, white, and male. Ginsberg's reading of Catullus ultimately allowed him to detach the idea of classicism from the Greek and Latin canon and transpose its authority to alternative social identities and cultural traditions, including those of the East.

Marguerite Johnson ("Radical Brothers-in-arms: Gaius and Hank at the Racetrack") analyses Charles Bukowski's close and complicated relationship to Catullus's poetry through the model of Catullus's own relationship to his "comites" (companions, tent-mates, brothers-in-arms) Furius and Aurelius, who are at once his companions, his rivals, and the objects of his vengeful mockery. Through allusion, imitation, and parody, Bukowski embraces Catullus as a like-minded precursor in a form of poetic invective that gives voice to feelings of social marginalization and disempowerment and a defensive masculine rage against promiscuous, rejecting women.

For Robert Creeley, as Nick Selby shows ("Riffing on Catullus: Robert Creeley's Poetics of Adultery"), Catullus was notably a poet who worked in a demanding metrical form and so, in that way, a master of the "beat." But the formal challenges of recreating Catullus's poetry in English were echoed in its subject matter, especially given the context in which Creeley's poem "Stomping with Catullus" was composed (as a bitter and ironic counter to his former friend Paul Carroll's translations of Catullus; the two had a falling out in 1954 over a domestic squabble). For Creeley, as Selby argues, the issues of domestic breakup, poetic rivalry, restless dissatisfaction, and questionable fidelity all coalesce in his act of translating Catullus.

The next group of papers returns to the Greeks and to the affiliations established by a diverse set of Beat and Beat-related poets with particular lyric and epigrammatic writers. Jennie Skerl ("Sappho Comes to the Lower East Side: Ed Sanders, the Sixties Avant-Garde, and Fictions of Sappho") considers the appropriation of Sappho by Ed Sanders, one of the major poetic voices of the sixties counterculture and deeply influenced by the Beat aesthetic—we might call him "post-Beat." *Tales of Beatnik Glory* is Sanders's fictionalized memorial to the Lower East Side avant-garde after its demise. The climax of volume two is "Sappho on East Seventh," in which Sappho appears in a vision to an aspiring bohemian poet, performing the role of poetic mentor, muse, heterosexual partner, teacher, and spirit guide. Sanders foregrounds the countercultural and protofeminist aspects of Sappho's poetry, Skerl argues, and reimagines her as a critic of patriarchal society—both our own and that of ancient Greece.

Victoria Moul ("Robert Duncan and Pindar's Dance") offers a close analysis of Robert Duncan's "A Poem Beginning with a Line by Pindar," which reveals the depth, consistency, and structural importance of Pindarism to Duncan's poetic project. His attraction to, and deployment of, key Pindaric motifs—the dance, the lyre, the bow, the loom—are founded on an appreciation of their productive richness as aesthetic metaphors, as images of a mode of art that is at once something we admire (watch, listen to, read) and something that we (readers or audience as well as writers) create and do.

Kenneth Rexroth's modernist, proto-Beat poetry was consistently informed by the Greek classics; Gideon Nisbet ("Kenneth Rexroth: Greek Anthologist") explores the particular influence of the *Greek Anthology* (a collection of [mostly] ancient epigrams compiled in the tenth century CE). Focusing on Rexroth's *Poems from the Greek Anthology* (1962), a collection of his own translations/versions, Nisbet shows how Rexroth transformed these poems in accordance with an aesthetic that could claim ancient poetic continuities but sought at the same time a contemporary voice—free-er, Beat *avant la lettre.*

A final group of papers presents case studies that bring to light the idiosyncratic combinations of influences—the personal canons—out of which individual poets forged their distinctive Beat practices. Jane Falk's study of Philip Whalen ("'A Walking Grove of Trees': Philip Whalen and the Classics") highlights the influence of midcentury Great Books curricula on Beat poetic practice; Whalen was exposed to the main texts of the classical tradition in the required Humanities sequence at Reed, and they became foundational for his own writing and continued reading. Equally important was the ongoing interest of the classics to contemporary writers and scholars whom Whalen especially admired, including Jane Ellen Harrison, Denys Page, Robert Duncan, Kenneth Rexroth, and Charles Olson. Out of these diverse influences, Whalen developed his own "New Paideuma," which was rooted in classical learning even as it incorporated critical views of Western values and sought to break down barriers between Eastern and Western thought.

The fusion of West and East sought by many Beats has been a paramount goal for Diane di Prima, as Nancy Grace and Tony Trigilio show in their analysis of her syncretic, visionary book-length poem *Loba* ("Troubling Classical and Buddhist Traditions in Diane di Prima's *Loba*"). In *Loba,* di Prima pays homage both to classical epic and to Buddhist practice, and challenges her readers to recognize the twining and twinning of these traditions. Di Prima's reworkings of classical myth restage female identity as subject rather than object through an emphasis on the female body thriving in its outsider relationship to masculinized religious cultures; the agency of this reborn female self is, in turn, the essential basis for a truly feminist experience of the Buddhist path to enlightenment.

Finally, Richard Fletcher ("Toward a Post-Beat Poetics: Charles Olson's Localism and the Second Sophistic") details Charles Olson's reliance on Greek writers of the Second Sophistic (the flowering of Greek culture under the Roman empire) to articulate his own wary relationship to the Beats. Olson drew in particular on the travel writers Pausanias and Maximus of Tyre in developing the particularism and localism which underlie his own poems set in Gloucester, Massachusetts, and which he saw as akin to the impulses to travel and see for oneself manifested by such Beat writers as Kerouac and Ginsberg. The cultural belatedness of Second Sophistic writers, and their straddling of local and global identities, made them apt mediators of Olson's own relationships with the distant past of the earlier archaic and classical Greeks and with the more recent past of the Beats.

Bibliography

Budelmann, Felix, and Haubold, Johannes. 2010. "Reception and Tradition." In *A Companion to Classical Reception*, edited by Lorna Hardwick and Christopher Stray, 13–25. Malden, MA: Wiley-Blackwell.

Corso, Gregory. 1958. *Gasoline*. San Francisco: City Lights Publishers.

———. 1960. *The Happy Birthday of Death*. New York: New Directions.

———. 1962. *Long Live Man*. New York: New Directions.

———. 1981. *Herald of the Autochthonic Spirit*. New York: New Directions.

Ferlinghetti, Lawrence. 1958. *A Coney Island of the Mind*. New York: New Directions.

Gewirtz, Isaac. 2007. *Beatific Soul: Jack Kerouac on the Road*. New York: New York Public Library and Scala Publishers.

Ginsberg, Allen. 1985. "I Am Not." *American Poetry Review* 14.6 (Nov/Dec): 17.

Grace, Nancy M., and Skerl, Jennie. 2012. *The Transnational Beat Generation*. New York: Palgrave Macmillan.

Hardwick, Lorna. 2003. *Reception Studies: Greece and Rome New Surveys in the Classics, No. 33*. Oxford: Oxford University Press.

Kerouac, Jack. 1958. *The Dharma Bums*. New York: Penguin.

Martindale, Charles. 2013. "Reception—A New Humanism? Receptivity, Pedagogy, the Transhistorical." *Classical Receptions Journal* 5: 169–83.

Morgan, Bill, ed. 2003. *An Accidental Autobiography: The Selected Letters of Gregory Corso*. New York: New Directions.

Olson, Kirby. 2002. *Gregory Corso: Doubting Thomist*. Carbondale: Southern Illinois University Press.

Pound, Ezra, 1973. *The Cantos of Ezra Pound*. New York: New Directions.

Skerl, Jennie, ed. 2004. *Reconstructing the Beats*. New York: Palgrave Macmillan.

CHAPTER 1

Beats Visiting Hell

KATABASIS IN BEAT LITERATURE

STEPHEN DICKEY

I

In the spring of 1959, the Wagner College literary magazine known as *Nimbus* renamed itself more concretely the *Wagner Literary Magazine* and announced a special issue. Its editors had sought commentary on the Beat movement from major modernists like E. E. Cummings, Robert Lowell, Marianne Moore, and William Carlos Williams. Responses were mixed—many negative, a few evasive—and some critics simply declined the offer. On a form letter of his own devising, Edmund Wilson checked the box labeled, improbably, "Edmund Wilson regrets that it is impossible for him to supply opinions on literary or other subjects" (1959, 29). The scholar who took the charge most seriously was Dorothy Van Ghent, whose specialty was the English novel of the eighteenth and nineteenth centuries. She began her three-paragraph contribution thus:

> The distinguishing characteristic of the Beat Generation is . . . the fact that they have a myth. The myth follows authentic archaic lines, and goes something like this. The hero is the "angelheaded hipster." He comes of anonymous parentage, parents whom he denies in correct mythological fashion. He has received a mysterious call—to the road, the freights, the jazz-dens, the "negro streets." This is the night journey or journey underground. . . . Where he goes is hell, the realm of death, ruled by the H- or Hades-Bomb.

> The hero is differentiated from the mass of the population of hell by his angelic awareness: he knows where he is. He knows that in hell it is silly to act as if you were in heaven, so he acts like a damned soul. His tortures—the heroic "ordeals" of myth—send him into ecstasy and he bursts into song, song filled with metaphors of destruction. . . . The Beats say they are a religious movement, and the Beat literature constantly indicates the far and visionary goal of the hero's quest—the return to the Kingdom, the transcendent kingdom of love and brotherhood and life. (1959, 27)

The following essay pays homage to Van Ghent by seeking to refine and apply some of her claims about the mythic Beat journey as a *katabasis*. Literally "a down-going," the term can mean any descent—as an army to the sea, or a wind down a mountain[1]—though more specifically it is used of a journey to the land of the dead as iterated through ancient epic—*Gilgamesh, The Odyssey, The Aeneid*—then Christianized in literary treatments of the Harrowing of Hell and, in its most sustained elaboration, Dante's *Inferno.* Although in Van Ghent's formulation, the Beat quester is distinguished spiritually "by his angelic awareness," in the most basic sense, a katabasis requires the traveler to be a living physical presence—corporeal, weighty, and warm—in vivid distinction to his or her spectral surroundings. From a narrative standpoint, in turn, the defining feature of the journey is that it is round trip: katabasis requires anabasis to render it something other than death. Thereafter, the traveler can report the experience to the living—as when Odysseus recounts his adventures to the Phaeacians, or tells Penelope of "the day that I went down to the House of Death" (ἤματι τῷ ὅτε δὴ κατέβην δόμον Ἄϊδος εἴσω, *Od.* 23.252).[2] The katabant must subsequently, in some fashion, carry back into life the knowledge or burden gained from the dead, some permanent—or at least permanently fading—alteration of the traveler's sense of both world and self.

The underworld as an image of earthly existence may have attached readily to the Beats in their time not just because so many of their works mention the atomic bomb—in Van Ghent's formulation, the newest god of hell—but because the Beats themselves found it so useful a topos. John Clellon Holmes, whose *Go* (1952) has a good claim to being the first Beat novel, originally conceived of it "as the first volume of a trilogy that would be structured on Dante's

1. The examples used in the *OED* to illustrate its definitions of the word: the first is derived, of course, from Xenophon, the latter from meteorology. The *OED* nowhere cites "katabasis" as a term designating a literary episode.

2. Translation by Fagles. The term is used in the *Odyssey* in other contexts to describe, e.g., a god's descent to earth (6.281, 20.31) or sliding down a gangplank to escape a boat, as when the disguised Odysseus invents for Eumaeus the story of his arrival at Ithaca (14.350).

Divine Comedy. Go was to be my *Inferno,* describing the circles of disbelief, descending from the upper world of young urban professionals, through the Bohemians, through the Beats, down into the outright underworld of criminality" (Holmes 1988, xxii).[3] Other Beat works—*Naked Lunch* most memorably—satirize social conventions through far more outlandishly diabolical caricatures than Holmes used in *Go,* making plausible the idea of the Beats as katabants who go underground—socially at least—for their inspiration, and who replicate the journey in their works. Such is one implication of William Carlos Williams's introduction to the first edition of Allen Ginsberg's *Howl and Other Poems,* ending, "Hold back the edges of your gowns, Ladies, we are going through hell" (Ginsberg 1956, 8), or of Norman Mailer's testimony during the censorship trial of William Burroughs's *Naked Lunch*: "To me this is a simple portrayal of Hell. It is Hell precisely" (Burroughs 1966, xvi). Comparing the author to Hieronymus Bosch, Mailer argues that Burroughs provides us "with an intimate, detailed vision of what Hell might be like, a Hell which may be waiting as the culmination, the final product, of the scientific revolution."[4] As if echoing Van Ghent, Mailer then winds up his testimony by proposing that *Naked Lunch* has a positive or "redeeming" social function for the court to consider because it is Burroughs himself who has made the journey underground: "A Great Society can look into the chasm of its own potential Hell and recognize that it is stronger as a nation for possessing an artist who can come back from Hell with a portrait of its dimensions" (Burroughs 1993, xvii).

Mailer's comments shift the focus from the work of art to the artist himself and, in so doing, from the merely emblematic hell of any dystopian vision to the writer as katabant. This essay will argue that not only did the major Beat writers share this general view of themselves but their works demonstrate a close familiarity with the traditional features of literary katabasis. Examples

---

3. In his retrospective introduction, Holmes added crucially, "As I wrote, I saw that the same hungers activated us all, and the thesis evaporated," although his original scheme survives in the title of the third and final section of *Go*: "Hell" (1988, 223).

4. Mailer's depiction of *Naked Lunch* is close to Burroughs's own early vision of the work, as set forth in a letter to Allen Ginsberg in February of 1955: "The novel is taking shape. Something even more evil than atomic destruction is the theme—namely an anti-dream drug which destroys the symbolizing, myth-making, intuitive, empathizing, telepathic faculty in man, so that his behavior can be controlled and predicted by the scientific methods that have proved so useful in the physical sciences" (Burroughs 1993, 268). Closer still to Van Ghent's concept of the Beats as nuclear age writers was Burroughs's initial summary of *Naked Lunch.* In a mock blurb he imagined for the cover of his yet unpublished manuscript, Burroughs wrote, "Suppose you knew the power to start an atomic war lay in the hands of a few scientists who were bent on destroying the world? That is the terrifying question posed by this searching novel" (ibid., 255).

treated here include Allen Ginsberg's "A Supermarket in California," which directly alludes to the geography of the classical underworld, and "Howl," which takes us on an emphatically vertical journey down, up, and through the Beat cosmos. Jack Kerouac's titles *Orpheus Emerged* and *The Subterraneans* also imply a katabatic vision, especially as the latter novel tells its "history of the hip or beat . . . or subterranean generation" whose members leave their apartments on Heavenly Lane to see films like Kurosawa's *The Lower Depths* before they go out drinking at Dante's Bar (Kerouac [1958] 1974, 133).[5] Yet *The Subterraneans* takes place entirely within the hipster underworld—a space also metafictionally defined as the narrator's room where he writes the novel[6]—and thus lacks the requisite physical movement of the katabatic traveler from life to death and back. With the publication of *Big Sur* in 1962, however, Kerouac most fully descends into, and most thoroughly exploits, the katabasis of classical epic. Rewriting this crucial episode for the purposes of what Van Ghent calls their "authentic archaic" myth, the Beats must inevitably respond to post-classical treatments, yet it is striking how frequently, and how specifically, Beat literature burns for the ancient underworldly connection.

II

The Whells of Subways

—ALLEN GINSBERG, "HOWL," PART 2, FIRST DRAFT

Allen Ginsberg's "A Supermarket in California" is a modern *nekyia*—an episode distinct from, but often subsumed under, the term katabasis—in which, after the performance of certain prescribed rituals, the hero converses with a prophetic or ancestral figure among the ghostly dead. The *locus classicus* of this event is in *Odyssey* 11, where the hero speaks with numerous shades—former comrades, noble women, warriors, his own mother—but only after receiving instructions about his homeward journey from the seer Tiresias. In Ginsberg's poem, these dead interlocutors are all combined into a single figure: Walt Whitman, who, in 1856, included a new poem in the second edition of *Leaves of Grass* that would become better known, after some revisions,

5. Kerouac's comment on the cover of the Norwegian edition of 1960 is also to the point: "The book is modelled after Dostoevsky's *Notes from the Underground*" (quoted in Bartlett 1981, 124).

6. As at the start and end of the novel: "Angels, bear with me—I'm not even looking at the page but straight ahead into the sadglint of my wallroom" (2); "And I go home having lost her love. And write this book" (111).

as "Crossing Brooklyn Ferry." With the audacious intimacy characteristic of his poetic voice, Whitman assures future generations of his transcendent and enduring presence:

> Closer yet I approach you,
> What thought you have of me now, I had as much of you—I laid in my stores
> in advance,
> I considered long and seriously of you before you were born.
> (7.1–3)[7]

One century later, a conversation between the dead and the living is joined through the camaraderie of allusion in Ginsberg's "A Supermarket in California" (1956):

> What thoughts I have of you tonight, Walt Whitman, for I walked down the sidestreets under the trees with a headache self-conscious looking at the full moon. (1)

The link is formed not just by Ginsberg's verbal inversion of Whitman's line, but by his ironic extension of Whitman's imagery to establish the precise setting of their encounter: a supermarket.[8] Yet if Whitman's stores were full, Ginsberg's are not, and for much of the poem the living speaker is more of a phantom than the dead but still vital Whitman whom he haunts:

> In my hungry fatigue, and shopping for images, I went into the neon fruit supermarket, dreaming of your enumerations!
> What peaches and what penumbras! Whole families shopping at night! Aisles full of husbands! Wives in the avocados, babies in the tomatoes!—and you, Garcia Lorca, what were you doing down by the watermelons?
>
> I saw you, Walt Whitman, childless, lonely old grubber, poking among the meats in the refrigerator and eyeing the grocery boys.
> I heard you asking questions of each: Who killed the pork chops? What price bananas? Are you my Angel?
> I wandered in and out of the brilliant stacks of cans following you, and followed in my imagination by the store detective.

7. All citations from Walt Whitman are from Whitman 1982.

8. Whitman's phrase, "I laid in my stores in advance," plays off the idiom "lay in store" and thus implies that he will enjoy yet more abundance, even after life, through the future generations he has already contemplated—a major implication of "Crossing Brooklyn Ferry."

> We strode down the open corridors together in our solitary fancy tasting artichokes, possessing every frozen delicacy, and never passing the cashier.
> (2–7)

Whitman's original title for "Crossing Brooklyn Ferry" was "Sun-Down Poem," imparting the elegiac nuances of endings and approaching death to the commuters' ordinary ferryboat ride that Ginsberg's conceit will extend backwards, as it were, into the classical afterlife in the equally mundane setting of the supermarket. In this light, Whitman's poem can be understood as a kind of inverted nekyia whereby the now physically dead poet sends his spirit forward to address the living reader across the existential divide:

> It avails not, neither time or place—distance avails not;
> I am with you, you men and women of a generation, or ever so many generations hence;
> I project myself—also I return—I am with you, and know how it is.
> (3.1–3)[9]
>
> What is it, then, between us?
> What is the count of the scores or hundreds of years between us?
>
> Whatever it is, it avails not—distance avails not, and place avails not.
> (5.1–3)

"Supermarket" reverses the encounter and restores it to that of a classical nekyia, wherein the living seek out the dead, hungry for guidance.

> Where are we going, Walt Whitman? The doors close in an hour. Which way does your beard point tonight?
> (I touch your book and dream of our odyssey in the supermarket and feel absurd.)
> Will we walk all night through solitary streets? The trees add shade to shade, lights out in the houses, we'll both be lonely.
> (8–10)

Thus at the poem's melancholy close, each figure returns to his proper realm as the dream-vision poet, belated with respect to both the classical

9. The wording of the first line and the entire third line in this passage are from "Sun-Down Poem" and the earlier versions of "Crossing Brooklyn Ferry," and do not derive from the edition of *Leaves of Grass* (1891–92) used in the Library of America text, otherwise quoted here.

and romantic traditions as well as to "the lost America of love," now feels "absurd" while reflecting on his "odyssey." Clearly there is a kind of antic humor throughout Ginsberg's poem absent from the descents or underworld conversations of ancient epic, but "Supermarket" nonetheless captures something of the subdued grief in such scenes, a pathos increased by the encounter with a dead parent. Just as Odysseus longs to embrace his mother Antikleia, and Aeneas his father Anchises, and just as both heroes fail thrice in their attempts, so Ginsberg transforms the "childless, lonely old grubber" Whitman into a paradoxical "dear father" whom he too must lose:

> Will we stroll dreaming of the lost America of love past blue automobiles in driveways, home to our silent cottage?
>
> Ah, dear father, graybeard, lonely old courage-teacher, what America did you have when Charon quit poling his ferry and you got out on a smoking bank and stood watching the boat disappear on the black waters of Lethe?
> (11–12)

The imagery of the classical underworld remains powerful here, but Ginsberg has altered the landscape to serve his own topical purposes. Charon, the ferryman of the dead, traditionally (and almost unanimously) navigates the river or lake of Acheron, or secondarily the Styx, neither of which pertains to the faculty of memory.[10] Here, though, Whitman's shade has been made to cross Lethe. Following the *Aeneid,*[11] this could mean that his spirit is not yet able to return to a new corporeal existence—to be "struck from the float" (5.9) anew, in one sense of the famous image of Whitman's poem—though here it seems more suggestive of a mutual obliviousness between America and her bard despite all those brave assurances in "Crossing Brooklyn Ferry":

> Who was to know what should come home to me?
> Who knows but I am enjoying this?
> Who knows but I am as good as looking at you now, for all you cannot see
> me?
> (7.4–6)

---

10. One minority report comes from Propertius 4.7.91–92, where the shade of Cynthia describes the return, at dawn, of spirits to the underworld: *luce iubent leges Lethaea ad stagna reuerti: / nos uehimur, uectum nauta recenset onus.* (At the light of dawn the laws order them to return to the Lethean pools: we are carried across, and the boatman surveys the cargo he's carried). Statius, *Thebaid* 12. 557, also refers to Charon as *Lethaei portitor amnis*, or "the toll collector of Lethe's rivers."

11. See *Aeneid* 6.703 ff., where Lethe is associated with the oblivion that must precede rebirth.

Whitman's ferryboat may subtly evoke Charon's vessel—everyone, after all, "shall cross from shore to shore years hence" (1.5)—yet the poem reassures us of the continuing relationship between the dead and the living in "the similitudes of the past and those of the future" (2.3), and celebrates the sheer materiality of life with exuberance but without resentment for the fact of personal mortality. (Indeed, in projecting himself toward the future reader, the speaker of "Crossing Brooklyn Ferry" sounds as if he is already speaking from the dead.) Ginsberg's last lines, however, make the underworld reference explicit, uncomfortably so, and far less positive. While Whitman's poem concedes that the future "cannot see" him, he nonetheless implies his continuing presence there and thereafter, but Ginsberg transfers that blindness to the dead poet who, in the final verb of the poem, can only watch the ferry "disappear." And though the living Whitman crossed the East River asserting his love for those "others who look back on me because I look'd forward to them" (4.4), Ginsberg makes the westernmost Lethe the last word in his revisionist vision, leaving the dead Whitman of "Supermarket" with a question about what, if anything, remains of his America and how much, if any, of his wisdom or guidance is now remembered. Time passes—the century, say, from 1856 to 1956—and Whitman's "Sun-Down Poem" has declined below the horizon into Ginsberg's underworld poem, set not when the sun is "half an hour high" (1.2) but at night, the journey done, adding shade to shade.

Compared to the necessarily fleeting nekyia of "Supermarket," "Howl" sets forth on a more exhaustive and exhausting journey to and from the underworld, traveling not only underground but throughout the cosmos meeting ghosts, demons, angels, and an entire subculture of living human beings, many in torment, some in ecstasy, a few in both (as Van Ghent describes the archetypal Beat). This is Ginsberg's Dantean journey of death and rebirth, navigated by a Blakean compass of innocence and experience. Read as a katabatic narrative, the work has a clear structure, with a linear trajectory surprising in so notoriously unruly a poem. Each of the four parts of "Howl" has its own structural mandate, its own rhetoric, its own sound arranged around a single word, but together they accumulate to a modern, miniature *Divine Comedy.*

The first, and longest, part of the poem is a single sentence running to seventy-eight often very long lines. It contains the core assertion of the poem as a visionary and metaphysical statement—"I saw . . . minds" (1.1)—before detailing a number of episodes in the lives of Ginsberg and his camarados through a series of increasingly independent clauses beginning with "who." It takes place on earth, mainly in Manhattan, though an earth that blends features of other Dantean afterworlds as the "angelheaded hipsters" (1.3) "purgatoried their torsos" (1.10). Yet while the population of the poem endures much physical torment, even the nightmarish sufferings of the hipsters—"who chained themselves to subways for the endless ride" (1.14), or "disappeared into . . . volcanoes" (1.29), or "walked all night with their shoes full of blood" (1.45), or "were burned alive in their innocent flannel suits" (1.56)—are prelude always to reappearance (1.30) or ecstasy (1.41) or resurrection whereby "the madman bum and angel beat in Time, unknown, yet putting down here what might be left to say in time come after death / . . . rose reincarnate in the ghostly clothes of jazz" (1.76–77).

The absence of an underworld in the first section of "Howl" is partly explained by the itinerary of the poem as a whole, since it will be part 2 that takes us to hell.[12] This section begins with one question followed by a series of exclamations, many of which have to do with "Moloch," whose name acts as an incantatory refrain. Moloch is the fire idol who demands that parents place their eldest born children, living, into the oven of his mouth. The Book of Leviticus forbids his worship (18:21, 20:2), and in *Paradise Lost* Moloch is "the strongest and the fiercest" of the fallen angels, "now fiercer by despair" (2.44–45), who counsels immediate and all-out war with heaven as Milton reshapes him around the deadly sin of wrath: a "horrid king, besmear'd with blood / Of human sacrifice, and parents' tears" (1.391–92).[13] In "Howl" Moloch is reimagined as an embodiment of the most destructive, dystopian aspects of the modern world. Not just the "electricity and banks" (2.7) of capitalism, not just the withering of joy by commerce and conformity, Moloch is also, plainly, the atomic bomb, the old-new fire god to which all parents, now, have to imagine someday sacrificing their children. This, then, is the katabatic section of the poem, taking place in hell, or on the earth that we have turned into a precinct of hell while self-destructively idolizing death: "They broke their backs lifting Moloch to Heaven" (2.11).

Ginsberg began the first of eighteen drafts of part 2 with a fragment of handwriting at the bottom of a typewritten draft of part 1. It does not begin, as do later drafts, with a question, but with an answer followed by a question: "Moloch, Moloch! Whose hand ripped out their brains and scattered their minds ~~on~~ the the whells of subways?" (Ginsberg 1986a, 58). Though when he typed up the second draft, Ginsberg immediately corrected "whells" to "wheels" (also retracting his initial miscorrection of "on the" to "the the"), and though the entire phrase vanishes by the third draft, the word "hell" is visible at the start of part 2, a Dantean slip of the pencil pushing its way forward in

12. There is a pun on "hell" in the phrase "who bared their brains to Heaven under the El" (1.5), and an indirect reference (1.15) to Judgment Day via allusion to "the crack of doom" (*Macbeth* 4.1.116), but the emphasis in part 1 is on the purgatorial sufferings of life on earth.

13. Milton 1998.

the misspelling of "wheels" as an early warning of the poet's conception. First thought, best thought.

Part 3 of "Howl" is an assertion of solidarity and love between the poet and his dedicatee, Carl Solomon.[14] Factually speaking, the two men had met and formed their friendship in 1949 at the New York State Psychiatric Institute of Columbia Presbyterian Hospital, but having revised the underworld riverways in "A Supermarket in California," Ginsberg now alters earthly geography by relocating their meeting to a different, nearby institution known simply as Rockland. I suggest that this is an artistic choice made so that "Howl" can bring us back to earth through the reassuringly sturdy (and much briefer) choric phrase "I'm with you in Rockland" (3, passim), thus supporting the poem's anabatic trajectory of a return from the military–industrial hell of Moloch to earth, to the rock, the bedrock land. (As the great absurdist himself, Carl Solomon, noted with mock outrage some years later, "I was never in Rockland. . . . Neither of us has ever been in Rockland. Ginsberg never even on a tour" [Ginsberg 1986a, 143].)

Part 4 of the poem has its own title, "Footnote to Howl," but despite that marginalizing gesture, this section was, until a later stage of composition, placed between what thereafter became parts 2 and 3.[15] The key word that it deploys, puns on anatomically, and harps on angelically, is "Holy." "Footnote" begins with fifteen "Holies" in a row, as if providing one to balance each verse in the Moloch section.[16] Completing the structural logic of the poem, part 4 takes place in heaven, or on earth at its most heavenly—the earth of beat friendships, loves, bodies, and souls—and thus "Howl" concludes by beatifying the beaten down and returning, as Van Ghent puts it, to "the transcendent kingdom of love and brotherhood and life."

Howl. Who. Moloch. Rockland. Holy. Howl. Not merely an echo of "Hell," the title of the poem indexes the interconnected sounds of the poem, and those key terms, those beat words, summarize the poem's movement from earth to hell, returning to earth, thence to heaven. It is a travelogue not just of Manhattan and its Charonesque subways, not just of the narcotic underground, not just of the now unlocked closet of Ginsberg's sexual identity, but of the moral universe.

---

14. Usefully for Ginsberg's purposes, Carl Solomon's last name brings to mind the biblical Solomon who, for all his wisdom, was for a time apostate in the worship of Moloch. See 1 Kings 11:7.

15. Ginsberg 1986a, 88–95, shows that not until the fourth draft (of five) did Ginsberg label the "Rockland" section as part 3, and "Footnote" became part 4.

16. "I set it as *Footnote to Howl* because it was an extra variation of the form of part 2" (Ginsberg 2000, 230).

III

Helling Headbent

—JACK KEROUAC, *BIG SUR*

Q: "Will you tell us which writers have had an influence on you, if any, on your writings I mean? Did any writers have an influence . . . ?"
A: "Not Dante!"

—JACK KEROUAC, INTERVIEWED ON ITALIAN TELEVISION BY FERNANDA PIVANO, 1966[17]

William Carlos Williams's foreword to Ginsberg's "Howl," though square, was true: hell is a likely place for howling, and Dorothy Van Ghent in 1959 was correct to quote the poem as the touchstone of her mythic reading of the Beats. Perhaps the only reason she did not quote Jack Kerouac's *Big Sur* instead was that it had not yet been written, for nowhere in the Beat oeuvre is the katabatic paradigm more intricately and kaleidoscopically applied than in Kerouac's novel of 1962.[18] Van Ghent's insight into the deepest narrative structure of Beat literature—its archaic myth, now seen anew in the blinding light of the atomic age—reaches its own prophetic fulfillment with this novel, for if the Beats collectively recorded their generational quest through the new Hades of postwar America, *Big Sur* depicts an individual journey wherein the hero performs sacrificial rites to enter a more private realm where he encounters the ghosts of his past, reckons his own mortality, and at last undergoes a melancholy renewal of his life's purpose. He must "accept loss forever"—Rule #19 of Kerouac's "List of Essentials" for writers of "Modern Prose" (Kerouac 1959, 57)—before returning transformed to the upper world, marked by death.

17. The disingenuousness of Kerouac's claim is audible in the humorous tones of the 1966 interview, wherein the denial of influence slyly advertises it. See http://www.youtube.com/watch?v=kOMyzslIP-o. Note too, that Kerouac quotes Dante's *Paradiso* (17.128–9)—*Tutta tua vision fa manifesta, e lascia pur grattar* (make plain all thy vision—and then let them scratch [trans., Sinclair 1974])—in an episode in *Visions of Cody* he also recycled for his final column in *Escapade* (April 1960), three months before traveling to Big Sur. (See "The Last Word," reprinted in Kerouac 1993, 188.)

18. Gregory Stephenson notes that "*Big Sur* records Duluoz's descent into hell" and ably analyzes the novel as a sequel to *Desolation Angels* that thus completes an essentially Christian journey culminating in "grace and vision, the ultimate boons of the hero-quest" via "a sort of downward ascent" (1990, 42–43). My discussion will undertake a complementary reading by focusing on the katabatic and other more classical elements of the novel.

Along the way, Kerouac signals his debts to classical literature with a number of details drawn from both ancient epic and Dante's *Divine Comedy.*

Triadic in plot and structure, *Big Sur* is a fictionalized account of the author's trip to the West Coast in late July 1960, punctuated by three visits to a small cabin owned by Lawrence Ferlinghetti. The invitation was initially a lifeline to Kerouac, who had been enduring what one biographer calls "a season of shame and disgrace" (Clark 1984, 184).[19] But what began as the promise of refuge to allow a productive period of writing ended in the disaster of a personal breakdown. A year later, Kerouac shaped those events into a work of fiction, using the katabasis model, which served him not merely for the occasional allusive glance, but as the novel's most deeply embedded structural principle. From the start, *Big Sur* immerses us in a flood of underworld tokens and scenarios as its protagonist, Jack Duluoz, makes his first, solitary visit to the cabin below the Bixby Canyon bridge.[20] This first descent functions as something of an overture, establishing the underworld motif for the rest of the novel: "What in the hell is this?" (10), "What the hell's going on!" (11).[21] Duluoz's epithets, initially inaudible as casual slang, gradually disclose their more literal, ominous nuances as he enters a place "even *darker* down there than anywhere," where "ferns of horror" grow and "humid mists rise coldly like the breath of death" (12). Completing the preliminary journey with its necessary anabasis, he crosses the bridge and discovers "a dreamy meadowland" beyond a fence: "Then I crawl thru the barbed wire and find myself trudging a sweet little sand road winding right thru fragrant dry heathers as tho I'd just popped thru from hell into familiar old Heaven on Earth, yair and Thank God" (13). Descriptive details from the following chapter, when Duluoz takes stock of his surroundings in the daylight, support the infernal ambiance with words like "doom," "death," and "evil"; bats "flying silently around" (18)

---

19. See Clark 1984, 176–84. A series of satires (most notably John Updike's *New Yorker* piece "On the Sidewalk" (Feb. 1959) and hostile reviews extending well beyond the reliably antagonistic *Time* magazine had aggravated Kerouac's paranoia. The premiere of the quintessential Beat movie *Pull My Daisy* was poorly received at a film festival even in San Francisco. Having agreed to visit Neal Cassady, then serving time in San Quentin, and to address an inmates' study group, Kerouac went on a three-day bender beforehand, remained passed out through the appointed time, and never responded to rescheduling efforts. In June 1960, Hollywood's travesty of his novel *The Subterraneans* was released, an event that so mortified Kerouac that he withdrew even further from his dwindling circle of friends.

20. The narrator's eventual breakdown is signaled by an apt *memento mori* from (and for) the author of *On the Road* when Duluoz sees that an "automobile that crashed thru the bridge rail a decade ago and fell 1000 feet straight down and landed upsidedown, is still there now, an upsidedown chassis of rust in a strewn skitter of sea-eaten tires, old spokes, old car seats sprung with straw, one sad fuel pump and no more people" (Kerouac 1992, 15).

21. Page citations are from *Big Sur* (Kerouac 1992).

as he reads *The Strange Case of Dr. Jekyll and Mr. Hyde*[22] with "those damned silent black wings flapping and throwing shadows" (19); and related imagery of vampires and ghosts, not to mention the sound of the creek that will later become "the babble and rave of evil angels in my head" (20).

The second section of the novel contains sporadic, though more than incidental, references to death, hell, infernal punishments, and descents both literal and figurative, but it is in the last third of the novel that such details again grow more frequent and intense. Here, the narrator charts his final descent to Big Sur, along with his lover Willamine, or Billie, to a penultimate encounter with death. Her presence in the novel combines Circean traits of guile and guidance with underworld torment. Variously described as "an ancient Salem housewife or Salem witch" (185), "an unconscious witch . . . she's witching me" (187), part of "a great witching force" and one of the "evil forces gathering down all around" (191), as well as "a member of the expert poisoning society" (199) whose young son, Elliott, is "a warlock disguised as a little boy" (206), Billie is the focal point—both target and source—of Duluoz's paranoia. He begins to suspect her of not just predatory matrimonial designs but even, at the emotional climax of the novel, a sacrificial or downright murderous intent toward her own son. After days of various threats to kill herself, or Elliott and herself together, and disturbing alternations of maternal punishment and embrace, Billie digs a garbage pit as they are packing up to leave the cabin. To Duluoz, it resembles "a neat tiny coffinshaped grave" (213) and as he hurriedly fills it with garbage the child grabs the shovel and begins to scream as if he himself is being buried alive. Billie fills the rest of the pit before she turns ominously to Duluoz:

> "Do you want to finish the job yourself?—"What do you mean?"—"Cover the earth on, do the honors?" "Why did you make it look like a grave?" I finally yell—But Billie is only smiling quietly and steadily at me, over the

22. The reference to Stevenson's novel ([1886] 2008) is both factual and conveniently symbolic, much like Kerouac's inclusion of the detail that Ferlinghetti's dog was named "Homer" (53). *The Strange Case* was—"of all things" (18)—the book in Ferlinghetti's cabin when Kerouac stayed there, and its "last elegant sentences" read "at dawn" (20) by Duluoz depict Jekyll's awareness of the death of his identity within Stevenson's story and, now placed within Kerouac's, a metanarrative moment signaling the fragility, indeed the fracturing, of both narrators' personalities as they "seal up [their] confession[s]." As Hyde's powers have grown to supersede Jekyll's, the latter claims that "this is my true hour of death, and what is to follow concerns another than myself" (Stevenson [1886] 2008, 66). By alluding to Stevenson's ending early in his own novel, Kerouac implies that *Big Sur* will not just parallel but continue the story of a dead or disintegrating narrator in an act of posthumous autobiography. Like Jekyll, Duluoz is another "down-going"—literally katabatic—man (ibid., 5).

grave, shovel in hand, the kid weeping tugging the shovel, rushing up to block my way, trying to shove me back with his little hands." (214)[23]

Admittedly, there is no mention of sheep's blood, and Duluoz—more Elpenor than Odysseus—seems already to have drunk the libations himself, but the polluted ritual of this bizarre, incomplete burial ceremony recalls the underworld precedents and promises of ancient epic[24], while signaling the nearly simultaneous beginning and end of Duluoz's last journey to the underworld. "The hell with all this madness!" he says, before passing out. "Just one short minute later" he awakens in "blessed relief . . . everything has washed away." He sees "fields and flowers," sits "smiling in the sun," hears "the birds sing again," and feels a "golden wash of goodness spread over all and over all my body and mind—All the dark torture is a memory—I know now I can get out of there" (215–16). Reversing the moment early in the novel when he first tried to find his way down to the cabin, liminal between land and sea, life and death, the protagonist has now come back to the region of life: anabasis perfects katabasis.

Duluoz's other and more constant companion throughout the novel is alcohol, which performs its own predictably bestializing sorcery, functioning at different times as entrance to, and punishment within, his personal hell. At the end of chapter 1, Duluoz wakes up in a cheap hotel named The Mars, "drunk, sick, disgusted, frightened, in fact terrified" by the sound of church bells through which rise the words of a sermon "*Satan* is the cause of your alcoholism" (5–6). Aptly framed by references to the classical pantheon and the Bible, Duluoz at this point is a character poised between two worlds or modes, corresponding to the liminal phase of the katabatic initiate: the upper and under worlds, liveliness and ghostliness, sobriety and drink, prophecy and nostalgia, or separation and reintegration, to use Van Gennep's formula.[25] Recalling Dante's lost path from the start of *The Inferno,* Duluoz has "gone the way of the last three years of drunken hopelessness which is a physical and spiritual and metaphysical hopelessness" (7), and he experiences in delirium tremens a mundane compendium of Dante's underworld punishments updating those of the Gluttons of the third circle, sloshing in putrid water and mud; the Avaricious of the fourth pushing weights around uselessly; the Wrathful

23. Having achieved some distance from these events a year and a half later, Kerouac described the novel, then being considered for publication, in a letter to Carolyn Cassady. About the character of Billie, who had been based on Carolyn's then-husband Neal's then-mistress, Kerouac wrote demurely, "The book outlines the possibility that she's a witch" (1999b, 322).

24. As Odysseus's to Elpenor, Aeneas's to Misenus and Palinurus.

25. Van Gennep [1909] 1960.

of the fifth sunk in perpetual muddy combat; and the Violent-to-others in the boiling blood of the seventh circle.[26] In this exemplary passage, Duluoz describes his flogging by the Demon Rum:

> The feeling of being a bentback mudman monster groaning underground in hot steaming mud pulling a long hot burden nowhere, the feeling of standing ankledeep in hot boiled port blood, ugh, of being up to your waist in a giant pan of greasy brown dishwater not a trace of suds left in it—The face of yourself you see in the mirror with its expression of unbearable anguish so hagged and awful with sorrow you can't even cry for a thing so ugly, so lost. (8)

Other classical and specifically underworld allusions crowd the early portions of the narrative: a Cerberean ocean, "barking . . . like a dog" when the lost Duluoz tries to figure "how can the sea be underground" (10); another body of water, a nearby creek with "so many voices . . . sudden choruses of other singers and voices . . . the voices of the creek amusing me so much at first" (19–20), pointing the way to the explicit Aristophanic allusion in the concluding poem, "Sea: Sounds of the Pacific Ocean at Big Sur," where "Pluto eats the sea" and the Ocean says "Kek kek kek!" (231–32).[27] There is also reference to "Vulcan's forge" (22), "a huge knot in a redwood tree looking like Zeus' face" (25), and even a "ghostly" (31) and "immortal" (26) donkey that might recall Ocnus's underworld ass, perpetually eating rope (though Duluoz names this "ancient sacred myth character. . . . Alf the sacred burro" [16] in tributary tribute to another fabled underground river, that of Coleridge's "Kubla Khan").[28]

---

26. See in particular *Inferno* Cantos 6.34 ff., 7.25ff., 7.100ff., and 12.46ff., respectively.

27. "Kek, kek, kek!" alludes to the sound made by the chorus of frogs that Dionysus encounters as he enters the Underworld with his slave Xanthias in Aristophanes' *Frogs* (209–67). Aristophanes transcribes the sound as "*brekekekek koax koax!*" (220).

28. The appended poem may make one final allusive gesture to the classical tradition by referring—rather obscurely, it must be admitted—to Tennyson's "Enoch Arden" ([1864] 1958), an Odysseyan variant wherein the hero returns home ten years after his presumed death at sea, but with different domestic results. Arden returns to discover that his wife has "with slow consent" (704) remarried his childhood friend and one-time rival for her love, and with him produced another child to join Arden's two surviving children. Living for another year as "a dead man come to life," (754) Arden does not disclose his presence or identity except by posthumous report. In *Big Sur,* Kerouac had referred to Tennyson twice earlier in "Sea" (1992, 233), and the last lines of that poem, and hence of the novel, are "be deep I see you / Enoc'h / soon anarf / in Old Brittany" (241). Kerouac himself had become increasingly interested in his own Breton ancestry, and Tennyson's manuscript notes to "Enoch Arden" mention that "something like the same story is told in Brittany and elsewhere" (H. Tennyson 1897, 2.7). Perhaps the convergence of these details led Kerouac to associate Duluoz with Enoch Arden, another figurative katabant.

Big Sur is, plainly, a highly allusive novel, yet the allusions are not mechanically dropped in but rather emerge plausibly from the protagonist's specific situation: his soul sickness; his fears of walking alone through strange, steep terrain in pitch blackness; the intensifying paranoia of the alcoholic. For both ancient heroes and this modern protagonist, the way out is the way through; or, in katabatic terms, the way up is the way down. This cycle of descent and return, quasi-death and recovery, occurs three times in the novel, conveyed not just by the physical locations of the protagonist but by scattered images combining diverse motifs of the underworld and the afterlife. These include a vignette of a Persephone-like young girl "jongling and jiggling through the fields to look for flowers" in what appears to her as a "Garden of Eden" but to the narrator as "this tortured human canyon" (122), and numerous descriptions of leaves violently blown into the surf that mingle Vergilian and Dantean nuances of lost souls awaiting burial, transport, or judgment:

> Besides I suddenly notice as if for the first time the awful way the leaves of the canyon that have managed to be blown to the surf are all hesitantly advancing in gusts of wind then finally plunging into the surf, to be dispersed and belted and melted and taken off to sea—I turn around and notice how the wind is just harrying them off trees and into the sea, just hurrying them as it were to death—In my condition they look human trembling to that brink—Hastening, hastening—In that awful huge roar blast of autumn Sur wind. (181–82)[29]

The novel even offers something like an updated show of heroes, as apparitions from Duluoz's past—chiefly Cody (known formerly as Dean Moriarty)—return to visit: "Suddenly, boom, the door of the cabin is flung open with a loud crash and a burst of sunlight illuminates the room and I see an Angel standing arm outstretched in the door!" (124). Duluoz's subsequent recollection of "the time in Mexico" when his companion "drove an old car over a rutted road very slowly as we were all high on tea and I saw golden Heaven" (125) presents Cody's appearance in *Big Sur* as an incursion from the heroic past of *On the Road*.[30] Duluoz, though, is beating a different path now, with a less paradisal angle of vision, and turns explicitly to Vergil to reflect upon "*lacrimae rerum*, the tears of things, all the years behind me and Cody" (136)

29. See also passages in *Big Sur* on pages 36, 188–89, 204. The relevant predecessor texts are *Aeneid* 6.305 ff. and *Inferno* 3.112 ff.

30. See *On the Road* part 4, chapter 5.

before describing himself as now "helling headbent" (141) to his final descent.[31] This anthimeria revises the more standard expression *heading hellbent* by constructing *helling* as an active verb to imply that Duluoz's existence even now is an unfolding, ongoing experience of damnation as he makes his Dantean journey through "an insane revolving automatic directionless circle of anxiety, back and forth, around and around" (199). Moreover, *headbent* suggests not just that Duluoz is being beaten down and driven under but that he is actively heading, as the epic hero must, toward a fate chosen as much as assigned. And though Duluoz is granted a vision of the Cross—a fairly common epiphany in Kerouac's fictions—it does not save him from the Boschian nightmare of "the underground Hell" (210) to come. Not surprisingly, these last portions of *Big Sur* read somewhat like *Naked Lunch,* though predicated on the use of and withdrawal from alcohol, not junk: an A-bomb, not an H-bomb, to recall Van Ghent's characterization of Beat mythography in the nuclear age. It is as close as the book gets to a sustained description, rather than a fragmentary glimpse, of hell as a lived experience:

> Instead of being really dead we'll be taken to the Underground Slimes to walk neck deep in steaming mucks pulling huge groaning wheels (among small forked snakes) so the devil with the long ears can mine his Purple Magenta Square Stone that is the secret of all this Kingdom—You end up down there groaning and pulling thru dead bodies of other people even your own family floating in the ooze. (209–10)

Fittingly, this last section ends with one more salute to the classical traditions of katabasis and nekyia. When Odysseus meets the shade of Achilles in the underworld, the great warrior rejects his fame in death:

> By god, I'd rather slave on earth for another man—
> some dirt-poor tenant farmer who scrapes to keep alive—
> than rule down here over all the breathless dead.
> (Fagles 11.556–8)

The Beat version of this pronouncement, belated and hungover, is Duluoz's vow: "This sickness has got me wishing if I can ever get out of this I'll gladly become a millworker and shut my big mouth" (211). In substituting "millworker" for "slave" in this formula, Jack Kerouac, native son of Lowell, Massachusetts, knows whereof he speaks.

---

31. See *Aeneid* 1.462.

IV

I dwelled in Hell on earth to write this rhyme.

—ALLEN GINSBERG, "AFTER READING KEROUAC'S MANUSCRIPT *THE TOWN AND THE CITY*"

In 1959 Dorothy Van Ghent understandably situated the Beat underground in the Atomic Age as humanity's latest version of hell, but Beat katabasis is a matter of literary fusion as well as nuclear fission. The Beats were not heirs to romanticism exclusively—certainly Burroughs was not—but much more proximately to the Modernists for whom, as T. S. Eliot wrote in his review of Joyce's *Ulysses*, the "mythical method" provided "a way of controlling, of ordering, of giving a shape and a significance to the immense panorama of futility and anarchy which is contemporary history" (Eliot 1923, 483). To those Modernists, in the words of a recent study, "the single most important myth [is] the descent to the underworld" (Smith 1990, 1).

By now, moreover, it should no longer be necessary to address Allen Ginsberg's observation that the most common misconception about the Beats was that they were illiterate, by which he meant not literally but literarily illiterate.[32] Burroughs in the mid-1930s at Harvard, home of Charles W. Eliot's "five foot shelf" of Harvard Classics, and Ginsberg and Kerouac in the early '40s at Columbia, were exposed to curricula in which classical literature was prominent and foundational. The "Literature Humanities" syllabus at Columbia in the years 1940–42, Kerouac's only years of attendance, included the *Iliad*, the *Frogs*, the *Aeneid*, and the *Inferno*.[33] Though the *Odyssey* was not listed, Kerouac (again through his Duluoz persona) refers to reading both Homeric epics in college (Kerouac [1968] 1994, 66), a claim that does not contradict his disavowal of schoolwork elsewhere: "Read and studied alone all my life.—Set a record at Columbia College cutting classes in order to stay in dormitory room to write a daily play and read, say, Louis Ferdinand Céline, instead of 'classics' of the course" (Kerouac [1960] 1970, viii). In fact, Kerouac's studious habits went back to Lowell High School, where he took off one day a week in his senior year to work his way through, among other volumes, the Harvard Classics (Johnson 2012, 61). Completing the innermost Beat circle was Gregory Corso whose extraordinarily hard childhood of parental abandonment, foster homes, homelessness, and prisons, made him (along with Neal Cassady) even more authentically an autodidact. Despite these circumstances,

32. Interviewed by Kristine McKenna, *Los Angeles Times*, February 16, 1994.

33. See http://www.college.columbia.edu/core/1937.php.

Corso nonetheless absorbed many classical authors and made frequent, not merely miscellaneous, allusion to them in his poetry.[34] Indeed, when teaching at the Naropa Institute in 1977, Corso's syllabus included *Gilgamesh,* a katabatic text he applied to his fellow Beats by "constantly referring to Gilgamesh and Enkidu as proto-Kerouac and proto-Cassady, two friends in search of the mystery of everlasting life" (Olson 2002, 75).[35] (In a later poem, "Ancestry," Corso would return to this analogy, alluding to Kerouac's most famous novel while depicting the epic Sumerian proto-Beats as "both on the unpaved road of antiquity" [1981, 20].) Thus, on the basis of their journals, interviews, and allusions, it would seem that even if all the Beats cut all their classes, we must credit them with wide and canonical reading beginning in what Kerouac called the happiest time of his life, his "book-devouring boyhood."[36]

One work written not long after that boyhood, Kerouac's *Orpheus Emerged* (1945, published posthumously in 2002), reminds us by its title that there are figures who make the katabatic journey outside of the epic tradition and that, while all of them return, not all of them return successfully. The legend of Orpheus is, of course, an extremely flexible allegory of the artist as a figure both inspired and destroyed, and at least some version of this myth was present in the minds of Jack Kerouac and Allen Ginsberg early in their careers, later proving useful to William Burroughs, as well. (Though Ginsberg referred to Corso as "great Orpheus of these States," Corso himself invested much more of his poetic identity in the god Hermes who, as psychopompos, made the katabatic journey a regular commute.)[37] While such analogies always risk tendentiousness, they may offer some suggestive, if disturbing, insights into the way the Beats—artists at once self-conscious and self-destructive—viewed their own works and lives, and found artistic opportunity and purpose in their personal underground sojourns.

In one of his earliest works—the third in his *Collected Poems*—Ginsberg goes underground for explicitly aesthetic reasons. In two occasional sonnets entitled "After Reading Kerouac's Manuscript *The Town and the City*" (1948), the first line of the first poem, responding to the first novel of his new friend,

---

34. See introduction to this volume, 4–7.

35. See also Corso's interview with Michael André (*Unmuzzled Ox* 22 (1981): 123–58, "Gilgamesh was the first thing written down. You know why it's important to me? Because I like to go back to the sources" (quoted in Olson 2002, 75).

36. The quotation comes from *Doctor Sax* (1987, 203), which Kerouac subtitled *Faust Part Three.*

37. Ginsberg's characterization of Corso is from "I Am Not," *The American Poetry Review* 14.6 (Nov/Dec) 1985, 17. For Corso's allusions to Hermes see, e.g., "In the Fleeting Hand of Time" in *Gasoline* (1958) and both "Ancestry" and "Columbia U Poesy Reading—1975" in *Herald of the Autochthonic Spirit* (1981).

begins: "I dwelled in Hell on earth to write this rhyme" (Ginsberg 2006, 13). In fact, Ginsberg might be said to have visited there throughout his career. Among his other works that conjure with the katabatic tradition are "Siesta in Xbalba" (1954–55), a poem set where the Mayan gods of the underworld preside, and "Plutonian Ode" (1978) which mines this tradition further by aligning the classical underworld with the nuclear age while, in Ginsberg's words, "accounting Homeric formula for appeasing underground millionaire Pluto Lord of Death"[38]. Addressed in part, like "A Supermarket in California," to "Father Whitman" (18), the poem summons details from classical myth to depict:

> . . . this magma-teared Lord of Hades, Sire of avenging Furies, billionaire
> Hell-King worshipped once
> with black sheep throats cut, priest's face averted from underground myster-
> ies in a single temple at Eleusis,
> Spring-green Persephone nuptialed to his inevitable Shade.
> (4–6)[39]

A later work that functions as a comic sequel to "Kaddish," "White Shroud" (1983) provides a further instance of Ginsberg's use of the nekyia as he journeys "To the Great City of the Dead" (2) and converses with his mother before returning "from the Land of the Dead to living Poesy" to write "this tale of long lost joy, to have seen my mother again!" (126–27).[40] More intimately, "Dream Record: June 8, 1955" inverts the nekyia pattern by having the dead question the living. This brief, powerful lyric details a ghostly visit from Joan Burroughs in which the dreamer updates the murdered woman on those still living, but when he questions her of what the dead might know or remember, she fades away into cryptic silence: "The next instant / I saw her rain-stained tombstone / rear an illegible epitaph" (31–33).[41]

Joan Vollmer Burroughs had received what "Dream Record" calls "the bullet in her brow" (11) from her husband, William Burroughs. In his introduction to an early work, *Queer*, not published until 1985, Burroughs writes, "I am forced to the appalling conclusion that I would never have become a writer but for Joan's death, and to a realization of the extent to which this event has motivated and formulated my writing" (xxii). By mythologizing his own career thus, Burroughs implicitly presents his art as an attempt to rescue Joan

38. This phrase comes from the back cover of *Plutonian Ode: Poems 1977–1980* (1982).
39. Ginsberg 2006, 710–13.
40. Ginsberg 1986b, 47–50.
41. Ginsberg 2006, 132.

if not from death, at least from meaningless death, thereby making that infamous "William Tell" game of 1951 not "just an absolute piece of insanity"[42] but something more akin to a sacrifice that enabled his own work. This retrospective analysis of *Queer* continues in terms that suggest an analogy to the artist's Orphic descent and return: "I live with the constant threat of possession, and a constant need to escape from possession, from Control. So the death of Joan brought me in contact with the invader, the Ugly Spirit, and maneuvered me into a lifelong struggle, in which I have had no choice except to write my way out." The introduction then closes with an italicized section. It begins: "*I have constrained myself to escape death*" (xxii).[43]

By endorsing Joan as a Eurydicean figure, never quite able to return from the dead herself but inspiring him to do so, and to pursue his own art thereafter, Burroughs could be said to have appropriated the Orphic legend for autobiographical purposes. One might object that Orpheus himself did not shoot his wife in the head, though in Ovid's account it was Eurydice's wedding that in some sense led to her death, a death rendered permanent when Orpheus turns around: the one violation of his contract with the underworld that he knew would prevent Eurydice's return.[44] The artist emerges alive and alone then, without a wife, but also as a katabant with new elegiac material for his art.

If William Burroughs functions in this modernized myth as both the serpent, whose bite fatally stings Eurydice, and Orpheus, the bereaved husband who attempts to redeem her death through his work, perhaps Jack Kerouac combines a different pair of roles from later in the story: the ecstatically destructive Maenads, whose wine-darkened senses cannot hear or heed the divine art of Orpheus whom they will tear apart, and the singer Orpheus himself, now newly emerged, isolated and gynophobic, but granted the theme of his own self-destruction. After all, when Kerouac sends Duluoz on his downward and inward quest in *Big Sur*, at least one of its goals is to furnish him with a song: the long lyric poem "Sea" (composed "mostly with eyes closed,

---

42. William Burroughs discussing his shooting of Joan Burroughs in *Burroughs: The Movie* (dir. Howard Brookner, 1984).

43. See also James Grauerholz, "The Death of Joan Vollmer Burroughs: What Really Happened?" (2002) at http://www.artifacting.com/blog/wp-content/uploads/2003/11/deathofjoan-full.pdf: "Other commentators have taken Burroughs' statements in the *Queer* introduction as a sort of 'key' to the writer's oeuvre, again taking his words at face value: to redeem himself of the sin of murder, William Burroughs dedicated his life to writing. But this apologia may be just a bit disingenuous, because Burroughs had already written a nearly complete draft of *Junkie* by December 1950, eight months before Joan's death" (61).

44. *Metamorphoses* 10.8–10.

as if blind Homer"[45]) that he retrieves from his experience and appends to the text of the novel. Thus again, from what Van Ghent calls "his tortures—the heroic 'ordeals' of myth" that "send him into ecstasy," the Beat protagonist "bursts into song, song filled with metaphors of destruction," as if the ancient Orphic urge keeps him singing of the "Sea" even after the novel ends, like the mythic lyrist's head as it floats away downstream.[46]

Bibliography

Bartlett, Lee. 1981. *The Beats: Essays in Criticism*. Jefferson, NC: McFarland.

Brookner, Howard, dir. 1984. *Burroughs: The Movie* (Criterion Collection DVD, 2015).

Burroughs, William S. 1966. *Naked Lunch*. New York: Grove Press.

———. 1985. *Queer*. New York: Penguin.

———. 1993. *The Letters of William Burroughs: 1945–1959*. Ed. Oliver Harris. New York: Viking.

Clark, Tom. 1984. *Jack Kerouac: A Biography*. New York: Da Capo Press.

Corso, Gregory. 1958. *Gasoline*. San Francisco: City Lights.

———. 1981. *Herald of the Autochthonic Spirit*. New York: New Directions.

Dover, Kenneth J. 1993. *Aristophanes: Frogs*. Oxford: Oxford University Press.

Eliot, T. S. 1923. "*Ulysses*, Order, and Myth." *Dial* 75.5: 480–83.

Fagles, Robert, trans. 1996. *The Odyssey*. New York: Viking-Penguin.

Ginsberg, Allen. 1956. *Howl and Other Poems*. San Francisco: City Lights.

———. 1982. *Plutonian Ode: Poems 1977–1980*. San Francisco: City Lights.

———. 1985. "I Am Not." *The American Poetry Review* 14.6: 17.

———. 1986a. *Howl*. Ed. Barry Miles. New York: Harper.

———. 1986b. *White Shroud: Poems 1980–1985*. New York: Harper.

———. 1994. Interview, *Los Angeles Times*, 16 February. http://articles.latimes.com/1994-02-16/entertainment/ca-23540_1_allen-ginsberg

———. 2000. "Notes Written on Finally Recording *Howl*." In *Deliberate Prose: Selected Essays 1952–1995*, edited by Bill Morgan. New York: Harper Collins.

———. 2006. *Collected Poems: 1947–1997*. New York: Harper.

Grauerholz, James. 2002. "The Death of Joan Vollmer Burroughs: What Really Happened?" http://www.artifacting.com/blog/wpcontent/uploads/2003/11/deathofjoan-full.pdf

Holmes, John Clellon. 1988. *Go*. New York: Thunder's Mouth Press.

Johnson, Joyce. 2012. *The Voice Is All: The Lonely Victory of Jack Kerouac*. New York: Viking-Penguin.

---

45. Letter from Kerouac to Ginsberg, September 22, 1960. See Morgan and Stanford 2010, 459.

46. Particular thanks to Ralph Rosen and Joseph Farrell for their scholarly advice, precise information, and timely questions. Grateful thanks as well to the Friends of English at UCLA for its support in the publication of this essay.

Kerouac, Jack. 1958. *The Subterraneans.* New York: Grove Press.

———. 1959. "Belief & Technique for Modern Prose: List of Essentials." *Evergreen Review* 2 Spring: 57.

———. 1966. Interview, http://www.youtube.com/watch?v=kOMyzslIP-o

———. 1987. *Doctor Sax.* New York: Grove Press.

———. 1992. *Big Sur.* New York: Grove Press.

———. 1994. *Vanity of Duluoz: An Adventurous Education, 1935–46.* New York: Penguin.

———. 1999a. *On the Road.* New York: Penguin.

———. 1999b. *Selected Letters: 1957–1969.* Ed. Ann Charters. New York: Viking.

———. 2002. *Orpheus Emerged.* New York: ibooks.

Milton, John. 1998. *Paradise Lost.* Ed. Alastair Fowler. London: Routledge.

Morgan, Bill, and Stanford, David. 2010. *Jack Kerouac and Allen Ginsberg: The Letters* New York: Viking-Penguin.

Olson, Kirby. 2002. *Gregory Corso: Doubting Thomist.* Carbondale: Southern Illinois University Press.

Oxford English Dictionary. http://www.oed.com/

Perseus Digital Library. http://www.perseus.tufts.edu/hopper/

Sinclair, John D., trans. 1974. *Dante's Inferno.* New York: Oxford University Press.

Smith, Evans L. 1990. *Rape and Revelation: The Descent to the Underworld in Modernism.* Lanham, MD: University Press of America.

Stephenson, Gregory. 1990. *The Daybreak Boys: Essays on the Literature of the Beat Generation.* Carbondale: Southern Illinois University Press.

Stevenson, Robert Louis. [1886] 2008. *The Strange Case of Dr. Jekyll and Mr. Hyde.* Oxford: Oxford University Press.

Tennyson, Alfred. 1958. *Poems of Tennyson.* Boston: Houghton Mifflin.

Tennyson, Hallam. 1897. *Alfred Lord Tennyson: A Memoir.* New York: H. T. Thomas.

Van Gennep, Arnold. 1960. *The Rites of Passage.* Chicago: University of Chicago Press.

Van Ghent, Dorothy. 1959. *Wagner Literary Magazine* Spring: 27–28.

Whitman, Walt. 1982. *Whitman: Complete Poetry and Prose.* New York: Library of America.

Wilson, Edmund. 1959. *Wagner Literary Magazine* Spring: 29.

CHAPTER 2

"Thalatta! Thalatta!"

XENOPHON, JOYCE, AND KEROUAC

CHRISTOPHER GAIR

Jack Kerouac's association with members of the Greek American population of Lowell, Massachusetts, has been, and continues to be, well documented. Most notably, in terms of his aspirations as a writer, his friendship with Sebastian "Sammy" Sampas is credited with introducing Kerouac to their school's literary club and, later, to the "young Prometheans," moves which not only exposed Kerouac to a range of new authors but also convinced him that becoming a writer was a realizable ambition for a boy from his background in industrial small-town New England. Much later, Sam's sister Stella would become Kerouac's third wife. More widely, the Greek American community to which Sampas belonged in Lowell continued to uphold a traditional Greek appreciation of the arts in ways that were less apparent in the Irish and French sections of the town that Kerouac also frequented, and this interest had a profound impact on the cultural life of a would-be artist such as Kerouac (Nicosia 1983, 82).

Greece, too, played a wider role in the development of the Beat consciousness, in a tripartite manner that embraced ancient Greek mythology and literature, British romanticism's engagement with this past and with the revolutionary struggle of the early nineteenth century, and a (rather naïve) conception of post–World War II Greece as a space in which to escape the crushing pressures of modern America. Gregory Corso was well versed in the Greek classics from his time in Clinton Prison, and the letters sent during his three-month sojourn in Greece in late-1959 are characterized by allusions to the Acropolis, Homer, and the "Gods of Greece," coupled with customary tales of drunkenness and urgent notes to Lawrence Ferlinghetti and others, requesting money (Corso 2003, 210–22).[1]

Unsurprisingly, given their affiliations with romanticism and transcendentalism, many Beat writers were drawn both to the literary and philosophical traditions of ancient Greece and also to the relationship between Byron and the Greek war for independence that led to the birth of the modern Greek nation. Significantly, when Jack Duluoz meets Sabby Sayakis (Sebastian Sampas) in Kerouac's *Vanity of Duluoz* (1968), he notes how Sabby would "yell Byron at me: 'So we'll go no more-a-roving / So late into the night . . .'," lines whose introduction chronologically anticipates Duluoz/Kerouac's own years of "roving" while—at the moment that he is writing—illustrating his retreat to life with Stella and Mémêre and the tacit acknowledgement that his roving days are now behind him (Kerouac 1982b, 70). Alan Ansen (*On the Road*'s Rollo Greb) lived in Athens for around forty years, while many of the major Beats traveled extensively in Greece, celebrating a place of ancient culture, natural beauty, and hospitality, where the status of the artist was very different from their experience of the midcentury United States. Last—but by no means least—the ancient Greeks' concepts of homosexual love between men and of the homosocial relationships that underpin the generation of art serve as direct precursors of the associations that, for Allen Ginsberg, were a necessary precondition for artistic creativity and that, in later life, saw him adopt a role akin to the ἐραστής (*erastês*) in the ἐραστής-ἐρώμενος (*erastês-erômenos*) relationship characterizing an ancient Greek education in military, civic—or, in Ginsberg's updated version, artistic—affairs.

This summary hints at what can be perceived as the central paradox of the Beat generation. In one respect, it stands as a quintessential American movement, looking back to Whitman and Thoreau, celebrating individualism in language generally drawn from the "American Grain" and highlighting aspects of American life threatened by an encroaching and pervasive modernity. On the other hand, Beat voices are also self-consciously pluralistic, drawing upon the aesthetic traditions of (among others) the East, of Europe (from the classics, through romanticism to modernism) and of Native American mythologies to construct their works. The paradox continues when international responses to Beat writing are considered: a corpus generally seen from within as counterhegemonic in its critiques of the cultural and political constraints of life at American midcentury is often read by non-Americans as the embodi-

1. See too Gustave Reininger's 2009 documentary, *Corso: The Last Beat*, in which the sixty-seven-year-old poet returns to Italy and Greece and muses on their significance in the formulation of his Beat persona.

ment of an American freedom unavailable elsewhere. The reading of Kerouac's relationship to Joyce and Xenophon that follows should be taken within the context of this introduction, since what I hope to illustrate is a significant interconnectivity between the literatures of ancient Greece, early twentieth-century European modernism and the fiction and poetry of Jack Kerouac.

Much of Kerouac's engagement with Greek literature and culture (both ancient and modern) comes, unsurprisingly, in the novels chronicling his Lowell childhood. In *Maggie Cassidy* (1959), Jacky Duluoz (the Kerouac stand-in) describes a newspaper picture in which he sees himself as a "Greek athletic hero with curly black locks, ivory white face . . . noble youth neck," and recalls G. J. Rigopoulakos's mother, "an old Greek widow the death of whose husband fifteen years ago left her still in blackest mourning, sat in a rocking chair . . . with an old Greek bible on her lap, and grieved, and grieved, and grieved," in two representations bordering on the stereotypical (Kerouac 1982a, 126, 14). A more significant moment occurs in *Doctor Sax* (1959), in what—at first glance—could pass for a simple duplication of the latter scene:

> [G. J.'s] mother who can't understand English . . . is rocking back and forth with her Greek bible, saying "Thalatta! Thalatta!" (Sea! Sea!)—and in the corner of G. J.'s house I smell the dank gloom of Greeks and shudder to be in the enemy camp—of Thebans, Greeks, Jews, Niggers, Wops, Irishmen, Polocks. (Kerouac 1984)

While the incident ends with Duluoz seeing G. J.'s "almond eyes" and pulling back from the notion that Greeks are "raving maniacs," their inclusion in a list of derogatory racial epithets hardly encourages a sense of identification (Kerouac 1984, 14). Yet such a conclusion conceals a more interesting moment of literary circulation that sheds light on Kerouac's reminiscences: "Thalatta! Thalatta!" is an ancient variant of what in modern Greek would be "Thalassa! Thalassa!" ("The Sea! The Sea!"). It is not, as Kerouac here seems to imply, a quotation from the Bible, but from the account of the retreat of the "Ten Thousand"—an army of Greek mercenary soldiers—from the Plain of Cunaxa to the Black Sea in 401 BCE, which is the subject of Xenophon's seven-book epic, *Anabasis.* It is unlikely, however, that the teenage Duluoz would know this, or uncertain even that Kerouac would have read *Anabasis* by the time that he wrote *Doctor Sax.*[2] Indeed, if he had, he would probably not have

2. This is not to understate the significance of the *Anabasis* which, as Tim Rood has noted, achieved "an extraordinary prominence as the text used for learning Greek in schools" in the United States in the second half of the nineteenth century (Rood 2010, 2). In an immensely useful, detailed history of the place of the *Anabasis* in American culture, Rood

implied that "Thalatta! Thalatta!" was taken from the Bible. It is possible, of course, that "Memory Babe" is offering a precise recollection of what he heard, even if he does not fully comprehend what he records. More likely, however, is that he is adopting the line more circuitously, drawing on the opening scene of James Joyce's *Ulysses* (1984, 4), where Buck Mulligan—discussing the sea—tells Stephen Dedalus, "Thalatta! Thalatta! She is our own sweet mother." If this is the case (and, given his unusually close attachment to Mémêre, the identification of sea and mother in Kerouac's representation is a provocative association to which I will return later), then a pattern emerges in which the adult writer draws upon his Greek American inspired knowledge of (Irish) modernism to reconstruct a moment from his teenage years before he had read Joyce and when he is in the early stages of what will become a significant, lifelong engagement with both ancient and modern Greek culture. Such a reading illustrates the complex transmission of ideas and language within which the sense of Kerouac's Greek Beat aesthetic outlined in what follows should be understood.[3]

The rather circuitous road to Xenophon should not be taken to suggest that Kerouac's identification with Ancient Greek literature and mythology is insignificant. It recurs regularly and is perhaps stressed most plainly in *Vanity of Duluoz,* which places Duluoz's life within the framework of Homeric epic. Possibly because he has dedicated the book to "Σταυρουλα" (his wife, Stella), he begins by recounting how he read Homer's *Iliad* "in three days" (Kerouac 1982b, 9) and represents, among other examples, a teenage football game as "Homeric battle" (16). In addition, in a letter to poet Philip Whalen, dated January 16, 1956, Kerouac chides Whalen for "wasting yr time with that idiot Gertrude Stein," and urges him to "read the great writers, stick to Rabelais, stick to Homer, stick to [Omar] Khayyam" (Kerouac 1995, 542). Likewise, many other works, most notably *Visions of Cody,* are laced with references

---

notes that it has "often been received second- or third-hand—except where children have plodded wearily through it at school" (218). While Rood does not mention Kerouac or other Beats, Kerouac's usage here does appear to fit the pattern he identifies.

3. This circulation is further complicated by the presence of Thomas Wolfe as a significant role model for Kerouac. Wolfe (who Kerouac read shortly before he moved on to Joyce) was heavily and openly indebted to Joyce—calling *Look Homeward, Angel* his "*Ulysses* book" (Rood 2010, 37)—and may well have influenced Kerouac's decision to read *Ulysses.* In addition, in *Look Homeward, Angel* (1930), Wolfe had planned to include clear and repeated allusions to Xenophon's *Anabasis.* These, however, were largely removed from the original 300,000-word manuscript, which was only published in full, as *O Lost: A Story of the Buried Life,* in 2000, and which, as Rood suggests includes, "by far the richest [literary] use of Xenophon in conveying and also interrogating the ideology of American growth" (ibid., 31). Although a passing reference to *Anabasis* remains in *Look Homeward, Angel,* it is improbable that this would have made a significant impression on Kerouac. See ibid., 27–50.

not only to the *Iliad* and the *Odyssey*, but also more widely to ancient Greek literature. Thalatta/the sea is a key motif throughout Kerouac's work, from the Thomas Wolfe-esque title of his very early novel, *The Sea is My Brother* through *On the Road*, *Visions of Cody*, and *Lonesome Traveller* and on to its central place in the prose narrative and accompanying poem of the Pacific (with the title, "Sea") of *Big Sur*.[4]

While this summary explicitly argues that the reference to *Anabasis* is a trace, filtered through at least one other narrative, that trace is significant as a kind of classical unconscious that highlights important formal continuities across Western literature. The *Anabasis* serves as an ancient precedent for Kerouac's modern, secular, autobiographical version of the epic journey, with a shared desire to reach the sea that differs from the island-based topography of Homer and Joyce.[5] In this context, it is worth assessing the structure and form of Kerouac's fiction within the frame laid out by Xenophon. As a starting point, I shall consider *On the Road* (1957), since the fact that it is a work well known to so many readers means that key themes can be identified swiftly. I will not be proposing that it is a direct retelling of *Anabasis* (either on a conscious or subconscious level), but rather suggesting that the terns "anabasis"—a journey inland from the coast—and its opposite, "katabasis" (that is, an expedition from the interior to the sea, but also, more widely, a descent into the underworld, or into madness, or other similarly hellish situations) provide the structural foundations for Kerouac's novel and that Sal Paradise's journeys resonate with echoes of Xenophon—albeit echoes that undermine or parody the intensity of Sal's quest through contrast with the magnitude of the original *Anabasis*.

On the Road begins with Sal Paradise's plan for his own version of anabasis: in a pattern reminiscent of Greek and Roman epics, such as the *Iliad*, the *Odyssey*, and the *Aeneid*, the narrative commences at a moment of despair, with Sal "feeling that everything was dead" after the breakup of his marriage and recent recovery from a serious illness (Kerouac 1972, 7).[6] His plan for

4. For another reading of the place of anabasis and katabasis in *Big Sur*, see Stephen Dickey's "Beats Visiting Hell: Katabasis in Beat Literature" in this volume. Dickey notes that "nowhere in the Beat oeuvre is the katabatic paradigm more intricately and kaleidoscopically applied than in Kerouac's novel of 1962." While I share Dickey's view of the novel's representation of a katabatic descent into mental turmoil, my argument will locate this fall as part of Kerouac's "one vast book" (as he calls it in the preface to *Big Sur*), the Duluoz narrative as a whole, while Dickey's focus links *Big Sur* to Allen Ginsberg's verse and to the Beat canon more widely.

5. I am grateful to the editors of this volume for their help in identifying this key point.

6. Thus, the *Iliad* commences with the Greek army enduring the plague sent by Apollo and the feud between Achilles and Agamemnon; the *Odyssey* begins a decade after the end of

spiritual rejuvenation involves a quest for self-discovery through a journey across America to the Pacific Ocean. But this journey needs to be subdivided, beginning with an episode of anabasis, as he heads to Denver, followed by the katabasis (here, essentially, in its most straightforward sense of a journey down to the sea) of the trip to the West Coast and a feeling of spiritual, if not actual, homecoming. Much of the remainder of the novel reenacts these moves in ways that carry traces of Xenophon's narrative, which, it should be remembered, also focuses more on katabasis than anabasis. Thus, attempting a linguistic American Grain vernacular that matches Xenophon's straightforwardly told epic, *On the Road* features similar scenes of struggles with nature in deserts, snowstorms, and mountain ranges; of hunger and other hardships; and, notably, of the need to overcome the hostility of local authority figures, such as the cops who seem keen to apprehend Sal Paradise and Dean Moriarty at every opportunity. The parallels continue with the parodic cameo appearances of the pseudo-Socratic Slim Gaillard and George Shearing, and in the emphasis on spiritual development as explicit rejection of what Sal sees as the pervasive materialism that is increasingly coming to define the postwar United States. Finally, as Sal reaches the coast and climbs the "big side of the canyon that led mysteriously to the Pacific Ocean," he enacts his own moment of "Thalatta! Thalatta!" akin to that of the Ten Thousand on Mt. Thebes:

> It was Sunday. A great heat wave descended: it was a beautiful day, the sun turned red at three. I started up the mountain and got to the top at four. All those lovely California cottonwoods and eucalypti brooded on all sides. . . . There was the Pacific, a few more foothills away, blue and vast and with a great wall of white advancing from the legendary potato patch where Frisco fogs are born. Another hour and it would come streaming through the Golden Gate to shroud the romantic city in white, and a young man would hold his girl by the hand and climb slowly up a long white sidewalk with a bottle of Tokay in his pocket. (76)

While this passage offers a vision of apparent integration for Sal, as the sea sweeps in to envelop the city in a romantic haze that replaces the images of loss and sickness at the start of the book, it is also (again, as with Xenophon's *Anabasis*), something of a false resolution. Where Xenophon's Greek soldiers must continue their battles, even when back within the Greek world, Sal also still has far to travel and will ultimately reject the promises of the West

---

the Trojan War, with Odysseus still far from home; and the *Aeneid* with the storm that wrecks the Trojan fleet and with Aeneas's recounting the tale of the Trojan Horse and fall of Troy.

and return to his aunt's house in the East. The lure of the Pacific will return through much of Kerouac's fiction, but it is never again able fully to represent the moment of utopian promise offered as Sal looks down from the California heights.

•

While I have been suggesting here that Kerouac is working within an epic form (and, of course, the Legend of Duluoz is conceived of by him as an epic in its own right), and while I have noted some similarities in the patterns of the *Anabasis* and *On the Road,* I do not wish to push the analogy too far. As I proposed above, "Thalatta! Thalatta!" provides a trace of a text, but it is a trace that seems unaware of the original source. Instead, I argue that the citation is more directly a reference to the opening pages of James Joyce's *Ulysses* and that Joyce serves as a mediating presence in Kerouac's appropriation of the classical epic and, in particular, in his construction of the sea as the central trope of potential liberation from the constraints of modern American life.

There is no doubt that the discovery of Joyce was a pivotal moment in Kerouac's quest to become a writer. In a letter to Donald Allen, dated October 1, 1959, Kerouac recounts how, as a young man, he "read Joyce and wrote a whole juvenile novel like 'Ulysses' called 'Vanity of Duluoz'" (Kerouac 1999, 248).[7] The point is more fully developed in the 1968 novel that bears the same title, when Duluoz (who appears to be practically indistinguishable from Kerouac here) notes that,

> I had just [in 1942] discovered James Joyce and I was imitating *Ulysses* I thought (really imitating "Stephen Hero" I later discovered, a real adolescent but sincere effort . . .). I had discovered James Joyce, the stream of consciousness, I have that whole novel right in front of me now. It was simply the day-by-day doings of nothing in particular by "Bob" (me), Pater (my Pa), etc., etc., . . . an attempt to delineate all of Lowell as Joyce had done for Dublin. (Kerouac 1982b, 118)

Ulysses, therefore, served as a key component in the emergence of Kerouac's stylistic and ideological practices. I will turn to the formal significance of Joyce's text later in this essay, but wish, first, to address the magnitude of Buck Mulligan's utterance as a signifier of a profound shift in attitudes toward Xenophon's *Anabasis* in the early twentieth century. In *"The Sea! The Sea!"*

7. This "Vanity of Duluoz" is not to be confused with Kerouac's 1968 novel of the same name.

The Shout of the Ten Thousand in the Modern Imagination (2004),[8] Tim Rood has traced the influence of the *Anabasis* in European and (to a lesser extent) American literature, noting that, because of its relatively simple language, it became a staple text for the Victorian and Edwardian European and American elites who insisted upon childhood Latin and Greek education. As a result, the theme was extensively used in Western adventure stories set in the East. "The sea! The sea!" would be a cry of triumph for any protagonist who survived the trials of a dangerous journey through the East and a staple of popular literature. Even before this, "Thalatta! Thalatta!" had served as the subject of Benjamin Robert Haydon's *Xenophon*, a painting representing the shouting army looking down on the sea from Mt. Thebes, which was probably the preeminent inspiration for the Philhellenic romances of the early 1800s.[9]

While Rood is keen to emphasize the manner in which *Anabasis* has been rewritten because of its ability to offer a transhistorical narrative of suffering and triumphant homecoming, he also acknowledges (more briefly) the tendency of modernist and postmodernist texts to question the very possibility of finding an authentic home. It is here that Joyce becomes so significant, given, as critics since Adorno have pointed out, that Stephen Dedalus and Leopold Bloom share an understanding of the extent to which alienation defines the human condition. Like Bloom, Kerouac's alter egos, such as Sal Paradise and Jack Duluoz, refuse to conform to the rules of the masses and—like Joyce and his central characters—believe that language can serve as the pivotal tool in expanding consciousness.

While, beyond Buck Mulligan's early utterance (and an essential Xenophonic echo of it, to which I will return later in this essay), the "Nausicaa"

8. Rood 2004, *passim*. Also see Hanson 2005, *passim*.

9. Rood 2010 maps the significance of the *Anabasis* within the political, literary, and philosophical culture of the United States. Among other examples, he notes the ways in which Xenophon was applied to Sherman's march and by the CIA in their (then secret) "Anabasis project" designed to "undermine Saddam Hussein's rule in Iraq by sabotage, infiltration, and disinformation, and by working with dissident Kurdish leaders in the north" (1). Rood also records how in a letter of 1763, future President John Adams cited Xenophon as his "favourite author," while the retreat of the "Ten Thousand" was invoked "as a parallel to Benedict Arnold's 1775 advance on Quebec . . . and to two of George Washington's celebrated marches" (54). Rood concludes, having studied numerous examples, that the United States has a long political and cultural tradition through which "imperialist exploitation of antiquity has been accompanied by a highly uncritical presentation of the ancient Greeks in popular history. The creation of the myth of America has been paralleled by the creation of an equally buoyant image of Greek democratic courage and discipline" (213). He does, however, also point to instances of challenge to this paradigm: one section of Cormac McCarthy's dystopian western, *Blood Meridian* (1985), is named "The Katabasis," while Walter Hill's cult movie, *The Warriors* (1979) reworks the *Anabasis* as an account of a New York gang's battle from the Bronx back to their home in Coney Island (216).

episode, and occasional metaphorical references, the sea's presence in *Ulysses* is largely implicit in the structured retelling of Homer's *Odyssey* rather than explicit as a constantly recurring motif, the patterns deployed by Joyce also anticipate Kerouac's fiction (most notably, *The Subterraneans, Visions of Cody,* and *Big Sur,* but also many other works) in significant ways. Northrop Frye's seminal *Anatomy of Criticism,* published in 1957, the same year as *On the Road,* describes this connection, in a manner that usefully historicizes Kerouac's reading of Joyce. For Frye,

> If a reader were asked to set down a list of things that had most impressed him about *Ulysses,* it might reasonably be somewhat as follows. First, the clarity with which the sights and sounds and smells of Dublin come to life, the rotundity of the character-drawing, and the naturalness of the dialogue. Second, the elaborate way that the story and the characters are parodied by being set against archetypal heroic patterns, notably the one provided by the *Odyssey.* Third, the revelation of character and incident through the searching use of the stream-of-consciousness technique. (1990, 313)

The combination of attention to the sensory details of daily life, the parodic appropriation of archetypal patterns and the use of stream-of-consciousness is familiar to anyone who has read Kerouac, while the fact that his own appropriation of these archetypal patterns can only come through the additional mediation of a hypercanonical modernist novel highlights the extent to which alienation has become a pervasive presence in the arts after the Second World War.

To illustrate the point, I would like first, briefly, to consider the "Joan Rawshanks in the Fog" section of *Visions of Cody,* the novel in which Joyce's formal influence on Kerouac is most pronounced, before concluding with a more detailed look at *Big Sur.* In *Ulysses,* Buck Mulligan calls the sea "our great sweet mother'; in *Doctor Sax,* Kerouac also associates the sea with the mother figure. In *Visions of Cody,* the two are torn apart. Where Sal takes the road to the Pacific with the expectation of revelation, the Duluoz of *Visions of Cody,* about to set off once more for California, claims that he has "nowhere to go except the water, the terrible terrible dark sea water, leaving behind the fields of life and my mother the great and final protector of my life and soul" (Kerouac 1980b, 138–39). The imagery contrasts sharply with parts of the letter that Duluoz writes to Cody (the Dean Moriarty of *On the Road*), prior to his departure, in which the death of June (Joan Vollmer) and other events lead to the fear that he "might have gone under," but also to the positive assertion that "now I'm a big seacaptain again" (73), but it is the former impression that creates the tone to be developed once Duluoz reaches San Francisco.

While *On the Road* draws upon (and parodies) the positive archetypes of Xenophon's *Anabasis,* "Joan Rawshanks in the Fog" can only recount the redundancy of these archetypes in a world obsessed with the two-dimensional banalities of the aging movie star. As such, Duluoz's return to the Pacific functions in a more complex manner, representing it as katabasis not only as a journey to the coast but also in terms of a fall into an anomie that will come to foreshadow an even bleaker descent into mental breakdown in *Big Sur* (1962). Witnessing take after take of Crawford running up some steps and fumbling with her keys, Duluoz loses any remaining ability to mythologize the West. Following a lengthy stream-of-consciousness recollection of his younger self's romanticized vision of Hollywood crews at work "in the California night, by moonlight . . . or some dreaming copse [or] . . . best of all . . . in the San Joaquin Valley of California, on a warm night . . . with the ghosts of old outlaws hanging from the cottonwood limb . . . and on the road itself Hopalong Cassidy, in his white hat and on his famed pony, loping along intently with beck and bent . . . all pure California night scenery and landscape," Duluoz concludes (with another classical allusion), "I had never imagined them going through these great Alexandrian strategies just for the sake of photographing Joan Rawshanks fumbling with her keys at a goggyfoddy door while all traffic halts in real world life only half a block away and everything waits on a whistle blown by a hysterical fool in a uniform" (Kerouac 1980a, 373–74).

Perhaps most significant in this episode is the near total exclusion of the sea from the scene. Whereas, in *On the Road,* the Pacific sends a romantic fog swirling through a city of young lovers, at this moment in *Visions of Cody,* that fog signifies nothing but the universal alienation of a modernity encapsulated by Hollywood's star system. Where once the sea was central to a vision of the possibilities of the West, here it becomes an invisible, ghostly presence, sending a "shroudy wind . . . smack from the great hidden dark bay" that also now houses "King Alcatraz . . . the sleephouse of two thousand dead criminals" (371).

•

Big Sur opens—like *On the Road*—with an extended period of crisis. In *On the Road,* Sal Paradise famously commences his narrative with the declaration that "everything was dead," planning to take off for the Pacific Ocean with fifty dollars in his pocket (Kerouac 1972, 7). The crisis at the start of *Big Sur* is brought about by a victory as pyrrhic as that of the army of the Ten Thousand at Cunaxa in Xenophon's *Anabasis.* After years of poverty and struggle, the success of *On the Road* had turned Kerouac into an overnight sensation, the "King of the Beatniks," unable to find any time or privacy to write (Kerouac 1980a, 7). Again, the response is to head West and—after a drunken false start in San Francisco—Jack Duluoz awakes in Monterey, "amazed and well again smelling sea air" (11). The events are a more-or-less direct transposition of Kerouac's own actions, but Duluoz's return to California suggests that the dystopian transformation of the nation is now complete and that the sea can no longer offer the kind of sublime transcendence it previously promised. On his first morning at Monsanto's cabin, Duluoz spots the wreck of a car beside the sea "like a terrifying poem about America one could write":

> The automobile that crashed through the bridge rail a decade ago and fell 1000 feet straight down and landed upside down, is still there now, an upsidedown chassis of rust in a strewn skitter of sea-eaten tires, old spokes, old car seats sprung with straw, one sad fuel pump and no more people—. (16)

Ever the quintessential Beat philosopher, Duluoz sees the wreck as a metaphor for the dangerous forces unleashed by technology. The car, rather obviously, symbolizes Kerouac's vision of the inevitability of the exhaustion of the American Dream and, more widely, the destruction of the human race, with metal rusted and tires eaten by a ravenous, insatiable ocean, itself far removed from the "blue and vast" backdrop to young lovers in *On the Road.* As John Tytell has noted, Duluoz's return makes him realize that the West of his dreams has now become a "tentacled megapolis" (Tytell 1976, 207), an image that succinctly combines memories of Frank Norris's California of the late nineteenth century with those of the sea monster that has superseded the sea mother. Where San Francisco had always represented the Frontier for Kerouac, as in *The Dharma Bums* or "October in the Railroad Earth," in *Big Sur* that Frontier has been overrun and the old heroes "have been hemmed in and surrounded and outnumbered—The circle's closed on the old heroes of the night" (Kerouac 1980a, 61).

In another way, however, the wrecked automobile suggests something more personal in the collapse of Kerouac's own dream of Beat generation freedom as realized in the transcontinental ana- and katabasis that shape some of the most joyous passages in *On the Road. Big Sur* is the moment when Kerouac finally admits to the hollowness of his own dreams, with the implication that he has been deceived all along and is revealed as the gullible immigrant, the wandering Bloom, who had believed what he had been told about the nation. Whereas in the early volumes of the Duluoz Legend, Kerouac incorporated mass cultural devices as a way to shape his own material, in *Big Sur,* he self-consciously rejects them, at one point cutting through a "big designed mankind cartoon of a man standing facing the rising sun with strong shoulders with a plough at his feet" to reveal a "necktied governor" manipulating the illusion. At last (perhaps acknowledging the inescapability of popular cultural referents and drawing upon an echo from another archetypal text, *The Wizard of Oz*), he admits that the America he had once cherished is no more than a pop cultural construction, and that "his" West was merely an internalized retelling of that narrative.

Big Sur (and the poem, "Sea," with which it concludes and to which I shall return below) goes beyond a simple recognition that Duluoz/Kerouac has been duped, suggesting that Kerouac now identifies his own complicity in the culture industry that he has come to despise. Whereas, in an earlier work such as *The Dharma Bums* (1958), the Duluoz character (here named Ray Smith) claims that his period of solitude on Desolation Peak brings rejuvenation and a renewed bond with Nature, Duluoz's visit to Monsanto's cabin even marks a rejection by the sea, which is here, for him, the key symbol of the natural world. In anticipation, he imagines that his sojourn will give him "peace" and the chance to "go back to childhood, just eat apples and read [his] Catechism—sit on curbstones, the hell with the hot lights of Hollywood." Quoting Emerson's assertion that "life is not an apology," Duluoz tries to convince himself that, "once again I'm Ti Jean the child." The early days of his time at the cabin represent a life of simple pleasures, in which he attempts to recreate and celebrate Emerson, Thoreau, and Whitman's vision of America. And yet, by the fourth day, he wonders whether he is "already bored?" and starts to long for cities that he knows will be "sickening." This yearning for company is equated with a recognition of an unbridgeable gap between Man and Nature, feeling that the sea "didn't want me there. . . . The sea has its waves, the man has his fireside, period" (Kerouac 1980a, 20, 30, 39 73). Where, in *On the Road,* the katabasis of the first arrival in San Francisco represented symbolic homecoming, here it is equated with absolute estrangement and with a psychological descent into the paranoia that dominates the second half of the novel.

The closing lines of (the prose section of) *Big Sur* appear, superficially, to offer an escape from the katabatic nightmare of the previous pages. Duluoz finally manages to sleep and awakes feeling that "everything has washed away—I'm perfectly normal again. . . . All the dark torture is a memory." He imagines an anabatic return to his mother, going "back home across autumn America," in which "it'll all be like it was in the beginning" (Kerouac 1980a, 180–81). But, while it is tempting to share Duluoz's optimism, and to recognize its potential as neat formal resolution in which, as Stephen Dickey puts it (see chapter 1, 28), "anabasis perfects *katabasis*," I would suggest that such a reading needs to be treated with caution.[10] First, these closing lines echo the opening pages of the novel, in which Duluoz envisages a joyful six weeks by the Pacific, "alone and undisturbed . . . just chopping wood, drawing water, writing, sleeping, hiking, etc., etc.," accompanied only by a "hopeful rucksack all neatly packed with everything necessary to live in the woods" (7, 10). Of course, this vision has been shattered before he even reaches the cabin; given both the events of the novel and the patterns of hopeful ambition swiftly replaced by desolate reality that shape so much of the Legend, it seems improbable that such a utopian fantasy will come to fruition. Second, the language of this concluding page, with its images of birds singing, a sleeping child, smiling adults, and religious purity, draws on precisely the kinds of popular cultural, sentimental, clichéd signifiers that Duluoz has earlier exposed (and which I discuss above) when he reveals the "necktied governor" manipulating the "big designed mankind cartoon of a man standing facing the rising sun with strong shoulders with a plough at his feet." Again, given the impassioned demolition of the culture industry and of his place within it, it is hard not to identify the irony in this ending. Is Duluoz truly envisioning a "golden and eternal" future, or is he surrendering to the logic of a culture he has previously rejected? Either way, the conclusion seems to be packed with self-mockery and a sense of personal complicity with all that he purports to oppose.

In any case, *Big Sur* ends not with this final passage of prose, but with the long poem, "Sea," dated August 21, 1960. Conceived as an attempt to capture the sounds of the Pacific, the verse develops—like the novel, itself—from an effort to regain the optimistic harmony between man and nature into the recognition of Kerouac's absolute separation from what had been a central symbol of his search for freedom. From something "Loved as Mother & fog," through "Glum sea, silent me" (Kerouac 1980a, 185, 190), the sea becomes yet another example of the modernity for which it once promised some compensation:

> Ah Ratatatatatat—
> The machinegun sea, rhythmic
> balls of you pouring in
> with smooth eglantinee
> (204)

As such, it is no longer something that can grant Kerouac any kind of solace. The Pacific is a "liar," that refuses to respond to the imputation, "Sea speak to

10. See Dickey's essay in this volume for a more optimistic reading of the conclusion to *Big Sur* than the one I provide here.

me, speak," and Kerouac asks, "Tiresome old sea, ain't you sick / & tired of all this merde?" (186, 191). For him, "The sea'll / only drown me" and "the attempt to "make our way / in self reliance" is thwarted by waves that "scare me" into a fear that "I am going to die / in full despair" (197).

Even his self-styling as a writer whose spontaneous prose marks him out from the calculated standardization of the United States at midcentury and as heir to the modernist tradition of literary experimentation (exemplified by Joyce) is no longer enough to save him from complicity in the appropriation and transformation of nature. Reiterating and developing the theme explored in the prose section of *Big Sur,* Duluoz writes of how, as best-selling author, his works appear on "gentle tree pulp pages / which've nothing to do / with your crash roar." Whereas Duluoz is able to recall a time when he was "still innocently playing with words," his literary endeavor now becomes merely another example of fallen, modern humankind's inability to see nature as anything more than commodity, with the pun on "pulp" summing up Kerouac's belief that his work is no different from any other kind of hegemonic popular culture (185–86, 177). The poem asserts that Kerouac is not alone in this complicity: bringing us full circle to G. J.'s mother's cry of "Thalatta! Thalatta!" and Buck Mulligan's "Thalatta! Thalatta! She is our own sweet mother," "Sea"—a title whose singular reference downplays the poetic and psychological intensity of the repeated "Thalatta! Thalatta!"—puns on the resemblance between the French words for sea, shit, and mother (mer, merde, and mère) in what is once more referred to as "Thalatta" (196). Although the allusion to Xenophon remains undeveloped, or indirect, filtered, once again, through Kerouac's responses to another narrative, that trace remains important as a marker of Western literary continuity across space and time, and as an example of the classical unconscious that pervades the Legend of Duluoz. As such, it usefully condenses the much more extensive genealogy that I have examined throughout this essay. There seems to be no doubt that Joyce is implicated here as (once more) an indispensable mediating presence. For example, in *Ulysses,* hearing "his boots crush crackling wrack and shells," Stephen Dedalus mulls upon the poetic qualities of the sea:

> *Won't you come to Sandymare,*
> *Madeline the mare?*
> Rhythm begins, you see. I hear. A catalectic tetrameter of iambs marching.
> No, agallop: *deline the mare.*[11]
> (Joyce 1984, 43)

11. Grace (2007, 181–89) provides a detailed discussion of the Joycean "inheritance" in Kerouac's "Sea," focusing on Stephen Dedalus "strolling along Sandymount Sand contemplating his

Joyce's play on mare's aural resemblance to "mer" (and, perhaps, too, to mère) anticipates Kerouac's own punning in "Sea," while the twinned play on sea/see suggests the process that moves from hearing the sounds of the sea to transforming them into poetry "agallop" with "iambs marching" that anticipates Kerouac's own methodology in "Sea."

Likewise, in *Ulysses,* Joyce included a few lines of prose that offer a close parallel to Kerouac's own onomatopoeic verse:

> Listen: a fourworded wavespeech: seesoo, hrss, rsseiss, ooos. Vehement breath of waters amid seasnakes, rearing horses, rocks. In cups of rocks it slops: flop, slop, slap: bounded in barrels. And, spent, its speech ceases. It flows purling, widely flowing, floating foampool, flower unfurling. (55)

In *Ulysses,* these lines—focalized through Dedalus—come shortly before Leopold Bloom's moment of nihilistic/katabatic "Desolation" (a word, of course, that would later reside near the heart of the Kerouac lexicon) when he muses on a "dead sea in a dead land," concluding with his vision of the Holy Land as "the grey sunken cunt of the world" (63). As such, they foreshadow Kerouac's equally desolate verse, in which America has become the dead land and Joyce is named directly, with his vision of "wavespeech" abandoned: "Joyce—James—Shhish— / Sea—Sssssss—see / —Varash / —mnavash la vache / écriture—the sea don't say / muc'h actually" (192).

This rejection of the symbolically positive power of the sea and its allusion to Joyce (and Xenophon) resonates even further, although in a somewhat different manner, when Kerouac's text as a whole—that is, the Legend of Duluoz—is considered alongside *Ulysses. Doctor Sax* records some of the earliest moments in Duluoz's life: although, chronologically, it is preceded by *Visions of Gerard* (1963), *Doctor Sax* is the novel in which Duluoz is properly initiated into reading literature and, tentatively, into dreams of becoming a writer. *Big Sur* marks the end point (bar the 1966 novella, *Satori in Paris,* which is largely devoted to a search for information about French ancestors) of this journey: as I noted above, Kerouac/Duluoz, exhausted by the trappings of his Beat celebrity, seeks solace by the Pacific but, instead, experiences mental disintegration.

This plot of decline, however, in which the nightmarish qualities of katabasis supersede the promises of freedom and enlightenment offered by the Pacific in *On the Road,* runs counter to the redemptive closing moments of *Ulysses,* where Molly Bloom's reference to "the sea the sea" (Joyce 1984, 706) provides formal counterpoint to Buck Mulligan's "Thalatta! Thalatta!" and a

self-imposed exile" and tracing the extent to which Kerouac is "carrying forward the Joycean sea project" in "Sea."

reiteration of Joyce's acknowledgement of Xenophon. In contrast to her husband's bleak vision of a/the "dead sea," Molly recounts how "the smell of the sea excited me of course" and concludes with lines that evoke the lust for life that Bloom and Duluoz have lost:

> O and the sea the sea crimson sometimes like fire and the glorious sunsets and the figtrees in the Alameda gardens yes and all the queer little streets and pink and blue and yellow houses and the rosegardens and the jessamine and geraniums and cactuses and Gibralter as a girl where I was a Flower of the mountain yes where I put the rose in my hair like the Andalusian girls used or shall I wear a red yes and how he kissed me under the Moorish wall and I thought well as well him as another and then I asked him with my eyes to ask again yes and then he asked me would I yes to say yes my mountain flower and first I put my arms around him yes and drew him down to me so he could feel my breasts all perfume yes and his heart was going like mad and yes I said yes I will Yes. (Joyce 1984, 704)

The emphasis on physicality and passion, accompanied by the explosion of natural colors at the end of Joyce's novel, is far from the Duluoz of *Big Sur*, whose impotence and alienation from those around him represent what he sums up as "lonely inhuman isolation" from the natural world and from other people (Kerouac 1980a, 178). Molly's memories evoke, up to a point, the desire that prompts Sal Paradise to head west, away from his dry college friends, and his subsequent eulogizing of the American landscape. More closely, they anticipate the role of Neal Cassady/Dean Moriarty/Cody Pomeray in the Duluoz Legend. Cassady's difference from the friends that Kerouac left behind mirrors the contrast between, on the one hand, Molly and, on the other, Stephen Dedalus and Leopold Bloom, whose narratives have framed all, bar the final section of *Ulysses*. Like Molly, Dean's speech is marked by the multiple repetition of "a thousand yeses" and, more importantly, by a form of stream of consciousness that bears little resemblance to formal English (Kerouac 1972, 8).[12] Yet, for the Kerouac of *Big Sur*, stream of consciousness—or, for him, "spontaneous prose"—has become the means to express not the joy and kicks of *On the Road*, but, instead, the mental torture of delirium tremens and spiritual alienation.

---

12. While this is not the place to develop the significance of the similarity, the parallel seems to go even further: as is well known, Joyce based Molly's soliloquy on letters written by his wife, Nora Barnacle. Likewise, Kerouac claimed to have been inspired to develop spontaneous prose by the "Joan Anderson" letter he received from Cassady on December 30, 1950, which, for Kerouac, "has all of Joyce at its command" (quoted in Nicosia 1983, 337).

Bibliography

Corso, Gregory. 2003. *An Accidental Autobiography: The Selected Letters of Gregory Corso.* Ed. Bill Morgan. New York: New Directions.

Frye, Northrop. 1990. *Anatomy of Criticism: Four Essays.* New York: Penguin.

Grace, Nancy. 2007. *Jack Kerouac and the Literary Imagination.* New York: Palgrave Macmillan.

Hanson, Victor D. 2005. "Thalatta! Thalatta!" In *The New Criterion.* http://www.newcriterion.com/articles.cfm/Thalatta—Thalatta—1368

Joyce, James. [1922] 1984. *Ulysses.* Harmondsworth: Penguin.

Kerouac, Jack. 1972. *On the Road.* New York: Penguin.

———. 1980a. *Big Sur.* London: Panther.

———. 1980b. *Visions of Cody.* St. Albans: Granada.

———. 1982a. *Maggie Cassidy.* St. Albans: Granada.

———. 1982b. *Vanity of Duluoz: An Adventurous Education, 1935–46.* St Albans: Granada.

———. 1984. *Doctor Sax: Faust Part Three.* London: Panther.

———. 1995. *Selected Letters, 1940–1956.* Ed. Ann Charters. New York: Penguin.

———. 1999. *Selected Letters, 1957–1969.* Ed. Ann Charters. New York: Penguin.

Nicosia, Gerald. 1983. *Memory Babe: A Critical Biography of Jack Kerouac.* New York: Grove Press.

Rood, Tim. 2004. *"The Sea! The Sea!" The Shout of the Ten Thousand in the Modern Imagination.* London: Duckworth.

———. 2010. *American Anabasis: Xenophon and the Idea of America from the Mexican War to Iraq.* London: Duckworth.

Tytell, John. 1976. *Naked Angels: The Lives and Literature of the Beat Generation.* New York: McGraw-Hill.

CHAPTER 3

"The Final Fix" and "The Transcendent Kingdom"

THE QUEST IN THE EARLY WORK OF WILLIAM S. BURROUGHS

LONI REYNOLDS

William S. Burroughs is perhaps best known as an experimental writer, iconoclast, and countercultural figure who wrote frankly about his drug use and transgressive sexuality. Several scholars, however, have observed that Burroughs's outwardly avant-garde writing follows the traditional linear structure of a "quest," at times with striking parallels to the heroic quests we associate with classical myths and epics such as Homer's *Odyssey* and Virgil's *Aeneid.*[1] While on the surface, *Junky* (1953), *Queer* (written in 1951–53), *The Yage Letters* (written in 1953), and *Naked Lunch* (written in 1955–57) may seem to be anarchic, hedonistic narratives of drug-fueled kicks, these early novels are, at the same time, structured around the framework of a single, continuing quest.

This chapter builds on important work by Stull (1981) and Skerl (1985) on the shaping presence of the quest in Burroughs and argues that classical versions of the quest can illuminate Burroughs's own systematic and sustained engagement with the theme, specifically in his early novels. Burroughs did not explicitly evoke parallels to classical myth as, for example, Jack Ker-

1. Skerl (1985, 6) picks up on the apparent dissonance between Burroughs's famously dissipated life and the traditional quest theme, stating that "[Burroughs's] own description of the following years [after he left Harvard in 1936] is one of aimless drifting and boredom. But a close look at his wanderings reveals an underlying quest." Skerl echoes Stull (1981, 15): "On close inspection, the 'newness' of Burroughs' vision fades and the stronger lines of a familiar pattern appear: the quest."

ouac did,[2] but as we will see, his work is informed by those traditional elements of the classical quest to which Dorothy Van Ghent called attention in other Beat writers—the denial of parents, the "mysterious call," the "journey underground" into "the realm of death," the "ordeals," and finally, "the far and visionary goal of the hero's quest—the return to the Kingdom, the transcendent kingdom of love and brotherhood and life."[3] In view of Burroughs's stated intention to *escape* traditional forms and create a "mythology for the space age" (a phrase which Burroughs began using in the mid-'60s to describe his work; Skerl 1985, 107), his relation to the classical tradition was necessarily indirect, but this does not mean that it was inconsequential.

It is evident from his letters that Burroughs was aware of antecedents in classical literature through his education and wide reading.[4] Even if Burroughs does not seem to have been unusually fascinated by the classical tradition, as was Corso, for example (see pp. 4–7 in this volume), and he did not draw explicitly on classical literature, the motivic and structural configuration of his novels can be helpfully illuminated through comparison with classical myth and epic.

My methodology in this essay bears some similarities to that of Vladimir Propp in his comparative study of folktales. Propp isolates certain narrative structures that do not depend on authorial intentionality but seem to recur across cultures as "motifs" or "type-scenes." Propp's work moves beyond individual intentionality toward something more universal or structural as an element of literary narrative and allows the comparison of works that may be—like Burroughs's writing and classical quest narratives—disparate in content, characterization, or purpose. The approach taken by the classicist R. G. Edmonds (2004, 8) is similar: he states that the narrative of a myth contains "traditional motifs, patterns of action, plot elements and sequences" and in his own work identifies and compares these aspects of several mythic *katabases*. Within Beat studies, Grace (2007, 4) takes a similarly structural approach in her analysis of the quest theme—and its parallels in the gnostic pearl tale—in Kerouac's work. Although she "makes no claim that Kerouac modeled *On the Road* after the pearl tale," stating instead that he "drew upon it as a general cultural reference," Grace maintains that "the pearl template as an interpretive template is relevant as a source of experience that even today

---

2. See Gair's chapter in this volume, and Skerl 1985, 22.

3. Van Ghent, quoted by Dickey above (15).

4. He calls "the Welfare State" a "Trojan Horse" in a 1949 letter to Ginsberg (1994, 57); refers to a "satyr . . . a mythological Greek creature characterized by insatiable lust" in a 1951 letter to Kerouac (75); and calls working on an early version of *Naked Lunch* "a veritable labor of Hercules" in a 1955 letter to Ginsberg (287).

holds significance and power." She continues: "By examining *On the Road* as a variation of that much older story, one can see how particular features of the mythic plot and characterization remain viable" (ibid., 84).

I will argue in this chapter that, like the work by Kerouac that Grace discusses, Burroughs's early novels can also be seen as "variations" of a "much older story," that of a quest, particularly as it was variously explored by the classical authors whom Burroughs would have encountered as part of his educational formation. We will find that some of the shared narrative structures of such quest narratives, like those discussed by Propp and Edmonds, and others detected in the Beats by Van Ghent, turn out to be strikingly present in Burroughs's early novels, as well.

For anyone wishing to analyze the perceived similarities between otherwise disparate narratives (historically or chronologically), Propp emphasizes the need to move beyond localized contingencies—an author's intentionality, for example, or the tale's relationship to the culture that produced it—in order to get to the deeper structures that recur with remarkable predictability across cultures:

> If we are incapable of breaking the folktale down to its components, then we shall be unable to make a correct comparison. And if we don't know how to compare, then how can we throw light upon, for instance, an Indo-European relationship or upon the relation of the Greek fable to the Indian, etc.? If we cannot compare one folktale to the other, then how is the folktale to be compared to religions or to myths?" (Propp 1968, 14)

Or, we might ask, how are we to compare classical myth and epic to the work of one of America's most avant-garde writers if we are unwilling to move beyond the question of how well (or how poorly) acquainted Burroughs was with a classical tradition that *seems*, at any rate, to inform some aspects of his writing? Burroughs's oblique engagement with the classical quest accords with the centrality of myth to Beat literature, which other scholars have noted.[5] This aspect of Burroughs's early work not only extends the range of expressive forms of myth in Beat writing but also reveals the power of the quest motif as a recurrent mechanism for organizing even that chaotic and aberrant experience that Burroughs sought to recount.

Toohey's (2010) working definition of the epic hero will serve as the foundation for our examination of Burroughs's conception of such a figure, which is central to his expression of the quest motif. For Toohey, the epic hero is

---

5. See Dickey in this volume.

someone who is "of superior social station and physique, is pre-eminent in fighting, courage, and perhaps in intelligence. Usually, as a result of a crisis or a war or an enforced quest, this hero will undergo some form of a change in status. After a period of being at odds (emotionally, physically, or even geographically) with his human and divine community he will assume his responsibilities and his duties to both groups" (Toohey 2010, 46).

The prologue of *Junky* introduces the theme of a quest and manifests the characteristics Toohey lists here, as well as those discussed by Van Ghent.[6] William Lee, the protagonist of the novels and Burroughs's fictional alter ego, is certainly of "superior social station" as the scion of a wealthy Midwestern family who lives a "safe, comfortable way of life" (Burroughs 1977, xi). The "crisis" he experiences, the call that inspires him to begin his journey, is self-determined and internal: it is the alienation he experiences in his community, which is made clear in the prologue. Lee feels not only as though the suburb in which he was raised was "cut off from contact with the life of the city" but also that "all contact with life was shut out" in this affluent milieu (xii). The phrases "cut off" and "shut out" and their contrast with the repeated term "contact" underscore the almost bodily separation and distance Lee feels from the society around him. Lee's quest begins when he sets out from this "comfortable" upper-class setting of his youth (xi), which he considers barren of opportunity for connection, stating that his early "environment was empty" (xiii).

The prologue of *Junky* also establishes the major objective of Lee's quest, which is the same across all four early novels. The dissatisfaction and yearning for a more exciting, more genuine mode of existence and a connection with others inspires Lee to set off on his journey.[7] But even after leaving his hometown and traveling, he cannot shake his sense of alienation. In the prologue, the phrase "cut off" is repeated, now with reference to the cushion of his trust fund; because of it, Lee states, "I was still cut off from life as I had been in the Midwest suburb" (Burroughs 1977, xiv). He contrasts his drug of choice, opiates, or "junk," with his sense of alienation, viewing it as a genuine, regenerating form of existence. In the last lines of the prologue, Lee states, "Junk is not a kick. It is a way of life" (xvi). This attitude toward junk persists into the main

6. Quoted by Dickey (15).

7. Propp refers to the "lack" that can serve as a character's motivation: "Prior to the beginning of the narrative, the situation in question [may have] gone on for years. But the moment comes when the dispatcher or searcher realizes what in particular is lacking, and in this moment originates the motivation for either dispatch or an immediate search" (1968, 69). Additionally, "a lack may at times be imaginary" (70).

text of *Junky*: initially, Lee sees junk as a vehicle for experience—a literal way of (experiencing) life—that would not have been available to him otherwise.

In *Junky*, as well as his later novels, Lee becomes frustrated by alienation and the limitations of physical existence and seeks to overcome these constraints through an expansion of consciousness that puts him in touch with a larger, universal reality, a more connected form of life. Such a goal, directed toward escaping the limitations of the alienated self, aligns Lee's desires with those of other classical heroes, who also yearn for transcendence and some form of union with other humans. In classical myth and epic, such goals are expressed in various ways, symbolic or physical, typically at the end of a quest; one thinks of the union between lovers, such as Odysseus and Penelope or Orpheus and Eurydice, a long-sought homecoming, such as Odysseus's delayed *nostos* to Ithaca after the Trojan War, or Aeneas's cosmically ordained foundation of Rome after his own search following the Trojan War. Lee's own search for union has various objectives, including drugs, closeness with a romantic partner and a community that will accept him, but his driving force throughout is his desire for a self-transcending life.

In the analysis that follows, I discuss the quest as a central theme in each of Burroughs's early novels along with analogues in the classical tradition. Noteworthy shared motifs, for example, are the journey to the underworld, or *katabasis*, in *Junky*; the search to escape the prison of the self in *Queer* and *The Yage Letters*, even as Lee's choices of vehicles for self-transcendence—homosexuality and drug use—mean that he remains "at odds" with the mainstream community; the hero's return in *Naked Lunch*. In his afterword to *William S. Burroughs at the Front*, Burroughs makes a statement that illuminates his idea of "mythology for the Space Age," asserting that his "purpose in writing has always been to express human potentials and purposes relevant to the Space Age" (Burroughs 1991, 268). I hope to demonstrate the ways that Burroughs expresses and updates the traditional elements of the quest narrative, so concerned with such "human potentials and purposes," which is deeply rooted in classicism. Such analysis illuminates how Burroughs, like his Beat cohorts presents the "hip vision of antiquity" discussed in the Introduction, that "makes new" and newly relevant and resonant, the mythic imagination of the ancient world at the dawn of postmodernism.

In *Junky*, Lee's decision to enter the world of junk begins a descent—his own heroic *katabasis*[8]—from a sheltered world of privilege to a dangerous yet enticing underworld. This downward movement from middle-class respectability into an underworld of experimentation with drugs, crime, and homo-

8. See Dickey and Gair in this volume for other Beat *katabases*.

sexuality is a major aspect of Lee/Burroughs's journey in *Junky* as well as in the other early novels. Paradoxically, though Lee's overarching goal is to attain the "transcendent kingdom of love, brotherhood, and life," he must journey through the land of the dead to attain this objective.

The various settings of *Junky* are characterized as, or in some cases are literally, either underground or related to death. After his initial experiences with junk, Lee is arrested and "taken to the Tombs" (Burroughs 1977, 27), the nickname for the Manhattan Detention Complex. His wife bails him out, but immediately after physically leaving the Tombs, he envisions "New York in ruins. . . . Weeds were growing up through cracks and holes in the pavement" (28): it is clear his *katabasis* is only beginning. After his release, Lee and an acquaintance, Roy, attempt to make money by "lush-working': descending into the subway and stealing money from the pockets of revelers intoxicated to the point of unconsciousness, a process which they call "working the hole" (33).

Lee's description of the junkies he meets during this time reads like a register of shades. These junkies, like the "hollow shades" of the unburied that Virgil describes waiting out their allotted term before being allowed to cross the river Styx, seem to inhabit a liminal space between life and death: they, too, can be seen as "shadowy likenesses of those deprived of light" (*Georgics* 4.472: *simulacra luce carentum*). Bill Gains has a "talent for invisibility" (Burroughs 1977, 55), while others "all looked like junk. There was Irish, George the Greek, Pantopon Rose, Louie the Bellhop, Eric the Fag, the Beagle, the Sailor, and Joe the Mex. Several are dead now, others are doing time" (30). The use of the euphemistic argot "doing time" also recalls the suspended limbo of the shades of the unburied: a state outside the normal passage of time yet still controlled by it. Lee's description of another underground acquaintance, Mary, as having "something boneless about her" and "look[ing] at you through a viscous medium she carried about with her" recalls the moment in Homer, *Odyssey* 11 (219–20) when Odysseus's mother describes her own incorporeality in the land of the dead: "Sinews no longer sinews hold the bones and flesh together"; thus, she "slipped through" Odysseus's arms when he attempted to embrace her (cf. *Od.* 11.205–6).

Even when Lee eventually travels on, leaving the subway, his shady acquaintances, and the Tombs behind, there is no resurrection: when he heads south to New Orleans, he describes the city as "present[ing] a stratified series of ruins" (Burroughs 1977, 68). Moving on to the Rio Grande Valley marks a further descent: "The Valley is a place where the new anti-life force is breaking through. Death hangs over the Valley like an invisible smog" (106). Burroughs's description of the Valley is similar to Ovid's depiction of the underworld through which Orpheus and Eurydice traverse: "thick with darkened vapor" (Ovid, *Met.* 10.54: *caligine densus opaca*). Its noxious "invisible smog" also makes it resemble Avernus of the *Aeneid*, "above which no creatures flying could / ever makes its way with its wings unharmed: such a vapor pouring forth from / its black jaws made its way to the vaulted sky" (Virgil 6. 239–41).[9] Again, the people Lee meets, particularly those connected to the junk underworld, are portrayed as ghostly; now, they are overtly described in spectral terms: "Old Ike, the pusher . . . often manifested himself like a poltergeist, throwing something or knocking on the walls" (Burroughs 1977, 134). Stull, too, (1981, 22), sees this part of Lee's quest as paralleling the descent of epic heroes into the land of the dead. He states that, toward the end of *Junky*, Lee comes back from this experience "a new person . . . who knows the junk equation and can sense when it is time to move on," but Lee's *anabasis*, his return to life and home, does not come about so quickly. In later work, Lee will arrive at "the knowledge or burden gained from the dead . . . [and] alteration of the traveler's sense of both world and self," to use Dickey's phrase in the preceding chapter (16), but not yet: he must acquire further experience in the land of the dead.

Lee's need for junk grows stronger and stronger as *Junky* progresses, and through his experiences with addiction, he comes to realize that junk not only contains in it the promise of life but also the danger of death. This dangerous aspect of junk connects it to another recurrent element of heroic quest narratives: the ordeal. By endangering the life of its user, junk functions as an initiatory ordeal, of the sort detailed by Propp (1968, 54–55).[10] Not only does Lee travel through the underworld and meet those shades who occupy a liminal space between death and life but he also comes to occupy that space himself through his drug use; he must pass through such an ordeal before he can become "a new person."

While in New Orleans, Lee overdoses, and his experience of the incident is described much as one would describe physical death. "Holy Jesus, this man is dying!" Lee's friend, Pat, who witnesses the overdose remarks (Burroughs 1977, 75), and Lee's own report of the overdose could easily be mistaken for a description of the process of death. He narrates: "As soon as I took the needle out of the vein, I knew it wasn't all right. I felt a soft blow in the heart. Pat's

9. quam super haud ullae poterant impune volantes
tendere iter pinnis: talis sese halitus atris
faucibus effundens supera ad convexa ferebat . . .

10. See also Nagy (1990, 136–45) on the ritual ordeals that Greek athletes undergo in competition. Nagy notes the frequent analogies of athletic ordeals in Pindar's epinician poetry to those of figures from myth (see, e.g., 137).

face began to get black around the edges, the blackness spreading to cover his face. I could feel my eyes roll back in their sockets" (74).

It is not just the effects of junk use that bring Lee closer to death, but the withdrawal from the drug. Lee, incarcerated in New Orleans and unable to use junk, describes the experience:

> The worst thing is lowering of blood pressure with consequent loss of body liquid, and extreme weakness, as in shock. It is a feeling as if the life energy has been shut off so that all the cells in the body are suffocating. As I lay there on the bench, I felt like I was subsiding into a pile of bones. (92)

These symptoms parallel the process of dying: first weakness, then a feeling that "life energy has been shut off," and then, "subsiding into a pile of bones." Again, we are reminded of the body's postmortem decay in Homer's description of the dead in *Od.* 11 and that final state in which the body can no longer "hold bones and flesh together." Now junk is associated with fragile and corruptible bodily existence, rather than the expansive, integrating, transcendent life that Lee originally sought. While he initially believed junk might bring him the latter, he has discovered that it only brings him the former, trapping him within his addicted body.

Lee fully identifies junk with death by the end of the text. After becoming addicted once more, while in Mexico City, he remarks: "Junk is an inoculation of death that keeps the body in a condition of emergency" (127). Lee's junk ordeal has taught him that the drug will not bring him the life he seeks. He now invests his hope for self-transcendent experience in other drugs, such as peyote and *yagé*.[11] Lee states:

> I decided to go down to Colombia and score for yage. . . . I am ready to move on south and look for the uncut kick that opens out instead of narrowing down like junk. . . .
>
> Kick is momentary freedom from the claims of the aging, cautious, nagging, frightened flesh. Maybe I will find in yage what I was looking for in junk and weed and coke. Yage may be the final fix. (152)

Here, the phrase "claims of the aging, cautious, nagging, frightened flesh" describes the life cycle, in which Lee is subordinated to his physical needs, "narrowed down" to the mindset of an animal. What he desires, though, is to

---

11. Burroughs consistently misspells the name of the drug *yagé* as "yage" in his writing. I have preserved this idiosyncrasy when quoting from his texts, but use the correct spelling in my own writing.

open up—rather than to contract—his psyche. What Lee seeks now is not so much life as transcendence of the limitations of (physical) life, and at the end of the text, Lee is hopeful that the new object of his quest, *yagé*, will serve as his salvation, his "final fix" (Burroughs 1986b, 57).[12] Lee continues his quest for transcendent experience in *Queer.* Although it was written in 1952, directly after *Junky, Queer* was not published until 1985. This delay is due to the novel's frank homosexual content, which would have been considered unpublishable during the period in which it was written. Burroughs initially envisioned the two, along with *The Yage Letters,* as part of one book about his experiences with junk (Burroughs 1994, 244). The action in the first half of *Queer,* which takes place in Mexico City, overlaps chronologically with the Mexico City section of *Junky.* In this novel, Lee's quest continues, but his object subtly shifts. Lee begins to look for *yagé*, but his search for the drug is subordinated to his search for what Van Ghent (quoted by Dickey, 16) terms "brotherhood" in her discussion of the Beat quest: human contact, companionship, and extreme intimacy. This shift of interest may seem surprising, but underlying it is the same longing to overcome the limitations of the body and the self that Lee experiences in *Junky.* Lee hopes, in his mainly homosexual relationships with others, to surpass the limitations of the body and mind in the form of a complete, literal fusion of two people. He wishes not only to enter his lovers' bodies sexually, but literally: to think as they think, to experience things as they experience them, and ultimately, to escape the alienating prison of the self, which by its nature prevents such intense identification.

In *Queer,* it is clear that Lee is much more interested in others around him, which foreshadows his longing for the perfect union. This work is written in the third person, which distances the reader from Lee and reflects his attempt to reach outside the self. Lee's attitude toward *yagé* changes in this text, reflecting his new longing for human communion. He no longer describes it as a personal "final fix" but as a vehicle for the ultimate connection of minds: telepathy. Rather than wishing to expand his own consciousness and enable a different subjective experience of reality, he now longs to link his own mind to that of others and participate in a form of communication that does not neces-

---

12. Burroughs's concern with escaping the limitations of the body, and the connection between this concern and his understanding of myth, is made evident in a March 1964 BBC interview. Burroughs states, "I feel that the old mythologies are definitely broken down and not adequate at the present time. . . . Heaven and hell exist in my mythology. Hell consists of falling into enemy hands, into the hands of the virus power, and heaven consists of freeing oneself from this power, of achieving inner freedom, freedom from conditioning" (quoted in Stull 1981, 19). Burroughs sees a mythic struggle between personal autonomy and a "virus power": the use of the word "virus" to characterize this villainous power strongly evokes associations to the body: its weakness to disease, its physical vulnerability.

sitate verbal expression. The drug is first mentioned in the text in conjunction with telepathy: "In South America at the headwaters of the Amazon grows a plant called Yage that is supposed to increase telepathic sensitivity" (Burroughs 1986b, 57).[13] Lee's desire for a superhuman, psychic link stems from his feelings of failure in connecting romantically with an acquaintance, Eugene Allerton, in a normal manner. He mentions the drug when his relationship with Allerton is not progressing ideally—just before, Lee speaks of it: "Allerton was somewhat sullen, and Lee felt depressed and ill at ease" (55). This failure only intensifies his wish for some form of perfect merger.

This desire is expressed even more intensely when Lee and Allerton see Cocteau's *Orpheus* at a cinema. A rare direct classical reference in Burroughs's work, the myth the film re-imagines can be seen as a parallel to *Queer*'s quest: a hero journeying through hell—in his case, a psychological hell of rejection and uncertainty—hoping for union with a loved one, yet ultimately unable to achieve that objective. As the two watch the film, Lee yearns for a physical union: "Lee could feel his body pull towards Allerton . . . straining with a blind worm hunger to enter the other's body, to breathe with his lungs, see with his eyes, learn the feel of his viscera and genitals" (48). Although Lee is attempting to overcome his bondage to his own body by entering Allerton's, the language in this passage reveals that this very urge is underscored by a base, bodily longing that overpowers Lee, as did his desire for junk. Lee's wish to surpass corporeal limitations is always brought about by a feeling of enslavement to physical needs.

Lee's longing for human connection intensifies when he and Allerton travel to South America, searching for *yagé*, and this craving for a connection overshadows his desire for the drug. The point at which Lee's wish for intimacy is made most evident comes when he is walking the streets of Guayaquil:

> [Lee] walked on, looking at every face he passed, looking into doorways and up at the windows of cheap hotels. An iron bedstead painted light pink, a shirt out to dry . . . scraps of life. Lee snapped at them hungrily, like a predatory fish cut off from his prey by a glass wall. He could not stop ramming his nose against the glass in the nightmare search of his dream. (92; ellipsis in orig.)

Now, rather than searching for life (the object of his overall quest) in junk or even *yagé*, the things Lee considers to be "scraps of life" are the faces of oth-

13. For my analysis of *The Yage Letters*, I use the latest edition of the work, which is entitled *The Yage Letters Redux*. The parenthetical references throughout my discussion of *The Yage Letters* refer to this work.

ers, and the items of everyday, domestic humanity. He feels that the integrated existence in which he sees other people take part is unachievable for him, as though he is separated from it "by a glass wall," which only intensifies his sense of desire and frustration. This expression of alienation through an image of separation is reminiscent of those in the Prologue of *Junky.* At this point in *Queer,* despite having traveled far from his hometown, Lee has the same problem he experienced there; such a lack of progress indicates that he is far from attaining the goal of his quest.

As Lee's desire intensifies, so does his yearning for a physical union: now, he actually imagines himself in the body of a boy, who "vibrated with life like a young animal," whom he sees on the streets of Guayaquil. Lee "could feel himself in the body of the boy. Fragmentary memories . . . the smell of cocoa beans drying in the sun, bamboo tenements" (93; ellipsis in orig.). In this passage, again, "life" is associated with other people, from whom Lee feels alienated. Lee then imagines a sexual experience between the boy with whom he identifies and another boy (93–94). But the fantasy is only fantasy, and when it ends, it leaves Lee feeling unfulfilled (94). Ultimately, Lee's yearning for intense human connection—elevated by the intensity of his desire to the status of the "transcendent kingdom," the union and integration that is the goal of the hero's quest—only leaves him more frustrated, more aware of his confinement and isolation within his self. At the end of *Junky,* while the quest remained unrealized as it does here, Lee set forth a specific new course of action, the search for *yagé,* which would bring him fulfillment. But here, there is no such new course of action, and the ending is much more uncertain.

Lee's quest for transcendent experience continues, though, in the "In Search of Yage" section of *The Yage Letters* (Burroughs and Ginsberg 2006, 16–22). *The Yage Letters* followed *Junky* as Burroughs's second published work, due to the delay in the publication of *Queer,* and in many ways follows directly from its conclusion. In this work, Lee gives up his search for intimacy with others, and now is fully focused on the goal set out at the conclusion of *Junky:* that of *yagé* as the "final fix" that will admit Lee to the "transcendent kingdom." In addition, the first-person viewpoint used in *Junky* is restored, reflecting this text's focus on personal fulfillment and an inward quest.

Early sections of the text emphasize Lee's frustration with the limitations of the human condition. This frustration is symbolized by Lee's movement on his quest, which alternates between Sisyphean circularity—for example, his backtracking due to a mistake with his tourist card[14]—and stasis. When Lee is

14. Under the category "The hero acquires the use of a magical agent," Propp includes an agent that is "eaten or drunk," which then produces magical results (1968, 41).

delayed in Peru, he writes: "This place gives me the stasis horrors. The feel of location, of being just where I am and nowhere else is unendurable. Suppose I should have to live here?" While Lee's frustration with both circular motion and stillness may at first seem contradictory or simply peevish, both conditions evoke feelings in Lee of being trapped, triggering his longing for transcendence. Whether confined in a cycle of junk addiction, a dreary Peruvian town, or his own body and mind, Lee cannot bear to be "just where I am and nowhere else" (ibid.).

In Mocoa, Lee has another, stronger experience with *yagé*, which, far from providing transcendence, only further confines him within his physical self. Lee describes the experience:

> I vomited violently leaning against a tree and fell down on the ground in helpless misery. . . . I kept trying to break out of this numb dizziness. I was saying over and over, "All I want is out of here." An uncontrollable mechanical silliness took possession of me. Hebephrenic meaningless repetitions. . . . I was on all fours convulsed with spasms of nausea. (Burroughs and Ginsberg 2006, 27)

In this passage, Lee's body takes over with strong physical sensations such as vomiting, numbness, and "mechanical silliness." Phrases like "trying to break out" and "all I want is out of here" reflect Lee's intense, but unfulfilled, desire to transcend these physical sensations and limitations.

The text ends with a letter describing Lee's second experience with *yagé*. Although this experience seems to be more fulfilling than the previous one, it is still unclear whether the drug has allowed him to surpass the borders of his body and self. Initially, Lee's impressions of his *yagé* episode point to some sort of transcendence being achieved: the experience is described in terms of fully unimpeded motion. He states, "Yage is space time travel," and under the influence of the drug, he has the sensation of moving "through" not around, seeing "migrations, incredible journeys through deserts and jungles and mountains." His consciousness can be seen to expand in that he is able to experience the various effects of extensive travel at once, having visions of various landscapes—"minarets, palms, mountains, jungle"—and their inhabitants in an instant. Also, being under the influence of *yagé* gives Lee a sense of "brotherhood" with "many races, Negro, Polynesian, Mountain Mongol, Desert Nomad, Polyglot Near East, Indian"; he feels their "blood and substance" as they "[pass] through [his] body" (50): precisely the integration with others Lee longed for in *Queer*. *Yagé* provides Lee with all the exhilarating sensations of a journey—a sense of motion and knowledge of the various areas and peoples of the world. While, as we have noted above, *yagé* can certainly take its toll on the body in the search for spiritual transcendence, the outward physical exertion one normally associates with heroic quests here takes place internally. It is a continual effort for Lee to triumph over the obstacles of alienation and stasis he faces along his journey, and it is *yagé*—the "magical agent" in Proppian terms[15]—that helps him accomplish this.

The final images from Lee's *yagé* experience suggest that while the drug may have temporarily expanded Lee's consciousness, his larger quest for the "transcendent kingdom" remains unfulfilled. One of Lee's later visions is that of a "Composite City," which, far from being a place where human limitations are overcome, offers detailed imagery of the bodily processes Lee longs to conquer, such as eating, sexuality, and excretion. There are "bars and rooms and kitchens and baths, copulating couples on rows of brass beds, criss cross of a thousand hammocks, junkies tying up, opium smokers, hashish smokers, people eating, talking, bathing, shitting back into a haze of smoke and steam" (50–51). These descriptions are overwhelming in their scope; it is as if Lee experiences the sheer proportion of human life and its manifold daily tasks all at once.

The final image of the composite city—and of the letter and the text itself—also suggests that complete transcendence has not been achieved. In the last sentences, Lee describes the city as "a place where the unknown past and the emergent future meet in a vibrating soundless hum. Larval entities waiting for a live one" (53). These last lines make the narrative end on a note of anticipation, rather than satisfaction. While the penultimate sentence begins with a potential image of unity, the past and future remain vague, not fully realized: "unknown" and "emergent." They only "meet" like two strangers: they do not become one. The image of "larval entities" suggests a sense of dormancy preceding growth and the realization of purpose, and the phrase "waiting for a live one" indicates the lack of such fully realized life. The "larval" image also points to the role of the biological cycle in limiting that maturity: the larval stage is a limiting, yet inescapable part of the life cycle of the organism that must be endured on the way to adulthood. Such an ending for this narrative implies that Lee's overarching quest has not been completely fulfilled. Although Lee's consciousness has been expanded via the *yagé* experience, the unclear note on which this text ends prevents a sense of ultimate achievement and final resolution.

Naked Lunch narrates the final stage of Lee's quest. In some ways, the novel seems to suggest that Lee is far from achieving the transcendence and renewal

15. See Skerl 1985, 20; Stull 1981, 227.

he desires. With recurrent imagery of violence, death, and decay that is more intense than that presented in the previous novels; it is as if, in the final step of his quest, Lee finds himself again in the land of the dead. America is presented as "old and dirty and evil" (Burroughs 1993, 24), one nation under "the black wind sock of death" (176). Its "dead armadillos in the road and vultures over the swamp" (25) evoke a contemporary Cocytus, the "unlovely swamp with its sluggish water" (Virgil *Georgics* 4.479: *Cocyti tardaque palus inamabilis unda*). The fragmented style of *Naked Lunch* differs markedly from the linear structure and factual tone of the three works which precede it, and this stylistic change means the quest lacks the sense of forward motion that previously propelled it through its moments of stasis.

In *Naked Lunch,* the two main means by which Lee previously sought transcendence—junk and sex—no longer serve as opportunities for redemption. Now, as a result of the knowledge he has gained during his quest, he presents them to the reader as enslaving systems of control. As at the end of *Junky,* junk serves as a manifestation of death: junkies are described as having "the cancelled eyes of junk" (84, 88) and voices "strangely flat and lifeless" (152). In scientific, distanced tones, Lee calls junk the opposite of "the whole life process" and states that it "suspends the whole cycle of tension, discharge and rest" (41). The life of a junky contains none of the ordinary activities that characterize human life: "No sexual outlet, no social contacts, no work, no diversion, no exercise, nothing but morphine" (195).

Sexuality, in which Lee earlier sought a kind of communion, is now presented as a sadistic act characterized by exploitation, waste, and bodily fragmentation. An early fantasy sequence reads:

> One youth hath penetrate his comrade, while another youth does amputate the proudest part of that cock's quivering beneficiary so that the visiting member projects to fill up the vacuum nature abhors and ejaculate into the Black Lagoon where impatient piranha snap up the child not yet born nor—in view of certain well established facts—at all likely. (45)

Here, the act of amputation makes the sexual act depicted serve the opposite of its typical unifying function: bodies are divided, not joined. The act is anonymous: the participants are nameless "youths," "comrades," and "beneficiaries"; it is not a moment of creation but of waste and loss. There is no womb in which the semen can grow; instead, it is rent by the teeth of piranha. Burroughs's use of the word "child" for the semen makes the waste of a bodily fluid into an act of murder, increasing the sense of horror and loss, and reflects Burroughs's conclusion that sex will never be the "final fix."

In a later scene evocative of *Queer,* sexual longing is similarly characterized by fragmentation; it is also, like junk, allied with death and spectrality. Watching boys playing outside a school, Lee "project[s] [him]self . . . across the street, a ghost in the morning sunlight, torn with disembodied lust" (58). Here, Lee is doubly divided: not only is his ego fragmented through the psychic tearing that enables his projection, it is his lust—typically a craving for unity—which is the reason for the rupture. Furthermore, this lust is characterized as "disembodied": Lee divorces sexual desire, a biological drive, from its typical locus. These multiple acts of splitting mirror physical death, rendering him a lifeless "ghost," again recalling the katabatic underworld of *Junky.*

The failure of junk and sex to bring Lee transcendence, however, and the fact that in *Naked Lunch* Burroughs ultimately seems to end up in the same land of the dead where he began, does not repudiate his earlier quests for transcendence. His condemnation of the things he previously viewed as potential routes to transcendence reflects the experience he has gained on his journey. As Dickey makes clear in chapter 1, the classical hero may pass through the land of the dead, but he does not join their ranks; the separation between the living hero and the dead is clear. In *Junky,* this line is blurred: Lee did become one of the shades, experiencing death-within-life through his drug experiences. But in *Naked Lunch,* he remains separate from the junk-using shades, and his goal takes on a different form. Although it is clear that Lee now equates junk with death and totalitarian power, his drug experiences have opened his consciousness. As Skerl and Stull point out, junk use has revealed to Burroughs that addiction is the human condition and has aided his progression to a mature fictional form that allows him to communicate his new knowledge to his audience.[16] Through his writing, Lee/Burroughs is able to achieve the transcendent unity he has sought throughout his quest, connecting with readers and thus the wider community in a form of hero's return. Lee/Burroughs's overall objective is not *just* the knowledge of the "junk universe," as Stull suggests, but the corpus that this knowledge allows him to create and the connections this corpus can facilitate. Although Lee/Burroughs still inhabits the land "under the black wind sock of death," the text of *Naked Lunch* allows him simultaneously to remain there and yet "return" to his community of readers with some measure of enlightenment.

Paradoxically, *Naked Lunch* facilitates a successful and heightened union of author and reader through its fractured form. Skerl states that the work's

16. Burroughs discusses his view on the role of the reader in shaping literary texts in the essay "Critical Reading" in *The Adding Machine* (1986a); his discussion of "intersection reading" (42–43) is an example of how the reader's perceptions at the time of reading influence the text itself.

"montage" style "asks the reader to make connections between the elements that are set next to each other. The new mental associations are a form of expanded consciousness" (Skerl 1985, 44). Burroughs makes this didactic element of the novel clear in various paratexts that instruct the reader; the Atrophied Preface at the end of the work states that "*Naked Lunch* is a blueprint, a how-to book" that can explain "how-to extend levels of experience by opening the door at the end of the long hall" (176–77). In order for such a transformation of consciousness to occur, the reader's active participation is required: he or she must also undertake a quest—a "long hall/haul"—of his or her own, must decide how to relate the text to lived experience. As Murphy (2000, 96) states, "*Naked Lunch* doesn't offer a single coherent linear reading but an irreducible multiplicity of lines. . . . It is up to the determined reader to decide which of those lines and directions to follow from the text out into the world." The reader's enhanced role serves to connect him or her closely to the author: the two, in a way, "collaborate" in the experience of *Naked Lunch.*

Naked Lunch also connects reader and author through its status as a direct "record of the writer's consciousness." The novel is highly personal, and reading it is a literal glimpse into the author's mind: "the mythic content is autobiographical. . . . The plot, his inner conflicts; the structure, that of his actual experience" (Skerl 1985, 44). By presenting his consciousness to the reader in this way, Lee invites the fusion of minds he craves in *Queer* and *The Yage Letters* but fails to achieve. In the Atrophied Preface, Lee states: "The Word is divided into units which be all in one piece and should be so taken, but the pieces can be had in any order being tied up back and forth, in and out fore and aft like an innaresting [*sic*] sex arrangement. This book spill off the page in all directions" (Burroughs 1993, 180). These images of unity within fragmentation provide insight into how *Naked Lunch*'s splintered structure brings together author and reader, describing the relationship between the two in terms of sexual intercourse. Although the Word is externally fragmented—"divided into units"—there seems to be an unassailable, almost magical accord behind them: despite their division, they remain "all in one piece." This transcendent unity is framed in terms of sexual possession: the reader is invited to "take" and to "have" the words Lee offers. This can be done as the reader pleases, and this highlights his or her enhanced power in the experience of *Naked Lunch.* Each of the following three phrases—"back and forth," "in and out," and "fore and aft"—exemplify wholeness within fragmentation: although each phrase contains two words that have opposite meanings, these phrases are taken as single expressions in everyday speech, serving as apt examples of separate "units" that can be seen to remain "all in one piece." These images of fragmented unity build up to the orgasmic, dynamic "spill" of the book "in all directions." Such a description suggests the novel's myriad possibilities, such as the reshaping of the reader's consciousness; it is an image of the consummation of the union between author and reader. Unlike the wasted orgasms of the young "comrades" and the hanged man, unlike the failed grasping toward Allerton in *Queer, Naked Lunch*'s "spilling out" to the reader has the potential for true union. For Burroughs, the sexual act is one of violence, bodily fragmentation, waste, and loss, but the textual act serves to unify even amidst the novel's multiplicity of interpretations and splintered structure.

In *Junky, Queer, The Yage Letters,* and *Naked Lunch,* William S. Burroughs provides the narrative of a quest that bears parallels to those present in classical myth and epic. His hero Lee casts off his "superior social station" and undergoes a "change of status" as he attempts to escape the alienation characteristic of twentieth-century humanity and find an integrated form of life. Lee first undergoes a katabatic ordeal in the underworld of junk, populated by those whom the drug has rendered living specters; in *Queer,* he seeks to escape alienation through a homosexual relationship that, even as it promises unity, places him at odds with the mainstream community. When this fails, Lee places his hope in the mystical herb *yagé,* enduring the further ordeals that finding and using it bring. Finally, Lee/Burroughs achieves a hero's return through the writing of *Naked Lunch.* This *anabasis* may seem unconventional—he remains physically in a liminal state, still inhabiting an underground milieu that he sometimes characterizes as the same land of the dead that he passed through in *Junky.* But if his quest has taught him anything, it is that it is only from this place, the place that Norman Mailer called "hell precisely," that Lee is able to carry himself back into life. By serving as a "record of the writer's consciousness" and "intersection point" for author and reader, *Naked Lunch* serves as a spectral literary return that has the potential to reshape the consciousness of a nation. More of an Aeneas founding a new home than an Odysseus returning to an old one, Burroughs is able to create, through his writing, a novel community, a "transcendent kingdom," in which he can escape the limitations of the self, experiencing a sense of affinity and integration at last.

Bibliography

Burroughs, William S. 1977. *Junky.* New York: Grove Press.

———. 1986a. *The Adding Machine: Selected Essays.* New York: Grove Press.

———. 1986b. *Queer.* London: Penguin.

———. 1991. "Afterword: My Purpose Is to Write for the Space Age." In *William S. Burroughs at the Front: Critical Reception 1959–89*, edited by Jennie Skerl and Robin Lydenberg, 265–70. Carbondale: Southern Illinois University Press.

———. 1993. *Naked Lunch*. London: Flamingo.

———. 1994. *The Letters of William S. Burroughs 1945–1959*. Ed. Oliver Harris. London: Penguin.

———, and Ginsberg, A. 2006. *The Yage Letters Redux*. Ed. Oliver Harris. San Francisco: City Lights.

Edmonds, Radcliffe G., III. 2004. *Myths of the Underworld Journey: Plato, Aristophanes, and the "Orphic" Gold Tablets*. Cambridge: Cambridge University Press.

Grace, Nancy. 2007. *Jack Kerouac and the Literary Imagination*. New York: Palgrave Macmillan.

Homer. 1951. *The Odyssey*. Trans. E. V. Riu. Harmondsworth, UK: Penguin.

Murphy, Timothy S. 2000. "Intersection Points: Teaching William Burroughs's *Naked Lunch*." *College Literature* 27.1: 84–102.

Nagy, Gregory. 1990. *Pindar's Homer: The Lyric Possession of an Epic Past*. Baltimore: Johns Hopkins University Press.

Perelman, Bob. 2009. "Zukofsky at 100." In *Radical Poetics and Secular Jewish Culture*, edited by Stephen Paul Miller and Daniel Morris, 40–48. Tuscaloosa: University of Alabama Press.

Propp, Vladimir. 1968. *The Morphology of the Folktale*. Austin: University of Texas Press.

Skerl, Jennie. 1985. *William S. Burroughs*. Boston: Twayne Publishers.

Stull, W. L. 1981. "The Quest and the Question: Cosmology and Myth in the Work of William S. Burroughs, 1953–1960." In *The Beats: Essays in Criticism*, edited by Lee Bartlett, 14–29. Jefferson, NC: McFarland.

Toohey, Peter. 2010. "Roman Epic." In *The Cambridge Companion to the Epic*, edited by Catherine Bates, 31–54. Cambridge: Cambridge University Press.

Weston, Jessie. 1913. *The Quest of the Holy Grail*. London: G. Bell and Sons.

CHAPTER 4

The Invention of Sincerity

ALLEN GINSBERG AND THE PHILOLOGY OF THE MARGINS

MATTHEW PFAFF

> The Academic Study of Western Classics has . . . been sabotaged by sexual psychopaths. . . . Why have the Loeb library texts been translated so as to leave out the balls? Have they not? I seem to remember for instance certain Catullus poems & lines were simply excluded for reasons of gentility.
>
> —ALLEN GINSBERG, "THE CLASSICS AND THE MAN OF LETTERS"

From the rise and reign of "Great Books classicism" in the first half of the twentieth century, to the development of the New American Poetry[1] and the Free Speech Movement in the '50s and '60s, things did not fare well for classicism.[2] The classics during this period enjoyed new degrees of democratic availability to the culture at large, but also faced new criticisms and a

1. The title of the New American Poetry comes from an influential anthology that represents a loose consortium of a number of avant-garde movements active particularly in the first decades after World War II, including the Black Mountain School, the poets of the San Francisco Renaissance, the Beat generation, and others. See Allen 1960 for the definitive anthology of poetry. The same editor has also collected statements of poetics under the title of *The Poetics of the New American Poetry in Allen* (1973).

2. Ginsberg was a participant in Columbia's Great Books curriculum, as were prominent modernists before him such as Louis Zukofsky, whose homophonic Catullus translations exerted a powerful influence on the New Americans, and whose early "Poem Beginning 'The'" satirizes the poet's experience as an undergraduate student in John Erskine's Great Books class at Columbia. See Zukofsky 2011. Both Columbia and Erskine himself were innovators in and spokesmen for Great Books as a novel pedagogical model. Research into the intersections of this concrete institutional context and experimental classicisms could shed light onto the particular valences, reactions, and counterreactions to the classics in modernist and later experimental poetries, as well as a particularly detailed account of one of the more influential mediums for the perpetuation of institutional classicism. For a brief popular history of Great Books, see Beam 2008.

growing displacement from their cultural centrality. In "The Classics and the Man of Letters," a questionnaire published in *Arion* in 1964, Ginsberg articulates a series of criticisms that express openly what earlier criticisms had tended to express only obliquely. "Whose Classics?" writes Ginsberg, "Three-fourths of the world's ancient literature is left out. Where's *Mahabharata?* The *Ocean of Story?* The *Puranas?* . . . The man of letters is also generally a finky old bore" (Auden et al. 1964, 54).[3] For Ginsberg, the historically situated, highly particular, and internally diverse body of Greek and Roman letters has come to function as a narrowly Western medium of ethnic and cultural mores. He paints the classics as a co-opted expression of the cultural center and an (occasionally not so) covert reification of "the universal, humanist subject" as peculiarly straight, white, and male, and repeatedly calls for the diffusion of the cultural authority afforded to Greek and Latin. He is happy to point out the artifice involved in the institutional mediations of "the Classics" in order to maintain "a monopoly on Latin-Greek" and seizes on a telling example: "Why have the Loeb library texts been translated so as to leave out the balls? Have they not? I seem to remember for instance certain Catullus poems & lines were simply excluded for reasons of gentility" (ibid., 56). He refers to the Loeb edition's refusal to translate Catullus's promise to "face-fuck and sodomize" his poetic enemies.

For Ginsberg, the omission is telling, and he latches onto it as the most visible face of classicism's role in regulating identity. Classicism's censorship of a queer and overtly sexualized past normalizes its material, such that it excludes "censored" social realities.[4] Thus, he offers the censored past as a figure for the excluded present. It is a key point that Ginsberg stages the conflict with "academic classicism," and offers the Loeb series as a knowing straw man for the institution in toto in order to *identify* with the classical text. What has been censored from Catullus, and by extension, the canon, is nothing less than Ginsberg himself.

For Ginsberg and other writers of the New American Poetry, the classics occupied a critical staging ground in the conflict for the meaning of the past, cultural capital in the present, and a window onto the processes that might reshape the cultural future. Due in part to his success in creating a viable

3. For Ginsberg, special elevation of Greek and Latin classics above various world literatures amounts to epistemological racism. Although the classics as texts themselves are useful, their presence at the head of an allusive pantheon is not. "The elements," writes Ginsberg, "of reference have . . . multiplied" (54).

4. By "censored" I mean that the Loeb edition, produced by faculty at Harvard since the 1830s, literally excised all references to "fucking" in every classical text until the 1940 edition. Then they started publishing full texts, but only in Latin until 1960.

public identity as homosexual ("America I'm putting my queer shoulder to the wheel") and self-described "Buddhist-Jew," and giving a communicable voice to censored identities, Allen Ginsberg came to represent one of the most visible and well-known faces of the counterculture. His cultural renown and presence in the popular imagination reflect his poetics, which fashion the self as public, intelligible, sincere, and transparent. From *Howl*'s obscenity trials to Ginsberg's public appearance before the Senate Judiciary Committee, staged exorcisms of the Pentagon, or any number of poetic representations ("who let themselves be fucked in the ass"; "Catullus sucked cock in the country"),[5] Ginsberg's poetics "naturalized" the cultural center's disavowed, censored margins—its queer or oriental or bohemian others—and fed them back into the system as public spectacle. He extended—and was a vital force in shaping—the New American Poetry and its public reception.

Ginsberg occupied an ambivalent position vis-à-vis classicism, both as a means of reception and as a series of received texts. He was at pains to emphasize the gap between "the Classics themselves" and "the basic literary stupidity of institutional (academic) Classicism in XXth Century," evincing distaste for "institutional . . . Classicism" and its transformations of Greco-Roman texts into reflections of the cultural center (ibid.). He also adopted many of its strategies, acknowledging classicism's peculiar lessons in the mechanisms of identity construction, the codification of cultural hegemonies, and the production of social intelligibility. In the same document, for example, Ginsberg brazenly employs the strategies he criticizes, translating the classics into his own milieu by valorizing "the spirit" of Greek and Latin literature rather than its form, its universality rather than its particularity ("Anacreon at a crucial point turned me on to HUMANITY"; ibid., 54), and so on. Although "Pindar's variable stanzas . . . encourage freedom," the idea of imitating set, classical "prosody" inspires derision: "Ugh!" Ginsberg quips, "That would be a monkey-like stupidity" (ibid., 55). It is the bluntest but most easily obscured of claims: Ginsberg and other writers of the New American Poetry, like the modernists before them, saw themselves less as countercanonical rebels of the new than as living classics.

Ginsberg borrowed in ways that are sometimes immediately apparent. More often, however, his classical debt is visible only in hindsight and with the intervening accrual of scholarship. This is true for the influence of Oswald Spengler's orientalist conceptions of core and fringe cultures on Ginsberg's apocalyptic poetics, and for the equally powerful influence of romantic con-

5. Unless otherwise noted, I have referred to Ginsberg 2006 for all quotations of Ginsberg's verse.

structions of prelapsarian Eastern cultures and Eastern religions on Ginsberg's "Eastern turn," at least in its germinal stages.[6] Likewise, the degree to which these discursive histories branch out from nineteenth-century philological models of ancient Greek and Roman culture sheds light on Ginsberg's egalitarian allusions. One of Ginsberg's primary strategies is to expand the aura of cultural authority accorded to the Greek and Latin classics to alternative world literatures, as well as his own milieu.[7] In mimicry of the Western Academy in its formative stages, when constituting various Buddhist, Hindu, Greek, or Sanskrit pasts as stable objects of knowledge, an ancient "classical" Greek and Latin past invisibly supplements Ginsberg's multicultural present.[8] His classical engagements both proceeded from and catalyzed a heightened sense of the formal dimensions of social experience, in which the objective, universal, and given is revealed as built (Catullus the singer of plainspoken American English is revealed as a local invention), and the attendant realization that that which had been built could also be demolished or modified (if the classical can become straight or American and the American, classical, then why can't the Beat become classical and the classical, Beat?).

Rather than examining a particular poem, this chapter traverses the broader arc of Allen Ginsberg's poetic career in light of his early Catullus translations, paying particular attention to the question of Catullan (and Beat) sincerity. Through close comparison with the Latin original—and the formal techniques by which that original is both preserved and erased—I argue that Ginsberg's adaptation represents a complex usurpation of classicism's "philology of identity." I then extend these readings into a renewed understanding of the progressive "classical silence" that descends on Ginsberg's later career, where he transposes the ideal of classical authority ever Eastward. Perhaps

6. John Lardas's book, *The Bop Apocalypse,* details the strong early influence on Ginsberg, Kerouac, and Burroughs of Oswald Spengler's apocalyptic orientalism in *The Decline of the West.* See Lardas 2000. For an alternate account that reads the influence of Buddhism on Ginsberg's poetics, see Trigilio 2007.

7. In a seemingly incidental remark in her 2001 article, "German Orientalism," intellectual historian Suzanne Marchand writes, "Orientalist philology [of nineteenth-century Germany] . . . provided the foundation for the deep critique of 'Eurocentrism' handed down to the anti-colonial and counter-cultural youth movements of the 1960s" (466). By linking orientalism to the critique of Eurocentrism, she makes room for a nonstandard conception of orientalism, generally conceived as a reflection of Eurocentric power relations. She then points toward the strong presence of such an orientalism in mid-twentieth-century American culture, in "the anti-colonial and counter-cultural youth movements of the 1960s" and suggests an uncanny historical community of this twentieth-century American orientalism and nineteenth-century German scholarship.

8. Masuzawa 2005 offers a detailed intellectual history of the discourse of "world religions" and a compelling case for its foundations in Western models of classical and biblical philology.

Ginsberg's primary insight is into the portability of classicism's power to invent social centers and govern public identities. If the modernist project showed the New Americans the plasticity of classical texts, it is only a short step from there to the divorce of classicism's cultural and hegemonic authority from a static reading list of Greek and Latin authors. Therefore, in examining Ginsberg's classical engagements, I attempt to demonstrate the processes whereby Ginsberg detaches the idea of the classical from Greek and Latin material texts, and transposes it onto alternative texts and social identities. In other words, Ginsberg's verse attempts a usurped and *perfected* classicism. Thinking through these broad questions in terms of Ginsberg's reception of a particular classical text reframes them as discrete philological practices, compelling us to reconsider the hypercontemporaneity of Ginsberg's poetics, the "organic" antiformalism of his verse, and the historical displacement of "the new" in terms of a very specific type of textual practice: a philology of the margins.

"sabotaged by sexual psychopaths"

> . . . the sense of old reality of Catullus, dead so long but his worries are still sad and true, and [I] can hear his voice in poems.
>
> —QUOTED IN SCHUMACHER, *DHARMA LION: A CRITICAL BIOGRAPHY OF ALLEN GINSBERG*

Perhaps because of his vocal critique of institutional classicism, elevation of the oriental classics above those of Greece and Rome, and the progressive absence of Greek and Latin language and literature in his published verse, none has yet systematically examined the role of classicism and classical reception as an urgent context for Ginsberg's poetics. There are many reasons to do so now, not least of which is the role of Greek and Latin at critical turning points in his career. "Malest Cornifici tuo Catullo," a short engagement with the Roman poet Catullus and his Latin, is well known as a transitional work, composed over several months in the period leading up to the composition of "Howl." During the same period, Ginsberg was poised on the brink of capitulation to a radically different way of life. In the midst of physical illness, he contemplated ending his burgeoning relationship with Peter Orlovsky and "becoming heterosexual." He considered exchanging poetry for the study of "Greek or prosody" at Berkeley, a very real possibility if not for Kerouac's stern response ("It's a Buddhist, AN EASTERN FUTURE ahead," "[Greek poetry] is child's play"; Charters and Kerouac 1999, 306). In this period of crisis prior to the composition of "Howl," his characteristic style hung in the balance, as well as the career that would carry him to public notoriety and a fraught but determined commitment to life as a public homosexual and advocate for the cultural margins. At the same juncture, he fiddled endlessly with "Malest," "work[ing] and rework[ing] the poem, checking its metric scheme against the Latin and the English translation of the Catullus poem" (Schumacher 1992, 192). Correspondence contemporary with the composition of "Malest" reveals a Ginsberg that sharply contrasts with the boisterous anti-academicism of the more familiar cultural icon:

> You would like Catullus. I read a collection of translations edited by an Aiken, and am reading him in Latin now with aid of a pony. . . . I am doing some real study on metrics. . . . Trouble is a real study involves knowledge of music, Provencal, Greek, etc. It all relates directly to history or basic theory of metrical practice and notation. I don't know how far I can go with the crude education I have. . . . There is a difference between the kind of fine classical education you can get in private school and the vague generalities of public high schools. Write sometime. I'll let you know when anything happens. Love, Allen. (Ginsberg and Morgan 2008, 100)

Ginsberg saw his work with Catullus as an attempt to remedy his "crude education" and attain the cultural capital ("knowledge of . . . Greek," "history of basic theory of metrical practice") that a "fine classical education" would have granted him. If we take this sentiment as an interpretive framework for "Malest," we see that he located the regulation of literacy (complex manipulation of poetic form, literary-historical knowledge) in the institution; and at least in part identified with the Great Books ideal "of fine classical education." In this time of personal crisis, Ginsberg turned to the Latin text and devoted painstaking attention to its linguistic, philological minutiae. Ginsberg became a philologist by proxy.[9]

The exact relationship of "Malest" to its source text resists easy categorization. In the same *Arion* questionnaire in which he attacks academic classicism, he describes his practice in "Malest" as "paraphrase." There could be no term *less* suited to Ginsberg's philological practice vis-à-vis the Catullan

9. Years later in the *Arion* questionnaire, Ginsberg goes to great lengths to dismiss this very faculty of classicism and its objects: "The spirit of Anacreon, sure. But greek prosody? Ugh!" He goes so far as to argue that study of philology should not be taught to undergraduates studying the classics and that, even in graduate school, philology qua philology should be emphasized only if the student demonstrates a remarkable aptitude. At each point, Ginsberg is at pains to pin classicism's foibles on its investment in the linguistic minutiae of its objects.

text than "paraphrase," or its implication of rough, sloppy approximation. The poem skips over paraphrase as "different words approximate sense," practicing extremes that fall on either side. The poem moves between extremes of relation and nonrelation that at no moment inhabit the "middle way" of paraphrase, but instead jarringly alternate between direct linguistic and semantic modeling and complete linguistic and thematic departure. There is no gradation between these disparate modes, and the abrupt jumps highlight the staggered, discontinuous transmissions of the Catullan source. Just as remarkable as the mode of adaptation itself is the fact that its complexity is visible only at the level of comparison with the Latin, because the resulting surface of Ginsberg's poem is seamless. The English poem qua English poem reveals none of the suturing points where it leaps from direct modeling to pure invention. The idea of paraphrase conceals extremes of stylistic mimesis, invention, and linguistic rigor combined with complete transformation of affect, register, and cultural context, and in many ways, speaks to the genius of Ginsberg's self-effacing philology.

I would like to situate Ginsberg's later poetics in terms of "Malest," and argue that they find their seeds in this sustained philological encounter with the Latin of Catullus. Ginsberg's "Malest" works to produce a formal surface and a cultural present whose dependence on its classical original is indistinguishable from invention, whether that relationship is in fact dependent or relatively arbitrary. Close comparison of the Latin with Ginsberg's "Malest" reveals a poet who lavishes attention on the forms of the Catullan original, and an adaptation with an exquisitely nuanced relationship to every formal aspect of its source. It lavishes this attention, however, not in the service of reproducing the original forms—the directive of the "faithful" translator in most traditional theories of translation—but rather in order to systematically disrupt those forms *while still producing a recognizably Catullan and classical text.* We might read "Malest" as a question Ginsberg poses to classics: to what degree is the ideal of "the classical" reducible to the particular forms of its preservation and mediation? Can there be a classical translation independent from a classical original? "Malest" answers with a resounding "Yes." It successfully "extracts" the formal means of creating the ideal of a classical past from the classical text. In this sense, we have Ginsberg the radical formalist, whose poetics produce a classical present, no matter their degree of separation from their model. Yet at the same time, the "sincerity," "universality," and "organicism" of the resulting poem is seamless, perfectly executed—visible only at the level of comparison with the Latin source. The formal mechanisms that translate the classical erase their own presence, creating the semblance of an organic and unmediated classical past into the Beat poetics of Ginsberg's milieu. "Malest" represents a treasure trove of material for contextualizing his immanent breakthrough to a poetics of naturalized public identity.

The choice of source text is by no means arbitrary. Taken together, Catullus 38 and "Malest" form a kind of thematic chiasmus. As is Ginsberg's "Malest," Catullus 38 is a homosocial address between men bound together by their status as agents of desire:[10]

malest cornifici, tuo catullo
malest, me hercule, et laboriose,
et magis magis in dies et horas
quem tu, quod minimum facillimumque est
qua solatus es allocutione?
irascor tibi, sic meos amores?
paulum quid lubet allocutionis
maestius lacrimis Simonideis.

For your Catullus, Cornificius,
it's bad; it's bad, by Hercules, and trying,
and daily and hourly gets much worse and worse.
Yes—least and most easily done—with what
consolation have you comforted him?
I'm in a rage with you—so much for my love?
A little sympathy, please, however small,
and sadder than the tears of Simonides.
(Lambert 2007, 60)

The overall theme of Ginsberg's poem reverses the original's affective register, as Malest's initial "I'm not doing well" becomes "I'm happy":

---

10. Wray 2001 has enriched my reading of Zukofsky's Catullus. Wray offers a lucid disciplinary history of Catullus scholarship and piercing insight into the particular historical discourses whereby Catullus comes to be constructed as "Romantic": the transparently biographical Catullus, the lyric poet Catullus, characterized by his "spontaneous overflow of powerful feelings" (Wordsworth 2009). Wray situates the history of Catullan scholarship—and therefore the ideological accretions engaged by poets such as Ginsberg—in terms of a broader history of lyric theory. He cogently historicizes the "Catullus" deconstructed and drawn on by Ginsberg, and thereby shows the ways in which the Catullan text is a site of contest and antagonism for successive and cycling ideas of self, voice, and verse. In general, Wray's book helps contextualize what is at stake in any engagement with the Catullan text.

I'm happy, Kerouac, your madman Allen's
finally made it:

At the same time, he keeps to the original's general subject matter and tone of homosocial address.

discovered a new young cat,
and my imagination of an eternal boy
walks on the streets of San Francisco,
handsome, and meets me in cafeterias
and loves me. Ah don't think I'm sickening.
You're angry at me. For all of my lovers?
It's hard to eat shit, without having visions;
when they have eyes for me it's like Heaven.
(Ginsberg 2006, 131)

The original Catullus 38, which is the object of Ginsberg's adaptation, comments on the sincere transmission of emotions as an interpersonal medium. The poem's subject ("your Catullus") teasingly addresses his male friend, Cornificius, chastising him for his lack of sympathy. The original dances around the subject of sincerity. On the one hand, the poem's speaker both gives and demands sincerity. The sincerity and depth of Catullus's "distress" is the substance of the space of address, along with his displeasure at the lack of reciprocal sincerity from Cornificius. On the other hand, the speaker's self-conscious histrionics signal the performative and manufactured nature of his distress—its insincerity—and likewise chides the addressee for refusing to manufacture a false emotion "pathetic as the tears of Simonides." The poem, then, is about the fabrication of sincerity as a necessary condition for egalitarian community and interrelation.

The poem's transformations and appropriations of its Latin source are both deliberate and heterogeneous, and address each of the poem's nested layers of significance—from meter, to phoneme, morpheme, syntax, and line—with discrete procedures. Though rules govern these procedures, their formalism is such that they systematically disrupt predictability. Metrically, "Malest" is a study in the systematic disfiguration of its source. The poem disrupts metrical equivalence with its source meter's hendecasyllabic (xx–⏑ ⏑–⏑– ⏑–x), but also within its own individual lines. Catullus's unvaried meter gives way to a dizzying sequence of metrical variations, and the uniform parameters of Catullan meter meet their inverse image in the measured, precise, and uniform *disparity* of each of Malest's parts (I = Invention, A = Adaptation):

A: I'm happy, Kerouac, your madman Allen's	11	(˘–/ ˘–/ ˘–) (˘–/ ˘–˘)
I: finally made it: discovered a new young cat,	12	(–˘ ˘ /–˘) (˘–/ ˘ ˘–/˘–)
A: and my imagination of an eternal boy	13	(–˘ ˘ /–˘–˘) (–˘ ˘–/ ˘–)
I: walks on the streets of San Francisco,	9	(–˘ / ˘–/ ˘–/ ˘–˘)
A: handsome, and meets me in cafeterias	11	(–˘ / ˘–/ ˘ ˘–/ ˘–/ ˘ ˘)
I: and loves me. Ah don't think I'm sickening.	10	(˘––) (–˘ /–˘ /–˘ ˘)
A: You're angry at me. For all of my lovers?	11	(˘–/ ˘ ˘–), (˘–/ ˘ ˘–˘)
I: It's hard to eat shit, without having visions;	11	(˘–/ ˘ ˘–) (˘–/ ˘ ˘–˘)
I: when they have eyes for me it's like Heaven.	10	(–˘ / ˘–/ ˘–) (˘ ˘–˘)

Outside of the deliberate mimicry in the call and response of lines 7 and 8, no two of "Malest's" lines scan alike, and no line in the poem scans as a hendecasyllabic. Even within Ginsberg's line, no two sides of a caesura mirror each other. "Malest" runs through a deft succession of metrical permutations—often from foot to foot—without repeating itself. Whereas Ginsberg's poem progressively extracts its source from the particular linguistic forms it inhabits, the original progressively animates those forms. The original Catullus 38 begins with the bare, mechanical reality of its meter, foregrounding the normally invisible artifice of metrical constraints. The first lines begin as performances of their own reduction to "mere" symptoms of meter: "It's bad. It's really bad. It's really really bad." They are zombie-like, lifeless, unvaried, and mechanical in their lack of metrical variation and constricted range of expression. The movement away from unvaried repetition is, at first, a mere twitch. Lines 1–3 are predetermined, passive, and subjected to their form, then evolve into repetitions with a ghost of variation, finally injecting expressiveness in line 3. Catullus 38 tells the formal narrative of the human struggling to invest the dull and dead materials of the predetermined form with life, while "Malest" tells the formal narrative of the human struggling to break free from its set, predetermined constraints. Taken together, the narratives told by the progression of the two poems' metrical structures forms a chiastic inversion.

In Ginsberg's adaptation, complex strategies of inversion, reflection, and invention continue at the level of line. The poem alternates between two distinct modes of transformations: inversion and invention. The invented lines stand in arbitrary relation to the semantic and linguistic form of the corresponding original lines, while the inversions attend carefully to the sound of the original line's language and syntactic relations while inverting aspects of its register. The first line of Ginsberg's "Malest" models the linguistic features of the original quite faithfully. The line's syntax and subject, apart from the affective reversal of "I'm happy," directly mirror Catullus. Ginsberg retains the affection of the poem's speaker diminutively referring to himself in the third person, adding "madman" as a descriptor, "your madman Allen." The addition of "madman," despite some expansion of length, only embellishes the sonic similarities of "your madman Allen" to "tuo Catullo" in terms of vowel distribution. Add this to the way that "Kerouac" evokes sonic similarities to "Cornificius," and the first line arrives at a marriage of sonic and thematic fidelity. Lines 3 and 7 likewise perform an inversion of affect, while modeling themselves directly on the concrete linguistic features of the original. "Imagination" sonically mimes "magis magis," and "an eternal boy" mimes the general syllabic distribution and sonic values of "in dies et horas." The relationship of semantic content to its original is slightly more complex than the simple reversal of line one, but nonetheless transforms the sense of quickening time of "in dies et horas" into the timeless "eternal" of the poem's idealized boy. What in the original line is an abysmal nadir of emotional state has come full circle as giddy wish fulfillment in "Malest." Line seven, like the others, mimics the syntax and sound of the original while effecting an affective reversal. Catullus's "I'm angry at you" becomes Ginsberg's pleading, "You're angry at me," and *sic meos amores* ("treat my love so?") becomes "For all of my lovers."

Of eight Catullan lines and nine of Ginsberg's, only three unequivocally model themselves after Catullus's sound or content. The other five lines of Ginsberg's poem have only the most tenuous connection to the Catullus. The connections extend little beyond the obvious framework of homosocial friendship and empathy given or received. Take, for example, the final lines of each poem. Only the most brazen interpretive doublethink can establish either sonic or thematic modeling. The "tenuous" lines exhibit features that are uncharacteristic of Ginsberg's poetics: a careful sense of enjambment, the subtle but persistent connective tissue between lines, a precision of address, and the polished, subtle but cutting barbs and appeals of Catullan wit. The poem's language is minimally generative, rather than the maximal and verbose generativity that becomes Ginsberg's modus operandi. The poem maintains the stylistic indicators of Catullan speech,[11] even in syntactic and semantic nonrelation: carefully placed terms of endearment ("your madman Allen"), polished inclusion of the vulgar ("it's hard to eat shit"), representations of verbal interjection ("ah"), embeddedness in geographical place ("streets of San Francisco"), variations in statement length, quick oscillations between report and address, the use of idiomatic phrases ("young cat"), and so on. The poem skillfully maintains the formal registers of Catullan voice. Where we might

11. One cannot escape the idea of voice in Ginsberg. I do not adopt the term uncritically, but rather as a description of the formal devices that create a textual semblance of voice in Ginsberg's verse.

perhaps describe Ginsberg's poetics as paraphrase (the three closely modeled lines), they invert semantic content but preserve linguistic form. Where "Malest" departs from the linguistic form of the original, it does so in a way that blasts through the gravity well of "approximate sense" and stands as pure invention.

The poem ends on a note of, if not insincere, at least facile, attraction. The "eternal boy" is idealized and unreal, and it is precisely the unreal "visions" that undercut and softly blunt the edges of the poem's self-satisfied preening. Nevertheless, the poem cannot resist the illusory flirtations that are "like Heaven": "when they have eyes for me it's like Heaven." Finally, the gaze flips around: Even as Ginsberg's poem translates its unreal classical fantasy into the stream of time and makes it real, the positions of source and target reverse. Now Ginsberg is the object of the gaze of the classical "eternal boy." Just as Ginsberg takes the Catullan text and translates it from the unreal, remote, and ancient past into the here and now, so too the "classical" Catullus that Ginsberg has recreated in the present translates Ginsberg himself into the past. "Malest" makes the classical real, which in turn makes "Malest" classical.

After going through these individual textual practices in detail, it is possible to step back and contemplate the science fiction insanity that is the translation machine of "Malest." For each of the source text's multiple planes of significance—from meter through phoneme, morpheme, syntax, line, and theme—"Malest" maintains multiple procedures of adaptation. We might productively distinguish between "horizontal" procedures of adaptation, which adapt Catullus 38 along the same plane of significance—say meter, for example—and "vertical" ones, which adapt Catullus 38 from one plane of significance to another—say from the metrical to the semantic, for example. Horizontally, "Malest" maintains at least two staggered, discontinuous modes of appropriation. Vertically, each plane duplicates some aspect of the planes above or below it—so for example, the alteration from invention to inversion at the level of line resonates with the shifting permutations from metrical foot to metrical foot, or the substitution of polar values at the level of morpheme—happy to sad—*while always* preventing seamless continuity of procedure. Moreover, it does this in such a way that the resulting poetic surface bears none of the marks of the artifice involved in its creation.

The way the poem cycles between direct relation and modeling—something quite close to translation—and indirect, transparent-seeming invention, self-consciously acknowledges its investment in the illusory "visions" and formal structures that, though artificial productions of reception, nevertheless create the seamless representation of voice, personhood, sincerity, and masculinity. It is specifically the invisibility of classicism's creation of sincerity, transparency, and normative identity onto which this piece latches. The primary formal goal of its engagement with the Catullan text is to reproduce the invisibility of the interface between text and ideology. It successfully reproduces classicism's ability to normalize or naturalize an otherwise foreign past. What I find remarkable about the resulting poetic surface is not so much the degree to which the ancient text is "updated," or the formal transformations whereby "Malest" appropriates the ancient text to make it its own—offering us now a queer Catullus, now a bohemian Catullus, now a hipster Catullus—but rather the complex ease with which the bohemian appears as classical. A contemporary landscape stands side by side with the ancient original in such a way that their disparity is indiscernible.

In "Malest," Ginsberg opposes an overtly queer Catullus to the sanitized Catullus of the Loeb edition that he so vocally criticizes in the *Arion* questionnaire. At the same time, the queer classical text emerges as a direct inversion of the hegemonic image. Whereas hegemonic classicism selects and represents only those aspects of a classical past that bolster the heterocentric present, censoring the rest to bolster the mores of "institutional (academic) Classicism XXth Century," Ginsberg flips it around and represents only the homoerotic Catullus. Even as the poem recovers a formerly censored aspect of the classical past, it holds it up as a guarantor of the censored (Beat) present: "Malest" guarantees the Beat present as a "living classic" precisely through analogy with the formerly censored aspect of Catullus. Similarly, "Malest" creates the past in the image of the present by updating its idiom to fit the particular social milieu it is meant to support (hipster, Beat, bohemian, and so on) and writing out the original text's meditation on poetic artifice and the construction of public emotion. Ginsberg's poem in no way "foreignizes" its queer content by means of the Catullan original. Rather than confronting the "straight" Catullus of hegemonic classicism with an image of difference and opacity, Ginsberg constructs a contemporaneity that is interchangeable with the classical past by naturalizing his queer Catullus. These are the formal processes whereby the classics are detached from the classical—the invention of "HUMANITY" and "the real human balls" from the "Ugh!" of "Anacreon's prosody." The subtle formal processes whereby Ginsberg's "philology of the margins" displaces the classical from the classic complicate our understanding of the unedited, sincere, or spontaneous in Ginsberg's poetics. If "Malest" is an early instance of the poetics of sincerity, transparent public image, and the unedited organicism of the self, then it calls for a substantial revision of our understanding of these terms in Ginsberg's poetics. They are "organic" in the way that organic food is so: we arrive at "natural" food not by backsliding to a primitive agricultural economy, but as the crowning achievement of high industrial food technology.[12]

Ginsberg's "Malest" personifies his usurpation of classicism's identity-regulating mediations. Ginsberg crafted a Beat classicism on the basis of discrete strategies of reception and mediation—in "Malest," those textual strategies are inversion, usurpation, and exclusion vis-à-vis the poem's source text. The poem seeks to reproduce and alter classicism's naturalization to reflect a marginalized queer identity.[13] With "Malest," Ginsberg discovered the ability of poetic form to naturalize the social margins in the period directly preceding the development of his characteristic poetics in "Howl." Ginsberg learned not only from the text of Catullus but also from the embedded series of institutional and ideological frameworks that mediated his access to Catullus and produced the immediacy of a living, directly accessible past.

Detailed analysis of "Malest" offers purchase for new perspectives on the broader arc of his poetics: Far more than in exploring the "organic" ancientness or mythical status of various traditions, Ginsberg invests in borrowing that status to create a self-mythologizing present: "Old life and new side by side, will Catholic Church find Christ on Jupiter Mohammed rave in Uranus will Buddha be acceptable on the stolid planets or will we find Zoroastrian temples flowering on Neptune" (Ginsberg 2006, 171). It is difficult to overstate the omnipresence of "naturalizing" strategies of reception as they gain complexity throughout Ginsberg's career. His verse consistently positions itself in relation to various frameworks of reference and reception, which by turns encompass historical and geographical facts; architectural landmarks; nationalist mythologies; religious, textual, and liturgical traditions; constellations of poets and poetic movements; and bodies of literature, organizing their inclusions in categories such as "American," "Oriental," "Biblical," and "Greco-Roman." Ginsberg's strategic use of these intertextual fields spans his poetic career, and operates at multiple levels, of which two of the most recognizable are (1) sustained *refiguration* and (2) *ambient allusiveness. Refiguration* refers broadly to the sustained engagement and *use* of an intertextual figure or trope, more robust than a brief allusion, lengthier than a line or two, and having a substantive function in the source, for example, the sustained use of Christo-

12. Davidson and others have noted the canny poise involved in the creation of Ginsberg's public image, "The change of Allen Ginsberg, market researcher, to Allen Ginsberg, poet, may not have been such a transition after all" (2003, 32).

13. Davidson characterizes it even more strongly, "Far from rejecting the cultural mainstream, the Beats embraced many of its more oppositional features"; "The Beats, to continue my first example, neither 'sold out' to the mainstream nor rejected it; rather, they worked strategically *within* it to develop an immanent critique" (Davidson 1998, 268, 269).

logical figures in "Howl," ("the eli eli lamma lamma sabachthani saxophone cry," "with the absolute heart of the poem of life butchered out of their own bodies good to eat a thousand years"; Ginsberg 2006, 139).[14] I coin the term *ambient allusiveness,* on the other hand, to refer to Ginsberg's idiosyncratic use of side-by-side allusions to eclectic intertextual fields. These lists function as egalitarian spaces in which disparate traditions share equal status and serve to generate allusive background noise rather than central poetic narratives, for example, when "The Big Beat" addresses a list of eclectic deities ("Kalki! Apocalypse Christ! Maitreya! grim / Chronos . . . / and Ganymede"; Ginsberg 2006, 357). This background noise tends to frame and lend atmosphere to otherwise highly contemporary engagements with current poetics and politics. In many ways, Ginsberg never rejected the poetics of naturalizing translation found in "Malest."

At the same time that this perspective contributes to our understanding of Ginsberg's poetics, it poses new questions and throws into relief several anomalies, including (1) the progressive absence of Greek and Latin intertexts in his verse, and (2) the sharp contrast of the apparent affirmation of "a fine classical education" with his subsequent and pronounced anti-institutionalism and anti-classicism. Firstly, the role of classical reception in "Malest" underscores a new intertextual peculiarity: remarkably, "Howl" represented Ginsberg's last sustained engagement with Greco-Roman classicism until late in his poetic career.[15] After "Howl," Ginsberg distanced his poetics from Greek and Roman texts as sites of poetic or linguistic authority, instead resituating its intertextual geography by prioritizing first a biblical, then an oriental, past, embracing Kerouac's "EASTERN FUTURE."[16] For a period of over a decade, Greek and Latin texts appeared *only* as members of egalitarian lists or as ambient allusions in Ginsberg's verse, and even then in small numbers, or as figures for hegemony itself: "Minerva, sexless cold & chill, ascending goddess of money . . . executive dyke, Minerva, goddess of Madison Avenue" (Ginsberg 2006, 194).[17]

14. See Hardwick 2003 for a critical vocabulary of reception studies including "refiguration" and many other terms. "Ambient allusion" is my own innovation.

15. A substantive refiguration rather than inclusion in a list of ambient allusions.

16. A search finds that the word "Greek" does not appear in *The Collected Poems* in pages 187–800; "Greece" appears once on page 347 as a place name; "classic" does not appear in pages 136–802; and "classical" not in pages 94–879 (except once on page 500 as "classical music").

17. One could possibly consider the brief (two-line) but thematically central use of Charon and Lethe in "A Supermarket in California" as a refiguration, but the poem is roughly contemporary with "Malest" anyway; or one could look at the broadest levels of genre and claim *Elegies for Neal Cassady* as a refiguration of classical elegy, but to my mind this is far too broad and indirect. The claim, too, limits itself to verse published in the collected poetry and stops

"Stotras to Kali Destroyer of Illusions" (1962) serves as a brief but representative illustration of this elision of Greek and Latin. Although the poem contains well over fifty proper names or direct allusions, including intertextual fields as various as American architecture, international politics, Medieval mysticism, "Bible," and Hinduism, only two of these ("Spouse of Europa"; "Maya") point to Greek or Latin sources. The contrast of this elision with the persistence of biblical and oriental refiguration underscores the peculiarity of Ginsberg's "classical silence." On the one hand, this excision was part of an articulated strategy to "let Occidental and Washington be transformed into a higher place, the plaza of eternity" (Ginsberg 2006, 163). On the other hand, Ginsberg's specific criticisms of classicism cannot fully account for the excision of Greek and Latin texts.

The disciplinary histories of biblical, oriental, and classical studies diverge at a relatively late point in history, and thus their codifications as coherent objects of academic knowledge share striking similarities. Nonetheless, Ginsberg took as perhaps the most stable intertextual feature of his work as the refiguration of the tropes, topoi, motif, and figures of "Bible" (e.g., "Tho I am not there for this Prophecy. . . . Take this, this Psalm. . . . This is the end, the redemption from Wilderness," in "Kaddish," Ginsberg 2006, 220) and "Orient" ("As the old sages of Asia, or the white bears of Persia / scribbled on the margins of their scrolls / in delicate ink / remembering with tears the ancient clockbells of their cities," 253). His verse hungrily assimilates a biblical and oriental past, while limiting the classical past to a nominal or token presence.[18]

Secondly, examining Ginsberg's later career from the perspective of the naturalizing classicism of "Malest" complicates the familiar narrative of "Howl" as an anti-institutional manifesto of countercultural transgression, as well as the timeline and motivations for his ultimate divorce from the ideology of "a fine classical education." The resonances of the formal strategies in "Howl" with those in "Malest"—in addition to Ginsberg's accounts and rebuttals of its critical reception—suggest that it was not until *after* the dismal institutional reception of "Howl" that he fully rejected (1) classicism qua Greek and Latin, and (2) the figures of "institution" and "academic classicism"

---

short of unpublished and archival materials, although I am unaware of any specific exceptions in them. By any account, we have a period of well over a decade following the composition of "Malest," spanning the height of his success as a poet and public figure, in which Greek and Latin intertexts take a back seat.

18. In general, a far more coherent and detailed account of the interrelationships between biblical, oriental, and classical philology in their formative periods is an absolute necessity to the coherence of classical reception studies; both an institutional and discursive genealogy of the same and of persisting formations of "the biblical," "oriental," and "classical" as literary topoi and sites of reception.

as privileged sites of cultural authority. "Howl" functions more as an extension and development of the classical "HUMANITY" in "Malest" than its revision or recusal. Like "Malest," "Howl" grounds itself in the "history or basic theory of metrical practice" and the literary historical archive governed by "a fine classical education," classical (Plotinus), biblical (eli eli lamma lamma), and modern (Cézanne, Whitman, etc.). Further, the terms of Ginsberg's defense of "Howl," the indignant incredulity with which he met its critical reception, and the strategic responses he subsequently developed, all suggest that he had intended "Howl" as a *practice* of "tradition" rather than its negation. He characterized it thus in his letters: "I ALSO believe it's the main "tradition," not that there is any tradition except what we make ourselves" (Ginsberg and Morgan 2008, 203).

In the same letter, his disdain encompasses the *mis*identification of "Howl" with "negative values" and "the whole sociological-tone-revolut whatever bullshit that everyone comes on with" ("the vulgarity . . . so called friendly from the same intellectual types . . . [of their] halfwit interpretations of "negative values" of Howl," ibid., 212) and his springs from the institution's wholesale misrecognition of the artifice, complexity, and literary-historical merits of Ginsberg's formalism:

> I get sick and tired I read 50 reviews of Howl and not one of them written by anyone with enough technical interests to notice the fucking obvious construction of the poem, all the details besides (to say nothing of the various esoteric classical allusions built in like references to Cézanne's theory of composition etc. etc.). (205)

With "Howl," Ginsberg had expected "the guardians of culture" to see their own reflections, or the poem's skilled manipulation of cultural capital, or at least some recognition of the formal achievement involved in recreating "tradition." "Howl" was meant to write itself into the Great Books tradition of universal "HUMANITY"—the "main tradition" and the institutional frameworks that he had formerly believed to be privileged entrances to classicism or canonicity.

Ginsberg's progressive disidentification with an academic classicism grounded in Greek and Latin resulted, I would argue, not from a rejection of that "tradition" or its attendant classicism, but from a progressive sense of the disjoint between "academic institution" and the cultural literacy required to regulate and reproduce canonicity: "Basically no one has insight into poetry techniques except people who are exercising them" (Ginsberg 2008, 203). The transition from "a fine classical education" to "the whole horror of Columbia"

(204) hinged on "the horrible irony of all these jerks who can't read trying to lecture me (us) on FORM" (205). For Ginsberg, the academic and high cultural reception of "Howl" compelled the realization that "the institution" and its representatives were relatively minor players in the regulation of cultural capital: "Just a bunch of dilettantes. And THEY have the nerve to set themselves up as guardians of culture?!?" (204). Ginsberg's version of classicism succeeded almost too well: The "horde of half educated deathly academicians" had mistaken Ginsberg's organic poetic surface as self-evident, missing or refusing to acknowledge the technical virtuosity involved in its production and its resonance with the procedures by which the very texts they claimed to represent had become the transparent semblance of affirmative "tradition."

The turning point in Ginsberg's final (at least for the ensuing years) disidentification was his realization that "the guardians of culture" had inherited a system of cultural production that exceeded them, and the operation of which they no longer understood. To borrow a phrase from "Wichita Vortex Sutra," Ginsberg now saw "the guardians of culture" as "bad magicians" who no longer spoke the arcane tongue from which they drew their power: "Not one yet, not ONE in all the colleges, magazines, book pages has said anything real, has got the point, either of spirit or prosody . . . NOT ONE" (Ginsberg 2008, 206). Ultimately, Ginsberg was a pragmatist of the first order, and it was this growing sense of the disjoint between "academic institution" and the cultural literacy required to regulate and reproduce "a contemporaneity for every period" that motivated his eventual, clairvoyant ultimatum: "UNLESS THERE IS MORE COOPERATION FROM THE SUPPOSEDLY RESPONSIBLE PARTIES IN UNIVERSITIES AND MAGAZINES," Ginsberg writes, "THEY CAN TAKE THEIR FUCKING LITERARY TRADITION AND SHOVE IT UP THEIR ASS—I don't need them and they don't need me" (ibid.).

Charles Altieri and others have characterized Ginsberg's multivalent occupation of the "mainstream margins" in terms of the nation:

> There is no doubt that Ginsberg feels wounded by the very nation that he wants to celebrate. But that is the aspect of contingency that he has to reconcile with the possibility of acknowledging the forces that have formed him. In fact, his sense of betrayal proves inseparable from ideals cultivated by that very nation. (Altieri 1999, 44)

While this analysis no doubt applies to questions of national identity, the present analysis suggests a more direct application to questions of "institution." "The very nation that he want[ed] to celebrate" becomes the "tradition" into which he sought entrance; and whereas his technical virtuosity allowed him to skillfully manipulate its formal networks of communication ("I don't need them [the universities and magazines] and they don't need me"),[19] he reserved his "sense of betrayal" by "the forces that had formed him" for "the horror of Columbia": "THEY CAN TAKE THEIR FUCKING LITERARY TRADITION AND SHOVE IT UP THEIR ASS."

---

19. As a compelling example of the many ways Ginsberg develops a "social formalism," and its similarities with the "naturalizing classicism" of "Malest," witness Ginsberg's testimony before the Judiciary Subcommittee on Juvenile Delinquency, investigating use of LSD:

> Dressed in a suit and tie, and speaking in a low, respectful tone, he [Ginsberg] began his address by admitting that he was uneasy . . . that the members might have prejudged him by his public "bearded image": "I am a little frightened to present myself—the fear of your rejection of me, the fear of not being tranquil enough to reassure you that we can talk together, make sense, and perhaps even like each other—enough to want not to offend, or speak in a way which is abrupt or hard to understand. . . . We can't treat each other only as objects, categories of citizens, role players, big names, small names, objects of research or legislation." (quoted in Schumacher 1992, 471–72)

Here is a moment when Ginsberg addresses *reception as a social question*, and a masterful negotiation of his public presentation, and the tissue-fine convergence of discursive strategies, and the legitimation of juridical authority. This direct encounter, his request to be allowed entrance into the field of juridical discourse, grounds itself in a nuanced social formalism. On the one hand, his appeal subtly criticizes the economy of public image, the unreality of its abstracted representations, and the ways in which it grounds juridical authority. At the same time, Ginsberg's strategies of *social formalism* offer the irreducible particularity of himself as "HUMANITY": resistant to the transformation of subjects into reified "objects," abstract "categories of citizens," "big names, small names," or "objects of . . . legislation." Ginsberg requests entrance into the highly charged and segmented public space as a human being, immediate and irreducible in his particularity.

Unlike "the guardians of culture" at an earlier point, the senators are not at all dismissive of Ginsberg's influence. Javits presents himself as fully aware of the threat posed by Ginsberg's formal mastery of the procedures that govern "legitimation" and makes explicit efforts to counter it:

> Q. Do you consider yourself qualified to give a medical opinion [concerning the use of LSD] which will determine the fate of my 16 ½-year-old-son?
> A. No. . . .
> Q. Of course you are not, and that is the important point that must be made to those who will listen to you.

Javits is speaking, not to Ginsberg, but to the matrix of public discourse. The senator exercises a strategy that strikingly resembles Ginsberg's own. The senator underscores the *formalism* and discursive artifice of Ginsberg's expertise, empiricism, objectivity, authority, intelligibility, and so on, as if to say: "Look! Though he sounds exactly like those that have been sanctioned as representatives of these various spheres of knowledge, and though he has exactly the same rhetorical arsenal and formal skill sets that they themselves exercise—he has not been sanctioned by the approved order." In effect, the senator is simultaneously drawing attention to the gap between the universality of discourses of reason, objectivity, empiricism, and reliance on fact and data, and their actual existence as subordinated to, situated within, and dependent upon highly contextual and contingent "legislative categories."

I would argue that Ginsberg's "classical silence" and disdain for academic classicism and its "tradition" had little to do with disavowing its textual capital or formal strategies. On the one hand, reading the elision only as a strategic move threatens to devolve into a flattening (and cold) critical judgment, dismissive of his ethical and multicultural commitments in a way that resonates ominously with his early institutional censure. On the other hand, my suggestion reflects the arc of Ginsberg's poetics themselves as they mature into self-reflexive critique and struggle with the contradictions involved in his classical usurpation: the symbiosis of critical innovation and the tradition from which it seeks to break; the "gap" between representation and its purported objects—public identity, sexuality, personhood, and so on; and the paradoxes of critical recidivism. That is to say that, although I argue that Ginsberg's poetics take as their starting point the strategies he identifies with the institution, they evolve. Ginsberg's basic critique of classicism is not that its strategies of identity reification and the creation of "images" of public identity are fundamentally insidious, but rather that they do not sufficiently nuance. The turn away from "Western" classics represents an evolving self-critique of his own classicism that begins at the level of represented content (resituating the intertextual stage of his naturalized, humanist, or American revisions onto ever more "foreign" or "unclassical" traditions) and finally turns against itself as a critique of representation as such.[20]

These tensions crystallize in the *Indian Journals* (1996), which stand as the culmination of an ongoing self-critique.[21] In the earlier period of "Malest" and

20. The shift in imaginary geography of Ginsberg's later work, especially the *Indian Journals,* in which the "outside" comes to be more and more exclusively located in the East, as well as the progressive Easternization of Ginsberg's post–*Indian Journals* poetics, represents an intensification of a textual and affective logic already implicit in "Howl," and deeply implicit in the romantic and transcendentalist tradition on which it draws so heavily. This mapping of a vertical geography of the metaphysical onto a horizontal geography, not to mention in combination with the degree to which, especially in his earlier poetry, Ginsberg takes on the role of the prophet (witness the repeated exclamation of "Moloch!" in "Howl" section 2, which transforms the poet into a Jeremiah, the poem into a Jeremiad, and America into a wayward Israel), might serve as concrete platforms from which to investigate Ginsberg's "neoromanticism." Ian Balfour, for example, has argued for the importance of the figure of the prophet in the crafting of romantic subjectivity and poetics in *The Rhetoric of Romantic Prophecy* (2002).

21. Two notable exceptions have paid a great deal of attention to the material in the *Indian Journals*: Hungerford 2005 and Watten 2002. This paper owes a great deal to Watten's formulation of the role of the East in the formation of an "outside" and his analysis of the *Indian Journals.* Watten's article, however, focuses on a political reading of the outside and focuses more narrowly on the *Indian Journals* themselves, rather than their relation to the longer arc of Ginsberg's work; and on the relationship of Ginsberg's post-India poetics to the emergence of Language poetry in the late '60s and '70s. To Hungerford's article, I owe many insights into Ginsberg's conception of a "supernatural" poetry of transformative power, although unlike

"Howl," Ginsberg's poetics articulate his "philological self-erasure." The osmosis of past to present, present to past, archaic to modern, center to margins, east to west, foreign to native, and so on, is the basis of his "linguistic supernaturalism" and creation of poetic immediacy, personhood, and presence. In India, Ginsberg encounters the material site of his "classical" projections. The *Indian Journals* mark a crisis in which Ginsberg confronts the "gap" between the "archaic time," liberated identities, and linguistic presence of his "oriental classicism," and the material reality of India as a measured present. To Ginsberg's credit, he does not shrink from the encounter, but follows its implications to their limits. The *Indian Journals* encounter the opacity of classicism's object in India and bring the question of language as an obdurate medium—resistant to stable reifications of identity—to the forefront in Ginsberg's work. After "Wichita Vortex Sutra," the Western classics return as a presence in his work. This return defers pride of place, but restores classical texts to viability and treats them as full interlocutors in a number of prominent poems, from "Ecologues" to "Plutonian Odes" and "τεθνάκην δ' ὀλίγω "πιδεύης φαίνομ' ἀλαία." Ginsberg's poetics evolve toward a self-aware critique or performance of their participation in practices of representation and image creation.

This chapter extends a close reading of "Malest" and Catullus 38 into a new appreciation of the arc of Ginsberg's career. It reframes the development of Ginsberg's poetics in terms of the highly particular mediation of a classical text and brings into a single lens a host of urgent issues, from censorship's influence on the content of Ginsberg's verse to the formal similarities between the cultural center and Ginsberg's "margins"[22]—and to what degree his poetics represent those margins by analogy with the center—issues of homosocial community and the economy of prestige, and the formalist "self-erasure" of his soon-to-be characteristic poetics of sincerity, authenticity, organicism, and "personhood." Reception studies allow us to articulate an early example of Ginsberg's poetics of public identity and "hegemonic marginalism" as grounded in highly specific modes of textual mediation. It contributes to and often revises our understanding of each of these issues and situates the histo-

Hungerford I emphasize the continuity of this emergence with logics already set in motion in Ginsberg's earlier poetry.

22. Perelman makes a number of provocative and compelling points vis-à-vis Ginsberg's relationship to Jewishness: "Another way of coming at Jewishness in innovative writing, what I'll call homeopathic Jewishness, will restore the commonsense fact that Ginsberg is a Jew, though in a non-commonsense way. . . . Crudely, the homeopathic model says that the more diluted the Jewishness the more Jewish the writer. . . . Back to "Ginsberg is more Jewish than Zukofsky." Really, isn't it simpler to reframe their difference-amid-genealogical-similarity as a difference in historical generation, both poetic and chronological? Zukofsky grew up speaking Yiddish; two decades later, Ginsberg grew up speaking English" (2009, 54–56).

ries of classicism and Western philology as potential contexts for Ginsberg's orientalism.

By examining not only the ways in which a critical poetics arises in opposition to, but also how it borrows from and shares similarities with "hegemonic classicism," this chapter participates in a growing body of scholarship that deepens our understanding of the New American Poetry by juxtaposing its impulse toward critique with its "reproduc[tion of] the very social forms [it] criticize[s]."[23] This critical development has ranged widely, recontextualizing the Beat generation's discourse of spontaneity and temporality in terms of the "burden of history" (Mortenson 2010, 1), the San Francisco Renaissance's "new, [homosexual] male subject," in terms of "a group ethos of male solidarity and sodality that often betrayed homophobic qualities" (Davidson 2003, 30), and the Black Mountain School's "production of new art forms and practice," in terms of "largely male forums . . . [and] the structure of homosocial relations, genitalized or not" (29). The marriage of classical reception and avant-garde studies allows us to resituate abstract negotiations of gender, sexuality, temporality, public identity, and intelligibility in terms of discrete textual mediations. Further, it contextualizes the dialectic of cultural critique and innovation in terms of the dance between a preexisting historical, cultural, and literary context and the horizon that strains toward "the new."[24] Examining the role of the classics in Allen Ginsberg's poetics offers a snapshot of the mechanisms of cultural development and identity construction as they operate at a particular literary and historical moment, and of the role that poetics and the mediation of key texts has played in broader processes of historical change.

---

23. Cf. Mortenson 2010, 1: "The Beats arrive in each new present with a burden of history (both individual and social) that complicates the ways in which they attempt to utilize the present."

24. It also offers the opportunity to rethink the classics themselves as originally avant-garde works of social critique that have been institutionally assimilated; and likewise of avant-garde works as bids for canonicity—works in the process of becoming canonical. The compulsory definition of experimental poets as "marginal" is thrown into striking relief when juxtaposed with the relative prominence in the popular imagination (and on the institutional reading list) some have attained: "The book [*Howl and Other Poems*] has sold more than 1,000,000 copies, its signature poem has been translated into two dozen languages and is anthologized in high school and standard anthologies worldwide as a literary classic" (Ginsberg et al. 2006); and as David Gates notes: "'Howl,' for all its affirmations, is a profoundly oppositional poem, and it counts on being opposed. . . . It's a radically offensive poem, or used to be" (quoted in Ginsberg et al. 2006). There is something vital in that seemingly incidental "used to be" that points to the dialectical nature of avant-garde critique and canonical affirmation.

Bibliography

Allen, Donald, ed. 1960. *The New American Poetry, 1945–1960*. New York: Grove Press.

Allen, Donald, and Tallman, Warren. 1973. *The Poetics of the New American Poetry.* New York: Grove Press.

Altieri, Charles. 1999. "Spectacular Antispectacle: Ecstasy and Nationality in Whitman and His Heirs." *American Literary History* 11: 34–62.

Auden, W. H., et al. 1964. "An *Arion* Questionnaire: 'The Classics and the Man of Letters.'" *Arion* 3.6: 6–100.

Balfour, Ian. 2002. *The Rhetoric of Romantic Prophecy.* Stanford, CA: Stanford University Press.

Beam, Alex. 2008. *A Great Idea at the Time: The Rise, Fall, and Curious Afterlife of the Great Books.* New York: Public Affairs.

Charters, Ann, and Kerouac, Jack. 1996. *Jack Kerouac: Selected Letters, 1940–1956.* New York: Penguin Books.

Davidson, Michael. 1998. "From Margin to Mainstream: Postwar Poetry and the Politics of Containment." *American Literary History* 10.2: 266–90.

———. 2003. *Guys Like Us: Citing Masculinity in Cold War Poetics.* Chicago: University of Chicago Press.

Ginsberg, Allen. 1996. *The Indian Journals.* New York: Grove Press.

———. 2006. *The Collected Poems, 1947–1997.* New York: Harper Collins.

Ginsberg, Allen, and Kerouac, Jack. 2010. *Jack Kerouac and Allen Ginsberg: The Letters.* New York: Viking.

Ginsberg, Allen, and Morgan, B. 2008. *The Letters of Allen Ginsberg.* Philadelphia: Da Capo.

Ginsberg, Allen, et al. 2006. "From the Poem that Changed America: 'Howl' Fifty Years Later." *American Poetry Review* 35.2: 3–10.

Hardwick, Lorna. 2003. *Reception Studies.* Oxford: Oxford University Press.

Hungerford, Amy. 2005. "Postmodern Supernaturalism: Ginsberg and the Search for a Supernatural Language." *Yale Journal of Criticism* 18.2: 269–98.

Lambert, John, trans. 2007. *The Poems of Catullus.* Chirchester: Scripsi.

Lardas, John. 2000. *The Bop Apocalypse: The Religious Visions of Kerouac, Ginsberg, and Burroughs.* Urbana: University of Illinois Press.

Marchand, Suzanne. 2001. "German Orientalism and the Decline of the West." *Proceedings of the American Philosophical Society* 145.4: 465–73.

Masuzawa, Tomoko. 2005. *The Invention of World Religions: Or, How European Universalism Was Preserved in the Language of Pluralism.* Chicago: University of Chicago Press.

Mortenson, Erik. 2010. *Capturing the Beat Moment: Cultural Politics and the Poetics of Presence.* Carbondale: Southern Illinois University Press.

Perelman, Bob. 2009. "Addendum: 'On the Jewish Question': Three Perspectives." In *Radical Poetics and Secular Jewish Culture,* edited by Stephen Paul Miller and Daniel Morris, 49–59. Tuscaloosa: University of Alabama Press.

Schumacher, Michael. 1992. *Dharma Lion: A Critical Biography of Allen Ginsberg.* New York: St. Martin's Press.

Trigilio, Tony. 2007. *Allen Ginsberg's Buddhist Poetics.* Carbondale: Southern Illinois University Press.

Watten, Barrett. 2002. "The Turn to Language in the 1960s." *Critical Inquiry* 29.1: 139–83.

Wordsworth, William. 2009. "Preface to Lyrical Ballads." In *Poetry and Cultural Studies: A Reader*, edited by Maria Damon and Ira Livingston, 20. Urbana: University of Illinois Press.

Wray, David. 2001. *Catullus and the Poetics of Roman Manhood.* Cambridge: Cambridge University Press.

Zukofsky, Louis. 2011. *Anew: Complete Shorter Poetry.* New York: New Directions.

CHAPTER 5

Radical Brothers-in-Arms

GAIUS AND HANK AT THE RACETRACK

MARGUERITE JOHNSON

si qui forte mearum ineptiarum
lectores eritis manusque uestras
non horrebitis admouere nobis . . .

if, oh readers, there is anyone who will
bravely touch my ramblings with their
own hands and not tremble . . .

—CATULLUS, *FRAGMENT* 14B

be self-taught.

—CHARLES BUKOWSKI, "NO LEADERS, PLEASE"

Charles Bukowski's poetic relationship with Catullus has received negligible attention from scholars, yet it provides significant insights into the reception of ancient verse by the Beats and their contemporaries. Bukowski's Catullus poems reveal intimate and personal readings and reworkings to articulate his own place in the world, often matching the poet's protestations of masculinity expressed through aggression and the grotesque. This chapter examines Bukowski's poetic solidarity with Catullus in terms of the concept of *contubernalis* in the Catullan sense, a brother-in-arms, a fellow traveler, and a peer. Catullus uses the term in *Carmen* 37 ostensibly to attack, but he does so cognizant of its traditional meaning (tent-companion or comrade) in order to underscore his awareness of the ties that bind him to the plethora of lovers surrounding Lesbia at the *salax taberna*.[1] He uses a similar expression in *Carmen* 11, *comites Catulli*, of Furius and Aurelius, playing on the standard mean-

1. On the use of *contubernalis* in *Carmen* 37, see Johnson 1999.

ing of *comes* (companion or comrade) in a poem that informs us intratextually of the irony implicit in this particular instance.[2]

Unlike Allen Ginsberg, Bukowski did not read Latin,[3] but he read and related to Catullus via the pages of an English translation.[4] His treatment of Catullus reflects an implicit simpatico with him that in turn translates into a Bukowskian dialogue with the poet.[5] In "what have I seen?" Catullus is directly addressed and ridiculed yet simultaneously lauded in a poem that channels the poet's playfully vitriolic voice (particularly *Carmen* 6). In "red up and down" and "the love poems of Catullus" in which the poet is not spoken to, but rather spoken about, the complexity of the intellectual and emotional bond is as equally strong. A less direct treatment is seen in "to the whore who stole my poems" in which Bukowski impersonates Catullus via *imitatio.* In each of the three approaches to Catullus—direct address, direct reference, and less obvious but specifically imitation-based composition—Bukowski establishes and reaffirms a bond between himself and Catullus, albeit grudgingly at times. He casts Catullus as his own Furius or Aurelius; his *contubernalis,* the object of ridicule and attack but also affection and admiration, depending on context and state of mind.

Before considering the relationship between the two poets, it is wise to address whether or not Bukowski can be classified as a Beat and, if so, what type of Beat. There is, of course, debate about whether or not Bukowski should be identified as a Beat writer. In fact, it could be argued that he does not belong to any creative enclave and is better situated as the artist-as-outsider.

2. See *Carmen* 16 for Catullus's most aggressive attack on Furius and Aurelius.

3. On Ginsberg's radically egalitarian approach to the classical canon, and also on his own translations of Catullus, see Pfaff in this volume.

4. It is uncertain what edition(s) Bukowski read. Bukowski owned almost no books, apart from editions of his own works, and used the public library as a young man, but less so later on (correspondence from Sue Hodson, Curator of Literary Manuscripts, The Huntington Library). However, in "red up and down" he mentions that the woman "walked out and sat on / my porch and read my copy / of Catullus" (1977, 14–16), clearly an indication he did have a copy, possibly his own. For the sake of convenience, Whigham's translation is used (except for the author's translation of *fr.* 14b and *Carmen* 41.1). The Latin text is from Catullus 1958.

5. This chapter positions Bukowski's treatment of Catullus outside debates surrounding autobiographical versus nonautobiographical readings of the poet. Such debates are anachronistic in relation to Bukowski's treatments of Catullus's verse because they do not surface in Catullan scholarship until the late 1980s (and elite literary criticism was antithetical to Bukowski's artistic creed, anyway). If pressed to take a position on how Bukowski understood Catullus's poems within such a paradigm, however, one may *suggest* that he read them as artistic artifacts as attested by his own reworkings of them combined with his own reinventions of Catullus's poetic persona. On the issue of identity, subjectivity, autobiography, and autobiographical fallacy in the poems of Catullus (an exhaustive scholarly enquiry), see Wray 2001 and also Gaisser 2009 for concise discussions.

The dissonance between Bukowski and the Beats is, essentially, one of his own making. Bukowski discusses his distaste for the Beats on numerous occasions, as illustrated in a letter to Jon Webb (*c.* October 1, 1962):

> Now, the original Beats, as much as they were knocked, had the Idea. But they were flanked and overwhelmed by fakes, guys with nicely clipped beards, lonely-hearts looking for free ass, lime-lighters, rhyming poets, homosexuals, bums, sightseers—the same thing that killed the Village. Art can't operate in Crowds. (Cooney 2007, 31)[6]

This excerpt shows Bukowski's unease with categorization and his intense dislike of belonging. His outsider status[7] protected his sense of identity and his creative process, and to preserve them, he could not be a part of any crowd, artistic or otherwise. Such sentiments are further voiced, indeed intensified, in later correspondence with Webb and his wife, Louise (December 7, 1963):

> The beats through their artefact of so-called brawny and courageous poeticism did more damage to the pure poem trying to breathe than Poetry Chicago has done accepting the accepted. The trouble with the BEATS: they gathered in crowds to gather SOLACE and when you take the gang-form you become the gang. (ibid., 96)[8]

If we take Bukowski's word for it, then, he was not, *is* not a Beat writer. Nevertheless, if we remove him from the classification process, he *was* and still *is* considered a Beat writer. Through his publishing relationship with the Webbs during the 1960s, most notably in relation to the magazine, *Outsider*, Bukowski was printed alongside Lawrence Ferlinghetti, William Burroughs, and Allen Ginsberg. In 1972, City Lights published his first collection of short stories, *Ejaculations, Exhibitions and General Tales of Ordinary Madness,* and he read at City Lights' Poet Theatre during the 1970s. This fluid association with the Beat movement, most strongly observed in Bukowski's links with publishers, thereby suggests a connection, even if he did not. There is also his interactions with the Beats, particularly, albeit briefly, Neal Cassady, "one of the few beat figures he admired" (Sounes 2000, 91) and his extensive correspondence with the "Queen of the Beats," Sheri Martinelli, another publisher of his early works.

6. Extract, letter to Jon Webb.

7. Bukowski was voted Outsider of the Year by *Outsider* magazine in 1962.

8. Extract, letter to Jon and Louise Webb, 7 December. On his vitriolic summation of Burroughs, see Bukowski 1973, 31–32.

Additionally, Bukowski's poetry, although highly individualistic, reflects the free verse, performativity and anti-authoritarian energy of the Beats.[9] But in terms of subject matter and lifestyle, he is not intimately part of their coterie, particularly as they themselves structured it. As Paul Clements suggests, Bukowski is part of the "outsider beat literature"[10] and, more importantly, a "materialist beat," a term Paul Whiston uses in relation to both Bukowski and Cassady. Whiston's emphasis here is on the literal meaning of "beaten down" as a cultural and social reality as opposed to the "'spiritual' beatific notion" of mysticism and vatic ecstasy[11] of bohemian Beats such as Ginsberg, Jack Kerouac, even Bob Dylan. In this literary and cultural classification of Bukowski's life and oeuvre within a more nuanced understanding of the Beat movement, we detect the interconnections and disconnections between him and its leading lights. Unlike some of them, Bukowski sourced no inspiration from professors and belonged to no university alumni. His was not a world of Columbia connections or any other academic ties; his institutional ties, if any, were to the post office. In this we see an emphasis on Bukowski as the "materialist beat;" the man who loathed the job and the institution that provided it, but who, nevertheless, had to work to sustain a livelihood in order to write. Rather than idealizing or even fetishizing the avant-garde rebellion against the American Dream via a championing of a free, itinerant, anti-establishment lifestyle that nurtured expression and insight, Bukowski lived that life through lack of choice, thereby embodying a Beat ideal, but never valorizing it. The American Dream rejected Bukowski long before he had the option to reject it himself.

The idea of Bukowski as an "outsider" Beat, a "materialist" Beat, is also in evidence in his approach to Catullus. In "what have I seen?"[12] Bukowski speaks directly to Catullus, admiring him while simultaneously modernizing him:

---

9. For the influence of the Beats on Bukowski's writing, see Clements 2013, 71–72.

10. Clements 2013, 6. For an insightful and early appraisal of Bukowski's outsider status, including a contrast to the Beats, see Rexroth 1964.

11. Clements 2013, 6, and Whiston 2000. Applying a Marxist reading of the Beats, Whiston argues that the lifestyles of Bukowski and Cassady, defined by social, cultural, and economic oppression that involved regular itinerancy, job-seeking, and hardship, were the catalysts for the Beat movement. This lived experience extended to the subject matter of Bukowski's writing and desired readership: "My genius stems from an interest in whores, workingmen, street-car drivers—lonely, beaten-down people. And those are the people I'd like to see reading my stuff, and I don't want to see too many learned comments, too much criticism, or too much praise get between me and them" (Bukowski in Blunden 2003, 166).

12. This version is from the manuscript dated June 28, 1979, and matches with one exception ("this great whale"), the audio recording of the poem during a reading at Sweetwater, Redondo Beach, California, in 1980 (released in 1994 under the title *Hostage*). For the published version, see Bukowski 2009, 110.

I like your way, Catullus, talking about the
whore who claims you owe her money, or
that guy who smiled too much—must have cleaned
his teeth with piss, or how about the poets
come with their blameless tame verse, or about
how this guy married a slut.
(Bukowski 1979, 1–6)

In the poem's second stanza, he both contemporizes and humiliates Catullus, making him a peer, a fellow punter at the racetrack:

you come right out and say things,
you're not like the others; but listen, Catullus,
didn't I see you at the racetrack bar last
Thursday? you had a great whale of a cunt
with you, must have scaled 190, one breast flopped
loose, dressed in a lavender sheet, I believe I heard
her pass wind in public—her teeth green, her buttocks
of sagging celluloid, and you drunk and pawing into
her anus . . .
surely that was not you, Catullus, at the racetrack
bar last Thursday?
(7–17)

Composed with a tonal mixture of admiration and mockery, "what have I seen?" shows a powerful intimacy between the two poets as Catullus is cast as Bukowski's *comes,* a "pal" he enjoys catching-out at the racetrack. The success of the poem, its tone, and content are reliant on Bukowski's familiarity with the Catullan oeuvre. Also necessary to poetic success is Bukowski's understanding of Catullus's direct, harsh honesty when it comes to vituperation and his liking for everyday, overtly untraditional subject matter as befitting the artistic creed of the *neoterics.* In stanza one, Bukowski references the Egnatius poems (*Carmen* 37 and *Carmen* 39), one of the two Ameana poems (*Carmen* 41) and the poem to Flavius (*Carmen* 6). As for his inclusion of "the poets" . . . "with their blameless tame verse" (4, 5),[13] his reference is more oblique and more interpretive, alluding to Catullus's occasional digs at bad verse and bad practitioners (men such as Caesius, Aquinus, and Suffenus, all of whom are mentioned in *Carmen* 14; Suffenus, again, in *Carmen* 22).

13. Perhaps an allusion to the Beat poets.

Bukowski's main theme in this poem, as signposted above, is twofold: admiration for the poet and mocking imitation of one of the poet's tropes, namely ridicule of someone he knows, someone in, out, or on the periphery of his "set," namely Flavius's girlfriend from *Carmen* 6. This dual theme is handled with sophistication and verve via Bukowski's use of imitation as a poetic weapon turned on the poet himself in order to augment, ironically, the compliment of imitation. Catullus in this sense becomes the object of his own vituperative style in a modern homage to him. Thus, as Catullus is praised in the line, "you come right out and say things" (7), he is exposed by Bukowski who copies the same technique by coming right out and saying things. As Catullus laughs and exposes Flavius for hiding a girlfriend who is suspected of being "as unattractive as / (doubtless) she is unacceptable" (*Carmen* 6.2–3),[14] he in turn is laughed at for avoiding Bukowski "at the racetrack bar last / Thursday" (9–10) because of an embarrassing girlfriend, namely "the great whale of a cunt" (10). This line, its vocabulary and imagery further exemplifies Bukowski's echoing of Catullus as illustrated in his additional attempts to demean Flavius via his girlfriend: "You are wrapped up with a whore to end all whores / and ashamed to confess it" (*Carmen* 6.5–6).[15] Bukowski, however, extends the insult via allusions to other poems in the Catullan corpus that ridicule enemies. For examples principally featuring women, we have Lesbia in *Carmen* 11.18 holding three hundred adulterers in her "embrace";[16] Ameana described as "that utterly fucked-out girl" in *Carmen* 41.1;[17] and Rufa who "sucks-off" someone called "little-Rufus" and who scavenges around graveyards, stealing from pyres in *Carmen* 59. Bukowski, the "beaten down" Beat, is drawn to the low-life cast members of Catullus's poetic dramas, seeing in them, perhaps, the down-and-out men and women of Los Angeles who were neighbors, coworkers, gamblers, sex workers, and drunks.

This image of Bukowski as a "materialist beat," illustrated in "what have I seen?" is accentuated when we consider a poem by Ginsberg that also pays homage to a poetic hero. In "A Supermarket in California" (1956),[18] Ginsberg imagines watching Walt Whitman shop for groceries.[19] Different to the direct and blunt nature of Bukowski, who sees and speaks to Catullus, Ginsberg

---

14. *illepidae atque inelegantes* (*Carmen* 6.2).

15. *uerum nescio quid febriculosi / scorti diligis: hoc pudet fateri.* (*Carmen* 6.4–5).

16. Perhaps echoed in "The Escape" (Bukowski 1977).

17. Author's translation.

18. On "A Supermarket in California," see Dickey in this volume (19); Dickey offers a different reading of the supermarket setting, regarding it as "mundane" (20) rather than my "middle-class."

19. I owe this comparison between the two poets to Leni Johnson.

establishes an artificial reverie to signpost that the encounter is not real or personal but imaginary and impossible:

> In my hungry fatigue, and shopping for images, I went into the neon fruit supermarket, dreaming of your enumerations!
> (Ginsberg 1956, "A Supermarket in California," para. 2)

Unlike the implied relationship revealed in Bukowski's address to Catullus, Ginsberg and Whitman are not "buddies," not *comites*, but share a student-master connection in the eyes of the student alone. The middle-class setting of the supermarket distinguishes Ginsberg's Beat world from that of Bukowski's racetrack:

> . . . Aisles full of husbands! Wives in the avocados, babies in the tomatoes!—and you, Garcia Lorca, what were you doing down by the watermelons?
> (para. 3)

The inclusion of Lorca amid the families is unorthodox and surprising; nevertheless, it too contributes to the markedly different world of Ginsberg and Bukowski. Not all, perhaps not many, of Bukowski's readers were familiar with Catullus yet this is of no consequence in terms of the poem's success. Bukowski simply talks to Catullus as he would to any other friend he spies in an embarrassing situation and wishes to mock. In contrast, Lorca is introduced as a poetic conceit that requires the reader to recognize the reference and juxtapose the poet to Whitman as two of Ginsberg's poetic and homosexual heroes. Walking with Whitman, passing Lorca and the families, Ginsberg's night-time supermarket is romantic; a world of poets, beautiful grocery boys, and a farewell image of Whitman disembarking Charon's boat and standing "on the black waters of Lethe" (32). This is in stark contrast to Bukowski's image of a drunken Catullus mauling a farting woman's anus at a racetrack in a poem stripped bare of classical adornment. Such a contrast—with an important echo ("I saw you, Walt Whitman" [10] / "but listen, Catullus, / didn't I see you" [8–9])—leaves a hint that Bukowski knew Ginsberg's poem and isn't just mocking Catullus.

This difference is evidenced further when we compare Ginsberg's "Malest Cornifici Tuo Catullo" (1958)[20] and Bukowski's Catullus poems. In 1955 Ginsberg was reading and translating Catullus[21] and this poem, an adaptation of

20. The poem appeared in the *Chicago Review* (1958) and in *Reality Sandwiches* (1963).

21. Raskin 2005, 150–51. See also Pfaff in this volume on Ginsberg's work on Catullus's verse.

Carmen 38 and addressed to Kerouac, is, like "A Supermarket in California," a polished, witty, self-consciously educated homage that captures the jouissance of Catullus when all is well with Lesbia or Juventius:

> I'm happy, Kerouac, your madman Allen's
> finally made it: discovered a new young cat,
> and my imagination of an eternal boy
> walks on the streets of San Francisco,
> handsome, and meets me in cafeterias
> and loves me.
> (Ginsberg 1958, "Malest Cornifici Tuo Catullo," 1–6)

Ginsberg's Latin, signposted in the title, establishes him as an aficionado, as one trained to mimic the poet in a "scholarly," innovative way.[22] Ginsberg's confident handling of the material is most overtly revealed in his style of replication: Ginsberg imitates Catullus by *becoming* Catullus.

"Malest Cornifici Tuo Catullo" is markedly different from Bukowski's Catullus poems. As a Latin-less reader, Bukowski could not title his poems in Latin, as Ginsberg did, nor could he echo Latin words or phrases. He overcame such hurdles, however, by amalgamating Catullan themes and imagery to write poems free from creative anxieties concerning the original language or a misguided imperative to capture linguistic fidelity. Such multipoem layering is evident in Bukowski's imitation of Catullus's poems about thieves in his "to the whore who took my poems":

> some say we should keep personal remorse from the
> poem,
> stay abstract, and there is some reason in this,
> but jezus;
> twelve poems gone and I don't keep carbons and you have
> my
> paintings too, my best ones; it's stifling:
> are you trying to crush me out like the rest of them?
> why didn't you take my money? they usually do
> from the sleeping drunken pants sick in the corner.

22. As discussed by Pfaff herein, Ginsberg (at times) liked to reject the stuffiness associated with traditional classics (prosody, for example). However, it is important to note that Ginsberg had the luxury of rejecting this elite tradition while at the same composing works that referenced his familiarity with it. The Beats' communion with antiquity is as much about class and, inextricably, education as it is about poetic aesthetics.

next time take my left arm or a fifty
but not my poems.
(Bukowski 1963, 1–12)

Bukowski laments the theft of his poetry and some of his best paintings, thereby joining Catullus in his own rants about thieves. In *Carmen* 12, Catullus rails against Asinius, a thief who employs similar strategies to Bukowski's whore, namely theft when his companions are drunk; and in *Carmen* 25, he attacks Thallus who made off with his cloak, napkins and writing tablets. It is *Carmen* 42, however, that is the main source of Bukowski's *imitatio.* Herein Catullus sends out his hendecasyllables to chase the whore who stole his writing tablets. Catullus's poem is more aggressive than Bukowski's condemnation: Catullus's thief is a whore (*moecha*) (employed five times), the word intensified by the use of the adjectives ugly (*turpis*) (3) and rotten or fetid (*pudita*) (11, 12, 19, 20).[23] Catullus continues to pile on the invectives: she strides with an ugly gait (*turpe incedere*) (8), laughs farcically and offensively (*mimice ac moleste / ridentum*) (8–9) with the mouth of a Gallic whelp (*catuli ore Gallicarni*), is filth (*lutum*) (13), not only a whore but the whorehouse itself (*lupanar*) (13) and, finally, a bitch (*canis*) (17). In fact, *Carmen* 42 is closer to Bukowski's "what have I seen?" in its squalid imagery of womanhood; in "to the whore who took my poems," he prefers to deride the woman via an emphasis on her actions and their effects rather than on her grotesqueness. Nevertheless, both are motivated by their belief in poetry as a means of exacting revenge and humiliation. Poetry as personal and cathartic is a consistent device throughout both poets' oeuvres, uniting them as brothers-in-arms—literally, in the thief poems—as they arm-up, sharpen their pens, and rail against the world.

In "the love poems of Catullus," Bukowski (2003, 177–78) writes a homage to the poet and the genre of the love poem itself:

she read his poems
she read them to the men waiting in her bed
then tore them up
laughing
and fell on the bed
opening her legs to the nearest convenient
cock.

23. Literally an "adulteress," but with the colloquial meaning of "whore." Whigham (1966) translates Catullus's Latin as "slippery whore" (*moecha turpis* [3]) and "unwholesome whore" (*moecha putida*, 11, 12, 19, 20).

> but Catullus continued to write love
> poems to her
> as she fucked slaves in back
> alleys, and
> when they were together
> she robbed him while he was
> drunk,
> mocked his verse and his
> love,
> pissed on his
> floor.
> (Bukowski 2003, 1–18)

The subject here is not only Catullus but Lesbia, the poet's principal object of desire. The two of them vie for Bukowski's attention as he defends the poet and damns his unworthy muse. Unlike the intimate brutality of "what have I seen?" here there is sensitivity toward the poet:

> Catullus was like
> most poets:
> I understand
> and forgive as I
> re-read him.
> (32–36)

Here is Bukowski at his introspective best; guard down, sentimental but, like Catullus, always in control of his craft. The heavy-handed slang and conversational style are still there but directed to express a different emotional and poetic energy; the defense of his artistic comrade, not his humiliation. The grotesqueness of the poem is linked to Lesbia.

The poem reflects three concerns on Bukowski's part: his imitation of Catullus's style to express his own views on Lesbia; his meditations on Catullus as a poet he knows, understands and forgives; and his biographical readings of the lives of both Catullus and his *puella.* Bukowski's treatment of Lesbia matches Catullus's hostile poems addressed to her. He presents her as equally whorish as her original lover does, emphasizing her utter unworthiness as a muse via the image of her reading the love poems of Catullus to the men in her bed, laughing at them, then tearing them up. Bukowski's fidelity to Catullus's account of the affair is evidenced in the references to her multiple lovers (*Carmen* 11, *Carmen* 37), to her "fuck[ing] slaves in back / alleys" (10–11;

see *Carmen* 58), and to her mockery of his love (*Carmen* 83). Bukowski also includes roughly comparable incidents from his own life—being robbed when he was drunk[24] and being with women who piss themselves[25]—but ascribes them to Catullus's experiences with Lesbia. This intrusion of his own experiences with women unites the two poets, valorizes their craft of love poetry despite its apparent futileness, and "pits" them against the world of women.

Such works operate as a testimony to their tenacity as poets, persisting in the composition of pointless love poems to faithless woman. This bond of intimacy is accentuated by Bukowski, who ends his poem with a biographical reading of the lives of Catullus and Lesbia. But here he seems to have made a spectacular error by conflating Lesbia with Sappho. Catullus, an ardent imitator of Sappho, named his mistress Lesbia in honor of her place of origin, Lesbos. But this conceit seems to have bypassed Bukowski[26] because he mentions that Lesbia committed suicide, thus mistaking her for the Sappho of the faux biographies of antiquity and later:[27]

Catullus who
otherwise
wrote brilliant
poems
faltered under the spell of
this wench
who
it is said
as she grew old
fled from him
begat a new life upon a far isle
where she ended up a

24. As in "to the whore who took my poems."

25. Pissing occurs comparatively regularly in Bukowski's writing; usually associated with him being drunk, but also associated with women; on the latter, see, "who the hell is tom jones?" (1977), "Piss" (1996), and the scene involving Lydia in *Women* (1978). Catullus also uses piss as vitriolic metaphor; see *Carmen* 37, *Carmen* 39, and *Carmen* 97. See Worman (2008, 234): "This obnoxious (and often anxious) emphasis on bodily appetites and urges has one of its important continuations . . . in the prose and poetry of male writers of the mid twentieth century. Poets like . . . Ginsberg and Charles Bukowski . . . reintroduced the rude comedy of the body into lyric form."

26. This is an unusual error in view of the fact that Bukowski read Sappho and should have been aware of the distinction between the real poet and Lesbia. On Sappho and the avant-garde of 1960s New York, see Skerl in this volume.

27. See Ovid, *Heroides* 15.

suicide.
(Bukowski 2003, "the love poems of Catullus," 19–31)

But maybe he didn't get it wrong but deliberately adopted the fake story of Sappho's death by suicide as a particularly fitting end for Lesbia—a poetic fantasy, a wishful death-as-punishment for the wrongs she committed against Catullus. Bukowski ends the poem by chronicling Catullus's biography, and here he may have intended a reference to *Carmen* 76, one of Catullus's most powerful poems, in which he presents himself as unwell and fatigued, but with poetic faculties fully charged, ruminating on his life, his health, and Lesbia:

he knew
as death approached
that it's
better to start out with a
strumpet than to end up
with one.
(37–41)

In "red up and down," Bukowski (1977, 171–72) describes another episode in a long line of meaningless yet meaningful encounters with women:

red hair
real
she whirled it
and she asked
"is my ass still on?"

such comedy.

there is always one woman
to save you from another

and as that woman saves you
she makes ready to
destroy.

"sometimes I hate you,"
she said.

she walked out and sat on
my porch and read my copy
of Catullus, she stayed out
there for an hour.
(1–17)

Bukowski frames this snapshot of life within the context of his copy of Catullus, a physical, potent memento he possesses, which leads him to meditate on the poet as he recalls an afternoon with a beautiful woman who is "red up and down." The pun of the title captures the woman's ambivalence toward Bukowski as well as her inherent mystique. She declares she hates him and promptly walks outside with his "copy / of Catullus" (15–16) and stays "out / there for an hour" (17), thus having "read" Catullus "up and down."

On returning indoors, she proves to Bukowski that she is also "red up and down," a natural red-head:

when she walked in I grabbed
her and pulled her to my lap.
I lifted my glass and told
her, "drink this."

"oh," she said, "you've mixed
wine with Jim Beam, you're gonna
get nasty."

"you henna your hair, don't
You?"

"you don't *look*," she said and
stood up and pulled down her
slacks and panties and
the hair down there was the
same as the hair
up there.
(24–38)

The sight of the seminaked woman leads Bukowski to Catullus in a perfectly evoked moment of confessional, stream-of-consciousness—Catullus too, no doubt, would have marveled at this beauty. Bukowski then thinks of Catullus's Juventius poems (*Carmen* 24, *Carmen* 48, *Carmen* 81, and *Carmen* 99), poems he never imitated because of his intense unease with bisexuality and homosexuality:[28]

> Catullus himself couldn't have wished
> for more historic or
> wondrous grace;
> then he went
> goofy
>
> for tender boys
> not mad enough
> to become
> women.
> (39–47)

In Bukowski's snipe at Catullus's liking for boys there is again a strong echo of the poet himself as he too rails against the sexuality of others when it suits. In *Carmen* 25 on Thallus and his theft of several of Catullus's belongings, he employs direct sexual invective as ridicule; beginning the poem with the vocative use of *cinaedus* (the passive recipient in sex), referring to the thief as soft (*mollis*)[29] and threatening to whip him (11), which will further demean him in the cultural/sexual hierarchy of Roman masculinity. Similarly, in *Carmen* 33 Vibennius and his son are attacked for thieving, with the son singled out for sexual humiliation in the same way as Thallus; he too is a *cinaedus* (2) and is additionally described as having an anus (*culus*) that is voracious (*vorax*) (4).[30] Likewise, his assaults on the women he casts as promiscuous are characterized by an aggressive, judgmental tone.

Such instances of Catullan machismo—accusing men of being soft and passive, threatening to render opponents passive[31] and humiliating women—are echoed in much of Bukowski's verse and prose. Clements suggests that Bukowski's hypervirility, expressed via extreme imagery is, however, a means of self-defense:

---

28. One of the additional reasons for his dislike of Ginsberg and Burroughs.

29. Catullus uses the comparative for emphasis, continuing the imagery in *l.* 10 with reference to his soft, gentle flanks and smooth hands (*ne laneum latusculum manusque mollicellas*).

30. The adjective used in the comparative as in *Carmen* 25.

31. See *Carmen* 15, *Carmen* 16, *Carmen* 21, *Carmen* 37.

> His excessive and continual focus on ugliness using grotesque humour is a foil and strategic mechanism to penetrate and expose hegemonic culture as well as prevent appropriation by it. (Clements 2013, 6)

Clements points to the use of obscenity, ugliness, and literary violence in Bukowski's work as a means of counterargument, yet this could be extended to consider the use of such themes, vocabulary, and imagery to reveal disempowerment. This is a possible reading of the grotesque and savage in Bukowski in view of the demoralized representation of himself in much of the writing that includes assaults on other personae.

In relation to Bukowski, the voice of disempowerment may be categorized as a form of "protest masculinity" in which the marginalized male embodies a claim to hegemonic power but lacks the resources and "institutional authority" that sustains it (Connell and Messerschmidt 2005, 847–48). In this situation, his machismo ironically demonstrates a lack of power. In "to the whore who took my poems," for example, Bukowski resorts to one of his standard words—"whore"—to rail against a thief. The word is part of his trade-mark "tough guy" persona, which was always performed in public, especially in interviews and poetry readings. And while the word signifies the power of Bukowski as the subject who vocalizes it, we also see his utter powerlessness, humiliation, and even victimization. All he has left is the word. Similarly, in "red up and down," Bukowski indirectly boasts of the woman in his house, casts himself as a hard-drinking womanizer, and demonstrates a dominant sexual energy; yet at the same time, he has doubts, thinking about those who would wonder "where such an ugly / old man could get / such beauty" (19–21). The uncertainty is replaced by a return to a protestation of his masculinity as he thinks of Catullus, who would appreciate the woman, but who was far less manly than himself, falling as he did, "for tender boys / not mad enough / to become / women" (43–46). Bukowski may be an ugly old man, but he isn't a faggot.

Likewise, while Catullus's *vituperatio* can be interpreted along the lines of a traditional Priapic model of iambic invective in which the poet adopts a menacing, threatening attitude to prove his virility and reassert his manhood (Richlin 1981, 42), there is also an anti-Priapic mindset at play that reveals his powerlessness. In invectives such as *Carmen* 11, *Carmen* 37, and *Carmen* 58, all of which are directed against Lesbia and employ obscene imagery to humiliate her, there are also powerful admissions of love, betrayal, and hurt, and, perhaps more revealing, impotence. In *Carmen* 11, for example, Furius and Aurelius are asked to deliver "non bella dicta" (17) to Lesbia:

live with your three hundred lovers,
open your legs to them all (simultaneously)
lovelessly dragging the guts out of each of them
each time you do it.
(Catullus 1958, 17–20)[32]

Whigham's translation captures the misogyny of the Latin, accentuated as it is by the reference to the excessive number of *moechi* penetrating Lesbia simultaneously and her rupturing (*rumpens*) their groins (*ilia*). Catullus's sense of social marginalization outside of the Roman system of gendered behavior, in which the freeborn male must always dominate and succeed in his sexual conquests, has been cauterized, hence his imagery of castration:

blind to the love that I had for you
once, and that you, tart, wantonly crushed
as the passing plough-blade slashes the flower
at the field's edge.
(21–24)[33]

On such vile outbursts in the Lesbia poems, Skinner (1991, 3) argues specifically for an impotent Priapic disposition on the poet's part:

> [The poems] in which Catullus helplessly deplores Lesbia's promiscuity, invert the Priapic model of obscenity by foregrounding the speaker's inability to do anything more than hurl feeble curses at those who have injured or betrayed him.[34]

Catullus's sense of being an outsider, primarily due to his Transpadane origins, is most strongly argued by Wiseman (1985, 111) who sees in Catullus's native Verona a community that was a "hard-working, straight-laced, traditional society that knew and valued Greek culture, was not inhibited about commercial profit, but took seriously the responsibilities of honest dealing." Wiseman argues that such an environment did not prepare Catullus for the fashionable elite society of Rome in terms of its values and lifestyle. While Wiseman may have a somewhat romanticized view of Catullus as an outsider,

32. *cum suis uiuat ualeatque moechis, / quos simul complexa tenet trecentos, / nullum amans uere, sed / identidem omnium / ilia rumpens* (*Carmen* 11. 18–22).

33. *nec meum respectet, ut ante, amorem, / qui illius culpa cecidit uelut prati / ultimi flos, praetereunte postquam / tactus aratro est.* (*Carmen* 11.21–24).

34. See Johnson 1999. There is a series of scholarly approaches to Catullus's aggression; for a discussion of the literature, see Wray 2001.

there are traces of a socially disenfranchised voice in poems other than the Lesbia cycle. Indeed, in his poems that deride members of the Roman elite, there is the same voice of disempowered protestation that characterizes his diatribes against Lesbia. In *Carmen* 28, for example, Catullus expresses his sympathy for Veranius and Fabullus for their time serving with Piso, comparing the latter's exploitation of them with his own experience in Bithynia with Memmius. The Priapic imagery is dominant and intensely graphic, yet as W. Jeffrey Tatum notes: "This poem is not primarily about sleaze: it is about ingratitude and exploitation, the exploitation felt by the municipal companion who has fulfilled his part of the bargain" (Tatum 1997, 495).[35] Skinner offers a more nuanced reading of Catullus's outsider status, particularly in comparison to Wiseman, suggesting:

> Throughout his poetry, Catullus appears to regard himself sometimes as Italian, at other times as Roman. Implicitly in poems 1 and 31, and quite explicitly at 39.13, he proclaims himself a *Transpadanus,* and therefore an outsider; but in 68a he insists that his *domus* is at Rome. (Skinner 2003, 34)

Skinner (ibid., 119) regards Catullus's Italian voice as "his familiar stage persona of Veronese outsider," which is particularly in evidence in poems dealing with men such as Piso, Memmius, Mamurra, and Caesar.

This is not to argue, however, that Catullus occupied anywhere near as socially and economically disadvantaged a background as Bukowski. Rather, it is to highlight the presence of "protest masculinity" in their works and to suggest that its origins lie in a self-identification with an outsider status on the part of both. In this sense, Catullus's violent responses to victimhood may have exerted a strong influence on Bukowski.

In a metaphorical sense, Bukowski, the Latin-less reader of Catullus, adopted a persona that suggests an uncanny understanding of the terms *contubernalis* and *comes* as ones redolent with affection; journeys taken; battles fought, lost, and won; disdain; disrespect; hate; and love. He recognized in Catullus not only a fellow traveler, racetrack companion, and poet but an outsider. Catullus's forceful protestations against the men and women who thwarted or belittled him, whether real, exaggerated, or imagined, struck a chord with Bukowski and gave him the voice with which to express his own life experiences, sometimes joyously ironic—even self-deprecatory—but most often, beaten down.

35. Tatum defines Catullus's Transpadane origins in terms of an ambiguous status, "Catullus, the Transpadane poet in Rome, remains always insider and outsider at once" (494).

Bibliography

Blunden, Ron. 2003. "Faulkner, Hemingway, Mailer . . . And Now Bukowski?!" In *Charles Bukowski: Sunlight Here I Am: Interviews and Encounters (1963–1993)*, edited by David Stephen Calonne, 160–67. Northville, NY: Sun Dog Press.

Bukowski, Charles. 1963. *It catches my heart in its hands*. New Orleans: Loujon Press.

———. 1973. *Notes of a Dirty Old Man*. San Francisco: City Lights.

———. 1977. *Love Is a Dog from Hell (Poems, 1974–1977)*. New York: HarperCollins.

———. 1978. *Women*. New York: HarperCollins.

———. 1979. Manuscript: "what have I seen?" In "Charles Bukowski Poem and Letter Manuscripts." http://bukowski.net/manuscripts/displaymanuscript.php?show=poem1979-06-28-what_have_I_seen.jpg&workid=4302

———. 1994. *Hostage*. Los Angeles: Rhino/Word Beat.

———. 1996. *Betting on the Muse*. Santa Rosa, CA: Black Sparrow Press.

———. 2003. *Sifting through the Madness for the Word, the Line, the Way: New Poems*. Ed. John Martin. New York: HarperCollins.

———. 2008. *The Pleasures of the Damned*. New York: Ecco.

———. 2009. *The Continual Condition: Poems*. Ed. John Martin. New York: Ecco.

Catullus. 1958. *C. Valerii Catulli Carmina*. Ed. R. A. B. Mynors. Oxford: Oxford University Press.

———. 1966. *The Poems of Catullus*. Trans. Peter Whigham. Harmondsworth, UK: Penguin.

Clements, Paul. 2013. *Bukowski, Outsider Literature, and the Beat Movement*. London: Routledge.

Connell, R. W., and Messerschmidt., James W. 2005. "Hegemonic Masculinity: Rethinking the Concept." *Gender Society* 19: 829–59.

Cooney, Seamus, ed. 2007. *Charles Bukowski. Screams from the Balcony: Selected Letters 1960–1970*. Sydney: HarperCollins e-books.

Gaisser, Julia Haig. 2009. *Catullus*. Oxford: Wiley-Blackwell.

Ginsberg, Allen. 1958. "Malest Cornifici Tuo Catullo." *Chicago Review* 12.1: 11–12.

———. 1956. *Howl and Other Poems*. San Francisco: City Lights.

———. 1963. *Reality Sandwiches*. San Francisco: City Lights.

Johnson, Marguerite. 1999. "Catullus, *C.* 37, and the Theme of *Magna Bella*." *Helios* 26.1: 85–96.

Ovid. 1977. *Ovid: Heroides and Amores*. Trans. G. Showerman. Ed. G. P. Goold. Cambridge: Harvard University Press.

Raskin, Jonah. 2005. *Ginsberg's Howl and the Making of the Beat Generation*. Berkeley: University of California Press.

Rexroth, Kenneth. 1964. "There's Poetry in a Ragged Hitch-Hiker." *The New York Times*, July 5.

Richlin, Amy. 1981. "The Meaning of *Irrumare* in Catullus and Martial." *Classical Philology* 76.1: 40–46.

Skinner, Marilyn B. 1991. "The Dynamics of Catullan Obscenity: cc. 37, 58 and 11." *Syllecta Classica* 3: 1–11.

———. 2003. *Catullus in Verona: A Reading of the Elegiac Libellus, Poems 65–116*. Columbus: Ohio State University Press.

Sounes, Howard. 2000. *Charles Bukowski: Locked in the Arms of a Crazy Life.* New York: Grove Press.

Tatum, Jeffrey W. 1997. "Friendship, Politics, and Literature in Catullus: Poems 1, 65 and 66, 116." *Classical Quarterly* 47.2: 482–500.

Whiston, Paul. 2000. "The Working Class Beats: A Marxist Analysis of Beat Writing and Culture from the Fifties to the Seventies." Sheffield: Sheffield University Press. Online Papers in Social Research. https://www.sheffield.ac.uk/polopoly_fs/1.71446!/file/2whiston.pdf

Wiseman, T. P. 1985. *Catullus and His World: A Reappraisal.* Cambridge: Cambridge University Press.

Worman, Nancy. 2008. *Abusive Mouths in Classical Athens.* Cambridge: Cambridge University Press.

Wray, David. 2001. *Catullus and the Poetics of Roman Manhood.* Cambridge: Cambridge University Press.

CHAPTER 6

Riffing on Catullus

ROBERT CREELEY'S POETICS OF ADULTERY

NICK SELBY

Written in the summer of 1954, Robert Creeley's "Stomping with Catullus" became a means for him to test his Beat credentials.[1] The poem is a translation, in the form of a theme and variations, of Catullus's poem "*Nulli se dicit*" (*Carmen* 70), but its explicit pushing at poetic limits (of translation and of rhythm) mark it as an important early instance of Creeley's experimental, countercultural, poetic practice. At the time he was writing this poem Creeley's first marriage was falling apart.[2] Angrily brought to task by his friend, poet Paul Blackburn, for recent adulterous affairs, Creeley bitterly denounced another friend's, Paul Carroll's, translations of Catullus, which had been strongly influenced and guided by Blackburn. Creeley described Carroll's translations as "awkward, stuttering, pompous," and blamed this squarely on the influence of Blackburn's wife, Freddie (Faas 2001, 172–73). "Stomping with Catullus" can be seen, therefore (and fittingly, given Catullus's reputation for vicious and vituperative poems) as Creeley's revenge on what he saw as a poetic betrayal and as a response to accusations of sexual infidelity (173–74). Given such circumstances, this essay argues that in "Stomping with Catullus" we see Creeley's performance of himself as a "Beat" poet eventuating from what I'm calling a poetics of adultery.

1. The poem was written "by August 26, 1954." See Novik 1973, 115. It was first published in the collection *All That is Lovely in Men* (1955).

2. The events surrounding this breakup are fictionalized in Creeley's novel, *The Island* (1963) and documented in Faas 2001.

While such a poetics of adultery rests on questions of fidelity (to poetic sources; between lovers) that are underscored by Creeley's use of Catullus, I want also to argue that it therefore underpins a broader, though no less troubled, negotiation with Beat aesthetics. And this, too, has broader implications for thinking about Creeley's place in the articulation of what has come to be known—after Donald Allen's influential anthology of 1960—as the "New American Poetry."[3] The issue of fidelity raised by "Stomping with Catullus" becomes, that is, a cultural—countercultural—and ethical issue within Creeley's poetics. The detailed reading of "Stomping with Catullus" that follows in this essay aims, then, to show how questions of fidelity are, for Creeley, more than simply subject matter—poetic "content"—made available to him via Catullus. Rather, Creeley's poetics of adultery comes to constitute an essential part of his poetic "stance toward reality" at this early stage in his poetic career.[4]

This means that the Beat pose adopted by Creeley in "Stomping with Catullus"—via what we might think of as his "adulterous" appropriation of the original Catullus poem—grounds his poetics in ethical—or, more properly, as I shall argue, *poethical*—questions. As we shall see, such questions are linked to the argument against Stoicism staged by Catullus's poetry and to Lucretius's discussion of things (as atomistic) and nature (as ethical) in *De Rerum Natura*. In effect, then, "Stomping with Catullus" also undercuts its own easy co-option to Beat aesthetics by asserting the larger poethical terms under which the New American poetics—experimental, countercultural, and profoundly unsettled—can be seen coming to operate in postwar America.

While Creeley's poetics of adultery helps chart these various aesthetic, poetic, and cultural maneuvers, it also—therefore—frames the ways in which "Stomping with Catullus" (alongside "The Whip" and "The Rain," which are discussed later in this essay) questions the idea of being a Beat poet and the relationship of Beat to classic. The aim of this essay is not so much, therefore, to plot Creeley's place within a genealogy of translations of Catullus into English (there have been many such translations subsequent to Catullus's first printing in England in 1684, so Creeley's reading strategy in respect of Catullus is hardly new [see Gaisser 2001, xxviii]). Rather, my delineation of Cree-

3. In the context of such a poetics of adultery, it is worth noting that among the Creeley poems selected by Allen for his anthology, *The New American Poetry*, are "The Whip" (discussed later in this essay), "A Marriage," "Ballad of the Despairing Husband," and "Just Friends," all poems dealing with marital breakup and adulterous relationships.

4. Charles Olson's famous and highly influential essay "Projective Verse" (1950) asserts that the new poetics, what he terms "OPEN verse" or "COMPOSITION BY FIELD," "involves a stance toward reality outside a poem as well as a new stance towards the reality of a poem itself." See Olson 1997, 239 and 246.

ley's poetics of adultery in "Stomping with Catullus" sees the "New Roman" (or "neoteric") poet as Creeley's means of exemplifying and embodying the concerns of a New American poetics to pull against '50s conformity and containment culture. This impulse is undoubtedly related to the concerns of the Beat generation, yet the readings of Creeley that follow—stemming from his "adulterous" poetic relationship to Catullus—contrast his poetic unsettledness, hesitation, and stuttering articulacy with a more assured, propulsive, Beat poetics. How far, the essay asks, *can* we read Creeley as a Beat poet when more seems to be at stake about the nature of things in his poetics than is encapsulated in Beat spontaneity and its mythologization of countercultural protest?

Before turning to a detailed examination of "Stomping with Catullus," it is worth noting an occasion where Creeley's performance of himself as a Beat poet is seen in relation to this poem. Speaking at a poetry reading in San Francisco in May 1956 (barely six months after the 6 Gallery Poetry reading there, which was—if we believe most literary histories—the event that launched the Beats into broader public attention), Creeley had this to say about his poem:

> This is actually the one poem of Catullus as [that] I could ever remember, having studied Latin a long long time ago. The first verse is a literal translation of the poem and those that follow are variations of it in a jazz idiom.[5]

Creeley's reading of such a poem, "in a jazz idiom," in San Francisco, in 1956, might very well be seen as certifying his Beat credentials. Much like Sal Paradise's motivations for going West at the start of *On the Road*, Creeley's reason for being in San Francisco at this time had "something to do with the miserably weary split-up" of his marriage (Kerouac 1957, 7). Indeed, "Stomping with Catullus" is a poem that (as can be heard emphatically in recordings of Creeley reading it) gives itself up, as it were, to the beat, to a sense of the rhythm of things.[6] However, the question of (poetic) fidelity that haunts Creeley's maneuver from literal translation to jazz idiom over the course of "Stomping with Catullus" significantly destabilizes the relationship of Beat to classic. This is witnessed in the poem's slippery status as a translation and set of variations, in its idiomatic speech and rhythms, and in its troubled sense of a lover's faithfulness, all of which might be broadened out into a wider cultural con-

---

5. The reading took place at the Telegraph Hill Neighborhood Association, San Francisco (May 20, 1956). A recording of it is available at https://diva.sfsu.edu/collections/poetrycenter/bundles/191193 (last accessed December 3, 2017).

6. As we shall see later, this can be related to a Heideggerian notion of poetic letting go, *Gelassenheit*.

cern with how a poem might be faithful to—come to represent—a particular moment: the Beats in the '50s, the turbulent Roman Republic in the 50s BCE.

Such worries about poetic and cultural fidelity are encapsulated, as we shall see, by the poem's attempt to make ironic play from the gap between what lovers say and what they do. Indeed, as Julia Gaisser has pointed out, not only does *Carmen* 70's repeated use of the word *dicit* ("she says") "hammer home a distrust of words and promises" by "implying an antithesis between words and actions," but the ironies of sexual infidelity insinuated by Catullus in this poem are modeled on an earlier text, Callimachus's *Epigram* 11 (Gaisser 2009, 32–34). Whether Creeley was aware or not of this longer literary history evoked by Catullus's poem, his act of translation of it certainly registers, and explicitly raises questions about, poetic origins and the authenticity of a poet's experience. And this pulls against the reification of spontaneity of expression in much Beat writing. If "Stomping with Catullus" is a Beat poem, we might wonder, what do its repeated readings—"variations" as Creeley has it—of Catullus tell us about a poetics of being-in-the-moment akin to Ginsberg's "first thought best thought" ideal? How does the diffidence, hesitation, and anxiety about the transience of a lover's declarations that is evident in "Stomping with Catullus" (and its going back over the same ground five times) square with a Beat poetics that is often associated with assuredness, declarative utterances, and onward propulsion (as in Ginsberg's *Howl,* or in jazz-like improvisation)?

We might also be brought to wonder why it is *this* Catullus poem that Creeley remembers. *Carmen* 70 is certainly not Catullus's most famous or commented upon poem (it's not the *Attis,* or "odi et amo" [*Carmina* 63 and 85]). Indeed, for a poet famed for bawdiness, and eroticism, this is remarkably diffident and restrained, enigmatic even, in its critique of the lover. What it witnesses is not a brash condemnation of Clodia's/Lesbia's adultery and political machinations (as in a number of the more famous poems), but a recognition of the very difficulties of coming to poetic terms with infidelity. It is precisely this, I think, that appeals to Creeley. It should also be remembered that *Carmen* 70 is a transitional poem; it is, as Kenneth Quinn has noted, a poem that "strikes a new note" (1972, 103).[7] In the sequence of Catullus's poems, it comes at a point where the longer middle poems give way to shorter, epigrammatic ones. Written in elegiac couplets, *nulli se dicit* is a poem very much about coupling. This too, I think, is why Creeley remembers it, and that

7. For Wiseman, this poem represents "a new tone in Catullus' love poetry—cooler and more analytical than the outbursts of joy or fury in the first book" (1985, 166).

will become more apparent when we look at the form that his translation and variations of the Catullus poem takes.

As we turn to take a closer look at the poem itself, Creeley's comment that "Stomping with Catullus" is in "a jazz idiom" serves to underline that which is absolutely explicit in the poem, namely its awareness of, and play with, the question of rhythm, of the Beat, or in a phrase favored by Creeley, its "sense of measure." The poem proceeds by developing an increasingly insistent sense of rhythm, a largely four-beat trochaic measure that pulls against the apparently conversational tone. This is important not only because such poetic stomping is central to the poem's affective power but because it also provides Creeley with a means of measuring ideas of the human and of relationship (as we will see later in his poem "The Whip"). The question of the beat that the poem embodies, then, becomes an insistently cultural question. Indeed, we might read the poem's jazzy syncopations as, themselves, setting in train a set of "adulterous" relationships in which we can hear a rhythmic pulling against the sorts of cultural and social four-square conformity that defines Cold War containment culture.[8]

The first section, comprising eight lines, of "Stomping with Catullus" provides, as it were, the theme upon which the subsequent four sections of the poem riff. Though Creeley describes this section as "a literal translation" of the Catullus original, it is clear from the outset that repetition and hesitation, even the very sounds the poem makes, are being used to significantly complicate the ways in which it might be working as "translation." Aware of its role in repeating an old theme—misunderstanding between lovers; misinterpreting their intentions—"Stomping with Catullus" opens directly into repetition as a means of marking the difficulty of that theme, the difficulty of saying what one means:

My love—my love says
she loves me.
And that she would never have
anyone but me.

Though what a woman tells
to a man who pushes her
should be written in wind and quickly

8. Nadel 1995. Gair (2007, 65) notes that jazz—and especially bebop—"offered a 'hip'—and thus, invariably, threatening—challenge to the hegemonic conventions of mid-century America."

moving water.
(Creeley 1982, 68)

The poem thus announces itself clearly as one that will test and explore sexual relationships. This is apparent in the play between the poem's speaker and his lover, and how this is broadened into a general (and presumably exemplary case) of "a man" and "a woman" in the second stanza.

The repeated "my" in the poem's first line means that its exploration of relationship is colored by an examination of ownership. Not only does the poet see his "love" as his possession but he is troubled by how he might, as a poet, possess the theme of love. While Creeley draws out these notes of ownership and repetition from his original (Catullus writes "*mulier mea*"—"my woman"—in his first line and repeats the use of "*mulier*"—a more generic reference to "woman"—in line 3 [Quinn 1972, 103, 288n30][9]), he undercuts Catullus's swagger though his own poem's stuttering rhythm. Creeley's speaker does not so assuredly possess his lover. Indeed, the awkwardness of Creeley's line breaks (and of his repetitions) in this opening stanza provide a sense in which his themes of love, possession, and fidelity will be drawn out for examination throughout the poem by the peculiar emphasis they are given as a result of the syncopated rhythm through which they are articulated. Effectively, then, Creeley's jazz idiom pulls apart the syntax of his first two sentences and thus sounds an off-key note that plays against his Catullus original.[10] What we hear in the opening moment of the poem, then, is a speaking voice that stumbles through the difficulties of sounding the enjambments between the stanza's longer and shorter lines. The question of the poem's beat becomes, therefore, Creeley's device for investigating the means and the efficacy of communication between lovers throughout the poem. It also—as we will see—signals a questioning of what might constitute a Beat poetics.

In these opening lines, we can also see how the idea of relationship inheres in the very act of repetition. Lovers—like poems—repeat old themes, actions, and words as they struggle to articulate their feelings. Pointedly, this occurs in the rhyme words of this first section of the poem. The repetition of "me" as the end-stopped rhyme in lines 2 and 4 builds on the theme of ownership and

9. The Catullus poem reads: "Nulli se dicit mulier mea nubere malle / quam mihi, non si se Iuppiter ipse petat. / dicit: sed mulier cupido quod dicit amanti, / in vento et rapida scribere oportet aqua." See Michie's translation, Catullus 1969, 186.

10. See Kerouac's (1959) description of Bop's transgressive cultural force as a "wild, impossible mistake in jazz . . . [in which] Thelonious [Monk] introduced a wooden off-key note to everyone's warmup notes" (51).

possession announced in the opening line and contrasts markedly with the rhyme of "her" and "water" in lines 6 and 8. Through the simple action of the rhyming pattern in these stanzas, the speaker's self-assuredness is thus undercut by his anxiety over the fidelity of the object of his love. Not only does the repetition of "me" come to sound like worried special pleading but the possessive pronoun ("her") that is attached to the generic "a woman" signals the slipping away of the actual lover into a type, into an example of love more broadly conceived. This then complicates the poem's opening contemplation of "My love," a phrase that—through its repetition in the poem's first line—sets up a play between the speaker's lover (as in "my love says") and the poem's investigation of the broader theme of love itself (as in the possibly more abstract-meaning "My love–"). Such slippages and complications are enacted in the poem's rhymes: the not quite perfect rhyme of "her" and "water" does indeed feel like water slipping through the poem's fingers.

The speaker's use of the trope of running water as a figure both for his lover's (and lovers', more broadly) inconstancy and for his anxieties about that inconstancy is, itself, a repetition of an old poetic image, one that Catullus himself was repeating from Greek poetry.[11] In Creeley's usage, the image is itself rendered slippery. First, it runs over the line break, thereby actualizing its theme of constant movement. And second, that enjambment serves to throw especial attention onto the adverb "quickly." The brief suspension caused by the line break in "written in wind and quickly / moving water" exposes the slipperiness of the relationship between verb and adverb, where "quickly" seems, initially, to apply to the verb "written" rather than as a qualifier for the "moving water" of the next line. The poet, it seems, must write quickly (in wind) of what his lover tells to him while also writing in water that is rapidly moving. Not only does this mark the impossibility for a poet of ever faithfully writing of love, or of inscribing faithfully his lover's words, it seems also to diagnose a broader problem about the relationship between actions in and experiences of the world. Exploring this broader problem—the difficult coupling of actions and things—is one of the consequences of Creeley's poetics of adultery. As we have seen, this problematic exploration emerges from the various couplings and miscouplings—of rhymes, repetitions, and lovers—that the poem performs and describes. It continues throughout the rest of the poem.

After the laying down of these themes in the poem's first section, the speaker's initial hesitancy is replaced by a more fluid sense of rhythm and by

11. Gaisser notes that this imagery "has various parallels in ancient literature. The closest one I know is a fragment of Sophocles: 'I write the oath of a woman on the water'" (2009, 136).

more determined, end-stopped rhymes in the four subsequent "variations" on the Catullus original. These subsequent stanzas settle into a pattern of rhyming couplets (they are thus more "faithful" to Catullus's original elegiac couplets), and the speaking voice in each successive section also becomes increasingly colloquial, as though Creeley is trying to test the limits of an off-hand, conversational, and spontaneous Beat argot. As with jazz players stepping up to take a solo on their particular instrument, each variation of Creeley's poem presents a different voice riffing on the same theme:

2.
My old lady says I'm it,
she says nobody else cd ever make it.

But what my old lady says when pushed to it,—
well, that don't make it.

3.
My old lady is a goof at heart,
she tells me she loves me, we'll never part—

but what a goofed up chick will tell to a man
is best written in wind & water & sand.

4.
Love & money & a barrel of mud,
my old man gives out for stud,

comes home late from his life of sin,
now what do you think I should tell to him?

5.
We get crazy but we have fun,
life is short & life gets done,

time is now & that's the gig,
make it, don't just flip yr wig.
(Creeley 1982, 68–69)

The poem develops, therefore, by presenting us with a series of shifting poetic and vocal perspectives. While continuing to enact the poem's theme of inconstancy and change, such shifts also allow Creeley to critique the initial pose and idiom adopted by the poem's male lover. We see the lover's possessiveness (signaled by "my love" in section 1 and "my old lady" in sections 2 and 3) being ironically and humorously countered by the woman's perspective in section 4 ("my old man gives out for stud"), which is, in turn, replaced by a collective voice ("We get crazy but we have fun") in the final variation, section 5. The act of variation, that is, pulls open the notion that the poem might be able to stay true to its original intentions. Precisely because Creeley writes the poem as a theme and set of variations he is able to investigate how a love poem might measure, or fail to measure, human relationships.

Similarly, though with different consequences, the poem's rhyme words—signaling both repetition and variation—put the poem at the limits of what might be able to be articulated by the lover. The rhyming of "it" four times with itself in as many lines in section 2 puts so much pressure on this pronoun, and on the question of to what it might refer on each occasion, that the lover's assertions collapse into all but nonsense. This sort of emptying out of the content of the poem by its gesturing to an absent referent might be seen as the result of, and the poem's means of, interrogating its status as a translation. It also further develops Creeley's opening up of a gap between a specific object of love—the poet-lover's "love," "old lady," or "chick"—and a more general sense in which the poem is addressing itself to, or apostrophizing, an abstract concept of love itself—"My love."

In section 4, the rhyme pattern further complicates the poem's themes of adultery and of the gap between the abstract and the particular. Seen from the woman's point of view (which itself complicates the poem's act of translation) the couplet, "Love & money & a barrel of mud, / my old man gives out for stud," is clearly critical of the male lover. Yet the specifics of that critique are blurred, one might say muddied, by the very means through which it is articulated. Rhyme and rhythm—instruments of feeling and affect—overpower these lines' sense and meaning. Here the poem obeys its own, earlier, advice by writing of a lover's infidelity (the presumed implication of "giv[ing] out for stud") in "water & sand," that is, in a "barrel of mud." Mud, of course, is a mixture of both water and sand, so a barrel of mud represents the adulteration of both those elements. Here, then, these strong full-rhymes continue, by a sort of poetic sleight-of-hand, the theme of adultery, not by an emptying out of the content of the poem's reference (as earlier) but by an overfilling of it, a barrel-full in a line packed with other big abstract nouns, "Love" and "money." And in the second couplet, the slippery sexual morality of the man is measured poetically by a slant-rhyme—"sin" and "him"—in which poetic and domestic fidelity come under simultaneous scrutiny.

Two related and important aspects of the poem are at play here. First, the woman's exasperation with her lover in this section picks up on a sense of suppressed antagonism and violence that runs through the whole poem. Though Creeley describes section 1 as a "literal translation" of the Catullus original, the injunction that a lover's words "*should* be written in sand" and the use of the verb "push" in "who pushes her" do not appear in Catullus's poem. These two additions add a sense of menace into the very way in which the lover describes his love. They signal his mistrust of his lover's words, the coerciveness of forcing a lover to speak of their love, and suggest that the relationship is underpinned by physical violence. The poem's "pushing" of the woman might well be seen as companion to its stomping and beating. In this case, Creeley seems to be investigating the ways in which misogyny is instrumentalized within beat poetics. Indeed the repetition of the imperative "should" in section 4 of the poem, but this time in the mouth of the woman and her rather exasperated (and dactylic) rhetorical question about her lover, "now what do you think I should tell to him?," indicates the poem's attempt to undercut the assumed power with which the poem's male lover speaks.

And second, such a question resonates powerfully with the poem's examination of miscommunication between lovers. In part this is because its rhythmical insistence leaves the very question open, in part because the question revolves around the gap between what lovers say, what they do, and what they tell to each other. Exploiting this gap—as it is set up in section 1 between a lover who "*says* / she loves me" and a mistrust of "what a woman *tells* / to a man"—is central to the poem's development of its critique of how lovers act together. The speaker's mistrust of his "old lady" is largely insinuated in section 2 because the use of the more passive-feeling verb "says," whereas in sections 3 and 4 the more active "tells" indicates the perception, on the part of the speaker, of a possible intention to deceive (in section 3) or to "tell off" the aberrant lover (in section 4).

The play between telling and saying, then, both underscores the poem's play of agency between its lovers and radiates outward to the reader and to our response to, and responsibility for, the poem before us (as is evident in the line "what do you think I should tell to him?"). Such poetic telling (and asking) cements the poem's anxious ethical positioning, which is heard in its final "variation." Here, human relationships are pitted not just against the ways and means through which we might *tell* them (and retell them as variations on an old poetic theme) but also against the ways in which they are played out in, and measured against, time and the things we might get done in time. If the phrase "life is short & life gets done" expresses a passive sense of agency in the face of life's shortness, it is balanced by an injunction not simply to give oneself up to time, but to "make" something (a poem, perhaps?) of it. But the balance here between a passive giving up of oneself to the way things are and an active making of something ("it") out of things brought together by the poem is precariously measured by Creeley's use of the ampersand in the final three variations. Tellingly, in section 5, this graphic device of verbal coupling replaces the "And" of section 1's third line and sets up a kind of internal rhyme *between,* and *within,* lines 2 and 3 of this section. In each line, the ampersand (or, copula) marks a caesura. These lines seem to be saying, therefore, that any coupling—whether verbal, poetic, or sexual—must recognize the fracturing upon which it is predicated.

What I want to suggest, then, is that Creeley's measure of things in this poem—via Catullus—is hardly a solid endorsement of a Beat aesthetics of giving oneself up to "IT" (as Sal and Dean famously do in *On the Road*), nor is it underpinned by the sort of Epicurean *ataraxia* that influences Catullus's anti-Stoic thinking. So, although Kerouac's "IT" remains an ambiguous concept, and thus only a partial measure of Beat thinking, the draw toward a "form of instant gratification, a thrill for the moment, an epiphany" that, according to Weinreich (1990, 54), it embodies is something that Creeley's poetics resists. Creeley's attention to *things* played, replayed, adulterated (rather than to a singular *IT,* a moment) sees the poem as a reality that is explored and into which he seeks to project meaning, as opposed to a reality that is transcended by, as Weinreich describes IT, "some form of isolated or radiating pleasure as a feeling and end in itself" (54). Creeley's poetics, that is, marks as profoundly ambiguous many of the tropes of spontaneity and "being-in-the-moment" that are commonly felt to characterize Beat writing. The indeterminacy, therefore, that results from Creeley's use of a jazz idiom in this poem, and of a theme and variations format, significantly undercuts its ostensibly "typical" Beat sensibility. The idioms of the poem's final line—"make it, don't just flip yr wig"—which sound very like those of a countercultural hipster, ring hollowly precisely because the earlier variations of the poem have demonstrated the provisionality of any single point of view. This impression is underscored by the increasingly stomping rhythms and resonant rhymes of the poem that pull forcibly against the sorts of subtlety and nuance that the poem has allowed to emerge earlier. What we witness here, at the end of the poem, are the ways in which it has effectively emptied itself out. Its pronouns are empty: to what, in fact, does the "it" refer?; is the poem about a real lover, or about Love itself?; is the object of its attention that lover, or Catullus's original poem? The closing image of flipping one's wig signals the poem's anxious frustration at its inability to speak of, or tell convincingly, the condition of love. That condition is, like a wig, an empty sort of mask that signifies the poetic disguises adopted by love poetry even as it seeks a poetic idiom to stop itself becoming adulterated.

As we have seen, the poem's structure as a theme and variations forces attention onto its *act* of translation whereby one version of Catullus is placed alongside another. This sets up a key theme of movement, restlessness, transition, and change that, in turn, sets up a poetics of adultery as a key mode for Creeley of enquiring into the condition of '50s America and into his position within "countercultural poetics." The poem's beat-ness (its riffing on jazzy sounds and rhythms) allows Creeley to interrogate what fidelity to self and nation, and to the avocation of being a poet might come to mean in such a turbulent cultural moment. And this sense of restlessness is, of course, a key theme for Beat writing more generally. However, the very form of the poem seems to cut against (as noted above) the assumed spontaneity of a Beat poetics, of the sort that Gair (2007, 38) has noted "most of the Beats preached (even if they did not practice)," and to proceed rather from an anxious poetics of hesitancy and a desire to examine closely—and then to reexamine—human and poetic relationships. The very measuredness of Creeley's poem, then, both argues for him as a Beat poet and against it. It certainly points up the slipperiness of Beat notions of spontaneity, as discussed further by Matthew Pfaff in chapter 4 of this current volume. What we hear—despite its jazz idiom—is that the poem's condition is *not* really one of improvisation, or of being-in-the-moment. It's a poem that cares more about *examining* its very processes than about giving itself up to process. In effect the poem is interested in the contrast between what one "says" in the moment and what one "tells" of the moment. And interestingly, this contrast, which goes hand in hand with revaluations of the power of spontaneity as a defining trope of Beat expression, runs through revisionist accounts of the Beat experience such as, for example, Johnson and Grace's (2002, 12–17) sense of how three different generations of Beat women commented back on the moment of the Beats via memoir and a developing feminist consciousness in the '60s, '70s and later; or Davidson's reading (1998, 269) of the Beats, in retrospect, as "work[ing] strategically within [the mainstream] to develop an immanent critique."[12]

"Stomping with Catullus" exposes, therefore, the adulterous relationship between being in the moment and commenting on the moment, between language—poetic language—and experience. It troubles, therefore, at how Beat aesthetics might be read as enacting an immanent critique within—however ambiguously framed—doctrines of spontaneous composition. And it is this fact of the gap between saying and telling that illuminates Creeley's poetics

12. See also Pfaff above in this volume.

of adultery and which provides him with a measure of what it means to be human, to have poetic agency. Creeley describes this sense in his essay, "A Sense of Measure," when he notes,

> I want to give witness not to the thought of myself—that specious concept of identity—but, rather, to what I am as simple agency, a thing evidently alive by virtue of such activity. I want, as Charles Olson says, to come into the world. Measure, then, is my testament. What uses me is what I use and in that complex measure is the issue. I cannot cut down trees with my bare hand, which is measure of both tree and hand. In that way I feel that poetry, in the very subtlety of its relation to image and rhythm, offers an intensely various record of such facts. It is equally one of them. (Creeley 1972, 34)

Creeley's sense of measure, then, is that which allows him to make poetically meaningful the distance between the "thought of [him]self" and what he is "as simple agency," an operation he investigates in his Catullus translations. And it is in this distance, I want to argue in this concluding section of the essay, that Creeley's *poethics* are grounded. I want, now, therefore to draw out a little further the relation here between the thought of the thing and the thing itself (the relation that "Stomping with Catullus" opens out in its initial hesitation, "My love—my love says") in order to examine how Creeley's poetics of adultery provides just such an intense record of facts. And I also want to begin to show how Creeley's poetic desire to "come into the world" has poethical bearing both on his work and, more widely, on the efforts of postwar American experimental poetry to epitomize a new "stance toward reality." Initially I will examine how the relationship between thought and thing is related to the imagery of hands, and holding, that is prevalent in Creeley's poetry. I will then, toward the essay's conclusion, consider how Creeley's poethics, and their resonances with Beat aesthetics, might be seen to emerge (via his dealings with Catullus) from Lucretius's *De Rerum Natura*.

In "Stomping with Catullus," it is the hand that "pushes" and that attempts to write on wind, water, and sand. In another poem, "The Whip," written at the same time as "Stomping with Catullus" and also published in the early collection *All that is Lovely in Men* (1955), the lover's hand signifies a compromised ethics or, at least, sexual guilt.[13] The act of a lover placing her hand on the poet's back in this poem allows the poet to see the consequences of his giving up of himself to things. This hand is the measure of his poetics and of how he might come into the world as a human; it is the measure of how

13. "The Whip" was first published in *Black Mountain Review* 1954, 23. See Novik 1973, 87.

Creeley's poetics of adultery might come to operate. The link between these two—the hand as a measure of the human and the hand as the sign of a poetics of adultery—is Heidegger. And it is clear that Creeley was aware of Heidegger's meditations on poetic being as early as 1948. In a letter to Bob Leed of *c.* August 1948, he notes, "when Heidegger . . . says that nothingness is the constitutive structure of the existent my understanding of his words produces an activity that is desperate in the extreme" (Creeley 2014, 17).

Throughout Heidegger's extended meditations upon Being (*Dasein*)—most especially in the first section of *Being and Time*—the hand plays a crucial figurative role. For him, the present-at-hand might be thought of as the way in which the world and its objects is (or seems to be) simply there, a disinterested ontological category that is distinct from human use.[14] It is, as Jonathan Goldberg has noted, "an unthinking everydayness in which objects seem simply to be there as objects" (Goldberg 1990, 295). Heidegger's point, though, would seem to be that the existence of things is never simply the result of an unthinking objectness.[15] He argues, in fact, that the present-at-hand arises from the ready-to-hand, or that which is—like a tool—available for human use. Things are present-at-hand, therefore, according to Heidegger, not as the result of an essential category of being, but because of the usefulness, the "handiness," of such things. Their Being depends upon their relation to the human in terms of use value or "in-handedness." In this sense then, the hand is the measure of their mode of Being. In Creeley's terms, the hand becomes the sign of the "complex measure" of the relation between "what uses me" and "what I use." It signifies a bodily relation to the object world, in which the poem itself transforms unthinking everydayness to poetic use. Such thinking against the instrumentalization of the body and of (poetic) experience is a ground shared by a Beat sensibility (of breath poetics; spontaneous utterance; and a return to uncensored bodily experience) seeking escape from the conformities and containments of '50s culture and by Heidegger's existentialist-inflected meditations on Being. Creeley's poetics—via its attempt to project meaning into its reality[16]—is an important bridge, therefore, between Heidegger's thought and the Beats.

The crucial transformation of unthinking everydayness into the poetic—in which Creeley's poethics is grounded—takes place in "The Whip." The poem acts out a scene of guilty, adulterous, desire. The domestic everydayness of the poet's love is here threatened by another love, one that is other, uncanny.

14. See Heidegger 2010, 69–88, and Inwood 1997, 14, 126.

15. See Goldberg 1990, 295, and Inwood 1997, 15.

16. See Creeley 2014, 17.

Noticeably in the first half of the poem, both women are unreadable signs, things toward which the poem addresses itself but which it can never fully encompass, much like the address to "my love" in "Stomping with Catullus." Both the whiteness and flatness of the first woman, and the returning to the poet of the other woman on the roof in a "fit"—like a returning of the repressed—sees these women turned into monstrous signs of the poet's inner turmoil. Though recalcitrant in their presence, they remain inscrutable.

> I spent a night turning in bed
> my love was a feather, a flat
>
> sleeping thing. She was
> very white
>
> and quiet, and above us on
> the roof, there was another woman I
>
> also loved, had
> addressed myself to in
>
> a fit she
> returned. That
>
> encompasses it.
> (Creeley 1982, 146)

Here, indeed, the first woman is made other not simply as an object in the poetic field—"a flat / sleeping thing"—but also in the description of her as a "feather." This effectively delivers a sense of the dislocation of the world of things and of signs—though she *is* "a feather" she is also an unreadable sign, "white / and quiet." Such a turning of the two women into signs of the poet's desire seems echoed by the poem's rhythmic turns, the syncopated music of its enjambed lines by which it measures the emotional space between the poet's "turning" in bed and the second lover's "return." The poem's title, and its difficult, hesitatingly articulated mistrust of, and desire for, its two women, clearly refers to Nietzsche's description of woman as the "Whip." But it also relocates Nietzsche's misogyny into a problematic fantasy about power over the (dreaming) body, and the poem's own relationship to the disciplinary structures of its own poetic embodiment as well as those of marital fidelity. It is beaten, that is, by the crippling dictates of '50s conformity.

This can be seen most clearly in the moment when the poem turns on a gesture of the body, the "thing" beside him in bed. The unthinking everydayness of the poet's desire, his inarticulate relation to the things of his love, is transformed by a touch of the hand (a loving hand, not one wielding a whip). As a result of this intimate gesture, he can now, like the poem itself, and however "wrongly," "think to say this." The hand is the sign and the measure of this transformation. The hand, that is, signals the poem's investment in coupling as the *act* that defines its poetic measure of humanness (and, like "Stomping with Catullus" it is written in couplets):

> But now I was
> lonely, I yelled,
>
> but what is that? Ugh,
> she said, beside me, she put
>
> her hand on
> my back, for which act
>
> I think to say this
> wrongly.
> (Creeley 1982, 146)

As with Creeley's act of translating Catullus, "The Whip" makes a claim upon the relationship between the *idea* of the lover's body and the actual *thing* that is the body. What this exposes as the act of Creeley's poetics is how a poem turns the world of things into signs (and thus exposes, or articulates, the gapped relation of the sign to the world). However, unlike "Stomping with Catullus," "The Whip" performs a counter movement whereby touch is healing, that which restores us to the world of things, rather than an empty poetic grasping at wind, sand, and moving water. "The Whip" can therefore be read as a poetic coming into the world because of its mediation between the thought it articulates and the things of its articulation. And, as we have seen, it is the corporeal (with the hand as its sign) that enacts this poetic transformation between thought and things (between, we might say, the present-at-hand and the ready-to-hand). The work of Creeley's poetics, then, is the pattern it makes out of its thinking to say things wrongly. But, of course, saying things wrongly is the originating condition for a poetics of adultery.

The sort of poetic thinking, as witnessed in these two Creeley poems, thus complicates, as discussed earlier, the "first thought, best thought" dictum of

Beat poetics because these are poems that attend to the act of making the poem sound, where what the poem says and what it tells may, uncomfortably, sit wrongly together. With this in mind I want to move toward a close by briefly thinking a little more about this giving up of oneself to the nature of things that Creeley's poetics investigates, and about another pattern of imagery—of rain and water—that "Stomping with Catullus" introduces into its investigation of the poetic conditions of being a Beat writer. This is less, perhaps, by way of a conclusion than it is an attempt to open up a few broader suggestions and examples of how a Beat aesthetics might be seen to resonate with the classics.

What I want to suggest is that the ways in which Creeley's—and Beat—poetics seeks to assert a relationship toward the things of the world finds some interesting parallels in Lucretius's *De Rerum Natura*. An interesting light—especially in terms of the poetics of the New American Poetry and Creeley's articulation of it—can be thrown on such parallels by Joan Retallack's notion of poetry's ethical force, the "poethical wager" it undertakes, in its assertion of a poem's investigation of our being-in-the world.[17] To give oneself up to the onslaught—the push, the beat, or the whip—of things, while it might be seen as a key Beat condition, is also the basis of Lucretius's Epicurean thinking. This is hardly surprising given the shared Epicureanism of Catullus and Lucretius, and the freedom principle and bohemianism that runs through these classical poets and the Beats. Indeed, Lucretius's discussion of things as atomistic and nature as ethical can be seen at play throughout "Stomping with Catullus" and "The Whip" and therefore provides a clue to reading Creeley's troubled negotiation of Beat aesthetics via his poetics of adultery. As Lucretius has it, atoms are in constant motion throughout the void of the universe, continually borne downward by their own weight. They are like raindrops falling, asserts Lucretius, and it is only because of their restless motion and their swerving from their straight path downward "in endless motion through the mighty void" that things can come into being (Lucretius 2.121–22; trans. 1997, 39). Nature, that is, results from collision, from the blows—or one might say, the beating—of one atom against another. For Retallack, Lucretius's description of the swerves and collisions of atoms as they "fall downwards like raindrops through the profound void" provide her with an image of how a poethics comes to operate.[18] The "poethical wager"—as she terms it—depends upon such "swerves," which have "made everything happen yet could not be predicted or explained" (Retallack 2003, 2). Such swerves are, we might say,

17. Retallack notes, "To speak of *poethics* is to foreground . . . writing/reading as a way of living in the world" (2003, 37–38).

18. Retallack (2003, 2) quotes, here, from Lucretius 2.222, Rouse's translation (1992, 113).

adulterous: through their unexpected collisions and changes of motion they deviate from a straight path. In this sense, then, Retallack's notion of the poethical swerve sees nature itself, poetic making, our being-in-the-world as predicated upon a poetics of adultery in which ethical responsibility inheres in the beat of one thing in nature against another. This means that for Retallack, the poethical wager entails a "certain poetics of responsibility with the courage of the swerve [that is] necessary to dislodge us from reactionary allegiances and nostalgias" (3).

Thought of in these terms, and seen through the lens of Catullus, Lucretius, and the Epicureanism they share, Creeley's poethics thus delivers a sense of the poem as a space in which to act (ethically) and the world in which it acts as an open field, an environment of ongoing, interacting engagements. The beat, or rhythm, of things and of the poem as a measure of the world we inhabit, the touch of a hand as the measure of the difficulty of human relations in—and with—the world are part, therefore, of Creeley's poethical wager. While the ongoingness and "courage" of Creeley's poethics are profoundly engaged with Beat aesthetics, his poetry can be seen to extend beyond this in its relationship to Olson's notion of open field, or projective, verse—of the poem as an environment in which we act—and which underpins the new "stance toward reality" of the New American poetics.[19] What this means is that the poethical trajectory of Creeley's poetics pushes beyond Beat understandings of the world as an implacable force against which humans are pitted because of the poetic attention he gives to "the kinetics of the thing."[20] The nature of things in Creeley's work—adulterous—and his poetic stance toward them—ethically tested—thus leads to a poetics in which a sense of measure pervades our being-in-the-world. For Creeley, the poem is an affective—and thus poethical—space. This links back to Catullus whose description by Julia Gaisser sounds uncannily like a description of Creeley: his poetry, she notes, "presents a complicated emotional landscape" in which "the poet places himself in the centre of a world of friends, enemies, lovers and other poets, where the highest values are personal and aesthetic" (Gaisser 2001, xxv, xxvii).

In conclusion, then, what is especially interesting in Lucretius's atomistic swerve, and in Retallack's use of this in her delineation of the poethical wager, is the imagery of rainfall and water it employs. Writing on water, as we have seen, is a key trope in Creeley's Catullus poem. It comes—unsurpris-

19. See Olson 1997, 246.

20. Olson describes the projective poem as concerned with "the kinetics of the thing" (ibid., 240). Wrighton 2010 examines the concept of a "poethical trajectory" in "certain strands of twentieth-century American poetry" (1–2). It is within this "trajectory"—broader in scope than most accounts of Beat aesthetics—that I am seeking to locate Creeley's work.

ingly—to express a sense of transience not only in human relationships, and the relation of one poet to another over the centuries, but also in the nature of things as they are, against which one is pitted. The "quickly / moving water" of Creeley's poem is the implacable force under which one is beaten down. It is also, therefore, his poethical ground. And this imagery recurs throughout Beat writing as can be seen in the following indicative examples. At the start of the version of Gary Snyder's poem "Night Highway Ninety-Nine" that appears in Ann Charter's *Portable Beat Reader*, we encounter a narrator who is on the move, hitching out of town. He is a figure for whom naming and raining come together to define the restlessness of the Beat experience and environment: "Too cold and rainy to go out on the Sound / Sitting in Ferndale drinking coffee" (Snyder 1992, 293). What is of interest here is the way in which the poem absorbs the various people (and their precarious experiences as archetypical Beat characters on the road) it goes on to describe into the very landscape it sees them traversing. At one point in the poem, a parenthetical detail about a part-time jobber who disappears into that landscape, seemingly recovered later, dead, from the river, asserts a weary, beat resignation to the way things simply are. His watery fate encapsulates the poem's Beat weariness, one in which raindrops, atoms, things, people are all seen as drifting in the void.

Throughout *On the Road*, too, Sal's promise of the West, the search for "IT" is oftentimes undercut by rainfall—torrential, drenching, fateful. Rain acquires a mythical status in Kerouac's novel, allowing Sal to assert a primal beat sensibility. He is described as the great beat goof who is abandoned to, and alone in, the wilderness of the rainy American night:

> I'd been poring over maps of the United States in Paterson for months. . . . Five scattered rides took me to the desired Bear Mountain Fridge, where Route 6 arched in from New England. It began to rain in torrents when I was let off there. . . . Not only was there no traffic but the rain came down in buckets and I had no shelter. I had to run under some pines to take cover; this did no good; I began crying and swearing and socking myself on the head for being such a damn fool. (Kerouac 1957, 15)

But at the heart of such abandon is, for Kerouac, a search for joy—as in Dean's pop-eyed awe at hearing George Shearing play one rainy night that is the "myth of the rainy night" (122). And so I want to recall Kerouac's description of the Beat generation in *Playboy* in 1959. Despite all the connotations for Kerouac of being beat—of being exhausted, pushed to it, despairing—the basis for the Beat generation is for him a quest for joyousness. He writes, "There is no doubt about the Beat Generation . . . being a swinging group of new

American men intent on joy" (Kerouac 1979, 359). According to Hadot (1995, 225), Lucretius's sense of the nature of things is one suffused (maybe "soaked") with a sense of Epicurean "joy and serenity . . . in the moment." In this sense, the beats might be seen to riff in a jazz idiom off the Epicureanism—the anti-Stoicism—of poets such as Lucretius and Catullus. But how, then, does Creeley's poetics—that I've characterized more as one of anxiety and hesitation—play off against the aim of Epicurean philosophy to help one live happily? As Ronald Melville has noted, "Epicurus aimed to give men peace of mind, what he called *ataraxia*, "being undisturbed" (Lucretius 1997, xvii).

Creeley's poetics of adultery pulls against this. He is perhaps less Beat, then, in the sense of an intention of joy, than in his recognition that the nature of things is something that beats us down, rains down on us. Thus the imagery of water and rainfall he frequently employs becomes a fascinating one in terms of his negotiation of the Epicurean and poethical possibilities of a Beat poetics. Through such imagery, Creeley figures the adulterating force of things against which a poem might set its process of thinking. His poem, "The Rain," provides a fitting conclusion, then, as it seems to epitomize his attempt to square up to the condition of the beat and to exemplify his poetics of adultery:

All night the sound had
come back again,
and again falls
this quiet, persistent rain.

What am I to myself
that must be remembered,
insisted upon
so often? Is it

that never the ease,
even the hardness,
of rain falling
will have for me

something other than this,
something not so insistent—
am I to be locked in this
final uneasiness.

Love, if you love me,

Lie next to me.
Be for me, like rain,
the getting out

of the tiredness, the fatuousness, the semi—
lust of intentional indifference.
Be wet
with a decent happiness.[21]

"The Rain" starts with sound and rhythm, the beating of rain on his roof; examines (in typical Creeley fashion) his existential angst, his unease, about his place within a universe of things and words ("what am I to myself / that must be remembered, / insisted upon / so often?"), and about the fidelity of lovers ("Love, if you love me, / *lie* next to me" [emphasis added]); and ends intent on joy. The poem's "semi-lust," its lovers lying to—and next to—each other, its intentional indifferences, and its blurring of things (their adulteration by being left out in the rain) are all coordinates of Creeley's adulterous poetics. The "decent happiness" with which the poem ends provides, finally—and because its affirmation is so troublingly downbeat—Creeley's measure of how far his poetics swerves from those Beat and classical models that he translates, improvises on, and turns into his own set of variations.

Bibliography

Allen, Donald, ed. 1960. *The New American Poetry, 1945–1960*. New York: Grove Press.

Catullus. 1969. *The Poems of Catullus*. Trans. James Michie. London: Rupert Hart-Davis.

Creeley, Robert. 1954. "The Whip." *Black Mountain Review* 3 Fall: 23.

———. 1955. *All That Is Lovely in Men*. Asheville, NC: Jonathan Williams.

———. 1959. "The Rain." *Nation* 189: 363.

———. 1962. *For Love: Poems 1950–1960*. New York: Charles Scribner.

———. 1963. *The Island*. New York: Charles Scribner.

———. 1972. "A Sense of Measure." In *A Sense of Measure*, 31–34. London: Caldar and Boyars.

———. 1982. *The Collected Poems of Robert Creeley, 1945–1975*. Berkeley: University of California Press.

———. 2014. *The Selected Letters of Robert Creeley*. Ed. Rod Smith, Peter Baker, and Kaplan Harris. Berkeley: University of California Press.

---

21. Creeley 1982, 207. This poem was written "Sept 15, 1959" and first published in *The Nation* 1959, 363. See Novik 1973, 92. It was subsequently published in Creeley 1962, the collection that included "Stomping with Catullus" and "The Whip."

Davidson, Michael. 1998. "From Margin to Mainstream: Postwar Poetry and the Politics of Containment." *American Literary History* 10.2 Summer: 266–90.

Faas, Ekbert with Maria Trombacco. 2001. *Robert Creeley: A Biography.* Hanover, NH: University Press of New England.

Gair, Christopher. 2007. *The American Counterculture.* Edinburgh: Edinburgh University Press.

Gaisser, Julia Haig, ed. 2001. *Catullus in English.* London: Penguin.

———. 2009. *Catullus.* Malden, MA: Wiley-Blackwell.

Goldberg, Jonathan. 1990. *Writing Matter: From the Hands of the English Renaissance.* Stanford: Stanford University Press.

Hadot, Pierre. 1995. *Philosophy as a Way of Life.* Trans. Michael Chase. Oxford: Basil Blackwell.

Heidegger, Martin. 2010. *Being and Time.* Trans. Joan Stambaugh. Albany: State University of New York Press.

Inwood, Michael. 1997. *Heidegger.* Oxford: Oxford University Press.

Johnson, Ronna C., and Grace, Nancy M., eds. 2002. *Girls Who Wore Black: Women Writing the Beat Generation.* New Brunswick, NJ: Rutgers University Press.

Kerouac, Jack. 1957; rev. 1975. *On The Road.* Harmondsworth, UK: Penguin.

———. 1959. "The Beginning of Bop." *Escapade* April 1959: 51–52.

———. 1979. *On The Road: Text and Criticism.* Ed. Scott Donaldson. New York: Penguin.

Lucretius. 1992. *On the Nature of Things.* Trans. W. H. D. Rouse. Cambridge, MA: Harvard University Press.

———. 1997. *On the Nature of the Universe* [De Rerum Natura]. Trans. Ronald Melville. Oxford: Oxford University Press.

Nadel, Alan. 1995. *Containment Culture: American Narratives, Postmodernism, and the Atomic Age.* Durham, NC: Duke University Press.

Novik, Mary. 1973. *Robert Creeley: An Inventory, 1945–1970.* Montreal: McGill-Queen's University Press.

Olson, Charles. 1997. *Collected Prose: Charles Olson.* Ed. Donald Allen and Benjamin Friedlander. Berkeley: University of California Press.

Quinn, Kenneth. 1972. *Catullus: An Interpretation.* London: B. T. Batsford.

Retallack, Joan. 2003. *The Poethical Wager.* Berkeley: University of California Press.

Snyder, Gary. 1992. "Night Highway Ninety-Nine." In *The Penguin Book of the Beats,* edited by Ann Charters, 293–304. London: Penguin Books.

Weinreich, Regina. 1990. *The Spontaneous Poetics of Jack Kerouac: A Study of the Fiction.* New York: Paragon House.

Wiseman, T. P. 1985. *Catullus and His World: A Reappraisal.* Cambridge: Cambridge University Press.

Wrighton, John. 2010. *Ethics and Politics in Modern American Poetry.* New York: Routledge.

CHAPTER 7

Sappho Comes to the Lower East Side

ED SANDERS, THE SIXTIES AVANT-GARDE, AND FICTIONS OF SAPPHO

JENNIE SKERL

Come o sacred lyre of mine! Speak out!
Gift yourself with speech. . . .

—SAPPHO 118 (TRANS. IN SANDERS, "A TRIBUTE TO SAPPHO")

Since I first translated Sappho
And memorized her meters
In Bluma Trell's Greek Lyric Poetry class
in 1964 at NYU
I have been in love, in awe, and deepest respect
For this great great poet!

—ED SANDERS, "A TRIBUTE TO SAPPHO"

"Each age, each generation invents its own Sappho,"[1] and Beat writer Ed Sanders follows in that centuries-old tradition. An experimental writer and performer who is also a student of Greek literature, Sanders employs Sappho to authorize the New York City avant-garde culture of which he was a part in the early 1960s and that he memorialized in his short story collection, *Tales of Beatnik Glory* (2004). Sanders's Sappho is an *exemplum*,[2] but rather than upholding traditional aesthetic forms or the ideology of the

1. Ellen Greene's observation introduces a collection of essays on Sappho's reception (1996b, 3), and similar statements have been made by several other scholars.

2. I use the term *exemplum* as defined by L. Hardwick (2003). She notes that *exempla* can involve "a mixture of artistic, verbal and political elements" and may contain a critique about contemporary matters (24).

dominant culture, the Sappho in *Tales* represents bohemian values that challenge convention: experimental art using contemporary media, frank eroticism and portrayal of the sexual body, and gender reversal that privileges the feminine as an alternative to aggressive masculinity. In constructing his countercultural Sappho, Sanders draws upon some of the biographical legends from the history of Sappho's reception, or what Joan DeJean calls the "fictions of Sappho"; in doing so, he foregrounds a reading of Sappho that is countercultural. This essay reviews the avant-garde culture in which Sanders played a major role and the history of Sappho's reception, leading to an analysis of how Sanders's poem, "Sappho on East Seventh," constructs a Sappho for his generation.

In the early 1960s, the Lower East Side of New York City was the locus of a new bohemia of young people, such as Ed Sanders, who self-identified as "beatniks" following in the footsteps of the older Beat generation of Kerouac, Ginsberg, and Burroughs. As artists began moving into this area in the late 1950s to avoid rising rents in the well-established bohemia known as Greenwich Village, they created what later became known as the East Village, a distinct avant-garde community that grew and expanded beyond the labels of Beat or beatnik. Beat poets interacted with other avant-garde poetry groups, such as the New York School and Black Mountain poets. Poets socialized with painters who had created a cooperative gallery scene on East Tenth Street and performance artists (playwrights, dancers, composers, and musicians) who created Off-Off Broadway. Underground film was born and new art forms emerged, such as the happening. Thus, from the late 1950s until the mid-1960s, the Lower East Side became a generational epicenter of avant-garde ferment. This early 1960s avant-garde was chronicled by participant observers, who described the East Side poetry scene from 1960–65 (De Loach 1972), surveyed the arts of "the new bohemia" of 1964–66 (Gruen 1966), observed "a new generation of scene-makers" congregating in the Lower East Side (Sukenick 1987, 127), and identified a "new consciousness" beginning around 1960 (Jones 1990, 126). Ed Sanders's fictionalized memoir, *Tales of Beatnik Glory* (2004), in its first two volumes, narrates the history of this arts community from 1957 to 1965 through the adventures of characters who illustrate the varied artistic and political activities taking place there.[3] Subsequently, Sanders published a documented memoir of the 1960s entitled *Fug You* (2011).[4]

---

3. *Tales of Beatnik Glory* consists of four volumes of short stories that were written over a period of thirty years. The stories in volume 1: 1957–62 were written in the 1970s and published in 1975. Volume 2: 1963–65 was written in the 1980s and published with volume 1 in 1990. Volume 3: 1966–67 and volume 4: 1968–69 were written in the 1990s and early 2000s. All four volumes were published in one book in 2004. All citations are from the 2004 edition.

4. A full-length critical analysis of the early 1960s arts culture is provided by Banes 1993; she identifies 1963 as the peak year, or most productive period. Banes's study is limited by her

Like previous avant-gardes, this community sought to create an alternative culture that served as a bohemian retreat from the dominant (bourgeois) culture, as a critique of mainstream values and social structures, as a force for social change, and as a crucible for art. Like the Dadas and Surrealists before them, this avant-garde sought to erase boundaries between art and life, to create art that, in Peter Bürger's words, could "organize a new life praxis from a basis in art" (1984, 49). The Lower East Side community was aware of its predecessors (some of whom, like Duchamp, were living in New York at the time) and built upon their achievements, but they also introduced new ideas and developed new art styles. Perhaps the most prominent characteristic of this avant-garde was the democratization of the arts (Sukenick 1987, 127; Banes 1993, 6; Bertens 1995, 5). Artists sought to create accessibility through low-cost materials or performances and an ethic of equality among artists and between artists and their audience. Thus, for example, poetry readings in bohemian cafes, such as Le Metro and the Tenth Street Coffeehouse, were egalitarian in structure, open to all with equal time to read, no censorship of material, and a nominal cost to the audience. Experimental poetry magazines, such as Ted Berrigan's *C*, Sanders's *Fuck You/A Magazine of the Arts*, and Diane di Prima and Le Roi Jones's *Floating Bear*, were mimeographed and stapled, given away for free or at low cost. New, relatively unknown poets were published along with recognized older figures. Experimental theater works and happenings avoided expensive productions and often used found materials; typically, a collection from the audience paid the performers (equally); and sometimes the audience was involved in the performance.

Democratization supported a drive toward eliminating hierarchies, both aesthetic and social. As Peter Schjeldal said in a piece about Andy Warhol, "The sixties were all about erasing boundaries" (1990, 102). The combination of materials from popular, mass culture along with the traditions of high culture—including the classics—was part of this art style, as was incorporating taboo subject matter and language, especially references to the body, sexuality, and drugs. Media and genre boundaries were also broken down by Lower East Side artists in an interdisciplinary art style that combined word and image and sound and performance and communal interaction among artists across media. Indeed, Gruen calls this bohemia "the combine generation." Stylistically, erasure of boundaries was conducted in a spirit of play and spontaneity; thus, the work–play boundary was also challenged. Sanders captures the

focus on the performing arts; thus, Sanders is mentioned but not discussed. Diggory 2009 covers this period within a broader encyclopedia. His introduction provides a succinct overview. Kane 2003 surveys the poetry community and discusses Sanders almost solely in relation to his magazine.

principle in this passage from *Tales*: "It was the best of times, it was the worst of times, but it was *our* times, and we owned them with our youth, our energy, our good will, our edginess. So let's party. . . . Poetry was a party. Work was a party. When I put out an issue of *Fuck You/A Magazine of the Arts* . . . that was a party. Fugs rehearsals were a party. Even demonstrations and long meetings planning the revolution" (2004, 277).

Physicality, the body as the focus of art, was also a mark of this avant-garde, especially its emphasis on the sexual body as the ground of a new aesthetic and an imagined social utopia. In his survey of the scene, Gruen devotes substantial coverage to Kerista (a commune practicing group sex), the predominance of sex in the little poetry magazines, sexual activity in underground films, the "body poetry" of the Fugs (Sanders's folk rock band), and the nude performances of cellist Charlotte Moorman. Nudity and explicit sexuality in the performing arts and film presented the shameless sexual body as a force for liberation.[5] Diggory has commented on the sexual energy underlying both Beat and New York School poetry in the 1960s, providing not only a basis for social and artistic freedom but also a vision of society expressed by the counterculture. In the early 1960s, much of the sexuality was projected from a largely unquestioned male—and male chauvinist—perspective; however, work by gay and female artists was prominent in the performing arts, which sometimes challenged gender borders and hierarchies.

This same bohemian community was also the home of many political activists in the antinuclear, antiwar, and civil rights movements, which in the 1960s were linked to movements for free speech, sexual liberation, and the legalization of marijuana. The political and artistic were intertwined in that many artists were also politically active or contributed their art to benefit political causes. Indeed, it is the mark of this generation that political protest was integrated into their art—in contrast to the comparative withdrawal of the earlier generation of Beats and other bohemians in the late 1940s and early 1950s. Group activity in politics and art fostered a strong sense of community, and the fusion of the aesthetic and the political created a utopian belief in the power of the avant-garde to change society by creating an alternative model: Bürger's "new life praxis" based on art. Sanders expressed this ideal as "Goof City," and a character in *Tales* writes a Goof City Manifesto, envisioning "a place of great freedom, affordability, cheap rents, adequate wages, wild times, plenty of leisure, guaranteed access to thrills and art, with streets so safe a person, man or woman, could walk naked at 4 a.m. and not be bothered or

5. Banes devotes an entire chapter to the body in the performing arts of the period.

touched" (2004, 429). (In fact, this utopia seems a literal description of the Lower East Side at the time.)

An aesthetic that celebrated the breaking of barriers or taboos, aspiring toward ecstasy through sex and drugs, and utopian dreams of social change embodied spiritual impulses. Spiritual quest had been a part of the Beat movement from the beginning. Kerouac insisted that Beat meant beatific (Kerouac 1999a), and he linked the Beats to an eclectic mix of religious traditions and American popular culture (Kerouac 1999b).[6] This eclecticism was also prominent in Beat "second generation" bohemia. Some created new religions. Sanders's friend and poet Al Fowler, described in *Fug You*, is an example: he claimed to be a member of the Free Catholic Church, wore a clerical collar, along with a large silver cross and an anarchist button on his lapel (2011, 40). He is the basis for the character Andrew Kliver in *Tales* who sports similar attire. The Kerista commune was also a new religion led by its founder. For some, art was religion. Poet Diane di Prima, active on the Lower East Side during this period, affirms in her memoir the community's spiritual sense of purpose: "It wasn't just the work, though the work was clearly blessed. Nor the rewards, which were none, as far as we knew. *It was the life itself*—a vocation like being a hermit or a samurai. A calling. The holiest life that was offered in our world: artist" (2001, 103). Several characters in Sanders's *Tales* echo di Prima's credo of art as a sacred vocation, and Sanders has stated that the Lower East Side in the 1960s was "a sacred zone" (Dougherty 1992, 8). Pop artists invested mass media images with religious power, such as Andy Warhol's serial images of Marilyn Monroe and the widowed Jackie Kennedy, transforming them into sexual/maternal goddesses. The film criticism of Jonas Mekas (also an experimental film maker) often discussed the new underground films in spiritual and moral terms. At the same time, two established churches in the Village—Judson Memorial and St. Mark's—reached out to the artistic community and provided venues for art as part of their ministry. In addition, the Catholic Worker movement, which plays a role in *Tales of Beatnik Glory* and *Fug You*, was active on the Lower East Side.

No other artist of that time and place better exemplifies the 1960s Lower East Side avant-garde than Ed Sanders. His art was inseparable from his politics and was a form of both protest and changing consciousness. His first published poem, *Poem from Jail* (1963) was written in jail after Sanders's arrest in a protest against nuclear submarines.[7] From 1962 to 1965, Sanders was also

6. See Prothero 1991 on the Beats' disaffection from mainstream organized religion in the postwar period, their exploration of a religious eclecticism, and radical ecumenism.

7. Publication of *Poem From Jail* by Lawrence Ferlinghetti's City Lights Press in 1963 gave Sanders important early recognition, linking him with the older Beat generation poets and their publisher.

an influential promoter and disseminator of avant-garde poetry through his self-published poetry magazine, *Fuck You/A Magazine of the Arts,* part of what Sanders calls the mimeograph revolution (2011, 2). The magazine also served as a manifesto for free speech issues, sexual liberation, and legalization of marijuana. The first issue was dedicated to "pacifism, unilateral disarmament, national defense thru [*sic*] nonviolent resistance, multilateral indiscriminate apertual conjugation, anarchism, world federalism, civil disobedience, obstructers and submarine boarders, and all those groped by J. Edgar Hoover in the silent halls of Congress" (quoted in Butterick 1983, 474). In 1964, Sanders opened the Peace Eye Bookstore on East Tenth Street, which sold small press poetry publications and provided a base for Sanders's diverse activities—the press, art shows, rehearsal space for his rock band, work on his experimental films, political organizing, and, of course, parties. According to Butterick, "For its time, Peace Eye was as vital as Lawrence Ferlinghetti's City Lights Bookshop had been on the West Coast during the previous decade" (477).

The culmination of Sanders's border-crossing and communal art during the 1960s was his folk-rock band, the Fugs, cofounded with Tuli Kupferberg, a pacifist anarchist who sold his poetry in the street. The name, the Fugs, refers to the euphemism that Norman Mailer was forced to use in his World War II novel, *The Naked and the Dead,* flaunting the unspoken obscenity and the censorship that the band defied. Writing their own songs, the Fugs combined music with poetry, political protest, social satire, sex comedy, and an anarchic style that usually ended performances with a Dionysian kind of happening with Sanders, in his own words, playing the role of "a modern-day American Bacchus" (2011, 393). From 1965 to 1969, the band had a cult following in New York and beyond. They also had a political role beyond protest songs, often playing to benefit the anti–Vietnam War movement or activists who had been arrested. Perhaps their most famous performance/protest was their exorcism of the Pentagon during the 1967 antiwar march in Washington, DC, described in Norman Mailer's *Armies of the Night* (1968).

The sexual body as the site of cultural struggle was prominent in Sanders's work of the 1960s. This aspect of his art gave him a certain notoriety as "an erotic provocateur" (Sukenick 1987, 176). Early poems, for example, were devoted to sex with animals, trees, and a goddess (Demeter). The title of his mimeographed poetry magazine announced the liberation of the four-letter word for sex. The editorial policy defined an openness with no restrictions: "Barf me your frick data, retch me in on your babble vectors, your arcanics, your spew. I'll print anything" (Sanders 2011, 30). Sanders's press also published several monographs that other publishers wouldn't touch because of obscenity issues, such as William S. Burroughs's *Roosevelt after Inauguration*

(1979). Like most rock and roll bands, the Fugs sang songs about sex, but theirs were more graphic and satirical of the genre, such as "Group Grope," "Wet Dream Over You," "Coca-Cola Douche."

Sanders's style in poetry, prose, and music employed the breakdown of hierarchies typical of the period and was very much a part of the 1960s avant-garde program of democratization and accessibility. His work playfully combined elements from popular culture, avant-garde art, and the poetic tradition going back to the ancient Greeks, producing an idiosyncratic collage of high and low culture, an interart mix of verbal and visual elements, accessible language, and his own characteristic humor made up of comic hyperbole, satire, slang, and neologisms.[8] Throughout Sanders's writing, Greek writers, history, and mythology appear as reference points, parallels, inspiration, and formal models; for at the same time that Sanders was active in the Lower East Side avant-garde, he was also studying the classics at New York University (located in Greenwich Village), completing a degree in Greek in 1964. Learning his craft as a poet and the study of the classics were parallel pursuits. From the beginning of his Greek studies and his artistic career, Sappho, in particular, had an important role. Over the years, Sanders paid homage to Sappho by translating her verses and setting them to music in his "Tribute to Sappho" and by reciting his poems accompanied by his lyre.[9] In *Tales of Beatnik Glory*, the long narrative poem, "Sappho on East Seventh," plays a central role in the series of autobiographical fictions set in the Lower East Side, bringing together Sanders's veneration for Sappho and the avant-garde milieu that nurtured him as an artist.

It is not surprising that a young poet studying the classics would be inspired by Sappho, who stands at the beginning of lyric poetry in the West (seventh century BCE)—a literary progenitor who has had a profound influence on the poetic tradition for centuries. In addition to his classical studies, Sanders absorbed a Sapphic poetics derived from his Anglo-American poetic forerunners and mentors who were part of the postromantic Sapphic tradition in English poetry. The romantics privileged the lyric, and the Sapphic ode was a model of sublimity and passion for both male and female poets during

8. Sanders's work displays many characteristics of early postmodernism as defined by Bertens 1995 and Huyssen 1986. Olsen 1999 calls Sanders's fiction "avant-pop," a species of postmodernism.

9. Beginning in 1977, Sanders began inventing electronic instruments, one of which is the pulse lyre, which he uses to accompany his poetry readings. Like Sappho and other ancient poets, Sanders partly recites and partly sings his poems. He often refers to himself as a bard. Sappho is also said to have invented a kind of lyre (Carson 2002, ix).

the nineteenth century.[10] Subsequently, the new scholarly editions of Sappho's fragments that appeared at the end of the nineteenth century stimulated one of the most important modernist movements in poetry: the "imagism" theorized by Ezra Pound and practiced in the early poetry of Pound, H.D., William Carlos Williams, Amy Lowell, and others who wrote short, free verse poems with concentrated concrete imagery, often imitating Sapphic fragments in form. In fact, some of Pound's and H.D.'s early imagist poems are free translations or imitations of Sappho. Imagism was influential in modern American poetry throughout the twentieth century, providing the basis for both short lyrics and long poems made up of fragmentary passages (e.g., T. S. Eliot's *The Waste Land,* Pound's *Cantos,* William Carlos Williams's *Paterson,* and Charles Olson's *The Maximus Poems*).

After World War II, imagism continued to influence American poetry movements through the poetic line of Pound, Williams, Olson, and Allen Ginsberg; these movements were labeled Black Mountain, San Francisco Renaissance, and Beat, and formally recognized in Donald M. Allen's influential 1960 anthology of avant-garde poetry: *The New American Poetry* (reissued in 1982 as *The Postmoderns: The New American Poetry Revised,* which included Sanders). These were the poetic forerunners and movements that influenced the young Ed Sanders as a poet, and both Ginsberg, one of the original Beats, and Olson, once the rector of Black Mountain College, were personal mentors.[11] Thus, Sanders's education in contemporary poetry and his own reading of the classics complemented each other and reinforced the importance of Sappho as inspiration, forerunner, model. As a student of the classics and of modern poetry, Sanders developed a stylistic fusion of poetic traditions in his own work. Throughout his poetic career, Sanders has composed in the open forms of his mentors while also experimenting with ancient Greek meters and imitations of Greek poets.

As "A Tribute to Sappho" shows, Sanders is familiar with the scholarship on Sappho as well as the poetry. Historically, the absence of knowledge about her or her society, as well as the fragmentary remains of her poetry, drew poets and scholars in each generation to invent a Sappho for their culture, their ideals, their social agenda. Sappho has been appropriated to support the values of many a reader, a scholar, a poet, an activist, and Sanders, in "Sappho on East Seventh," participates in a long chain of reception when he introduces

10. See Vanita 1996 and Prins 1999 for extended studies of the Sapphic tradition in nineteenth-century English poetry.

11. Sanders and others of his generation continued to look toward Pound's *Cantos* as a resource for contemporary poetry. In 1967, Sanders considered it a coup to have the opportunity to publish a group of the previously unpublished cantos, 110–16.

Sappho into his bohemia. By the twentieth century, a complex and contradictory array of images, themes, and biographical fictions had been transmitted and made available to Sanders.[12] His poem plays with these images of Sappho as well as alluding to her poetry.

Among the many contradictory "fictions of Sappho," several that were persistent over time and influential among scholars and poets are relevant to Sanders's poetic construction of a Sappho for *his* time. Most important to Sanders's conception of Sappho is the praise in antiquity that declared that Sappho was the Tenth Muse—an epithet repeated throughout history. Other legends from antiquity that Sanders recalls are of Sappho as the heterosexual and abandoned, suicidal lover of a young man (Phaon)—a legend told by Ovid and a prominent part of her identity through the nineteenth century—and the scandalous Sappho, the lover of women whose books were burnt by both Christian and Muslim religious authorities in late antiquity.[13]

Sanders rejects the "Victorian Sappho" of the nineteenth century who was chaste, virginal, and absorbed into an ideal of female sexual purity, but he draws on one facet of that figure—a spiritual, almost divine Sappho who could be associated with the Virgin Mary.[14] He also draws upon another prominent nineteenth-century fiction that remained influential into the next century—that Sappho was a teacher in a school that prepared girls for marriage by teaching poetry, music, dance, and deportment—and even sexual technique. Although the girls' school has been debunked (see Parker 1996), the idea of Sappho as a teacher persists in those contemporary critics who assert that Sappho's *poetry* instructs its readers, particularly male readers, in how to feel, how to love, or how to understand female desire.[15] Willis Barnstone's translation of Ovid supports this view: "What did Sappho of Lesbos teach / but how to love women?"(2006, xxvi, his translation of *Tristia* 2.363, *Testimonia* 49, in Campbell 1982).

12. Sappho's reception has become a scholarly field in and of itself, and several publications have traced the reception history. Important work includes books by DeJean (1989), Greene (1996a, 1996b), Lipking (1988), Prins (1999), Reynolds (2000), and Vanita (1996). Johnson 2007 sees "Sappho's lives" as illustrative of classical reception theory.

13. Contemporary scholars believe that the decline of learning from the sixth through the ninth centuries and thus neglect, rather than active destruction, led to the loss of much of Sappho's work. See Snyder 1989, 10.

14. DeJean 1996 and Vanita 1996 provide extended analyses of Sappho's association with Mary in the nineteenth century.

15. Critics who discuss what Sappho teaches men include Greene (1996b), Lipking (1985), Skinner (1996), and Stehle (1997).

Sanders's poem also reflects the early modern period when readers identified a lesbian Sappho[16] who coexisted with many other versions, as diverse modernist male and female poets found inspiration in a lyric precursor who could be fashioned into a literary mother, muse, collaborator, representative of heterosexual or homosexual passion, or a modern independent woman. It was not until the end of the 1960s that second-wave feminism enabled the construction of a lesbian and feminist Sappho, which is widely accepted today. Beginning in the 1970s, Sappho became an icon for lesbians participating in the women's liberation movement and the gay liberation movement. But in the early 1960s, the period Sanders chronicles in *Tales*, a sexually liberated, but not strictly lesbian, Sappho came into being: it is she who inhabits Sanders's poem. (For Sappho as a 1960s "swinger," see Reynolds 2000, 359.)

Finally, Sanders's Sappho parallels some feminist scholarship that interprets Sappho as a poet who disrupts patriarchal structures and hierarchies, offering a critique of the martial world of Homer and of fifth-century Athens, which has been idealized as the pinnacle of ancient Greek culture. Like these critics, Sanders's "Tribute" cites Sappho 16 where "what one loves" is declared to be more beautiful than troops or warships.[17] This Sappho represents a woman-centered world that offers an alternative to patriarchal control: a realm of eros, beauty, and pleasure. Sanders also explores the gender reversal that occurs in mythology when a mortal man has sex with a goddess, which several feminist critics have detected in a pattern of allusions in Sappho's poems to four myths about goddesses who take an active sexual role in relation to a young man: Aphrodite and Adonis, Aphrodite and Phaon, Eos and Tithonus, Selene and Endymion.[18] These myths can be interpreted as a trope that asserts women's autonomy and control over their sexuality.

Sappho and her historical reception play an important role in *Tales of Beatnik Glory*, as Sanders seeks to preserve the 1960s bohemia that he helped to create. In paying tribute to his generation, Sanders sought to ground his work and his vision of a bohemian community within a historical context that links the transitory art world that existed for a few years to traditions spanning centuries or millennia. Thus, in *Tales*, he claims precursors in the work

---

16. S. M. Gilbert and S. Gubar 1989 survey the sexual psychology of early modernist literature and the role of Sappho in writing by both men and women during this period. Benstock 1986 and Gubar 1996 analyze the aesthetics of the Anglo-American Sapphic community of writers in the early twentieth century.

17. See Snyder 1997 and du Bois 1996. Numbering of Sappho's poetry refers to the Loeb edition (Campbell 1982).

18. See Skinner 1996, Stehle 1996b, and Williamson 1995. Early in his career, Sanders had explored the experience of a man having sex with a goddess in the poem, "Holy Demeter Walking in the Corn Furrow" (1967).

of earlier activists, prior avant-gardes, and great writers of the past, especially the ancient Greeks. The stories in *Tales of Beatnik Glory* frequently allude to Greek divinities, philosophers, historians, and literature. A beatnik's mother-in-law who delivers care packages to the "underground" beatnik couple is a modern-day Demeter; a beautiful woman who disrobes in public is compared to Phryne; two artist friends refer to each other as Apo and Dio (Apollo and Dionysus); the Celestial Freakbeam Orchestra subscribes to the philosophy of Plotinus—these are just a few of the numerous classical reference points that Sanders weaves throughout the work, merging the high and the low and transforming both. However, one classical reference goes beyond brief allusions or comparisons: "Sappho on East Seventh," a story in verse that Sanders calls a "sho-sto-po," or short story poem. Significantly, the story about Sappho appears near the center of volume 2, the volume that narrates the years 1963–65, the peak years of the Lower East Side avant-garde. Sappho plays the role of the muse that validates the Lower East Side bohemian subculture and Sanders's personal commitment to its aesthetics and ethics.

Sanders chooses Sappho as the bohemian muse, not only because of his admiration for her poetry and his own poetic vocation but because Sappho can be aligned with an art that employs the sexual body as site of cultural change, with erotic pleasure as a source of creativity, and a politics of pacifism and sharing abundance. As feminist critics have pointed out, Sappho's woman-centered world offers an alternative to socially prescribed masculinity and patriarchal dominance. From Sanders's perspective, these characteristics can legitimate bohemia's hedonism and the avant-garde's critique of male-dominated bourgeois culture and American militarism. For Sanders, Sappho's poetry offers not just an escape from repressive social structures, but a reconstruction of the self and society based on alternative values. Sappho's anti-patriarchal poetry also supports Sanders's pacifist politics. Sanders, like other scholars, has cited Sappho 16 to support the thesis that Sappho represents a challenge to Homer and martial values:

> . . . poets are sometimes fascinated with bellicosity,
> but you won't find much talk of war in the
> shreds of Sappho
> but rather the melodies of love, tenderness, family,
> partying, arousal, longing, sadness, and fun.
> ("Tribute to Sappho" 4)

The Sappho in opposition to Homer is thus an attractive precursor for Sanders, the pacifist antiwar poet, who concludes *Tales of Beatnik Glory* with a song expressing the idealistic hope of his generation: "We are going to change the world without spilling a drop of blood" (2004, 766).

In "Sappho on East Seventh," Sappho appears in a vision to John Barrett, a bohemian poet and graduate student in classics (one of Sanders's alter egos in *Tales*) and, as his muse, she proceeds to educate him in art, eros, and an ethic of compassion. The Sappho who appears to Barrett is a supernatural being who is a constructed from several spiritual traditions, consistent with the eclectic spirituality of the Lower East Side. In the introduction to *Tales*, Sanders calls "Sappho on East Seventh" a ghost story that traces the religious yearnings of John Barrett, reflecting the spiritual hunger of the era (2004, 5). As a ghost of the ancient poet who acts as a spirit guide in the poem, Sappho reflects one kind of supernatural being—one which refers to the *Divine Comedy* in which Virgil leads Dante on a spiritual journey, a comparison made explicit at one point in the poem, creating a parallel in which an ancient poet guides a modern one. Sanders's Sappho is also a muse whom John Barrett has "called down" with a song accompanied by his homemade lyre, recalling Sappho's reputation as the Tenth Muse, the originator of lyric poetry and herself the inventor of a lyre. Barrett's invocation to Sappho alludes to several of Sappho's poems. He imitates the classical form of an invocation to a deity illustrated by Sappho herself in Sappho 1 (often called "Hymn to Aphrodite"), describes Sappho's milieu, paralleling the strategy or spell in Sappho 2 ("Hither to me from Krete"), and quotes Sappho 118: "Come my sacred lyre / make yourself sing" (Sanders's translation within the poem). Thus, Barrett's song invoking Sappho puts him in a position parallel to Sappho requesting the presence of Aphrodite, therefore implying that Sappho herself is a goddess of love, as well as a poetic muse. A muse is a goddess, and Sappho makes an awe-inspiring appearance through a rip in the sky, scattering kernels of grain, and accompanied by the chirping of birds.[19] Finally, after the ancient Greek Sappho leaves Barrett, she reappears to him later in the story in the form of a weeping woman reminiscent of the *mater dolorosa,* one of the images of the Virgin Mary, recalling the maternal aspect of the poet's muse. Thus, Sanders's Sappho is a hybrid construct drawn from Greek, Roman, and medieval sources, pagan and Christian, literary and folk images, but all pointing to female divine inspiration and authority, and reflecting the eclecticism of bohemian spiritual concepts.

---

19. In an email interview with the author (Skerl 2014), Sanders stated that the casting of seeds was important to his view of Sappho as a spirit since grain always seemed central to ancient Greek spirituality and religion, as in the myths of Demeter and Persephone. Birds are yoked to Aphrodite's chariot in Sappho 1.

By choosing Sappho as the presiding spirit of the avant-garde, Sanders identifies a precursor who stands at the beginning of lyric poetry in the West, linking the 1960s avant-garde with a long poetic tradition and ancient cultural authority. But by making Sappho a goddess, a divine force, he goes even further in valorizing the art of bohemia as the overarching goal and ultimate value. His character John Barrett's passionate devotion to art is a commitment that is a life-changing, world-changing spiritual vocation to him and his peers. Barrett's dedication had previously been established in volume 1 of *Tales* where he is described as enmeshed in the Lower East Side community, devoted to the "holy books" of his poetic mentors, and ready to record moments of inspiration in his notebook. In the brief prologue to "Sappho on East Seventh," we are told that he has created a shrine to Sappho in his apartment, with pictures of her, copies of tattered papyri containing her poetry, and his translations. At the same time as Sappho elevates Barrett's vocation by her presence, she descends to the decidedly shabby milieu of Barrett's apartment in an old tenement, with its mattress on the floor, splattered candles in chianti bottles, a nail for a clothes hanger, a shelf holding a hodgepodge collection of well-marked books, and a homemade lyre constructed from found materials in the neighborhood. This is literally a "comedown" for a goddess, typical of Sanders's style in the poem of comically merging the high with the low. The effect of this erasure of hierarchy is both to invest the ordinary, even the tawdry, with an aura of transcendence and, at the same time, to make the goddess a quotidian being. Furthermore, in his hybrid experimentation with forms, Sanders, the author, also embeds Sappho in a modern free verse poem that combines narrative and lyric, words and images. Drawings that function as illustrations are part of the poem, and one of the visual images is a portrait of Sappho, thus enclosing her picture in the work.[20]

Upon her appearance in Barrett's "beatnik pad," Sappho proceeds to act as a teacher and guide—in art, sexual technique, and compassion. Thus, Sanders draws upon the tradition of Sappho as a teacher of the male lyric poet. Sappho's first teaching concerns Barrett's artistic ambitions. Although her authority derives from tradition and the high status of the classics, she does not endorse imitation of traditional forms or established poets; rather, she authorizes the art of Barrett's generation by playing on Barrett's lyre rather than her own, by commending his collection of books by his contemporaries, by praising his translations as "better than Byron's" (256), and by recommending

20. The image is a profile bust of Sappho accompanied by a lyre and a bee, and enclosed in an oval. Sanders stated in an interview with the author that this image was taken from the Loeb Classical Library edition of Greek Lyric Poets, which he had used in his undergraduate class on Greek lyric poetry, taught by Bluma Trell.

that he find a "Muse for your age" (257).[21] She declares that this modern muse is Retentia, Muse of the Retained Image, that is, of film, photography, and recordings, which were very much a part of the Lower East Side avant-garde and Sanders's own multimedia experiments: "yours is the era / of captured sunlight / & oxide-dappled tape / Retentia / catches the beauteous flow" (258). She urges Barrett to pray to Retentia, "for each muse aids / in her measure / and the task / is to know / the mix of the muses' gifts / in your lines" (259).[22] Sappho says she longs to hear the maidens singing in Mitylene ("if only / I could *hear* / their image again!" 259, my italics), wishing that a recording existed and thereby approving new art using modern technology. Her song at this point recalls Sappho's poems of memory and longing (Sappho 94 and 96). Retentia, the new muse, herself appears in the poem: "forth stepped Retentia / in a blue-black gown / crackling on its surface with / tiny jiggle-jaggles of lightning" (259–60).

Sappho's next lesson is about eros, as she takes it upon herself to teach John Barrett to satisfy a woman through oral sex, first preparing his body with scented oil and unguents familiar from Sappho's poetry. (Retentia assists by providing the oils.) "How can you think / a woman like Louise / would love you?" she asks (260), since he has no oils in his cupboard and no skill as a lover. (Louise Adams, a painter introduced in volume 1, is a woman Barrett is longing for.) Her erotic desire for women is not denied in the poem: "Don't you make it only with, uh, *gunaikes?*" asks Barrett (264). Several lyrical passages describe her sensual attraction toward women, but the poem emphasizes an eroticism beyond the heterosexual/homosexual binary with its comically epic description of oral sex. Sanders's use of plant imagery to represent female genitalia parallels such imagery in Sappho's poetry: flowers, apples, other fruits, and plants.[23] The difference between Sappho's symbolism and Sanders's explicit comparison between the lithops and the clitoris is the difference between traditional sexual imagery (such as rosebuds or other flowers, pearls or other gems, a landscape that represents the female body) and the 1960s pursuit of sexual and literary freedom that included an openness to talking and writing about sex.

---

21. Quotations from "Sappho on East Seventh" are cited by page number in *Tales of Beatnik Glory* (2004).

22. Sanders has expanded upon his theory of multiple, contemporary muses based on new technologies in two poetry manifestos: *Investigative Poetry* (1976) and *The Z-D Generation* (1981).

23. See Burnett 1983 and Winkler 1996 on sexual imagery in Sappho. Winkler focuses particularly on clitoral imagery.

In constructing a Sappho who teaches sexual technique to John Barrett, Sanders reprises one strand of biographical speculation in the long history of Sappho's reception—Sappho the teacher. He literalizes this theory of Sappho's reception in his hyperbolic and comic style, as Sappho instructs Barrett in how to perform oral sex. Sanders's Sappho is definitely not the chaste, virginal poetess or Victorian schoolmistress, but a frankly sexual being who has no prudery about sexuality, and like Sanders himself gives important value to sexual expression. Her sexuality is not scandalous, but shameless in the positive sense of the 1960s avant-garde. The poem focuses on a sexual act that blurs the line between heterosexual and homosexual, and whose purpose is pleasure, not procreation, reflecting the sexual freedom of the early 1960s and the art that explored a variety of sexual acts and sexualities. Furthermore, in "Sappho on East Seventh," Sappho is herself a divinity representing both eros and poetry, and she links poetry and sexuality very literally, as she makes sexual knowledge a prerequisite for poetry: "Every bard must have / its perfect knowledge," she says (262). This Sappho is not the abandoned female victim of unrequited love for a man, but a dominant partner. Sexually, Barrett acts as Sappho's acolyte who submits to her instructions, a gender reversal, recalling the Greek myths about goddesses and mortals that appear in Sappho's fragments. Traditional male sexual dominance is replaced by mutuality, implying a broader cultural adjustment.[24]

Sanders constructs a twentieth-century Sappho whose eroticism is celebrated, in contrast to the many times in the reception history in which her sexuality was condemned or repressed. This modern Sappho specifically reflects the sexual revolution of the early 1960s, a time of sexual freedom for both the women and men of the Lower East Side in the post-pill, pre-AIDS era, and before second-wave feminism criticized the sexist assumptions of sexual liberation. What is important about this Sappho's sexuality is openness about the enjoyment of sexual pleasure and the freedom to portray the sexual body that was very much a part of the art of the Lower East Side. This pleasure-seeking Sappho affirms the hedonism of the 1960s portrayed in *Tales of Beatnik Glory* and that Sanders later defended in an interview: "We have to be hedonistic in a good part of our lives; otherwise, why live? . . . There's that double life-track of having fun while working for a better world" (Horvath 1999, 24). There is also a connection to the poetry of Sappho herself, which is often cited as a model for passionate intensity, sensuality, sensuous imagery, and the sublime. Several Sapphic fragments portray eros as a powerful force

24. Several critics have noted mutuality and reciprocity in Sappho's erotic poems: Snyder (1997, 13), Stehle (1997, 278; 1996a, 149), Winkler (1996, 108), and Williamson (1996, 263). K. J. Dover (1979) is cited in support.

to be honored: "Eros shook my being / as a wind / down a mountain / shakes the oak trees" (Sappho 47; trans. Sanders 2001, 8).

After their sexual union, Sappho acts as a spirit guide to other times and places, thereby providing another form of instruction, leading next to a lesson of compassion. She first takes Barrett to visit Emma Hardy in 1911, the estranged wife of the writer Thomas Hardy who has retreated to live in her attic boudoir while her husband corrects proofs in his study with his mistress. Sappho orders Barrett to relieve Emma's excruciating back pain with an oil from Mytilene—the erotic unguent transformed into a healing salve. In this episode, Sappho acts compassionately toward an abandoned woman rather than representing the abandoned woman herself: here, Sanders has transposed one of the most persistent "fictions of Sappho," her supposed unrequited love for the younger Phaon and her suicidal despair, to another figure—Emma Hardy.[25] Thus, Sappho does not suffer negative consequences from her frank erotic expression, but represents the positive power of eros and sympathy between women. Eased of her pain, Emma is able to feed the birds at her window, a compelling image of female nurture and a link to Sappho's kernels and the birds at the beginning of the poem.[26] This maternal fertility imagery is associated with ancient female goddesses and foreshadows Sappho's final appearance in the poem.

Before Sappho leaves Barrett, she transports him to an underground place, another motif from classical mythology: "a site of steam & fire" that reminds Barrett of Dante's hell with Sappho as his Virgil (268). Here Sappho becomes less a deity than a ghostly mortal who accepts her death and the loss of most of her poetry. Sanders's poem refers to the legends about the destruction of Sappho's poetry through wars and religious riots. Sappho has taken Barrett to the baths of Alexandria after the Muslim conquest, where papyrus books are being burned to heat the water—including some of the books of Sappho. Sappho calmly accepts the destruction of her poetry and slips into the bath with other women, returning to a women's society such as she enjoyed in her life and luxuriating in the sensual pleasure of the bath, a fitting farewell, but also a reminder of the piecemeal remains of Sappho's poems, that the Sappho we know is made up of fragments and she herself is mute—unknown. Barrett sees the last word of a page of Sappho burn—a play on Byron's oft-repeated phrase, "burning Sappho" (from *Don Juan*), here referring to burning books,

---

25. Hardy was an admirer of Sappho. He experimented with Sapphic meter, and after his wife died, he wrote memory poems about her that could be called Sapphic. Sanders's poem focuses sympathetically upon Emma, not Thomas Hardy.

26. Sanders explained the linking of the seeds in the poem in an interview with the author.

not burning passion. Sappho accepts the end of her poetry in her farewell to Barrett, which quotes the inscription on Keats's tombstone:

> And now it is time
> For ashes and chars
> To come to the
> mixolydian mode
> Some poets' words
> are written on water[27]
> Others make flame
> To make it moil.
> (270)

The poem has several conclusions in addition to Sappho's disappearance in the bath. First, there is a series of comic deflations, typical of Sanders's pattern throughout *Tales* of undercutting elevated ideals with scruffy reality, grandiose ambition with comic pratfalls. In an attempt to save a piece of a Sappho papyrus, Barrett slips in the bath and "wakes up" in his apartment, clutching a silver knob from a papyrus roll. He and Consuela, a classmate and a secret witness to his vision, fall into each other's arms, both overwhelmed with the experience that has brought them together. It is implied that John has sex with his next-door neighbor who is wearing a homemade chiton and peplos sewn from Lower East Side fabrics, including Ukrainian embroidery trim, common on bohemian blouses at the time, and dirty from kneeling on the fire escape. Thus, Barrett returns to his life embedded in bohemia. Friends mock his story, and he is unable to sing Sappho down again.

Deflation, however, is followed by another apparition that concludes the poem—Sappho as a maternal figure, another image of female divinity and another aspect of the muse. Barrett has an unexpected vision of Sappho for a second time near the St. Nicholas Carpatho-Russian church situated on Tenth Street in the heart of the bohemian district and a well-known landmark. Decked with Russian crosses, icons, and jewels (related to the Eastern rite church and the Ukrainian ethnic community of the Lower East Side), a weeping woman briefly appears in the street outside the church and is immediately identified by Barrett as Sappho. The vision appears without warning, utters a gnomic "you'll cry too," and disappears (274). A weeping woman associated with a sacred site is reminiscent of a facet of Mariology—the sorrowful mother (*mater dolorosa*) who relieves suffering through her own pain and

27. Keats, a Sapphic poet of the English romantic movement, requested these words on his gravestone: "Here lies one whose name was writ in water." The grave also displays the image of a lyre.

empathy, a female spiritual resource that can also be found in ancient Middle Eastern fertility goddesses.[28] Indeed, in a later story in volume 2, this apparition reappears and is identified as the "Carpathian Mother" (in "Cynthia," Sanders 2004, 322). The merger of Sappho and a mother goddess—never specifically identified as Mary—recalls the nineteenth-century conflation of the poet and the Virgin as exemplars of feminine authority, autonomy, and spirituality. Certainly, a maternal figure of compassion is an image that supports Sanders's political positions on ending war, sharing abundance, and peaceful change. There could also be an autobiographical element in Sanders's vision of Sappho as a maternal deity. He first decided to study the classics in college because his mother, who died when he was in high school, had told him that a gentleman knows Greek and Latin. He was introduced to Sappho by the noted teacher, Bluma Trell.[29] He met his wife in Greek class, and their daughter was born in 1964.

Sappho, the exalted female poet, also serves to recognize the women of bohemia as equal participants and representatives of bohemian values. The story-poem about Sappho introduces a cluster of stories at the center of volume 2 focused on strong female characters, for it is in this volume that Sanders purposefully emphasizes the women artists and activists who were very much part of the scene, but who were often overshadowed by men in a sexist era. This point was raised by Sanders in several interviews in which he regretted the chauvinism of the era and discussed the increased attention to women characters in volume 2. (See especially interviews with Horvath 1999 and Dougherty 1992.) Beginning in volume 2, Sanders restores women's historical presence and continues to integrate them into the group story throughout the next two volumes. This strategy reflects the time that volume 2 was written—the 1980s—after the cultural impact of second-wave feminism—and acknowledges Sappho as a precursor for women artists.

•

In "Sappho on East Seventh," Ed Sanders has created what Jane McIntosh Snyder calls a "productive fiction" (1997, 79). A seventh-century-BCE poet known only through her fragmentary texts is reconstructed as the muse of the early 1960s Lower East Side avant-garde. Just as bohemians choose a mode of living that functions as a critique of the dominant social order, so Sanders's choice of

28. Sanders has stated in an email to the author, "From a long study of Sappho fragments, I sensed that there was a *mater dolorosa* aspect to her, and thus the vision Barrett had." See Warner 1983 and Pelikan 1996 for the *mater dolorosa* of Mariology.

29. The *New York Times* obituary for Professor Trell (Thomas 1997) stated that her "unbridled enthusiasm brought ancient Greece alive to a generation of New York University students."

a female literary ancestor provides a source of alternative aesthetic and social values. Sappho lends her authority and status to a community of artists who created a counterculture that challenged the dominant culture: she endorses experimental art using new technology, the sexual body as an empowering creative force, and an ethic of compassion that opposes war. By "coming down" to John Barrett, Sappho participates in the collapsing of hierarchies that promotes equality, fusing the sacred with the everyday. Sanders also associates Sappho with female divinity, which is another countercultural move in a male-dominated society. The female goddesses Aphrodite, Demeter, the Muses, Mary (technically not a goddess, but nevertheless a spiritual authority) sanction bohemian alternatives to conventional middle-class mores and Cold War militarism—such alternatives as hedonism, eroticism, artistic freedom, compassion, equality, and sharing abundance. Sanders employs Sappho as an *exemplum*, but one which reverses that classical strategy: first, by using Sappho as a challenge to traditional values rather than to support authority, and, second, by telling a new story about Sappho, whereby Sanders invents rather than recalls the precedent.

As Hardwick has pointed out, modern appropriations of classical texts or motifs not only reflect contemporary contexts but also provide new perspectives on classical sources (2003, 4). In creating a countercultural Sappho, Sanders foregrounds the countercultural aspects of Sappho's poetry: poetry of eroticism, pleasure, and beauty in a woman-centered world can offer a critique both of our own culture and of the patriarchal society of ancient Greece. In presenting Sappho as a goddess, Sanders also foregrounds a submerged or subordinated tradition of female spiritual authority that points toward alternative religious concepts that can be the basis for social change. The goddesses of antiquity are alien to our contemporary modes of thought, but, for that very reason, they can pose a radical challenge.

Sanders's Sappho is also a bricolage of many "fictions of Sappho" from the past, the multiple aspects of Sappho in stories that have been told about her over time. As Sanders manipulates the legend, the reader realizes that Sappho herself has become a myth that can be selectively repeated and revised within different cultural contexts. Sanders's poem treats Sappho's reception history as a resource for new configurations—a paradigm according to Hardwick (2003, 90)—emphasizing that our knowledge of Sappho is filtered through successive reinterpretations. Whereas much of the scholarship on Sappho's reception history has focused on discrediting these fictions, Sanders's story about Sappho illuminates their positive role as "mediating texts" (112) that transmit Sappho to successive generations.

Bibliography

Allen, Donald M., ed. 1960. *The New American Poetry.* New York: Grove Press.

Allen, Donald, and Butterick, George F., ed. 1982. *The Postmoderns: The New American Poetry Revised.* New York: Grove Press.

Banes, Sally. 1993. *Greenwich Village 1963: Avant-Garde Performance and the Effervescent Body.* Durham, NC: Duke University Press.

Barnstone, Willis, trans. 2006. *Sweetbitter Love: Poems of Sappho.* Boston: Shambhala Books.

Benstock, Shari. 1986. *Women of the Left Bank: Paris, 1900–1940.* Austin: University of Texas Press.

Bertens, Hans. 1995. *The Idea of the Postmodern: A History.* London: Routledge.

Bürger, Peter. 1984. *Theory of the Avant-Garde.* Trans. Michael Shaw. Minneapolis: University of Minnesota Press.

Burnett, Anne Pippin. 1983. *Three Archaic Poets: Archilochus, Alcaeus, Sappho.* Cambridge, MA: Harvard University Press.

Burroughs, William S. 1979. *Roosevelt after Inauguration.* San Francisco: City Lights Books.

Butterick, George F. 1983. "Ed Sanders." In *The Beats: Literary Bohemians in Postwar America, Dictionary of Literary Biography,* vol. 16, part 2, edited by Ann Charters, 473–86. Detroit: Gale Research.

Campbell, D. A., ed. and trans. 1982. *Greek Lyric I: Sappho and Alcaeus.* Loeb Classical Library. Cambridge, MA: Harvard University Press.

Carson, Anne, trans. 2002. *If Not, Winter: Fragments of Sappho.* New York: Knopf.

DeJean, Joan. 1989. *Fictions of Sappho, 1546–1937.* Chicago: University of Chicago Press.

———. 1996. "Sex and Philology." In *Re-Reading Sappho: Reception and Transmission,* edited by Ellen Greene, 122–45. Berkeley: University of California Press.

De Loach, Allen, ed. 1972. *The East Side Scene: American Poetry, 1960–1965.* New York: Doubleday.

Diggory, Terence. 2009. "Introduction." In *Encyclopedia of New York School Poets,* vii–xiii. New York: Facts on File.

di Prima, Diane. 2001. *Recollections of My Life as a Woman: The New York Years.* New York: Penguin.

Dougherty, Sean Thomas. 1992. "Ed Sanders Interview." *Long Shot* 13: 87–90.

Dover, K. J. 1979. *Greek Homosexuality.* Cambridge, MA: Harvard University Press.

du Bois, Page. 1996. "Sappho and Helen." In *Reading Sappho: Contemporary Approaches,* edited by Ellen Greene, 79–88. Berkeley: University of California Press.

Gilbert, Sandra M., and Gubar, Susan. 1989. *No Man's Land: The Place of the Woman Writer in the Twentieth Century: Vol. 2. Sexchanges.* New Haven, CT: Yale University Press.

Greene, Ellen, ed. 1996a. *Reading Sappho: Contemporary Approaches.* Berkeley: University of California Press.

———. 1996b. *Re-reading Sappho: Reception and Transmission.* Berkeley: University of California Press.

Gruen, John. 1966. *The New Bohemia: The Combine Generation.* New York: Grosset & Dunlap.

Gubar, Susan. 1996. "Sapphistries." In *Re-Reading Sappho: Reception and Transmission,* edited by Ellen Greene, 199–217. Berkeley: University of California Press.

Hardwick, Lorna. 2003. *Reception Studies.* Oxford: Oxford University Press.

Horvath, Brooke. 1999. "Ed Sanders and His Fiction: An Interview." *Review of Contemporary Fiction* 19.1: 23–30.

Huyssen, Andreas. 1986. *After the Great Divide: Modernism, Mass Culture, Postmodernism.* Bloomington: Indiana University Press.

Johnson, Marguerite. 2007. *Sappho.* London: Duckworth.

Jones, Hettie. 1990. *How I Became Hettie Jones.* New York: Grove Press.

Kane, Daniel. 2003. *All Poets Welcome: The Lower East Side Poetry Scene in the 1960s.* Berkeley: University of California Press.

Kerouac, Jack. 1996a. "Lamb No Lion." In *Good Blonde and Others,* edited by Donald Allen, 51–54. San Francisco: Grey Fox Press.

———. 1996b. "The Origins of the Beat Generation." In *Good Blonde and Others,* edited by Donald Allen, 55–56. San Francisco: Grey Fox Press.

Lipking, Lawrence. 1988. *Abandoned Women and the Poetic Tradition.* Chicago: University of Chicago Press.

Mailer, Norman. 1968. *Armies of the Night.* New York: New American Library.

Olsen, Lance. 1999. "Divining the Avant-Pop Afterburn: Fame and Love in New York." *Review of Contemporary Fiction* 19.1: 99–100.

Parker, Holt. 1996. "Sappho Schoolmistress." In *Re-Reading Sappho: Reception and Transmission,* edited by Ellen Greene, 146–83. Berkeley: University of California Press.

Pelikan, Jaroslav. 1996. *Mary through the Centuries: Her Place in the History of Culture.* New Haven: Yale University Press.

Prins, Yopie. 1999. *Victorian Sappho.* Princeton: Princeton University Press.

Prothero, Stephen. 1991. "On the Holy Road: The Beat Movement as Spiritual Protest." *Harvard Theological Review* 84.2: 205–22.

Reynolds, Margaret, ed. 2000. *The Sappho Companion.* New York: Palgrave.

Sanders, Ed. 1963. *Poem From Jail.* San Francisco: City Lights Books.

———. 1976. *Investigative Poetry.* San Francisco: City Lights Books.

———. 1981. *The Z-D Generation.* Barryton, NY: Station Hill.

———. 2001. "A Tribute to Sappho—A Talk, with Music, Given at Poet's House in New York City, March 30, 2001." In *Woodstock Journal,* edited by Ed Sanders. http://www.woodstockjournal.com/pdf/sapphotribute.pdf

———. 2004. *Tales of Beatnik Glory.* New York: Thunder's Mouth Press.

———. 2011. *Fug You: An Informal History of the Peace Eye Bookstore, the Fuck You Press, The Fugs, and Counterculture in the Lower East Side.* Boston: Da Capo Press.

Schjeldal, Peter. 1990. "Andy Warhol: Museum of Modern Art." In *The 7 Days Art Columns, 1989–1990,* 101–4. Great Barrington, MA: Figures Press.

Skerl, Jennie. 2014. Email interview with Ed Sanders, January 12, 2014.

Skinner, Marilyn B. 1996. "Women and Language in Archaic Greece, or Why Is Sappho a Woman?" In *Reading Sappho: Contemporary Approaches,* edited by Ellen Greene, 175–92. Berkeley: University of California Press.

Snyder, Jane McIntosh. 1989. *The Woman and the Lyre: Women Writers in Classical Greece and Rome.* Carbondale: Southern Illinois University Press.

———. 1997. *Lesbian Desire in the Lyrics of Sappho.* New York: Columbia University Press.

Stehle, Eva. 1996a. "Romantic Sensuality, Poetic Sense: A Response to Hallett on Sappho." In *Reading Sappho: Contemporary Approaches,* edited by Ellen Greene, 143–49. Berkeley: University of California Press.

———. 1996b. "Sappho's Gaze: Fantasies of a Goddess and A Young Man." In *Reading Sappho: Contemporary Approaches,* edited by Ellen Greene, 193–225. Berkeley: University of California Press.

———. 1997. *Performance and Gender in Ancient Greece: Nondramatic Poetry in Its Setting.* Princeton: Princeton University Press.

Sukenick, Ronald. 1987. *Down and In: Life in the Underground.* New York: William Morrow.

Thomas, Robert McGill, Jr. 1997. "Bluma Trell, 94, Professor and Expert on Greece, Dies." *New York Times,* June 12, 1997.

Vanita, Ruth. 1996. *Sappho and the Virgin Mary: Same-Sex Love and the English Literary Imagination.* New York: Columbia University Press.

Warner, Marina. 1983. *Alone of All Her Sex: The Myth and Cult of the Virgin Mary.* New York: Vintage.

Williamson, Margaret. 1995. *Sappho's Immortal Daughters.* Cambridge, MA: Harvard University Press.

———. 1996. "Sappho and the Other Woman." In *Reading Sappho: Contemporary Approaches,* edited by Ellen Greene, 248–64. Berkeley: University of California Press.

Winkler, John J. 1996. "Gardens of Nymphs: Public and Private in Sappho's Lyrics." In *Reading Sappho: Contemporary Approaches,* edited by Ellen Greene, 89–109. Berkeley: University of California Press.

CHAPTER 8

Robert Duncan and Pindar's Dance

VICTORIA MOUL

Modernist poetics, rooted in the work of Pound and Eliot, is generally considered to be hostile to Pindar for both artistic and political reasons: Pound famously described Pindar as "the prize wind-bag of all ages."[1] In the modernist poet Robert Duncan (1919–87), however, despite the importance of Pound to his work, we find a thoughtful engagement with Pindaric form and imagery that was sustained across several collections.[2] That engagement centers upon, but is not limited to, one of Duncan's major poems that has often been anthologized, "A Poem Beginning with a Line by Pindar," published in the 1960 collection *The Opening of the Field*.[3] This piece is acknowledged for its particular significance by Duncan himself, as well as by

1. In a letter to Iris Barry (Paige 1950, 87).

2. Duncan's version of modernism, related closely to Pound, Whitman, and William Carlos Williams, but distanced from Eliot, links him to Beat poetry more widely. Although this article focuses on Duncan's use of Pindar, many features of "A Poem Beginning with a Line by Pindar"—and of Duncan's poetry as a whole—including the focus on the damage done by war and industry, a romantic appreciation of the land and spiritual experience, connect his work to that of Allen Ginsberg and Gary Snyder in particular.

3. This chapter is centered upon that impressive and rewarding collection, though I have also drawn from several of Duncan's other collections. In order of publication, they are: *The Opening of the Field* (1960), *Roots and Branches* (1964), *Bending the Bow* (1968), *Ground Work: Before the War* (1984) and *Ground Work II: In the Dark* (1987). Duncan himself considered his "real work" to have begun with *The Opening of the Field* (see O'Leary 1999).

various of his critics.[4] My attention was caught by the aural beauty of portions of Duncan's poem and by the extent to which it is, oddly and obliquely, suggestive of the experience of reading Pindar in Greek, despite its undoubted difficulty and elements, perhaps, of self-indulgence. This short article is an attempt to consider in more depth the Pindaric features of this poem, the presence of Pindaric motifs in Duncan's work more generally, and to what extent an appreciation of Duncan's engagement with Pindar might advance our reading of his work.

There have been, to my knowledge, only two scholarly articles devoted specifically to Duncan's Pindar poem, although several other critics discuss the poem briefly and acknowledge its importance. The first of these, published by Michael Heller in 1984, acknowledges that "Duncan's poem is an 'ode,' and in this, Duncan is consummately Pindaric," but does not pursue this observation, focusing instead on the features of the poem that link it to epithalamia (Heller 1984). The second piece, an article published by Frank Nisetich (1997), makes several useful observations, but his real target—and interest—is not Duncan, but rather persistent "misreadings" of Pindar of a particular kind, of which he considers Duncan's poem to be a recent and revealing example. Duncan's poem, he argues, has uncritically (and perhaps unconsciously) repeated a long-standing and mistaken view according to which Pindar's genius is characterized chiefly by its "emotional fervor" (Nisetich 1997, 120). Nisetich makes plain his disdain for this approach to Pindar. He contrasts it with recent scholarship, from Bundy onward, which has stressed the extent to which Pindar's verse works within constraints of generic convention (rather than being somehow freely inspired), and how Pindar takes pains to achieve the "delicate balance between just praise and proper restraint" (121). In fact, Nisetich spends only the final seven pages of his article discussing Duncan's poem rather than the traditional misconception of Pindaric style—as exemplified by Reuben Brower (1948)—of which he considers it an example. In response, I would like to examine those features of Duncan's distinctive form and tone that may be considered successfully Pindaric.

Duncan's poem begins and ends with clear references to Pindar's first Pythian ode, and the style of the poem (like much of Duncan's work) may be described as resembling that of Pindar in certain rather general ways: the poem is long, with a complex structure, and it is marked by elaborate meta-

4. Duncan comments on the importance of the poem within his work in "Towards an Open Universe" (1966a, 133–46). Other readings of the poem include Johnson (1988, 70–78) and Gunn (1991), where he remarks: "The only other poem of our half-century that I would place in the same class as the Pindar poem is Basil Bunting's *Briggflatts*" (22). I am indebted to Gunn's remarks on Duncan, in this article and elsewhere.

phors, strings of related images, multiple mythological and historical allusions (generally not clearly or fully retold), and by the poet's references to himself and to his work. Each of these features may reasonably be considered loosely Pindaric. This is particularly true of the combined concern with the author's inspiration and with national history and politics. "A Poem Beginning with a Line by Pindar" incorporates references to several American presidents, to Native Americans, and to the damage wrought by debt, war, and industry:

> Hoover, Roosevelt, Truman, Eisenhower—
> where among these did the power reside
> that moves the heart? What flower of the nation
> bride-sweet broke to the whole rapture?
> . . .
> There is no continuity then. Only a few
>   posts of the good remain. I too
> that am a nation sustain the damage
>   where smokes of continual ravage
> obscure the flame.
> (Duncan 1960, II.26–29, 45–49)

Pindar's victory odes are also deeply (if very differently) political, concerned as they are with the praise of kings and rulers, and the yoking of aristocratic virtue and military success to athletic victory and the poet's own achievement. *Pythian* 1, for instance (the ode to which Duncan's poem alludes directly), uses mythological references to Typhos, Philoctetes, Croesus, and Phalaris, and political references to contemporary battles at Salamis and Himera to evoke and discuss the civic and military power of Hieron of Syracuse, who had recently defeated the Etruscans at Kyme. This association of political and mythological themes with athletic victory—of Hieron's chariot in the Pythian games of 470 BCE—is typical of Pindar's epinicia.

Just as Pindar connects the glory of these victories with the poet's own power to memorialize (and in that sense, create) that glory, so Duncan's verse is also marked by its insistence upon the poet's perspective upon the events he describes or to which he alludes: "I too / that am a nation sustain the damage" (II.46–47). Duncan's poetry, here and elsewhere, returns repeatedly to the history and mythology of poetry itself. This particular poem alludes to several major American poets, including Ezra Pound, William Carlos Williams, Walt Whitman, and Charles Olson, to whom the third section of the poem is dedicated.

In common with other Beat and Black Mountain poets, Duncan's verse is marked by a very wide range of cultural and political models and references, including but far from confined to the classical world.[5] This poem is itself devoted in part to a description of and meditation upon Goya's *Cupid and Psyche,* and his work is in general dense with references both direct and implied to other poets and artists, ancient and modern.[6] He is by no means modeling himself solely upon Pindar, and nor is he a scholar of Greek poetry or performance.[7] But Duncan's engagement with Pindar is nevertheless not superficial: references to Pindaric images—especially of the lyre, the bow, and the cup—recur throughout his work, as I discuss below. In this chapter, I want to offer a reading of "A Poem Beginning with a Line by Pindar" that defends the coherence of Duncan's poem and its status as a meaningful and (for this reader, at least) a moving reception and interpretation of certain aspects of Pindaric style. Secondarily, I want to consider some ways in which an appreciation of what Duncan means by "Pindaric" adds to our understanding of *The Opening of the Field* as a whole, and beyond it, to some of the features and motifs of subsequent collections, especially *Bending the Bow.*

---

5. Donald Davie described the Black Mountain Poets (including Duncan) as "very learned poets, who write very learned poems" (1977, 179).

6. In a 1969 interview with George Bowering and Robert Hogg, Duncan remarked: "I'm always derivative. I derive all my forms, and they come from adoration and falling in love with poets" (1971, no page numbers). This comment is quoted and discussed by Stephen Collis (Collis and Lyons 2012, xi). Similar remarks are found in several of the interviews printed in "Part I: Derivation and Obedience" (Wagstaff 2012, 1–60).

7. There is, however, evidence that Duncan had at least some knowledge of Greek. In her essay on Duncan, Ellen Talman, a personal acquaintance of his in California during the late forties, reports: "At this time, Robert [Duncan] was a passionate student, auditing, if not attending, many English literature classes and various language courses . . . which included their struggling with Latin and being tutored in Greek" (2006, 64). Many of Duncan's poems include Greek phrases, drawn from Homer and Hesiod as well as Pindar. See for instance "Chords: Passages 14," "Spelling: Passages 15," and "Passages 30: Stage Directions" in *Bending the Bow* and "Passages 33: Transmissions" in *Ground Work: Before the War.* The long sequence "The Regulators," published in *Ground Work II: In the Dark,* concludes with a poem based upon a section of *Iliad* Book 2 (which is quoted in Greek at points throughout). Another, much later, poem, "Eidolon of the Aion," also springs from a line of Pindar, this time a fragment (1984, 155–58). More general references to Greek mythology are found consistently beginning in his first collection *The Years as Catches* (1966b). The artist R. B. Kitaj remarked that "Duncan is a high-pitched answer to Pound's question, what would America be like if the Classics had a wide circulation" (Bertholf and Reid 1979, 203–6).

Pindaric Features and Form in "A Poem Beginning with a Line by Pindar"

The line with which Duncan's poem begins is taken, as Nisetich notes, from Maurice Bowra's 1928 translation of Pindar's *Pythian* 1; it is marked as a quotation by italics:

> *The light foot hears you and the brightness begins*
> god-step at the margins of thought
>   quick adulterous tread at the heart.
> Who is it that goes there?
>   Where I see your quick face
> notes of an old music pace the air,
> torso-reverberations of a Grecian lyre.[8]
> (I.1–7)

The meaning of Bowra's line is itself rather unclear; Pindar's highly compressed sentence defies most translators. A painfully literal translation of the Greek might read "to you [that is, the lyre to which the ode is addressed] listens the step, of glory the beginning." In the Greek line, the foot is "light" in the sense of "bright" rather than "not heavy"—Bowra has effectively translated the Greek for "brightness," "ἀγλαΐας," twice.[9] But this is such an unexpected attribute of a foot in English that it is natural to misunderstand the meaning of the translation here, as Duncan in fact reports himself as doing:

> In "A Poem Beginning with a Line by Pindar," the germ of the poem quickened as I was reading one evening the *Pythian Odes* translated by H. T. Wade-Grey and C. M. Bowra. I have an affinity with Pindar, but here it was my inability to understand that began the work or it was the work beginning that proposed the words I was reading in such a way that they no longer belonged to Pindar's *Pythian I*: "The light foot hears you, and the brightness begins." In Pindar it is the harp of Apollo that the light foot of the dancer hears, but something had intruded, a higher reality for me, and it was the harp that heard the dancer. "Who is it that goes there?" the song cried out.

---

8. The quotation is from line 3 of the translation of *Pythian* 1 in Wade-Gery and Bowra (1928).

9. Quotations of the Greek are taken from Race's Loeb edition of Pindar (Race 1997a and 1997b). English translations are also based upon Race, though I have made some alterations.

> I had mistaken the light foot for Hermes the Thief, who might be called The Light Foot, light-fingered, light-tongued. The Homeric Hymns tell us that he devised the harp of Apollo and was first in the magic, the deceit, of song. But as Thoth, he is Truth, the patron of poets. (1966a, 144)

Duncan may have misunderstood the meaning of the phrase "the light foot," but his opening stanza continues to respond, with some success, to the nuances of Pindar's difficult sentence. The phrase "god-step" goes some way toward capturing the multiple resonances of "βάσις ἀγλαΐας ἀρχά," literally "the step, the beginning of glory." Ἀγλαΐα is a grand word—as well as "splendor," "beauty," or "glory," it is also the name of one of the Graces at *Olympian* 14.13; moreover, the word is linked to the αἴγλα διόσδοτος (*Pythian* 8.96), the "god-given gleam" of outstanding performance and of the fame that—via the epinician poet—arises from it.

In the Greek, as Duncan himself notes, the dancer's "step" listens to the lyre, the "Χρυσέα φόρμιγξ" of the ode's opening line ("Golden Lyre, the rightful possession of Apollo and of the violet-haired Muses"); in the following lines of the ode, the singers are also described as "obeying" the lyre, as if their song and their dance (the movements of their feet) were quite independent. Duncan's poem similarly both distinguishes and conflates physical movement (pacing, stepping, dancing) and the song (the poem) itself. The first lines of the poem, quoted above, and even its title use Pindar's opening lines to concentrate upon the idea of "beginning": the beginning of a song, or a dance, but also the "beginning" that is inspiration, linked to the choral dance by the motif of stepping or treading: "god-step at the margins of thought, / quick adulterous tread at the heart. / Who is it that goes there?" (I.2–4). The answer is Pindar himself, also the idea of the poem as it approaches the poet, and—in the myth of the next section—Cupid (Love) as he approaches Psyche (the Soul).

The certain or uncertain approach recurs in the second section of the poem:

> In time we see a tragedy, a loss of beauty
>   the glittering youth
> of the god retains—but from this threshold
>   it is age
> that is beautiful. It is toward the old poets
>   we go, to their faltering,
> their unaltering wrongness that has style,

their variable truth,
    the old faces,
words shed like tears from
a plenitude of powers time stores.

A stroke. These little strokes. A chill.
    The old man, feeble, does not recoil.
Recall. A phase so minute,
    only a part of the word in- jerrd.

    The Thundermakers descend,

damerging a nuv. A nerb.
(II.5–21)

The "faltering" of poets who sometime err, "their unalterable wrongness that has style" is linked here with the physical damage of a stroke, and the marred speech of the aged poet William Carlos Williams.[10] Their uncertain tread is perhaps linked too, to one of Pound's early poems, "The Return," which suggests a similar connection between physical uncertainty and the uncertainty that comes with the metrical freedoms of modernism:

See, they return; ah, see the tentative
    Movements, and the slow feet,
    The trouble in the pace and the uncertain
    Wavering!
(Pound, 1–4)[11]

In the prose passage at the end of the poem, Duncan associates a related feature of style with Pindar, whom he describes as going "too far" and even "toppling over." The "old poets" are both modern, living poets, now old, and ancient poets—the ancient sources to which the modern poet turns, and, chief among them, Pindar.

The "tread at the heart" marks the approach of the dancer, of love (Cupid), and also the "approach" that is involved in reading a poem (such as Pindar's, or Duncan's), or of looking at a work of art. That erotically charged footstep

10. Williams is not identified by name in the poem, but the identification is discussed, among others, by Johnson (1988, 72).

11. The metrical and aesthetic implications of Pound's poem are discussed in Patterson 2011, 180–84.

returns near the end of the poem, at the beginning of the fourth and final section:

> Oh yes! Bless the footfall where
> step by step the boundary walker
> (in Maverick Road the snow
> thud by thud from the roof
> circling the house—another tread)
>
> that foot informd
> by the weight of all things
> that can be elusive
> no more than a nearness to the mind
> of a single image
>
> Oh yes! this
> most dear
> the catalyst force that renders clear
> the days of a life from the surrounding medium!
> (Duncan 1960, IV.1–14)

The pacing of this "boundary walker" is associated with the "god-step," the "tread at the heart," and the cry of "Who is it that goes there?" in the opening lines of the poem, and in turn, with the dance that begins in the first line of Pindar's ode, and with which Duncan's poem ends. But Duncan also here links that *process* (of walking or dancing) with the "nearness to the mind / of a single image." This combination of a process (dancing, walking, moving) and an object (an image, a painting, a lamp) is fundamental to the poem, and to the *idea* of a poem, the genesis of a work of art: "The catalyst force that renders clear / the days of a life from the surrounding medium." We see the same progression from process to object and vice versa in the opening lines, as they move from Pindar's dance to Goya's painting, and again at the poem's close, as Duncan, evoking and imitating Pindar, "topples over" from a prose description of stasis (a mosaic) back into the movement of verse that itself describes a dance:

> (An ode? Pindar's art, the editors tell us, was not a statue but a mosaic, an accumulation of metaphor. But if he was archaic, not classic, a survival of obsolete mode, there may have been old voices in the survival that directed the heart. So, a line from a hymn came in a novel I was reading to help

me. Psyche, poised to leap—and Pindar too, the editors write, goes too far, topples over—listend to a tower that said, *Listen to me!* The oracle had said, *Despair! The Gods themselves abhor his power.* And then the virgin flower of the dark falls back flesh of our flesh from which everywhere . . .

A line of Pindar
moves from the area of my lamp
toward morning.

In the dawn that is nowhere
I have seen the wilful children

clockwise and counter-clockwise turning.
(IV.47–60)

Nisetich is critical of Duncan's summary of Pindar's style here: "Though scholars have from time to time compared his verbal arrangements to mosaics, Pindar did not have mosaic in mind when he denigrated sculpture. It was the *mobility* of his song that made it superior: unlike a statue, a poem can travel through space and time, carrying its message everywhere. And that is the important thing: the message" (1997, 128). Nisetich is right of course about the opening of Pindar's *Nemean* 5 ("I am no sculptor, to craft unmoving statues standing upon their own base. Instead, on every ship and every boat, sweet song, go forth from Aigina"). Duncan is in any case referring apparently to a commentator, not Pindar himself ("the editors tell us . . . the editors write").[12] But Nisetich's reading of Duncan is uncharitable: the structure and force of these closing lines describe the transition from the static text to the moving, dancing poem, as Pindar's own line "moves from the area of my lamp / toward morning," and becomes the choral dance with which both Duncan's and Pindar's poem began.[13]

12. Bowra alludes to Pindar's reputation for "extraordinary lapses" in the preface to his translation. In the comparison of verbal art to a mosaic, Duncan may also have been influenced by Basil Bunting's poem "Ode 34," which both makes and exemplifies this comparison. Duncan particularly admired Bunting.

13. Duncan himself makes clear that he intended the link between the changing direction of the dance and the structure of a Pindaric ode: "In the turn and return, the strophe and antistrophe, the prose and the versus of the choral mode are remembered the alternations of night and day and the systole and diastole of the heart, and in the exchange of opposites, the indwelling of one in the other, dance and poetry emerge as ways of knowing" (1966a).

Action and Image in Duncan and Pindar

In his brief but enormously perceptive comments upon Duncan's work in an article of 1991, Thom Gunn describes another poem from *The Opening of the Field*, "Poetry, A Natural Thing," as Duncan's "ars poetica," a kind of poetic manifesto. That poem is composed simply of two alternative descriptions of poetry itself, two metaphors for the poem:

Poetry, A Natural Thing

    Neither our vices nor our virtues
further the poem. "They came up
    and died
just like they do every year
    on the rocks."

    The poem
feeds upon thought, feeling, impulse,
    to breed   itself,
a spiritual urgency at the dark ladders leaping.
. . .
This is one picture apt for the mind.

A second: a moose painted by Stubbs,
where last year's extravagant antlers
    lie on the ground.
The forlorn moosey-faced poem wears
    new antler-buds,
    the same,

"a little heavy, a little contrived,"

his only beauty to be
    all moose.
(1–9, 21–30)

Of this poem, Gunn remarks:

> Here [Duncan] gives us two separate images for the poem itself, first as it appears to the composing poet, a process taking place, and then as it appears

> to the reader, an artifact like a picture. . . . The picture he shows us is a literal one, an oil-painting by Stubbs, of a moose: the moose is comic and rueful—old antlers on the ground, new antlers barely started—caught in mid-course antler-wise as it were, "his only beauty to be / all moose." . . . The moose is caught in a state of unfinishedness, and indeed the image follows the other apparently contrasting one in which we see poetry as an intense and driven *process*, in Romantic opposition to the orthodox-Modernist artifact. (1991, 18)

Gunn's identification of "Poetry, A Natural Thing" as a kind of "ars poetica" seems to me to be very acute. In fact, we find this double characterization of poetry—as both object and process—throughout *The Opening of the Field* and beyond, in the major collections that followed it. For Duncan, poetry both *is* and *is about* a combination of object and process; and it is this habit of thought that is key to understanding Duncan's interpretation of and attraction to Pindar. Pindar offers Duncan a paradigm for both elements of this formula, and (crucially) for their combination.

The poem "Under Ground" begins:

> first
> more-than-fire, then liquid stone, then stone . . .
> where there do the dead go?
> in utter subjectivity placated that
> turn upon their own steps?
>
> The old folks, no more than
> old thoughts, dressd in full regalia, dried;
> hung in thorn trees; potted;
> boxd, the polishd bones cleansed of rot;
>
> honord by verse that preserves
> Hippokleas, first of the boys
> in the double course at Delphi;
>
> Ford Madox Ford as well; or
>
> Mr W. H., half in half out of ground,
> the double-you that in the ache of Love
> survives, for Love's . . .
> Hate's a monument too! "all happinesse

and that eternitie
promised
by
our ever-living poet
wisheth
the well-wishing"
(Duncan 1960, 1–23)

"Hippokleas, first of the boys / in the double course at Delphi" refers to Pindar's *Pythian* 10, dating from 498 BCE. Pindar's earliest ode, it is printed first in Bowra's translation of Pindar, from whom Duncan has borrowed the phrase. It is relevant to Duncan's poem that this is the first of Pindar's odes—that is, the oldest—but also that it celebrates the triumph of a child or adolescent. Hippokleas, for all his great age, is preserved by the poet as a glorious boy; as—to some extent—is the mysterious "Mr W. H.," the unknown (so only imperfectly remembered) dedicatee of Shakespeare's sonnets.[14]

For all its unconventional appearance, this is at root a very traditional poem: a work concerned with the power of poetry as an agent of immortality. No poet has been more explicitly concerned with that power to spread fame than Pindar, almost every one of whose victory odes makes a direct promise of lasting memorialization. The hope for immortality is central to Pindar's celebrations of victory, which emphasize the necessity of achievement *and* the memory of that achievement for true glory.[15] But Duncan's version of the immortality-motif is typically double-sided: the great poets of the past and their subjects are caught "in action," preserved like Hippokleas in youth and energy, but they are also made into beautiful objects "dressd in full regalia, dried; / hung in thorn trees; potted; / boxd, the polishd bones cleansed of rot." Here we find a second example of the combination of action and object identified by Gunn in "Poetry, A Natural Thing."

"A Poem Beginning with a Line by Pindar" begins from and returns to an image for the poetic process—the dance in the meadow—that is, as we have seen, related directly to Pindar's victory odes, and is also a central motif for the collection as a whole.[16] Versions of this image recur in one form or another

14. A portion of the dedication page from the 1609 quarto is reproduced in Duncan's poem.

15. Instances of this theme in Pindar are so numerous that an exhaustive list would be extremely long. Examples can be found at: *Olympians* 4.10, 5.23–24, 10.91–93, *Pythian* 1.92–94 and 99–100, *Pythian* 3.107–15, *Isthmian* 4.40–42, *Nemean* 6.28–30 as well as *Nemean* 7.12–16 and 31–32.

16. "The dance in the meadow is a visionary pun on Charles Olson's poetics of 'composition by field,' a field which is both an open and a boundaried place; and is thus not only an image in the poetry but an image for it as well" (Gunn 1991, 21).

in almost every poem in *The Opening of the Field.*[17] Dancing is primarily a "process," an activity, rather than an object. But the dance (especially a circular dance) recurs in Duncan's work as an image both of movement and, in its imaginative permanence, of stability:

coupling and released from coupling,
    moving and removing themselves, bowing
and escaping into new and yet old
    configurations,
the word "*old*" appearing and reappearing
    in the minds of the youths dancing
. . .
and the dance, the grand séance of romancing feet in their numbers,
    forward and back—we were the medium
for Folk of the Old Days in their ever returning.
(from "An Interlude," in *The Opening of the Field*)

This is part of the force of Duncan's engagement with the opening of *Pythian* 1, in which the dance and the dancers of that dance are both the same and distinct.

Several of Duncan's other favorite images for the poetic "object" are similarly related to Pindar's own tendency to represent the ode itself as a precious building or possession.[18] A particularly clear example of this is at work in the opening lines of "The Question," also from *The Opening of the Field*:

Have you a gold cup
dedicated to thought
that is like clear water
held in a flower?

or sheen of the gold
burnishd on wood
to furnish fire-glow

---

17. There are too many examples to mention, but note for instance the opening poem of the collection ("Often I Am Permitted to Return to a Meadow"), the poem "The Dance," which follows it ("Lovely their feet pound the green solid meadow"), and the inspired and religious dance of "Evocation" ("At the dance of the Hallows I will tell my love").

18. The ode is, for example, imagined as a palace in the opening lines of *Olympian* 6 and a treasure-house at *Pythian* 6.7–9; as a drinking bowl at the beginning of *Olympian* 7, and a memorial column at *Nemean* 4.81. The lyre of the Muses at the opening of *Pythian* 1 is also a κτέανον, a "possession."

a burning in sight only?[19]
(1–8)

The combination of images in the opening lines of this poem is indebted to Pindar. *Olympian* 1 famously begins:

Ἄριστον μὲν ὕδωρ, ὁ δὲ χρυσὸς αἰθόμενον πῦρ
ἅτε διαπρέπει νυκτὶ μεγάνορος ἔξοχα πλούτου

Water is best, but gold, blazing like fire in the night, shines out, exceeding even noble wealth
(1–2)

The specific qualities of Duncan's poetic cup—golden, shining like fire, and like "clear water held in a flower"—all seem to relate closely to the opening of *Olympian* 1; as does the concern of the poem with the relationship between gold and money. The poem explores the distinction between artistic and monetary "wealth," and suggests in its final lines that the association between gold and spiritual or cultural riches is an ancient one:

O have you a service of rich gold
to illustrate the board of public goods?
as in the old days regalia of gold
to show wherein the spirit had food?
(45–48)

Olympian 1 associates Hieron's worldly wealth (the "rich and blessed hearth of Hieron," 10–11) with the "richness" of victory, and of the poet's celebration of that victory. Duncan suggests that ancient society (and poetry)—like that of Pindar or the Aztecs, whose use of gold is cited in the middle of the poem—recognizes spiritual and artistic "wealth," and marks it with material splendor and luxury.

This is not all that "The Question" derives from Pindar. The object in question—the image for the poem, or for poetic wealth—is a cup. *Olympian* 7 begins with an elaborate simile that compares the victory ode itself with a φιάλα, a drinking-cup or shallow bowl, another object described as "entirely gold" and "the crown of possessions":

19. We find the same motif, more briefly, in the fourth line of another poem of the collection, "At Christmas": "to fill the cup that is now the poem."

Φιάλαν ὡς ἔι τις ἀφνειᾶς ἀπὸ χειρὸς ἑλὼν
ἔνδον ἀμπέλου καχλάζοισαν δρόσῳ
δωρήσεται
νεανίᾳ γαμβρῷ προπίνων
οἴκοθεν οἴκαδε, πάγχρυσον, κορυφὰν κτεάνων,
συμποσίου τε χάριν κᾶ-
δός τε τιμάσαις ἑόν, ἐν δὲ φίλων
παρεόντων θῆκέ νιν ζαλωτὸν ὁμόφρονος εὐνᾶς·

καὶ ἐγὼ νέκταρ χυτόν, Μοισᾶν δόσιν, ἀεθλοφόροις
ἀνδράσιν πέμπων, γλυκὺν καρπὸν φρενός,
ἱλάσκομαι,
Ὀλυμπίᾳ Πυθοῖ τε νικών-
τεσσιν·

As when a man takes from his rich hand a drinking-bowl
foaming inside with dew of the vine
and presents it
to his young son-in-law with a toast from one home
to another—an all-golden bowl, crown of possessions—
as he honors the joy of the symposium
and his own alliance, and thereby with his friends
present makes him envied for his harmonious marriage,

so I too, by sending the poured nectar, gift of the Muses
and sweet fruit of the mind, to men who win prizes,
gain the favour
of victors at Olympia and Pytho.

The central role of a numinous object that is both the subject of the poem—an element of what is described—and also representative *of* the poem is markedly Pindaric. But the cup is not the only resonant motif Duncan borrows from Pindar. The lyre from *Pythian* 1 appears, as we have seen, in the opening lines of "A Poem Beginning with a Line by Pindar." It is present by implication, because in Pindar it is the lyre to which the dancers listen, just as the "light foot" of Duncan's poem hears something and asks "Who is it that goes there?" It is also named directly, at the end of the first stanza: "Where I see your quick face / notes of an old music pace the air, / torso-reverberations of a Grecian lyre" (I.5–7).

The "Grecian lyre" reverberating in "A Poem Beginning with a Line from Pindar" becomes central to Duncan's 1968 collection, *Bending the Bow.* Over a series of poems, in a sequence of associated images, he describes the composition of poetry in terms of drawing a bow, playing a lyre, and weaving on a loom: all activities linked, both literally and metaphorically, by the tightened string.

The sequence appears to begin in the fourth piece of the collection, "Such Is the Sickness of Many a Good Thing," as the poet describes his failure to express himself in terms of string so taut it "taunts the song":

> Such is the sickness of many a good thing
> that now into my life from long ago this
> refusing to say I love you has bound
> the weeping, the yielding, the
>   yearning to be taken again,
> into a knot, a waiting, a string
>
> so taut it taunts the song,
> it resists the touch. It grows dark
> to draw down the lover's hand
> from its lightness to what's
>   underground.
> (23–33)

Duncan makes an explicit connection between the bow (and arrow), the lyre and the shuttle of the loom in the poem "At the Loom—Passages 2." The poem begins with the "shuttle" of the poet's mind creating the web of the verse:

> my mind a shuttle among
>   set strings of the music
> (5–6)

and goes on to associate "that loom" with the lyre of ancient lyric:

> There was such a want in the old ways
>   when craft came into our elements,
> the art shall never be free of that forge,
>   that loom, that lyre—

the fire, the images, the voice.
(24–28)

In the second half of the poem, Duncan links the shuttle of the loom etymologically with a dart or arrow:

Let there be the clack of the shuttle flying
  forward and back, forward and
        back,

warp, *wearp, varp:* *"cast of a net, a laying of eggs"*
  from **warp-* *"to throw"*
. . .
And the shuttle carrying the woof I find
  was skutill "harpoon" - *a dart, an arrow,*
    or a little ship
(35–39, 45–47)

This transition from shuttle to weapon is important to the final third of the poem, which turns to epic themes, and finally the central confrontation of the *Iliad* between Hector and Achilles. Both the lyre and the bow are images of the poet's art found in Pindar, as is that of weaving.[20] Crucially, when Pindar evokes a loom or a bow in his verse, it represents both the poem itself and the *action* of the poem:

ἔπεχε νῦν σκοπῷ τόξον, ἄγε θυμέ· τίνα βάλλομεν
ἐκ μαλθακᾶς αὖτε φρενὸς εὐκλέας ὀ-
  ϊστοὺς ἱέντες; ἐπί τοι
Ἀκράγαντι τανύσαις
αὐδάσομαι ἐνόρκιον λόγον ἀλαθεῖ νόῳ . . .

Now aim the bow at the mark, come, my heart. At whom
do we shoot, and this time launch from a kindly spirit
  our arrows of fame? Yes,
bending the bow at Akragas,
I will proclaim a statement on oath with a truthful mind . . .
(*Olympian* 2.89–92)

20. Pindar uses metaphors of weaving to describe his work at *Nemean* 4.44–45 and 94, *Olympian* 6.86–88 and in fr. 179 (Snell). On the roots of this association in Homer see Snyder 1981.

"Bending the bow" is here a metaphor for the composition and the performance of the ode, as well as for its effect: to deliver the "arrows of fame" that will ensure the lasting reputation of Theron, and of his city, Akragas.[21]

The closest parallel in Duncan to this particularly famous Pindaric image is found in the fifth piece of *Bending the Bow*, a poem that shares its title with that of the collection as a whole. Here it becomes clear that the tightened string of the previous poem is not, as we might have imagined, the string of a lyre, but of a bow:

> We've our business to attend Day's duties,
> bend back the bow in dreams as we may
> til the end rimes in the taut string
> with the sending.
> (1–4)

Once again, the poem is about attempted communication (the writing of a letter, and the poem itself); and like "Poem Beginning" and "Poetry, A Natural Thing," it is structured by descriptions both of emblematic processes (drawing a bow, writing the letter, playing a lyre) and by an ekphrasis, a kind of "still life" image of objects and of art and of objects described as art. The lines quoted above continue:

> Reveries are rivers and flow
> where the cold light gleams reflecting the window upon the
> surface of the table
> the presst-glass creamer, the pewter sugar bowl, the litter
> of coffee cups and saucers,
> carnations painted growing upon whose surfaces. The whole
> composition of surfaces leads into the other
> current disturbing
> what I would take hold of. I'd been
>
> in the course of a letter—I am still
> in the course of a letter—to a friend,
> who comes close in to my thought so that
> the day is hers. My hand writing here
> there shakes in the currents of . . . of air?

---

21. Similar statements are found at *Nemean* 6.26–28, *Isthmian* 5.46–48, and *Olympian* 9.5–12.

of an inner anticipation of . . . ? reaching to touch
ghostly exhilarations in the thought of her.

            At the extremity of this
                Design
"there is a connexion working in both directions, as in
            the bow and the lyre"—
only in that swift fulfillment of the wish
                that sleep
            can illustrate my hand
                sweeps the string.

You stand behind the where-I-am.
The deep tones and shadows I will call a woman.
The quick high notes . . . You are a girl there too,
    having something of a sister and of wife,
        inconsolate,
and I would play Orpheus for you again.

                    recall the arrow or song
                    to the trembling daylight
                    from which it sprang.

(4–36)

In this extract, the first stanza or verse paragraph is concerned with the description of everyday objects—the creamer, the sugar bowl, coffee cups and saucers—all caught in the light and reflecting the image of the window. We recognize here the elements of a still life—that is, a piece of art. Although it is not marked out as a painting, this cluster of objects is evoked in such a way as to suggest both "Day's duties," the minutiae of daily life, and the composition of a work of visual art. Duncan in fact uses the word "composition."

Just at this point, the static image breaks into movement: "The whole / composition of surfaces leads into the other / current disturbing / what I would take hold of" and this sentence about "leading into" guides the poet and the reader into the following verse paragraph, concerned this time not with objects but with an activity—or rather, the interruption of that activity (writing a letter). The structure of this passage and the transition between the two sections—from object to action—resembles rhetorically that of the final part of "A Poem Beginning with a Line by Pindar," where the poem itself "topples over" from prose description into verse movement.

The importance of this transition is highlighted within the poem by the third section of the passage quoted above: "'there is a connection working in both directions, as in / the bow and the lyre.'" That "connection working in both directions" alludes both to the idea of communication involved in the interrupted letter and to the juxtaposition of object and process: both bow and lyre are for Duncan emblematic of that combination.[22] In the introduction to *Bending the Bow,* Duncan cites the source from which the quotation in this passage is taken: "Hermes, god of poets and thieves, lock-picker then, invented the bow and the lyre to confound Apollo, god of poetry. '*They do not apprehend how being at variance it agrees with itself,*' Heraklitus observes: '*there is a connexion working in both directions.*'"[23]

Of this cluster of images associated with Pindar—the dance, the lyre, the bow, the brimming cup—the lyre recurs more frequently in Duncan's work than any other. This cannot, of course, be attributed solely to the influence of Pindar: Duncan's lyre links him with the entire ancient tradition of lyric poetry of which Pindar is only one (albeit particularly prominent) member. At several points, Duncan combines the lyre with other classical motifs of poetic inspiration. In a sequence based upon Dante's prose, for instance, Duncan combines the poetic lyre with the spring of inspiration and (later in the poem) the soaring eagle—a series of images that respond to Dante's own reception of classical motifs:

> Let him first drink of the
>   Fountain, and then,
> adjusting the strings, draw
>   directly his measures
> keeping the beat of the
>   water falling.
> (Duncan 1984, "Let Him First Drink of the Fountain", 1–6)

---

22. The third verse paragraph closes with an allusion to Milton: "Begin then, Sisters of the sacred well, / That from beneath the seat of Jove doth spring, / Begin, and somwhat loudly sweep the string" ("Lycidas," 15–17). Taken from the opening invocation to the Muses, the reference is appropriate to Duncan's interest here in the sources of his own poetry. "Lycidas" is an elegy for Edward King, drowned in the Irish sea. Given the interrupted letter, and the references to "playing Orpheus," "ghostly," and "shadows" in Duncan's address to the unnamed women, I assume that she is herself either recently deceased or recently bereaved. Obviously, in focusing closely upon Duncan's engagement with Pindar, my readings of these poems omit a great deal; his intertextual richness in particular is of considerable interest and sophistication.

23. Duncan (1968, iv). A section toward the end of "Circulations of the Song" in *Ground Work: Before the War* also juxtaposes Hermes and the bow, although in that passage the speaking poet himself becomes the target of the arrow and of the song.

Duncan found various things in Pindar that he admired, and which connect Pindar, perhaps surprisingly, with the poetic tastes of the Beat generation as a whole: long poems of ambitious range and scope, a blend of political and mythological material, a strong authorial voice and a remarkable imagistic style. It is also clear that Duncan alludes at certain points to individual Pindaric odes. But the key to his engagement with Pindar, his self-declared "affinity," has to do not with local allusions, but with the double focus upon art—or rather the "work of art" in both senses—as both a beautiful object and a dynamic process. In Pindar's distinctive style and use of metaphor Duncan found a model for this feature of his work, as we saw in his version of the golden cup of *Olympian* 1; but he found, too, several specific images—the lyre, the bow and the loom—with which to evoke both aspects of his poetics. These beautiful items combine culturally and historically evocative objects with a metaphorical version of the poetic *process* itself.

In this use of Pindar, Duncan responds to only one aspect of Pindar's poetry among many others (we could mention the political and social role of the odes' content and performance, the idea of victory, or their religious attitudes, for instance). But the fact that Duncan does not offer in his verse a complete interpretation of Pindar does not detract from the interest of his engagement.

Thom Gunn's final collection of verse, *Boss Cupid* (2000), opens with a poem titled simply "Duncan." Gunn's own brief "Acknowledgements and Notes" at the back of the collection makes it clear that Robert Duncan is meant. Gunn's poem makes moving use of the imagery of "Poem Beginning with a Line by Pindar" as it describes the faltering steps not this time of the ancients or of William Carlos Williams or of Ezra Pound's version of the wavering poet, but of the aged Duncan himself:

> With plunging hovering tread tired and unsteady
> Down Wheeler steps, he faltered and he fell
> —Fell he said later, as if I stood ready,
> "Into the strong arms of Thom Gunn."
> ("Duncan", 25–28)

Gunn's appropriation of the terms of Duncan's poem is not limited to this motif. Tracing Duncan's life, the poem begins with an image of his youthful poetic energy:

> When in his twenties a poetry's full strength
> Burst into voice as an unstopping flood,

He let the divine prompting (come at length)
Rushingly bear him any way it would.
(1–4)

Readers who are familiar with the Latin poet Horace will recognize the allusion here. In the second ode of his fourth lyric book, Horace outlines the risk taken by those who seek to imitate Pindar, and describes Pindaric style with a famous simile,

Monte decurrens uelut amnis, imbres
quem super notas aluere ripas,
feruet inmensusque ruit profundo
  Pindarus ore,

laurea donandus Apollinari,
seu per audacis noua dithyrambos
uerba deuoluit numerisque fertur
  lege solutis.

Like a river rushing down from the mountain, which rain showers have swollen beyond its accustomed banks, Pindar seethes and rushes, immeasurably large and deep of voice,

Pindar, to whom Apollo's laurel is to be granted, whether he unrolls his fresh expressions in bold dithyrambs, and is borne along in metres free from all law. [The poem goes on to describe Pindar's hymns, epinicia, and epithalamia.]
(*Odes* 4.2.1–8)

The comparison of Pindaric style to a river in spate lies behind a long tradition characterizing Pindaric style as inspired, overwhelming and free from metrical constraint ("*numerisque . . . lege solutis*," although Pindar's complex meters are in fact highly patterned, as Horace was certainly well aware). Duncan's poetic experiments, and his characterization of the poetic footstep or dance that beats in his poems, are reflected by Gunn in both their most confident (Pindaric) mode, and their most tentative: the unsteady pace of an elderly man. Gunn's touching and perceptive poem pays tribute to the elderly Duncan by relating his frailty—and Gunn's own gesture of support—to Duncan's earlier description of Williams. As Duncan was to Williams, the senior poet, so now Gunn is to Duncan. But the "unstopping flood" of Duncan's Pindaric mode—marked by inspiration and freedom—is crucial to Gunn's tribute. It is, moreover, typical of Gunn to recognize the importance of Duncan's Pindarism, but to describe it in terms borrowed from Horace, a poet who, like Gunn himself, is traditionally associated with poetry of tighter control and a smaller scale.

I have tried to demonstrate in this study what Gunn's tribute suggests: that Duncan's Pindarism, though limited, is consistent and important both to individual poems and collections, and to his poetic *persona* overall. Duncan's ideas about Pindar are rooted in a tradition—ultimately a tradition of *poetic*, more than critical response—from which recent scholarship, as Nisetich pointed out, has tended to diverge: modern scholarship has largely reacted against the long tradition of response to Pindar as a poet of religious inspiration. A full treatment of Duncan's Pindarism, especially in the late collections *Ground Work: Before the War* and *Ground Work II: In the Dark* would have to engage in particular with his use of Pindar, and of Greek literature more generally, as the poetry of religious experience. But it is I think at least a useful starting point to note that Duncan's attraction to, and deployment of key Pindaric motifs—the dance, the lyre, the bow, the loom—is not superficial, nor limited only to that major poem, "A Poem Beginning with a Line by Pindar," but is rather founded upon an appreciation of their productive metaphorical richness: images of a mode of art that is at once something we admire (watch, listen to, read) and something that we (readers or audience as well as writers) create and do.

O song of the many changes,
Song of the one thing,

    I have only this song to send

    to take my place among the dancers.
("A Set of Romantic Hymns" V, final lines, from *Roots and Branches*)

Bibliography

Bertholf, Robert J., and Reid, Ian W., eds. 1979. *Robert Duncan: Scales of the Marvelous.* New York: New Directions.

Brower, Reuben. 1948. "The Theban Eagle in English Plumage." *Classical Philology* 43: 25–30.

Collis, Stephen, and Lyons, Graham, eds. 2012. *Reading Duncan Reading: Robert Duncan and the Poetis of Derivation.* Iowa City: University of Iowa Press.

Davie, Donald. 1977. *The Poet in the Imaginary Museum: Essays of Two Decades*. Ed. Barry Alpert. Manchester, UK: Carcanet.

Duncan, Robert. 1960. *The Opening of the Field*. New York: Grove Press.

———. 1964. *Roots and Branches*. New York: Scribner's.

———. 1966a. "Towards an Open Universe." In *Poets on Poetry*, edited by Howard Nemerov, 133–46. New York: Basic Books.

———. 1966b. *The Years as Catches: First Poems (1939–1946)*. Berkeley, CA: Oyez Press.

———. 1968. *Bending the Bow*. New York: New Directions.

———. 1971. *Robert Duncan: An Interview by George Bowering and Robert Hogg, April 19, 1969*. Toronto: Printed at the Coach House.

———. 1984. *Ground Work: Before the War*. New York: New Directions.

———. 1987. *Ground Work II: In the Dark*. New York: New Directions.

Gunn, Thom. 1991. "Adventurous Song: Robert Duncan as Romantic Modernist." *PN Review* 17.4: 14–23.

———. 2000. *Boss Cupid*. London: Faber and Faber.

Heller, Michael. 1984. "The True Epithalamium." *Sagetrieb* 3: 1.

Johnson, Mark Andrew. 1988. *Robert Duncan*. Boston: Twayne Publishers.

Nisetich, Frank. 1997. "Pindar's Modernist Debut: Reuben Brower, Robert Duncan, and the Pindaric Tradition." *Classical and Modern Literature* 17.2: 117–34.

O'Leary, Peter. 1999. "Notes and Comments." *Chicago Review* 45.2: 146–68.

Paige, D., ed. 1950. *The Letters of Ezra Pound, 1907–1941*. New York: Harcourt Brace.

Patterson, Ian. 2011. "Time, Free Verse, and the Gods of Modernism." *Tradition, Translation, Trauma: The Classic and the Modern*, edited by Jan Parker and Timothy Matthews, 175–89. Oxford: Oxford University Press.

Pound, Ezra. 2003. *Poems and Translations*. Ed. Richard Sieburth. New York: Library of America.

Race, William H., ed. 1997a. *Pindar: Olympian Odes, Pythian Odes*. Cambridge, MA: Harvard University Press.

———. 1997b. *Pindar: Nemean Odes, Isthmian Odes, Fragments*. Cambridge, MA: Harvard University Press.

Snyder, Jane McIntosh. 1981. "The Web of Song: Weaving Imagery in Homer and the Lyric Poets." *Classical Journal* 76: 193–96.

Talman, Ellen. 2006. "My Stories with Robert Duncan." In *Robert Duncan and Denise Levertov: The Poetry of Politics, the Politics of Poetry*, edited by Albert Gelpi and Robert J. Bertholf, 63–71. Stanford, CA: Stanford University Press.

Wade-Gery, H. T., and Bowra, C. M., eds. 1928. *Pindar: Pythian Odes*. London: Nonesuch Press.

Wagstaff, Christopher, ed. 2012. *A Poet's Mind: Collected Interviews with Robert Duncan, 1960–1985*. Berkeley, CA: North Atlantic Books.

CHAPTER 9

Kenneth Rexroth

GREEK ANTHOLOGIST

GIDEON NISBET

Nothing left but the broken walls—
The crumbling frescos scrawled with smoke
And the obscenities of Greek
Infantrymen.

—KENNETH REXROTH, *PHAEDRA*
(*BEYOND THE MOUNTAINS*, 1951, 27)

Poet, anarchist, critic, teacher, and self-taught polymath, Kenneth Rexroth (1905–82) was not best pleased when *Time* magazine dubbed him in retrospect the "Father of the Beats." His riposte has become famous: "An entomologist is not a bug." Rexroth had arrived before, and rated himself above, the San Francisco movement that he helped bring into the world. (When Ginsberg read *Howl* at the 6 Gallery in October 1955, Rexroth was master of ceremonies, and he was a witness for the defense at the obscenity trial that followed its publication two years later.) The movement's enthusiasms—the life of the road, the infatuation with Chinese culture—were to him old news; his early life had been a Kerouac novel before the fact.

As a writer and thinker, Rexroth considered himself a breed apart from the angry young men whom he angrily called the "unemployable, over-educated, miseducated members of the *lumpen* intelligentsia" (Rexroth 1986, 72).[1] He had taught himself to read numerous languages (if not perhaps very well),

1. From his journalism, damning Kerouac as a poor modern substitute for Petronius into the bargain. This was tit for tat: Rexroth the elder statesman of the San Francisco scene had been pastiched in Kerouac's *The Dharma Bums* (1958) in the character of Rheinhold Cacoethes, a speaking name ("Badcharacter") that mocks his Hellenic hobbyism. We meet Cacoethes again at chapter's end.

and he prided himself on his knowledge of the Great Books of the Western tradition. His influences were not theirs, or not in his reckoning. One of these influences, and one of long standing, is the subject of my chapter. Rexroth had cut his teeth as a writer in Chicago, the seedbed of imagism, and from the imagists—H.D., Pound, Aldington—he picked up a taste for the peculiar ancient classic that had inspired their movement: the Greek Anthology. He offered versions of poems from this Anthology in two major publications, the first near the beginning and the second at the peak of his poetic career: *The Phoenix and the Tortoise* (1944), and the explicitly titled *Poems from the Greek Anthology* (1962).

It is with the latter of these that my chapter is principally concerned. Published by the University of Michigan Press under its Ann Arbor Paperbacks imprint, *Poems from the Greek Anthology* (henceforth, *Poems*) was most recently reissued in 1999 with a partial concordance.[2] All references in this chapter are however to the original publication of 1962 (the text is identical). This first edition is worth seeking out for its fine linocut illustrations, by the artist and industrial designer Geraldine Sakall, who also illustrated Douglass Parker's translations of *Acharnians* (1961) and *Wasps* (1962) for Ann Arbor at around the same time. Sakall's artwork contributed tangibly to the book's favorable critical reception, and deserves its own critical treatment (concerns of space preclude its discussion here).[3]

Rexroth and the Tradition of the Anthology

As a hybrid work, neither entirely ancient nor conventionally a classic, and one not well known even among students of ancient literature, the Greek Anthology needs some brief explanation—all the more so since (for reasons peculiar to its genre) it has been so often misrepresented to the Anglophone reading public by translators and exegetes.[4] Its principal content is epigram, a genre of short poem, typically composed in elegiac couplets and most frequently running to two, four, or six lines. The Anthology contains about 4,000 such poems. Its tradition is authentically ancient, running right back to the

2. Otto Steinmayer supplements the latter at http://bmcr.brynmawr.edu/2000/2000-11-06.html (last accessed November 9, 2016).

3. On *Poems* as "art book," see Parker 1962, and cf. the anonymous reviewer for the *Saturday Review* 45.2 (1962): 43. Rexroth cared how his books looked: http://www.conjunctions.com/archives/c01-kr.htm (last accessed November 9, 2016).

4. I give an account of this peculiar reception history in a recent monograph (Nisbet 2013), taking the story as far as 1929; the current chapter brings it closer to the present day.

Garland of Meleager (first century BCE), but the Anthology we read today was compiled in tenth-century Byzantium. Its complex bulk tells tales on a millennium's worth of compilation, reediting and reordering, and expurgation.[5] In its present form it consists of sixteen books, inartistically arranged and often disorderly—not so much poetry books as repositories. Most, but not all, comprise epigrams of one particular type: dedicatory, for instance, or epitaphic. All are conventionally cited by the abbreviation "AP," for the best of its manuscripts: *Anthologia Palatina*, the Palatine Anthology.

For a work with such a garbled history and with such a mix of content, in character and period as well as quality—even on its best days, epigram is reckoned a "minor" genre—the Anthology managed to carve out quite a niche for itself in the Western tradition, even in the inferior and censored redaction known to the Renaissance (the "Planudean" Anthology).[6] It was much used in schools as a teaching text for classical languages, and former schoolboys often liked to tinker up versions of their own. In the later nineteenth century, it also became an important vehicle for popularizing critics who wished to communicate (their version of) the spirit of Ancient Greece to a newly literate mass public.

One of these critics demands our particular attention as a precondition for understanding the Anthology's place in twentieth-century American translation. He is John William Mackail, a charismatic educationalist whose books on classical topics were best sellers throughout the English-speaking world. His most enduring legacy was as the editor and translator of a modern Garland: *Select Epigrams from the Greek Anthology* (first edition 1890; henceforth, *Select Epigrams*). Mackail's 500 "best" poems, newly edited with explanatory notes and arranged into twelve "chapters," came with a translation into plain, clear modern prose. *Select Epigrams* was an immediate critical and popular triumph, supplanting its source text and becoming genuinely canonical in a way the Anthology had never quite managed for itself; for the coming decades, it *was* the Greek Anthology for English-speaking readers and writers across the world. No other translated text exercised such lifelong fascination; and in the United States, Mackail was loved more and loved longer even than at home.[7]

Mackail assiduously winnowed the Anthology to make it moral and patriotic—an ideal school text, and later the major poetic exemplar for remember-

---

5. The introduction to Livingstone and Nisbet 2010 gives a brief account and suggests further reading.

6. The surveys by Hutton (1935, 1946) remain valuable.

7. On Mackail's ascension to canon status, see Nisbet 2013, 256–58; on his American fame, 241–42, 247.

ing the British and Commonwealth dead of the Great War.[8] After the war, translators took it in a less martial direction as nature poetry, often with an erotic spin; Rexroth's major American prototype, Wallace Rice (1927), went further, turning the "Anthology" borderline-pornographic through free adaptation, expansion, and outright invention. Rexroth will follow this precedent.[9] Whatever their bent, *Select Epigrams* was the constant touchstone of fellow translators right through into the 1920s, and installed the Anthology as a key text of poetic modernism. Virginia Woolf became an Anthology addict when her brother Thoby gave her Mackail for her twentieth birthday:

> Your book has come, and delights me. These little Epigrams I think I appreciate most of all Greek—as the feminine mind would, according to my theory. And MacKail [*sic*] isnt so precious as I thought—and some—most that I know—of the epigrams are divine—I read them over and over again. (1975, 46–47)[10]

When H.D. worked up the versions from the Anthology that Pound (London, 1912) declared the sacred scripture of a new literary movement, dubbed on the spot "imagism," *Select Epigrams* was her source; we know she ended up owning at least three copies. Pound became a convert.[11] This imagist connection is how the Anthology came to hold such importance for Rexroth. His poetic trajectory and identity in many ways followed H.D.'s, notably in her conception of translation as an act of imaginative recreation. In pursuit of that goal, Rexroth followed in her footsteps toward other ancient classics, too—her fixation on reversioning Euripides pretty clearly set him on the same early career path of revisionist drama in Greek dress—but the Anthology seems to have got the deepest under his skin.[12] He quickly developed firm ideas about what it could be made to mean as a corpus, through slanted excerption:

---

8. On Mackail and Simonides, see ibid., 241, 244–45. On *Select Poems* and the war, see briefly but influentially Fussell 1975, 180–81; on Kipling, Vandiver 2010 delivers depth and nuance.

9. On Nature-poetry, see Nisbet 2013, 187–89; on the bucolic-erotic shift, 283; on Rice, 300–304, and cf. for context (268–69) on Rice's 1920s precursor in spicy American translation, Mitchell Buck.

10. See Kolocotroni 2005, 319n23; Collecott 2000, 51–52n10. Cf. Woolf's review essay on Paton's Loebs, "The Perfect Language" (1987, 114).

11. See Pratt 2008, 30; Collecott 2000, 51–52n10; Gregory 2011, 143, 146–47; Donoghue 1988, 237. On translators' Mackail-worship through to the 1920s, see Nisbet 2013, 281–84; Vosper (1951, 88) gives a couple of examples. On Pound, see Nisbet 2013, 285.

12. On H.D. the Euripideanist, see Gregory 2011, 143. Years later, Rexroth (1987, 174) still resents that she got to the Anthology first.

> The poems in this book might be considered as developing, more or less systematically, a definite point of view. That development proceeds genetically or historically. The classical paraphrases come first. . . . I have tended to select those that best show forth a sense of desperation and abandon in the face of a collapsing system of cultural values. In contrast, there are other epigrams of resignation. (Rexroth 1944, 9)

Phoenix helped put him on the map as a poet to watch, and its conception of the Anthology is distinctively imagist, that is, Mackailian.[13] But then, the sudden reversal: "[The epigrams] are mostly from Hellenistic, Byzantine *and Late Roman* sources, *and from Martial.*" (Rexroth 1944, 9, emphases added)

Separating the Truth from the Facts

> My pal at BTJ [perhaps the Miami technical school, Boys Town Jerusalem] has sent down the video-film of my reading there. If I had known I was being shot I would have tried to be more resolute. The reader is a pathetic old cripple who has to be helped to his chair at the microphone. His tremor is bad and he drops his pages on the floor; but a nubile young maiden rushes up to pick them up for him. He sighs a good deal . . .
>
> The best part is when he's reading those hot versions of the *Greek Anthology*; the camera pans around the audience and young ladies can clearly be seen rubbing their legs together. *Où sont les neiges.* (Laughlin 2006, 251)[14]

Rexroth enlisted Martial and the Latins because they were good for the grand narrative on which he had already determined: Decline and Fall (with, as recalled here, a side order of orgies after the manner of Wallace Rice). His taste for Latinizing the Anthology of the Greeks was to assert itself again eighteen years later in his second and more explicitly advertised bout of adaptation, *Poems,* to which we now turn our attention. The non-Greek content of this volume is one of its most striking features—it pretty explicitly gives the lie to the book's own title, something no "Greek Anthologist" before had had the nerve to try—and makes a sensible point of first contact for our engagement with the volume. The unpaginated preface shrugs away the anomalies:

---

13. E.g., Rexroth (1944, 9) "find[s] no epitaph" there for Harmodius and Aristogeiton—because there is none in Mackail or the Anthology *stricto sensu*; this hadn't stopped nineteenth-century translators packing them in from elsewhere.

14. Quoting a letter from his friend; the ". . ." would appear to be Rexroth's own punctuational heavy breathing rather than an ellipsis, per se.

> Along with the epigrams of the *Anthology* are a few lyric fragments and some bits of Latin. Once I thought I might do a book from the Latin Anthology, the Petroniana, Luxorius, Maximian's Fifth Elegy, Amare Liceat, Martial, Ausonius, some of the *Carmina Burana*, and the Plaints of Abelard. Actually Latin verse, with its rhetorical emphasis, does not interest me greatly, and it is unlikely that now I shall ever devote so much time to it. So these few pieces are scattered among the 100 Poems from the *Greek Anthology* as an extra dividend.

Continuity with *Phoenix* gives the lie to this tale. Rexroth did not simply happen to include a few bits and pieces he had lying around; instead he is deliberately rehashing and enlarging the cultural eschatology he sketched out all those years before. By design, the Latin authors of *Poems* trend late. Ausonius (late fourth century) studied Martial closely after a gap of centuries; Luxorius is sixth century, a poet of North Africa under the Vandals; Maximianus, an Italian of the same period, is conventionally called the "last of the Roman poets." *Phoenix* had already cast them as the last gasp of Late Antiquity ("desperation and abandon"), ushering in a very different and definitively post-classical world in which new kinds of voice and perspective, religious and romantic, were to dominate after a lapse of centuries (Abelard, *Carmina Burana*).

"Some bits," a "few pieces," "scattered"—the scale of Rexroth's misrepresentation becomes apparent when we run the numbers. Like every predecessor in translation from the Anthology, and with good reason, *Poems* ignores the clumsy historic form of its text, here dismissed as a technicality of interest only to specialists.[15] Its particular solution is to present its authors alphabetically, from Agathias and Ammianus to the obscure Tymnes and Zonas (we will examine the volume's opening and closing sequences later in this chapter). This is as good a scheme as any, rests on solid precedent, sells the book well by hinting at comprehensiveness, and has the incidental virtue of making it easy to track who purportedly wrote what. The roster is so extraordinary, it bears presentation in full, with the Latin elements emboldened. My frequent "[*sic*]"-ing reflects Rexroth's difficulties with ancient proper names:

> Agathias—Ammianos—Anixamandros [*sic*]—Anonymous (x 11)—**Anonymous Carmina Burana (Abelard?)**—Antipatros [*sic*] of Sidon

---

15. "I have provided no notes or other apparatus—the last word of scholarship on these things has been said long ago," Rexroth (1962) advises in his unpaginated foreword. Actually it had hardly begun.

> (x 4)—Antipatros [*sic*] of Thessalonika—Anyte (x 3)—Archilochos—Aristodikos of Rhodes—Asklepiades of Samos (x 9)—**Ausonius**, after Rufinus—Bassos [*sic*] (x 2)—The Delphic Oracle—Glykon—Hedylos—Ibykos—The Emperor Julian—Kallimachos—Krates—Krinagoras—Leonidas of Tarentum (x 14)—Lucian—Markos Argentarios [*sic*]—**Martial (x 7)**—Meleagros (x 3)—Nicharkos [*sic*]—Nossis (x 2)—Palladas (x 4)—Paulos Silentarios [*sic*] (x 4)—**Petronius (x 6)**—Philetas—Philodemos (x 7)—Plato—Poseidippos (x 2)—Sappho (x 4)—Sekundos [*sic*]—Simonides (x 3)—"Simonides, Antipatros, and others"—**Sulpicius Lupercus Servasius Jr.**—Thymokles—Tymnes—Zonas.

Some of these choices embrace conventionality. For instance, we get plenty of Sappho, who (though really not an epigrammatist) was an Anthology author as far back as Meleager's Garland, and whose poetry was Rexroth's own first foray into the joys of Greek. The genre's Hellenistic and Imperial Greek heyday is quite well represented—for example, by Antipater, Asclepiades, Meleager, Philodemus, and Posidippus—as are the Late Antique poets (Agathias and Paul the Silentiary), whose imitative poems had so often helped fill out the school textbooks. Simonides, too—a poet of Greece's classical age, famed for his verse inscriptions celebrating the Greek achievement in the Persian Wars—has a showing that reflects his traditional popularity, including with Mackail. Other inclusions, though, are so utterly obscure—Tymnes, Zonas—that their inclusion in a distilled, best-of-the-best "Greek Anthology" of a mere 109 poems seems deliberately perverse to a reader who knows the source material (though, of course, most will not).

And then there is all the Latin. "I know what the Greek says," declares the translator's preface, but much of his Anthology was never *in* Greek to begin with. At least Martial is an epigrammatist; Petronius is only rarely a poet, and then usually in the service of either satire or an obscure point of literary-critical polemic (his reader is usually clueless as to which). Rexroth's versions of them are fun, but we might wonder why in a small selection of a hundred-odd so-called "Poems from the Greek Anthology," a source text with many thousands of poems to its name, a baker's dozen of them—just under an eighth of the whole—are out of two *Latin* poets. Ausonius has the unusual distinction of being a poet as fluent in Greek as in Latin; but Rexroth chooses to go to his Latin side. Add in *Carmina Burana*, and nearly a seventh of Rexroth's "Greek Anthology" is Latin. What was he playing at?

Actually the facts—X was Greek, Y was actually Roman—did not loom large in Rexroth's scheme of things; what mattered was truth, and truth made

Romans and Greeks interchangeable. Introducing his first volume of collected journalism, *Classics Revisited,* he wrote:

> Eskimos, Polynesians, Romans, Chicagoans—all men have the same kind of bodies and the same kind of brains and cope with an environment in ways which would seem more uniform than not to an observer from another planet. (Rexroth 1986, vii)[16]

In Rexroth's estimation, a literary classic speaks truths that we all share; it "reveals . . . the fundamental dynamism of human life in the way, for instance, in which the operation of a power plant reveals the laws of physics" (vii–viii). His pessimistic vision finds no more progress in literature than in life—the human tragicomedy is forever being played out to the same script, dictated by genetics and environment—so all classics are equally modern:

> The greatest literature presents men wearing the two conventional masks: the grinning and the weeping faces that decorate theatre prosceniums. What is the face behind the double mask? Just a human face—yours or mine. That is the irony of it all—the irony that distinguishes great literature: it is all so ordinary. (ix)

His versions of epigram accordingly play a game of mix-and-match, as in this example, riffing on a sympotic epigram by Antipater of Sidon (AP 11.23):

> Fortune-tellers say I won't last long;
> It looks like it from the newspapers;
> **But there is better conversation**
> **in Hell than in an insane nation;**
> And a galloping jug will get there
> Quicker than these loud pedestrians,
> **Tumbling down hill witless in the dust.**
>
> ANTIPATROS [*sic*]
> (Rexroth 1962, 17, emphases added)

There is considerable expansion and alteration here: nearly half the poem (the emboldened parts) is outright invention, and "newspapers" is pretty loose; but these changes express what the poem is trying to say, or *ought* to be trying to

16. The passing shout-out to Chicago as a spawning-ground of literary colossi is cute.

say in the estimation of its modern translator. "There are no Classics that are untrue" (9). The whole gist of *Classics Revisited* is that the plain-speaking and nonspecialist critic (i.e., Rexroth) is ideally set up to nose out the great works, to remind us of their truths and tell us why they matter, just by virtue of being in touch with his natural and universal humanity—as scholars in universities are not. By this reckoning, a literal translation would be pedantic and therefore "false"; free adaptation is not so much licensed as made a duty.

Old Rhetorics, New Rhythms

Irresistible as they must have been to Rexroth the self-styled outlaw intellectual, these convictions only go part of the way to explaining the extraordinary liberties Rexroth has felt entitled or even impelled to take with this particular source text. Instead, Rexroth has fallen under the spell of—or perhaps is ironically channeling as part of a deadpan poetic persona-game—a long tradition of egregious and feckless garbling of the Anthology under the pretext of accommodating its authors to contemporary sensibility. This tradition came with built-in obsolescence and is distinctly pre-Mackailian. Its hinterland is the early years of the nineteenth century; even then it was mocked, and by the turn of the century it was dead and buried . . . but every once in a while it would still lurch from the graveyard moaning for brains. The Anthology's translator for the British mass market in 1929—Shane Leslie, a journeyman peddler of hand-me-down opinions of whatever vintage—glossed the epigrams of the Anthology as "read[ing] distantly from our civilisation, but a little modern dress brings some of them deliciously home. . . . The translations in this book are not always literal when they attempt the impressionism of the original"; and *that* attitude, peculiar to translators of the Anthology as of no other classical text, could justify all manner of mischief (1929, 9).[17]

So, there is proto-Beat literary machismo in Rexroth's comments and choices, to be sure, but also a certain toeing of the party line among translators of epigram, a pose of spontaneity that has hardened into a conventional mask. To his foreword ("these poems make no pretense of scholarship"; 1962, n.p.), compare closely Rice thirty-five years before ("Making no pretense to scholarship myself"; 1927, xvi)—but also, preceding Rice, the obscure Scottish translator Alexander Lothian ("I profess myself no very scientific student of

17. On adaptive translation of the Anthology in the early nineteenth century and the severe criticism that it provoked in some quarters, see Nisbet 2013, 56–60, and cf. 290–93, on Frederic Wright's cringeworthy *The Girdle of Aphrodite* (1923).

the Anthology"; 1920, n.p.) and, looser but decades down the line, Michael Kelly's translations from the heterosexually erotic AP 5 ("At university what pedantry, what dry as dust . . . I read English Literature"; 1986, 7).

The translators' rhetoric all points toward one conclusion: the Anthology's ideal translator is unscholarly and even careless. Not only does he (and it is almost always a "he") pay no regard to the form and content of his source—a source that in the Anthology's peculiar case is postclassical and therefore "untrue"; he does his best work impressionistically, without even looking at the text.[18] This kind of claim would shock readers of any other classical text in translation, but by Rexroth's time what had begun as conscious and provocative paradox (in large part born from the backlash against Oxford Uranism) had ossified into a reflex habit of thought. It would not even do to be too good at Greek—that was what dons were good for, and what did dons know about Life as it was lived by real men?[19]

With *Poems,* epigram now hikes and rides the rails. Ever since learning Greek with Sappho, says Rexroth, and in dialogue with his Chinese influences,

> on the freight trains of my youthful years of wandering, in starlit camps in desert and mountain ranges, in snow-covered cabins, on shipboard, in bed, in the bath, in love, in times of loneliness and despair, in jail, while employed as an attendant for the insane, and on many other jobs and in many other places, the *Anthology* and the lyric poets of Greece have been my constant

18. "Many of the translations came to me as I turned the Greek poem over in memory, with no text at all" (Rexroth 1962, n.p.)—compare, for example, to Lothian, whose habit it professedly was "in leisure times to carry [Mackail's Greek *editio minor*] about with me, not in my pockets only, but in my head and heart" as he walked his native hills (1920, n.p.). Translators often justified mangling the Anthology by claiming that they were taking it back to its roots in Meleager's Garland—not so much by reconstructing his lost book, but by themselves compiling the kind of selection they felt he *ought* to have been authoring, with scant regard for plausible chronology; see, for example, Neaves 1874, 14.

19. The Mackailians' originary motive was tacit homophobia; Rexroth's, the contrarian outsider's contempt for institutionalized and theorized Eng. Lit. Cf. his grudge-airing remarks on academia's unfitness to judge Mark Twain, conceived as his own ideal bohemian prototype in the 1959 essay reprinted in *Assays* (1961, 95). Kelly (1986, 8) continues the tradition, rhetorically counterpointing the bloodless, sexless Classics of the dons to his success at placing his own Anthology translations with the British men's magazines, *Mayfair* and *Club International.* In the United States, I know of two Christmas special issues of *Playboy* (December 1969 and 1970) that have carried loose anonymous paraphrases from the Anthology as installments in the magazine's long-running "Ribald Classics" series, illustrated by the talented freelancer Brad Holland.

> companions. . . . Now they are moving away from me to the printed page and I will miss them terribly. (Rexroth 1962, n.p.)[20]

As reported by Rexroth, the genre ticks off the activities and venues of Beat identity so thoroughly that one is amazed not to find the novels of Kerouac packed full of Simonides, Sappho, and Meleager. And again Rice is an important prototype for Rexroth's conceits: "much joy and a little learning has gone to the making of these pages, which I am happy in sharing with others, though with a little sadness that my work, certainly for a time, is ended" (Rice 1927, xvii). Rice and Rexroth alike present turning the Anthology into English for our time as a personal work in progress: a work *on* the self, as much as *for* others; it is a happening.

As a translator of epigram at least, Rexroth seems to have no idea what a cliché he is being when he brags of bringing a free and lusty spirit to its text and finding there a modern attitude. He is the text's ideal patsy—or just possibly is playing at being such, so straight-facedly as to own the role.

The remainder of this chapter brings these contextual strands together, in two sequential readings that explore how *Poems* frames its so-called "Greek Anthology." We begin with an examination of how the book begins. How does Rexroth create expectations and coach his reader on how to experience "Anthology" within the strictures of his alphabetical scheme? We then conclude by examining how the book ends. How does he close *Poems* down, within these same strictures? The chapter then concludes with some brief remarks on the afterlife of Rexroth's Anthology.

How *Poems* Begins

One lesson that classical texts teach us is that openings are important; they demand to be read carefully, and in the case of ancient classics are liable to be interpreted programmatically. In the case of a selection from a wider ancient corpus, editorial choices of structure and content amplify the drama. A sequential reading may be expected to inform on the individual translator's practice as a conscious reversioner of the classic, and on how s/he apprehends and relates to the source text in question. In the case of Rexroth and the Anthology, we may also read in a further, implicit position-statement about his priorities. One consequence of choosing to arrange alphabetically is to

20. Rexroth is at least setting up lots of plausible excuses, if we believe a word of any of this, for not having an edition of the Greek text to hand.

put all the anonymous poems under "A," very near the start—and Rexroth has chosen to include a lot of them (twelve in all, or a ninth of the book). So Rexroth front-loads the collection with the spontaneous poetry of the common man—not that it *is* that, in all likelihood, but that is the story that his arrangement implicitly tells. His "Anthology" is a folk document, the opposite of academic.

> Restless and discontent
> I lie awake all night long.
> And as I drowse in the dawn,
> The swallows stir in the eaves,
> And wake me weeping again.
> I press my eyes close tight, but
> Your face rises before me.
> O birds, be quiet with
> Your twittering accusations.
> I did not cut that dead girl's tongue.
> Go weep for her lover in the hills,
> Cry by the hoopoe's nest in the rocks.
> Let me sleep for a while, and dream
> I lie once more in my girl's arms.
>
> AGATHIAS SCHOLASTICOS
> (Rexroth 1962, 1)

The first epigram we meet, though, is by a named author: before Anonymous comes Agathias (AP 5.237), the Late Antique compiler of the *Cycle*, which was Cephalas's largest source when he compiled "our" Greek Anthology several centuries later. The original is in book five of the Anthology, the heterosexual love poems. This is a powerfully simple version, and quite faithful, as well; of the small liberties taken, the preface has given us fair warning. In the original, "your face rises before me" is third-person, and gives a name instead of a face: "Again the thought of Rhodanthe haunts my heart." Similarly, "I did not cut that dead girl's tongue. / Go weep for her lover in the hills" is an oblique version of the original. Agathias supplies the names that identify the myth within its own cultural system—Philomela and Itys; Rexroth adds mystery and avoids antiquarianism by stripping them out. The reader likely comes away bamboozled by this gnomic utterance, but the lines make a memorable impression; it's a good trade-off.

Dawn after dawn comes **on the wine**
Spilt on the books and music,
And on the stained and tumbled pillows.
And then, while we are paying
No attention, a black man comes,
And roasts some of us, and fries
Some of us, and boils some of us,
And throws us all in the dump.

AMMIANOS
(Rexroth 1962, 2)

The second epigram of *Poems* (AP 11.13) is from the Anthology's eleventh book, which uniquely in its rather wobbly scheme contains two separate types of epigrams, which its compiler reasonably claims to be related: sympotic and "skoptic" (roughly speaking, satirical—in other words, a good source of after-dinner jokes and maxims). This is from the shorter, sympotic section at the front of the book. The author, Ammianus, is an Eastern Greek of the second century CE who is best known for his poems in the later, skoptic part of book eleven, where he is the master of the elaborate pun and play on words.[21] Here, though, he expresses a straightforward sentiment characteristic of the symposium: drink and be merry, because life is short and enjoyment is fleeting. (The deaths by different methods of cooking are glossed by Paton in a footnote to his Loeb as deaths from disease: consumption, fever, and dropsy).

As previously, I embolden the invented material to clarify the extent and the libertine drift of the translator's fabrications. The genitive absolute ἀμελούντων ἡμῶν, "while we are paying no attention," is the jumping-off point for an elaborate ekphrasis in which the details are all Rexroth: the poem's scene shifts from the rule-bounded and homosocial world of the ancient symposium to one of the soirées at which Rexroth regularly held court in San Francisco.

The other peculiar feature of this translation is in line 5: "A black man comes." As in the opening poem—"I did not cut that dead girl's tongue"—we could say this is Rexroth trimming detail in pursuit of lapidary mystique. In the Greek, the man is not black but purple, πορφύρεος—nor is he specified as a man. Instead, ὁ πορφύρεος is pretty clearly Death personified; when blood gushes it is πορφύρεος, and consequently πορφύρεος θάνατος is a

21. For discussion of Ammianus see Nisbet 2003. The poet is the subject of a recent doctoral thesis (2011) by Francesca Ricciuti of La Sapienza, Rome.

familiar formulation in Homer. In Ammianus's Greek, our ultimate fate is the βάραθρον—the pit, or deep cleft in the rocks, into which Athenians hurled condemned criminals; by metaphorical extension, the word is used to mean "ruin" or "perdition." When Rexroth (who himself was actively antiracist) has the "black man" dispose of his victims' bodies in the "dump," one pictures dead refrigerators and car crushers; the image evokes the milieu of organized crime and must have played uneasily against the backdrop of racial politics in 1960s America.

The third poem in Rexroth's selection—the last before the Anonyma—is the end-product of a completely different kind of adaptation:

> **It is necessary that things**
> **Should pass away into that from**
> **Which they were born.**
> All things must pay
> To each other the penalties
> And compensations for all the
> Inequalities wrought by time.
>
> ANIXAMANDROS [*sic*][22]
> (Rexroth 1962, 3)

Its source text had never before kept company with any kind of "Greek Anthology," however loosely conceived, for the simple reason that it is not a poem. Anaximander (sixth century BCE) was an early Greek philosopher, and one of the first Greeks to write in prose. All we have of him is this one citation, quoted by the Byzantine philosopher Simplicius over a thousand years later (sixth century CE).

To make matters worse, not all of this "poem" is even Anaximander's. His words begin in line 4, "All things must pay. . . ." What Rexroth appears to have failed to realize is that his first three lines (which I embolden) are Simplicius presenting a proposition that he then illustrates by *quoting* Anaximander. Simplicius then marks the end of the quotation with a brief and snarky comment on Anaximander's highfaluting style: "as he somewhat poetically says." It is in this form that the fragment appears in editions, most obviously in Diels-Kranz's fragments of the Presocratics.

If Rexroth, who "knows what the Greek says," looked at the Greek even for a second, then the layout on the page must have made it very obvious

22. "Anixa-" for "Anaxi-" could be a typesetter's error but is as likely to be the poet's own misreading of his source.

that Anaximander's dictum is not poetry—"somewhat poetically" just means Anaximander uses flowery language that Simplicius thinks would be more at home in epic. The most straightforward explanation would be that the translator has come to this text at second hand in his general reading on philosophy, and has misconstrued *both* Simplicius's closing comment *and* the point at which the citation gets real: in other words, he has rewritten someone else's translation and done so carelessly. There were already firm grounds—notably his evident incompetence with names—for not taking Rexroth at his word when he claimed to "know what the Greek says" and this looks like further corroboration. Or is it? Setting aside disciplinary rigor, a more relaxed reader could surmise that the assertion is not so much a truth-claim as a performance of vatic authority in the service of a poetic persona. An outright partisan might even claim that the poet misconstrues the fragment and its context deliberately and playfully, as part of his creative process; which interpretation we prefer ultimately comes down to readerly judgment and to the expectations (if any) about Rexroth's talent and method with which we approach his palimpsestic text.

Ensuing poems in the early part of the book (there is no hard and fast rule by which one can call time on an "opening sequence," per se) may be dealt with rather more summarily. Rexroth's fourth choice is the first of his dozen Anonyma. Its source is a papyrus fragment in hexameters, P.Oxy.1.8, first published in 1898 and promptly assigned to either Alcman or Erinna. By the time Rexroth took it up, Maurice Bowra had called it for Erinna, in a work Rexroth (allegedly an *aficionado* of lyric) really ought to have known. However, reporting the fragment as "Anonymous" suits Rexroth's narrative of the Anthology quite well; perhaps unknown to him, he is not the first of epigram's modern exegetes to have found advantage in placing emphasis upon that very theme (Symonds, for one, leaned on it to flag up epigram's authenticity as a human document).[23]

The fifth poem derives from a genuinely anonymous epigram, AP 5.201; Rexroth expands it a little, making an eight-liner out of a four-line original, but none of his elaborations are outrageous. His sixth choice too is genuinely anonymous; it has the look of another AP 5 epigram, but appearances can be deceptive. Wine spilled on stained and tumbled pillows, half the garden tracked into the bedroom—the real gone chicks of *Poems* will have a lot of housework to get through once they're done taking care of their author's sexual needs:

23. Symonds (1920, 540–41), the closing comments of his chapter on epigram.

Flowers will do us no good on our tombstones;
Tears mixed with ashes only make mud.
Let's move half the garden into the bedroom,
Roll about, and moan in unison.

ANONYMOUS
(Rexroth 1962, 6)

Again, the additions are emboldened. The first couplet condenses an anonymous, four-line sympotic epigram from early in book eleven (AP 11.8), where exhortations to live for today are par for the course—garlands of flowers are a classic party-goer's accessory as well as an offering to the dead; the details are subtly updated (the mud of the original is from wine poured as a libation at the tomb, a custom we no longer keep). The second couplet, where "flowers" and "mud" cue up an earthy sex romp, has no source outside of Rexroth's priapic imaginings. Through creative expansion, he has sent the source poem in an entirely new direction—again, did he but know it, a move for which precedent goes all the way back to Symonds in the 1870s.[24]

Before concluding this section, let us pause to note the themes on which *Poems* has so far touched—themes that we have seen are sometimes not those with which the poems started off in the Greek. They make quite a sequence: love, death, death, death, love; the seventh poem is an epitaph. The following five are love poems, and as before, love really means sex: "the wage of wantonness, / And the joys shared with lovers" (Rexroth 1962, 9).[25] And the sequence cranks on thereafter, vacillating between the twin poles of elegiac cliché: love, love, death, love, love, death . . .

Conceived primarily in terms of male sexual entitlement, the erotic half of this thematic double-act is straight out of Wallace Rice, whose *Pagan Pictures* reimagined the Anthology as a hedgerow paradise of yielding maids and throbbing manhoods. (Rice also injected himself into the text in ways that upped the ante in the translator's self-fashioning as a heroic intervener—Rexroth's fabulations look almost modest when compared to his predecessor's wholesale literary impersonations.)[26] The morbid half is Mackail, whose canonic *Select Epigrams* gave inordinate weighting to thoughts of mortality.

24. Ibid., 531, butchering Strato of Sardis AP 12.258; for discussion see Livingstone and Nisbet 2010, 146–47.

25. A poem that is *both* erotic *and* funereal ("But the blessings of many / Possessions I leave behind," i.e., in death).

26. On Rice's undeclared, pseudo-classical *alter ego*, "Xenos Palaestes," see Nisbet 2013, 302–3.

How *Poems* Ends

> Behind the flutes and flowers change comes and the shadow of fate stands waiting. . . . For over all Greek life there lay a shadow . . . [in treating death], if anywhere, the Greek genius had its fullest scope and most decisive triumph; and here it is that we come upon the epigram in its inmost essence and utmost perfection. (Mackail 1890, 61, 64)

We may recall that Rexroth's choice of organizational scheme—the notionally nonnarrative solution of arranging *Poems* alphabetically by name of author—was a world away from Mackail's. *Select Epigrams* had proposed a more obviously prescriptive route through the Anthology's content, reallocating its winnowed content under twelve thematic "chapters," which the reader is invited to read sequentially; the intended upshot is a kind of morally uplifting and ultimately closural *Bildungsroman.* In Mackail's scheme, mortal thoughts found their natural home in the closing chapters (effectively the last four of the twelve, or a whole third of *Select Epigrams*; did I mention that Mackail was morbid?).[27] Rexroth, bound to alphabetization, ought not to be able to match this distribution—but he gives it his best shot.

There is an older context here, long predating Rexroth and Mackail both. From the earliest translators, explanations of the Anthology for English readers typically placed particular emphasis on the very same thematic binary—love and death—that we saw in Rexroth's opening sequence. This had made intuitive sense to them because of the uses to which antiquity famously put elegy and the elegiac couplet. In Roman literature in particular, elegy became the meter of love-poetry, but its funerary uses were already long established. The origin of the elegiac mode was popularly supposed to lie in laments for the dead: the ancient etymology, ἒ ἒ λέγειν (to cry woe!, woe!), loses none of its imaginative force for being philologically implausible, because the scenario is intuitively evocative. Before epigram was epigram in a literary sense, it was ἐπί-γραμμα—a text inscribed on a surface, which not infrequently would be that of a monument, which in turn would more often than not be funerary; and when epigram became a literary genre in the Hellenistic period, it began by taking existing inscriptional forms as models.

---

27. Mackail's twelve categories are: 1. Love, 2. Prayers and Dedication, 3. Epitaphs, 4. Literature and Art, 5. Religion, 6. Nature, 7. The Family, 8. Beauty, 9. Fate and Change, 10. The Human Comedy, 11. Death, 12. Life. Don't be misled by that last one; he means Life Everlasting. On how he briefs his readership to read sequentially for moral instruction, see Nisbet 2013, 250–53.

Early literary epigram also mimicked its lapidary prototypes at the level of compositional technique, pursuing highly iterative elaboration on (at first) a deliberately narrow range of themes and motifs. The result of these factors in combination is that there are more faux-epitaphic epigrams extant in the Anthology than any other single kind. The book in which the sepulchral poems are placed, AP 7, is longer (748 poems) than any other—and *much* longer than AP 5, the home of the heterosexual love poem (309 poems). The sepulchral poems are still very much a minority within the Anthology as a whole, but one would not think it from the rhetoric of the nineteenth-century translators, for whom the work's whole purpose often seems to lie in decorous *memento mori*.

The size of AP 7 gives no real grounds to suppose that the Greeks were especially morbid—the mock-epitaph simply happened to get a head start on most of the other subgenres that comprised literary epigram—but in the shared rhetoric of the Anthology's English afterlife, these poems became proof positive that the Greeks sensed the doom of their race. Death is the ever-present stranger at the feast—a feast conceived in alluringly Alma-Tadema-esque terms (flute-girls and flowers) in the quotation from Mackail with which this section began. And Mackail's formulation quickly became the decisive gloss on their lesson to modernity—a modernity which looked back to ancient Hellas for inspiration but need not share its sadness, because it knew salvation through the word of Christ. (That most of the authors of the Anthology are inconveniently of Roman or later date is a small detail easily elided once the rhetoric starts flowing.) Much of the introductory matter of *Select Epigrams* is expended on talking up Greek morbidity, and we have seen how the basic structure of Mackail's selection influentially gave pride of place to death and its inevitability. Epigram in his calculatedly quote-worthy summation was

> a metre which could refuse nothing, which could rise to the occasion and sink with it, and be equally suited to the epitaph of a hero or the verses accompanying a birthday present, a light jest or a profound moral idea, the sigh of a lover or the lament over a perished Empire. (Mackail 1890, 6)

It is in this light—the modern Anglophone reception of the Anthology as a meditation on love and death, but especially death—that we now wind up our encounter with Rexroth's collection.

Rexroth's column on the Anthology for *Classics Revisited* reveals how much he has bought into Mackail's old rhetoric that turned Greek funerary epigram into the symptom of a culture fixated on its own decorous demise:

> Melancholy saturates the later poets of the *Anthology* and even tinctures Meleager. . . . It is simply a more somber, more continuously haunting realization of the final term of the good, the true, the beautiful—and of the self and of civilization itself. (Rexroth 1986, 59)

Accordingly, the last ten poems of his selection are all to do with tombs, memorials for the dead, the inexorability of fate, and how soon our lives will be over. This reenactment of the narrative trajectory from *Select Epigrams* is no small achievement given that Rexroth has committed to an alphabetical structure; he must find examples that hit the right notes while still being written by poets whose names fall near enough to "Z."

Simonides is well represented here, with four poems (it is convenient that "s" falls late-ish in the alphabet). Accordingly, *Poems* includes a suitably spare version of his greatest hit, "Go tell it to the Spartans" (Rexroth 1962, 106). The last of the Simonidean quartet is an epitaph for Anacreon, with the faux-scholastic attribution, "Simonides, Antipatros [*sic*], and Others." Despite appearances, this is not an ancient collaboration. The Anthology contains a flurry of literary epitaphs for Anacreon (AP 7: 23–33), and what Rexroth has done is rifle through Paton's Loeb translations and throw together an impressionistic pastiche using whatever phrases strike him as evocative. For motives which may again be left to individual readerly speculation, he appears to have turned a blind eye to the facing Greek text.[28]

Following the Simonidean extracts, the closing roster heads into the Anthology's outfield of one-hit wonders. First up is the dazzlingly obscure "Sulpicius Lupercus Servasius Jr." whose poem (four from the end) I reproduce here in Rexroth's version:

> Rivers level granite mountains.
> Rains wash the figures from the sundial.
> The plowshare wears thin in the furrow;
> And on the fingers of the mighty,
> The gold of authority is bright
> With the glitter of attrition.

28. See Rexroth (1962, 107). For example, "wine bibber" is from Paton's AP 28; "the white marble," Paton on AP 30. We know Rexroth leaned on Loebs when translating classical authors; see Ben Pleasants's memoir of his visit with Rexroth in 1976, http://www.thiscantbehappening.net/node/562?page=4 (last accessed November 9, 2016). There is no shame in a literary author offering a "translation" based on a literal rendering by a Greek scholar—recent successes include David Grieg, whose *Bacchae* for the National Theatre of Scotland (2008) was no less acclaimed for his frank admission that he worked from a literal translation by the Glasgow classicist Ian Ruffell. Accordingly, one could wish that Rexroth had been honest about his process and not tried to brazen it out.

SULPICIUS LUPERCUS SERVASIUS JR.
(Rexroth 1962, 108)

Servasius is a poet of the fifth century, par for the course given the translator's long-established penchant for trawling Late Antique Latin authors for hints of decline. Rexroth probably came across him in the *Oxford Book of Latin Verse*, where this poem is given the very apt heading, "The Work of Time." Its themes are alluringly antiestablishment, at least by the time Rexroth is through with them; Servasius gives us three four-line stanzas of which Rexroth attempts only the second half, so we join the poem one-and-a-half stanzas in. The original is much more clearly a priamel, a persuasive list of examples illustrating the theme proposed at its outset, which is universal entropy:

Omne quod Natura parens creauit,
quamlibet firmum uideas, labascit . . .

Everything that mother Nature has brought into being,
however permanent it might look to you, is falling apart.

In other words, this did not begin as a poem about the crumbling of "authority" at all; only through selection and omission does it become in *Poems* the classical-or-thereabouts prototype of Dylan's "the times, they are a changing." The effect is smartly achieved.

Next up is Thymocles, perhaps the most obscure of the poets of the Garland of Meleager; this epigram on the fleeting nature of youth and beauty (AP 12.32), translated faithfully by Rexroth, is his only extant poem.[29] Tymnes follows, another Garland poet with rather more of an Anthology presence—seven epigrams in all, four of them funerary. This one is a beautiful and haunting version of AP 7.211, one of two epitaphs for animals that are preserved under his name among the Anthology's literary epitaphs:

Eumelos had a Maltese dog.
He called him Bull. He was the most
Loyal dog that ever lived.
His bark comes faintly up from Hell,
Lost on the night-bound roads.

TYMNES
(Rexroth 1962, 109)

29. Rexroth 1962, 109.

Last of all comes Zonas, a poet of the Garland of Philip (first century CE) of whom nine epigrams survive in various styles; this is his only extant sympotic poem and combines the themes of wine and death. Combined with a repetition ("earth") that is not there in the original, the double sense Rexroth draws out of "bore" (gave birth) and "bear" (carry) helps his version pack more punch than its rather conventional source text, AP 11.43:

Pass me the sweet earthenware jug,
Made of the earth that bore me,
The earth that someday I shall bear.

ZONAS
(Rexroth 1962, 111)

Since Rexroth includes no end matter, this is his Anthology's literal last word, and he has chosen to go out with a poem from the twelfth and final chapter of *Select Epigrams* (12.13 in Mackail's scheme): "Give me the sweet cup wrought of the earth from which I was born, and under which I shall lie dead." The Greek that Mackail translates as "cup," κύπελλον, is specifically a "big-bellied drinking-vessel, beaker, goblet" in the standard Greek lexicon of Liddell and Scott, at home in scenes of Homeric feasting; later is it used of receptacles for milk; perhaps on this occasion, Rexroth really does "know what the Greek says"?

More likely, I think, he supersizes his drink because a cup is just too respectable and bourgeois for the self-image of the outlaw intellectual. At the 6 Gallery reading of *Howl*, the wine was legendarily slurped straight from gallon jugs, a detail immortalized in the mildly fictionalized and very famous retelling of the evening in Kerouac's *Dharma Bums*. Witnesses recall that Kerouac led the audience response, beating time on an empty wine jug as Ginsberg declaimed:

> Everyone was there. It was a mad night. And I was the one who got things jumping by going around collecting dimes and quarters from the rather stiff audience standing around in the gallery and coming back with three huge gallon jugs of California Burgundy and getting them all piffed so that by eleven o'clock when Alvah Goldbrook was reading his wailing poem "Wail" drunk with arms outspread everybody was yelling "Go! Go! Go!" (like a jam session) and old Rheinhold Cacoethes [Kerouac's cipher for Rexroth] the father of the Frisco poetry scene was wiping tears in gladness.
>
> Meanwhile scores of people stood around in the darkened gallery straining to hear every word of the amazing poetry reading as I wandered from

> group to group, facing them and facing away from the stage, urging them to slug from the jug. . . . "Great, hey Rosie?" I yelled, and she took a big slug from my jug and shined eyes at me. (Kerouac 1958, 13–14)

This is the second jug of wine we have met in *Poems*: the first was the "galloping wine-jug" of Antipater AP 11.23, toward the start of the book. That first jug had no basis in the Greek at all, which merely specified wine. *Où sont les neiges . . .*

The Afterlife of *Poems*

Like Pierre Louys's *Chansons de Bilitis* (1894), Rexroth's confection fooled some of the people, some of the time—especially if they were predisposed to be taken in. Astonishingly, Chester Starr's popular *History of the Ancient World*—first published in 1965, when *Poems* was the latest and funkiest "Greek Anthology" to hand, and now in its fourth edition—is still recommending Rexroth's Anthology *as a translation,* alongside the versions of Dudley Fitts, for students of ancient history keen to get a sense of what ancient epigram was like. Did Starr have no idea that *Poems* was less a "translation" than a creative riff on a part-antique theme? More likely he chose to turn a blind eye; Fitts's versions, after all, explicitly bill themselves as paraphrases. It is probably no coincidence that Starr promotes these two poets as a double act: Fitts's period of creative engagement with the Anthology was spent as a New Directions author.[30] And it is *only* the Greek Anthology, so who cares?

Rexroth's legacy as a translator of Greek epigram is zealously curated by his latter-day acolytes. An essay by the artist and writer Gregory McNamee, "When We with Sappho" (never published in print as far as I can tell, but widely disseminated online), takes at face value the roster of authors in *Poems* as a full and faithful record of the actual Anthology's contents: Martial and Petronius are now members in good standing. This flies rather in the face of the mumbled admissions of Rexroth's own prologue: "Had Rexroth been French or Swedish, he might have been honored by his government with a

30. See Starr 1991, 432. Fitts's postwar efforts, notably (1957), are recycled from his shorter books of 1938 and 1941, both under the same New Directions banner as Rexroth. In Vosper's subject review (1951, 91–92), the early efforts of Rexroth and Fitts on the Anthology are paired stylistically.

medal and a nomination to some closed society of belles-lettristes for having recovered a literary monument."[31]

McNamee buys *Phoenix*'s rhetoric of decline as straight reportage of the intent of the Anthology's Byzantine compiler, or even of its sampled Hellenistic and Late Antique authors ("the Codex Palatinus documents the decline of Greek civilization in the Mediterranean"). His account of the history of the Anthology's publication is entertainingly imaginative—did you know the Greek text was only first published in 1911? "It befits his wide-ranging intellectual curiosity that Kenneth Rexroth somehow found the modern European edition, long before the Loeb Classical Library saw to it that an American edition was made available": not only his curiosity, but his unique ability to bend time.[32]

The reviewer of the 1999 reissue of *Poems* for the *Bryn Mawr Classical Review*, meanwhile—Otto Steinmayer, a classicist with sidelines in English Literature and comparative studies—was going all out to channel Rexroth in his prime:

> Kenneth Rexroth's *Poems from the Greek Anthology* has been by me nearly twenty years, and I welcome the reissue. In my role of Common Reader, I take the sincerest pleasure in Rexroth's poetry. I go back to his translations and his own poems time and time again, and have some of them by heart. As scholar, after long acquaintance, I have found no flaw in his handling of Greek; rather the opposite.
>
> When poems work, when words become charmed, it is easy to overpraise them, and to review them in the usual sense is to risk the hybris of tampering with the Muse.[33]

Steinmayer, too, believes or affects to believe in Martial as a Greek poet. Rexroth's loose ways with his sources are excused as "you're not reading it right":

> Yet for all that, Rexroth was a poet of ripe modernism (he midwifed the Beat movement), he followed the tradition of the greatest English translators from

---

31. For example, at http://www.gregorymcnamee.com/articles_and_other_writing/when_we_with_sappho_essay.pdf (last accessed November 9, 2016).

32. W. R. Paton's facing-text translation of the Anthology for the Loeb Classical Library appeared in five volumes between 1916 (not 1911) and 1918, when Rexroth was still a child. European publications of the text did indeed precede it, beginning in 1494 and becoming comprehensive and accessible with Friedrich Jacobs's edition for the Tauchnitz series in 1813–17.

33. http://bmcr.brynmawr.edu/2000/2000-11-06.html, as in my note 2.

> the classics. Like theirs, his ideal reader knew Greek, and Rexroth always invites us knowingly to study the play of original and translation.

(Never mind that, in the edition published in his lifetime, Rexroth gave his readers no clue as to where in the Anthology's 4,000-odd poems—if at all—any given "original" might be found.)

Where now for *Poems?* Michigan's commitment to the Ann Arbor Paperbacks will surely keep it in print long into the future, and thanks to the advocacy of its core fandom it may well continue to hoodwink the unwary into thinking it has much of anything to do with a curious Byzantine compilation called the Greek Anthology; it's a book that inspires peculiar passion.[34] Besides, Rexroth's versions are direct and forceful; his distinctive poetic voice is ageing well, and when he chooses or happens to be approximately faithful (hard to say which on any occasion; even a stopped clock tells the right time twice a day), he is still worth quoting even by classicists.[35] As poet and bullshitter alike, Rexroth's considerable talent deserves some posterity, and there is every chance that this elegant semi-imposture will be his most lasting monument.

Bibliography

Collecott, Diana. 2000. "'This pother about the Greeks'": Hellenism and Anti-Hellenism in 1914." In *Ezra Pound and Poetic Influence: The Official Proceedings of the 17th International Ezra Pound Conference Held at Castle Brunnenburg, Tirolo Di Merano*, edited by Helen May Dennis, 55–69. Amsterdam: Rodopi.

Cyrino, Monica. 2010. *Aphrodite*. New York: Routledge.

Donoghue, Denis. 1988. *Reading America: Essays on American Literature*. Berkeley: University of California Press.

Fitts, Dudley. 1938. *One Hundred Poems from the Palatine Anthology in English Paraphrase*. Norfolk, CT: New Directions.

———. 1941. *More Poems from the Palatine Anthology in English Paraphrase*. Norfolk, CT: New Directions.

---

34. Not many academic reviewers would go on, as Steinmayer did, to post a five-star review on Amazon: "Worthy to stand with Ben Jonson—Kenneth Rexroth is the best translator of the Greek Anthology since the Renaissance." Rexroth's groupies can be quite intense; see the essays and other resources amassed at the fan site, http://www.bopsecrets.org/rexroth/ (last accessed November 9, 2016).

35. For example, Cyrino raids Rexroth for AP 6.210 on Aphrodite (2010, 66), and why not? Peter Jay included many versions from *Poems* in his selection for the Penguin Classics (1973), sadly long out of print. Michael Wolfe, versioner of a recent (2012) selection from AP 7, credits *Poems* as the wellspring of his interest in epigram in the publisher's blog, http://jhupressblog.com/2013/01/page/2/ (last accessed November 9, 2016).

———. 1957. *From the Greek Anthology: Poems in English Paraphrase.* London: Faber and Faber.

Fussell, Paul. 1975. *The Great War and Modern Memory.* New York: Oxford University Press.

Gregory, Eileen. 2011. "H.D. and Translation." In *The Cambridge Companion to H.D.*, edited by Nephie J. Christodoulides and Polina Mackay, 143–57. Cambridge: Cambridge University Press.

Hutton, James. 1935. *The Greek Anthology in Italy to the Year 1800.* Ithaca, NY: Cornell University Press.

———. 1946. *The Greek Anthology in France and in the Latin Writers of the Netherlands to the Year 1800.* Ithaca, NY: Cornell University Press.

Jay, Peter, ed. 1973. *Poems from the Greek Anthology.* Harmondsworth, UK: Penguin.

Kerouac, Jack. 1958. *The Dharma Bums.* London: Andre Deutsch.

Kolocotroni, Vassiliki. 2005. "'This curious silent unrepresented life': Greek Lessons in Virginia Woolf's Early Fiction." *Modern Language Review* 100: 313–22.

Laughlin, James. 2006. *The Way It Wasn't: From the Files of James Laughlin.* New York: New Directions.

Leslie, Shane. 1929. *The Greek Anthology: Selected and Translated with a Prolegomenon.* London: Ernest Benn.

Livingstone, Niall, and Nisbet, Gideon. 2010. *Epigram.* Cambridge: Cambridge University Press.

Lothian, Alexander. 1920. *The Golden Treasury of the Greeks.* Oxford: Basil Blackwell.

Mackail, John William. 1890. *Select Epigrams from the Greek Anthology.* London: Longmans, Green Co.

Neaves, (Lord) Charles. 1874. *The Greek Anthology.* Edinburgh, UK: William Blackwood and Sons.

Nisbet, Gideon. 2003. *Greek Epigram in the Roman Empire: Martial's Forgotten Rivals.* Oxford: Oxford University Press.

———. 2013. *Greek Epigram In Reception: J. A. Symonds, Oscar Wilde, and the Invention of Desire, 1805–1929.* Oxford: Oxford University Press.

Parker, Douglass. 1962. Review of Rexroth 1962, *Classical World* 56: 43.

Pratt, William. 2008. *The Imagist Poem: Modern Poetry in Miniature.* New Orleans: University of New Orleans Press.

Rexroth, Kenneth. 1944. *The Phoenix and the Tortoise.* Norfolk, CT: New Directions.

———. 1951. *Beyond the Mountains.* New York: New Directions.

———. 1961. *Assays.* New York: New Directions.

———. 1962. *Poems from the Greek Anthology: Translated by Kenneth Rexroth.* Ann Arbor: University of Michigan Press.

———. 1986. *Classics Revisited.* New York: New Directions.

———. 1987. *World Outside the Window: The Selected Essays of Kenneth Rexroth.* Ed. Bradford Morrow. New York: New Directions.

Rice, Wallace. 1927. *Pagan Pictures. Freely Translated and Fully Expanded from the Anthology and the Greek Lyrical Poets, Variously Augmented by Modern Instances.* Chicago: Boni and Liveright.

Starr, Chester G. 1991. *A History of the Ancient World: Fourth Edition.* New York: Oxford University Press.

Symonds, John Addington. 1920. *Studies of the Greek Poets. Third Edition.* London: A. and C. Black.

Vandiver, Elizabeth. 2010. *Stand in the Trench, Achilles: Classical Receptions in the British Poetry of the Great War.* Oxford: Oxford University Press.

Vosper, Robert. 1951. "The Greek Anthology in English." *Classical Journal* 47: 87–92.

Wolfe, Michael. 2012. *Cut These Words Into my Stone: Ancient Greek Epitaphs.* Baltimore: Johns Hopkins University Press.

Woolf, Virginia. 1975. *The Letters of Virginia Woolf, 1888–1912. Volume 1: The Life of the Mind.* Ed. Nigel Nicolson and Joanne Trautmann. London: Hogarth Press.

———. 1987. *The Essays of Virginia Woolf, Volume 2: 1914–1918.* Ed. Andrew McNeillie. London: Hogarth Press.

CHAPTER 10

Philip Whalen and the Classics

"A WALKING GROVE OF TREES"

JANE FALK

In a 1964 panel discussion with fellow poets Gary Snyder and Lew Welch, subsequently published as *On Bread and Poetry,* Philip Whalen characterizes himself as a "poet like Homer was a poet, or like Ben Jonson," then compares himself to Callimachus (Snyder, Welch, and Whalen 1977, 18). Whalen's poetic affinities here reflect his historical and cultural milieu in the United States of the mid-twentieth century and his general interest in and knowledge of classical culture. Whalen, associated with the San Francisco Renaissance, is known primarily as a Beat generation poet.[1] A participant in the 6 Gallery reading in San Francisco in 1955, he joined East and West Coast poets to create an originary moment for a bicoastal Beat Movement, with Kenneth Rexroth presiding as master of ceremonies. As one of the Beat avant-garde who called into question Western values after World War II, he looked instead to Eastern philosophies and religion, especially Zen Buddhism. However, through his poetic influences and poetry, he demonstrates an extensive knowledge and firm grounding in Western literary and philosophical traditions, including classical Greek and Latin authors. This essay will view Whalen's relation to the classics through his historical context and in conversation with his poetic predecessors as well as contemporaries, his attitude being at times superficial, at times knowledgeable, and ultimately critical. Under the influence of Bud-

1. Donald Allen in his *New American Poetry* anthology (1960) categorized Whalen along with Gary Snyder and Michael McClure as having no geographical location in contrast to Beat, San Francisco Renaissance, or New York School writers.

dhism, he would eventually come to the conclusion that there had to be a synthesis or melding of Western and Eastern cultures.

Born in 1923, Whalen came from a working-class background. He was raised in The Dalles, a small town in Oregon on the banks of the Columbia, upriver from Portland, served in the army Air Corps during World War II, then attended Reed College on the GI Bill from 1946 to 1951. At Reed, a selective liberal arts college in Portland where he met fellow poets Gary Snyder and Lew Welch, he studied the humanities, concentrating in creative writing and literature.[2] Students were required to take Humanities 11 and 12 during their freshman year, from which they would have gotten a solid grounding in the classics as the fall semester was devoted primarily to Greek and Latin texts, the time frame of the class extending from Egypt to the Byzantine Empire. Humanities 11 used Michael Rostovtzeff's 1930 two-volume *A History of the Ancient World,* along with selections from the *Odyssey,* Thucydides, Aristotle, Herodotus, Aeschylus, Pericles, Plutarch, Sophocles, Euripides, Aristophanes, Demosthenes, Isocrates, Plato, Theophrastus, Plautus, Terence, Polybius, Lucretius, Cicero, Virgil, Horace, Juvenal, Lucian, and Marcus Aurelius, as well as Gibbon's *Decline and Fall of the Roman Empire.*[3]

Despite this background, Whalen was similar to those classics enthusiasts called out by W. H. Auden in his introduction to *The Portable Greek Reader,* a volume possibly familiar to Whalen.[4] Auden claims that the classics are an endangered species: "The days when classical studies were the core of higher learning have now passed and are not likely in any future we can envisage, to return. The educated man of today and tomorrow can read neither Latin nor Greek" (Auden 1948, 3). Whalen appears to be one of those "educated men" with a superficial knowledge of the classics because in his 1956 poem, "The Slop Barrel: Slices of the Paideuma for All Sentient Beings," the poem's speaker states, "Now let's regret things for a while / That you can't read music / That I never learned Classical languages" (2007, 90–92).

However, Whalen's numerous allusions to classical literature and myth, along with his use of Greek and Latin phrases, indicate his wide reading in the classics and his overall knowledge, expanded on from his freshman-year coursework. In "Since You Ask Me," the press release for a poetry tour he

---

2. For further biographical information, see Falk's (2007) Philip Whalen entry in *Encyclopedia of Beat Literature.*

3. Note that most of these readings were excerpts rather than complete texts. References to the 1946 Reed College Humanities 11A/12A syllabus are courtesy of Special Collections, Eric V. Hauser Memorial Library, Reed College, Portland, Oregon.

4. Whalen may have seen this book in Charles Olson's library when he visited Olson on an East Coast poetry reading tour with Michael McClure in 1959. See Maud 1996, 292.

made in 1959, and included as a prose poem in his 1960 volume, *Memoirs of an Interglacial Age,* he likens himself to Dr. Samuel Johnson in taking on the title of doctor or teacher, one who is "constantly studying." He adds, "I do not put down the academy but have assumed its function in my own person, and in the strictest sense of the word—*academy*: a walking grove of trees" (Whalen 2007, 8–10). This seems a somewhat oblique reference, but for those familiar with Greek classics, recalls the olive grove owned by Academus, reputed to be the site of Plato's Academy.[5] In this brief description of his poetic and pedagogic mission, Whalen indicates his interest in not only the British neoclassical tradition (Samuel Johnson), but the classical itself, as well as demonstrating the essentially didactic nature of his poetry. In this regard, in an interview of 1992 with Anne Waldman and Andrew Schelling, he notes that his work is "supposed to encourage you to learn things. . . . If nowhere else then just in what I'd written, to see what I was talking about . . . where Samuel Johnson said this or that, or Democritus, or Shakespeare" (Whalen 1994, 230–31).[6] In Whalen's letter of June 28, 1958, to fellow poet Charles Olson, he compares himself to Michael McClure ("a poet in the sense that Robert Graves means poet") stating, "Hell, I am a didactic poet. A pedant, a prig. In other words some sort of anti-poet." He goes on to classify himself among "Silver Age types. As I said before pedantical, priggish . . . commentators, like Lucian, Martial, Dante" (Whalen 1958, 1).[7] Here Whalen's self-identification with writers like Lucian or Martial indicates his privileging of the witty, satirical, and humorous over the lyrical and an interest in history and social commentary in the role of critic and teacher.

Part of his pedagogical duty, as he must have realized from his knowledge of Ezra Pound's various guides such as *Culture* (1938) or *ABC of Reading* (1934) (texts he mentioned reading at Reed in his 1971 interview with Anne Waldman [Whalen 1978, 28]), was to provide reading lists and scholarly advice. In a letter of 1968 to fellow poet and friend, Joanne Kyger, Whalen provides a reading list, noting that "a writer reads a lot," then proceeds to recommend a number of Greek texts, among them Homer, Hesiod, Greek lyric poetry, Pindar, Aeschylus, and Aristophanes, as well as Plato, Herodotus, Sophocles, and Plutarch. He includes Latin texts also, adding that "those English writers we must read all take it for granted that we know writers such as Virgil, Horace, Plau-

5. Rostovtzeff alludes to the *Academeia* as a grove consecrated to Academus in the first volume of his history (1930, 338).

6. Note Democritus's association with the Presocratic philosophers featured in Whalen's poem, "Sourdough Mountain Lookout."

7. Robert von Hallberg's use of the term "poet pedagogue" in regard to Charles Olson may be applicable to Philip Whalen here (von Hallberg 1978).

tus, Terence, Cicero, Ovid, and Martial" (Whalen 1968, 1–2). He mentions Liddell and Scott's *Greek Lexicon,* which he calls "an invaluable accompaniment" to the Loeb Classical Library, noted as "bilingual." This list demonstrates not only his familiarity with the classics but also his belief in the value he and any poet in the English and American literary tradition, should place on them.[8]

Moving from a consideration of Whalen's role as teacher to that of poet, numerous classical allusions in his poetry range from what one might call the ridiculous to the sublime. Whalen's most superficial, though humorous, use involves punning and word play, often in shorter poems. This could be considered as elitist name-dropping, but is often a clever and concise way to express his ideas. One of the more effective allusions of this type, in a later poem that shows that classical name-dropping never really left Whalen's poetic tool kit, comes in "Treading More Water," written in 1978 after Whalen had begun Zen practice under Richard Baker Roshi at the San Francisco Zen Center. The poem may be about a meditation session as it begins, "It is very hard to understand that / We are where we are at; I am here intentionally" (Whalen 2007, 1–2). The speaker's stream of consciousness continues, as he begins the third stanza, "Start again. Direct the imagination" (13), which implies control of the wandering mind. The poem concludes: "Seven minutes from now. You hear the words, 'Caught between Sybil and Charisma' / I am grown invisible and very wise" (21–23). Here the timing may relate to a period of sitting meditation coming to an end, while recalling Odysseus's journey and his escape from the Sirens with passage between Scylla and Charybdis. Thus Whalen presents the poem's speaker as caught between two ways of being viewed by others: Sybil or charismatic poet. These lines also convey the feeling that the speaker is caught between a rock and a hard place, spiritually treading water as the poem's title suggests.

In other poems, Whalen simply incorporates Greek or Latin expressions or stock phrases, one of the most frequently used being the Latin expression, *desunt cetera/ae,* meaning "the rest is missing." This phrase sometimes appears at the end of poems that seem unfinished, the phrase suggesting that something has been left out. This is despite the fact that he has reversed the usual order of this phrase (*cetera desunt*). For example, "Translation of a Lost Play by M. M." (1958), a possible reference to a play by Michael McClure, is a short dialogue between Maurice and Ferdinand about baby Moses. On hearing a baby crying, Maurice asks who and why, with Ferdinand's answer: "He weeps there for that he is already a prophet" (Whalen 2007, 11), followed by

8. Later, in his 1971 interview with Anne Waldman, Whalen refuted this kind of list-giving advice, noting that people have to find out for themselves (Whalen 1978, 28).

Maurice's "Ah, glorious wretched little! / *desunt ceterae*" (12–13). With this somewhat abrupt ending, is Whalen likening himself to a prophet to whom no attention is paid?

Some of these stock phrases occur as titles to poems, a hint at how the poem should be read. For example, Whalen uses "Poeta Nascitur," as title of a 1984 poem with reference to the aphorism, *poeta nascitur non fit,* meaning a poet is born not made. Although the poem does not directly address this issue, Whalen may be questioning his role as poet. A more nuanced use is the title of the short poem, "Gradus ad Parnassum" (1963), recalling the Latin title of a dictionary of prosody, which means "a step to Parnassus." The four-line poem appears to be a simple, literal description of an urban scene:

Palmetto tree, its shadow on the house corner
And the light upon them:
A single proposition.
(Where was the sky?)
(Whalen 2007, 1–4)

Whalen may have recalled the Latin phrase as he walked up Parnassus Street in San Francisco, a steep street in the Upper Haight. This movement upward may in turn have recalled the guidebook, what it takes to write a poem, and his gradual progress therein. The poem then becomes more than a simple description of light, tree, and shadow (what can be seen); it demonstrates what a poem can be made of. In addition, the poem may also pay homage to Ezra Pound and his *ABC of Reading,* prefaced by this explication of its title as frontispiece: "ABC or gradus ad Parnassum, for those who might like to learn. The book is not addressed to those who have arrived at full knowledge of the subject without knowing the facts" (Pound 1934, 9).[9]

Whalen also uses classical myths or personae in a more substantive way to comment on contemporary situations. For example, "To My Muse" is a short poem in which the poet/speaker is represented by Tithonus with his muse, Eos, goddess of Dawn:

9. Another of Whalen's poems with classical reference is "'Past Ruin'd Ilion,'" its title quoting and appropriating a line, "Past ruin'd Ilion Helen lives," (1), from W. S. Landor's "To Ianthe" (1964). Whalen, however, in contrast to Landor, launches into a stream of consciousness ramble about his contemporaries, not at all about Helen, Troy, or a lovely woman. Interestingly, Whalen may have found Landor's poem in Pound's *ABC of Reading*. Note that Pound, himself, echoed this line in his Canto IX, changing it to "Past ruin'd Latium," with reference to Isotta, love of Sigismundo Malatesta. Thus Whalen demonstrates the continued importance of the classics to the English literary tradition in the lineage of Ezra Pound, while similarly rewriting Landor.

Now I see my part in the story:
Tithonus, immortal & wrinkling
greying and fading, voice
from a big pot,
A seashell echo, prophesying

and you pink sunrise, Eos, ever young
opening
(Whalen 2007, 1–7)

Eos had a child, Memnon, by Tithonus, a mortal whom she had begged Zeus to make immortal. Since she forgot to also ask for eternal youth, he became old, while she, immortal, remained young. The retelling of this myth suggests not only the speaker's troubled relationship with the muse and doubts about his poetic ability but also a love relationship with someone he considered as muse.[10] Such short poems have an epigrammatic quality about them, perhaps one reason he associates himself with Callimachus and Martial.

A more literal and explicit type of classical allusion appears in homage poems, dedicated to figures Whalen admires in the world of classical studies, such as, "Spring Poem to the Memory of Jane Ellen Harrison (1850–1928)"; Edward Gibbon, "Life in the City, in Memoriam Edward Gibbon"; "For Kenneth Rexroth," a poem inspired by reading Rexroth's translations of the *Greek Anthology*; and "M" for Robert Duncan. This last poem highlights the letter *M* or *mu,* referring to Duncan's interest in alphabets of various languages as evident in his *Passages* series, especially the poem "Spelling." "M" also relates to Duncan's interest in *muthos* (myth), a term he found in Jane Ellen Harrison's work, which is evident in his long essay "The Truth and Life of Myth," with an epigraph from Harrison's *Themis*: "Possibly the first *muthos* was simply the interjectional utterance *mu*; but it is easy to see how rapid the development would be from interjection to narrative" (Duncan 1985, 1).[11]

In this poem, Whalen's references in relation to the letter *M* are somewhat esoteric as is typical of his poetic method: Kabala, Roman numerals (line 12 reads "In Rome M = 1000"), and Egyptian, Phoenician, and Greek alphabets: "μ *mu* in Greek / Aeschylus makes the Eumenides / cry 'μ μ μ μ'" (Whalen 2007, 8–10). This last line echoes the chorus's lines from Aeschylus's *Eumenides*

10. For a similar conflation of muse and lover, see Whalen's 1964 poem, "To the Muse."

11. Duncan read the *Passages* series at the Berkeley Poetry Conference, July 1965. "Spelling" was also published in the eighth number of *Open Space,* August 1964, a journal to which Whalen contributed. "M" also relates to Charles Olson's interest in *muthos* as evidenced by his using the same quote from Harrison in *The Special View of History.*

translated by George Thompson in the Auden *Portable Greek Reader*: "Chorus: Mu, mu! Clytemnestra: Ah, you may mew, but he is fled and gone; For he has friends far different from mine. Chorus: Mu, mu!" (Auden 1948, 343).

The classics were perhaps most significant for Whalen, however, as one aspect of his New Paideuma, a term first mentioned in his 1956 poem "The Slop Barrel: Slices of the Paideuma for All Sentient Beings." Here he references Pound's use of the term in *Culture*, a text with which Whalen was familiar. Pound goes to Frobenius for this term (probably a neologism derived from the Greek *paideia*), explicated as "the tangle or complex of the inrooted ideas of any period" (Pound 1938, 57). For Pound, this "New Learning . . . can imply whatever men of my generation can offer our successors as means to the new comprehension" (58). Whalen will make this term relevant to his own time, as evidenced in a letter to Gary Snyder of June 10, 1957, in which he complains about "kritics" misrepresentation of the Beat generation, adding that "the trouble is none of us has published anything like a manifesto" and concludes that whatever any of them may write "could present Slices of the New Paideuma" (Whalen 1957, 1).

Whalen's 1956 poem is about growing up and gaining knowledge, as well as about ways to write poetry using a new vocabulary, specifically one that juxtaposes several layers of language: American speech and slang ("Native Speech," as he titles several 1963 poems); Western (often classical); and Eastern (often Buddhist) terms and concepts. Thus three levels or kinds of language are combined in this title representing that triumvirate of colloquialism (slop barrel), Greek term, (*paideuma*), and Buddhist phrase (sentient beings). Whalen's title is thus typical of his method in this and other poems, introducing readers to new possibilities for poetry.[12] He will continue to use such juxtapositions as representative of his New Paideuma project in subsequent poems.[13]

An early poem exemplifying Whalen's method is the 1958 poem, "Hymnus ad Patrem Sinensis," which uses a Latin title to pay homage to classical Chinese hermit poets. Whalen also includes contemporary slang in the penultimate line in spondaic meter describing the poets: "& conked out among the busted spring rain cherry blossom wine jars / Happy to have saved us all"

12. Compare Pound's juxtaposition of languages in *The Cantos* as precedent for Whalen here.

13. Another possible influence here may be Kenneth Rexroth for the idea of combining Greek/Latin classics and Asian religion and culture as he does in his collections, *More Classics* and *More Classics Revisited*. For Rexroth's importance to Whalen, see Whalen's interview with Anne Waldman: "Rexroth, who is really one of the brightest and liveliest persons that I have known, and he's been of immense help to me getting things published and getting people to invite me to read, material and spiritual help of all kinds" (Whalen 1978, 29).

(Whalen 2007, 12–13). To some, this title may seem pretentious, but as part of Whalen's new Paideuma project, an effective demonstration of his method.[14]

"Sourdough Mountain Lookout," one of Whalen's best-known poems, exemplifies his assertion of a relationship between Western and Eastern philosophy. Here he juxtaposes quotations from the Presocratics and the Buddha to make direct and literal connections with the speaker's situation in the poem. The poem recounts a summer spent as a fire lookout, and the speaker's meditations on life as he observes the mountains, rivers, planets, and stars, the view from a ridge "encircled by chiming mountains" (Whalen 2007, 10). He quotes Heraclitus as he drowses in the sun, remembering his dreams: "'The waking have one common world / But the sleeping turn aside / Each into a world of his own'" (32–34).[15] Thoughts of what it is to be a man, "That there is more to a man / Than the contents of his jock-strap," (56–57) lead to a quotation from Empedocles:

> At one time all the limbs
> Which are the body's portion are brought together
> By Love in blooming life's high season; at another
> Severed by cruel Strife, they wander each alone
> By the breakers of life's sea.
> (58–62)

Later as his "sweat runs down the rock," (69), Heraclitus again comes to mind:

> The transformations of fire
> are, first of all sea; and half of the sea
> is earth, half whirlwind. . . .
> It scatters and it gathers; it advances
> and retires.
> (70–74)

He then quotes the Buddha on the transitory nature of life, which could relate either to Heraclitus on the flux and change of the world or Empedocles's Strife against Love. Whalen ends the poem with his departure from the lookout

---

14. Michael Davidson reads this poem differently, stating that Whalen's "ponderous Latin title is gradually debunked as his hymn of praise illustrates the endurance of the absolutely temporary" (1989, 118).

15. Whalen provides as a source for these quotes John Burnet's *Early Greek Philosophy* (1957).

at the end of the season and his slangified translation of the Prajnaparamita Sutra's conclusion:

Gone
Gone
REALLY gone
Into the cool
O MAMA!
(167–71)[16]

In a less well-known poem, "With Compliments to E. H." (1959), Whalen uses a similar approach. The poem appears to be about Zen and archery, the E. H. of the title referring to Eugen Herrigel and his book, *Zen and the Art of Archery*, a popular book on Zen in the 1950s, but is actually about the process of writing a poem. The classical reference is again to Heraclitus, archery recalling fragments 45 and 66, which Whalen adds as addenda to the poem:

> (45) Men do not know how what is at variance agrees with itself. It is an attunement of opposite tensions, like that of the bow and the lyre.
>
> (66) The bow . . . is called life . . . , but its work is death.
> (Whalen 2007, 94–97)[17]

Here Heraclitus's "attunement of opposite tensions" can apply to those inherent in the poem or the process of poetry, itself. Whalen also compares hitting the target to the making of verbal distinctions in poetry, the Zen approach being not so much to hit the target as to gain the correct attitude toward the process. As he juxtaposes West and East in the poem, he demonstrates that the poet can gain from both worlds, another way opposites are attuned.

It is in the long poem format, however, that Whalen's New Paideuma project becomes most evident. His long poems often originate in his journals and notebooks; he selects passages, types them into a draft, then collages the pages, "cutting" and "rearranging," as he puts it in his interview with Anne Waldman, often over a period of time. He adds that "any of the longer poems which took a year or so or more to write, have rewritings in them and cut-

16. This sutra is one of the key texts of Zen Buddhism. Note here Whalen's combination of Presocratic and Buddhist philosophy and his affinity with A. N. Whitehead's process philosophy, which privileges process over substance.

17. Interestingly, Octavio Paz makes reference to these same passages in *The Bow and the Lyre*. Whalen's source for these quotes is also given as Burnet (1957).

tings and are all worked out. The original material from which it's written is spontaneous writing. . . ." (Whalen 1978, 37). In many instances, his journal entries transform into poems, as in his *Scenes of Life at the Capital.* His poems often include quotes from his wide reading, which serve as meaningful commentary on the ideas he tries to express and a way to add other voices to the conversation of the poem.[18]

A long, collaged poem with multiple quotations, including some from classical authors, is "The Education Continues Along," dedicated to Clark Coolidge and written over the period of a year from 1965–66. This rambling poem about education and questions of epistemology reflects Whalen's thoughts about poetry, music, history, and science with specific allusion to a question from Coolidge regarding the Tesla coil, Tesla's invention of a "machine that could extract electric voltage out of the very ground on which he stood" (Whalen 2007, 121–22). A report on Whalen's research on Tesla is followed by "assertions about history" (228) in which the poet refers to an extended passage from Denys Page's *History and the Homeric Iliad* to supplement his own ideas.

Page's argument concerns the historical validity of the *Iliad* and specifically the historical record, who makes it, its reliability, and its truth value. Whalen has directed readers to a chapter in which Page discusses tablets from Pylos and Knossos and what can be learned of Mycenaean society from these documents, the point being that facts without context are not particularly useful. Page notes the "theoretical" nature of a reconstruction based on analogies between societies that "might be true, or it might be false." He adds that "the whole system is an hypothesis, a pattern not revealed by the Tablets but impressed upon them from outside" (Page 1959, 184). Whalen's use of Page adds to the nuanced view of history presented in this poem.

In the poem's conclusion, Whalen meditates further on history, using his New Paideuma approach with quotes from the colloquial, the classical, and the modern. He juxtaposes memories of his grandmother's sayings, "'None of it came to nothing in the end / None of it amounted to a hill of beans' / That's what my grandmother used to say," with fragment 173 of Alcaeus, a drinking song quoted in Greek and with translation: "And nothing will / come of anything." Whalen then quotes Gertrude Stein: "Let me recite what history teaches. History teaches" (Whalen 2007, 273–80). In these juxtaposed quotes, his grandmother's as important as Alcaeus's, Whalen demonstrates history as

18. Whalen's use of quotes and allusions resembles that of Lucian. In a letter to Snyder written on March 31, 1962, he mentions reading the new Penguin edition of Lucian's dialogues and satires.

record and process and points again to the difficulty of determining historical truth, even though humans continue to record their own versions.

Although Whalen's use of the classics in his poetry is ubiquitous and often provides a positive complement to his twentieth-century worldview, especially through his interest in the Presocratics, he is sometimes critical of this heritage. Such a position is in keeping with the penchant (shared by other Beats) to critique Western culture after World War II with memories of recent examples of barbarity: the atomic bomb at Hiroshima or the Nazi concentration camps of Auschwitz. An important influence on Whalen, especially in regard to the direction in which he moved away from classical Greek philosophy, was the work of poet Charles Olson.

When Whalen graduated from Reed, he moved to California, eventually making the San Francisco Bay area his home. Here he may have first encountered Olson at a series of lectures based on Olson's *The Special View of History* given at the San Francisco Poetry Center in 1957.[19] The epigraph for this work comes from Heraclitus: "Man is estranged from that with which he is most familiar," Olson's argument being that modern man has become estranged from a vital part of himself, as Heraclitus realizes. Olson notes that "man lost something just about 500 BC and only got it back just about 1905 AD," adding, as of the twentieth century, "the absolute or ideal has been tucked back where it belongs—where it got out of in the 5th century BC and thereafter" (Olson 1970, 15–16).[20]

Olson argues further that the problem lies with Plato, Socrates, and Aristotle. In one passage, Olson notes we inherited from Plato "an either-or, from the split of science and fiction," then blames Aristotle for classification which "divided up anything into its parts" (1970, 20). He adds that "an enormous fallacy called discourse invented by Socrates drove science, myth, history, *and* poetry away from the center" (1970, 21). The problem lies in the fact that the "rational mind hates the familiar and has to make it ordinary by explaining it in order not to experience it" (1970, 31). Olson had made his case against the Greeks as early as "Human Universe," an essay first published in 1951–52: "We stay unaware how two means of discourse the Greeks appear to have invented hugely intermit our participation in our experience, and so prevent discovery." He refers here to both "Socrates' readiness to generalize" and Aristotle's "logic

19. Whalen also corresponded with Olson, especially in the late 1950s and early 1960s after the San Francisco lecture series. The lectures were subsequently published in 1970.

20. Jane Ellen Harrison also figures in these talks. Olson is particularly interested in her intent to take the basis of Greek religion back to what might be considered primitive ritualistic practices. Olson notes of Harrison in these lectures, that she as a "modern has stated the mythological with some approximation to the reason of its practice" (1970, 21).

and classification . . . that have so fastened themselves in habits of thought that action is interfered with" (Olson 1967, 4). Plato, too, is implicated for his "world of ideas, of forms as extricable from content" (1967, 5). This division would become problematic in relation to the Beat interest in physicality, through an emphasis on the oral and performative aspects of poetry.

Whalen takes up Olson's critique of the Greek classics in his own poetry, for example, in "The Greeks" (1965). Here the speaker complains about the Greeks' division and fragmentation of the universe as the poem begins:

> divided it three ways
>   Underworld, earth and sea, heavens above
>
>   HADES   POSEIDON   ZEUS
>
>   3 ways
>   body, soul and spirit
> We've been fragmented ever since
> (Whalen 2007, 1–6)

The poem ends with an implicit comparison with the Sumerians who "were smart enough to combine sixes and tens / Their year was exact, their poetry / Who knows if their poetry scanned?" (32–34).[21]

Whalen further points out Greek inadequacies in several other poems. In "The Best of It" (1964), he records mind ramblings and considers various activities while listening to the sounds of the city:

> Read the Greeks, read nudist propaganda with bright colored
> photographs
>   The Greeks are enchanting
> as far as they go but there are many more things
> to know and discuss, more worlds of
> trouble and delight than they had time to know
> (Whalen 2007, 88–93)

Whalen makes a similar point in the long poem, "Minor Moralia," begun in 1959, returned to and completed in 1962, which posits an ideal relation of soci-

21. Whalen may again be echoing Olson. In "The Gate and the Center," another early essay, Olson notes, "We are only just beginning to gauge the backward of literature, breaking through the notion that Greece began it, to the writings farther back: to the Phoenicians . . . and, most powerful of all, the Sumerian poets" (1967, 20).

ety and the individual with instructions for living on a personal as well as social level. Although Whalen does not mention Plutarch in the poem, a case where the reader must make the connection, the title recalls Plutarch's collection of ethical essays *Moralia.* The first part of the poem begins with the quest for knowledge: "Looking at a man trying to decide what he knows" (Whalen 2007, 1), but moves to the need for action: "After you understand it all / How do you behave?" (69–70). Action is more significant as it involves feeding the hungry; an abecedarian logic is not the answer:

> The Greeks went "A, B, C, D, E. . . ."
> They kept slaves and superstitions
> They got cynical and vanished after letter "P"
> (Letter "N" standing for *Nicomachean Ethics).*
> (81–84)

Here as with Plutarch, Plato and Aristotle are not mentioned by name, although Whalen appears to suggest Plato ("P") and Aristotle ("N").[22] In the second part, "THE FINAL PART OF *MINOR MORALIA,* FOUR YEARS LATER, A NEW END A NEW BEGINNING, 27:x:62," Whalen claims that the "real problems of poverty, injustice, war, cruelty and ignorance / MUST BE SOLVED," adding a "(hiatus) . . . WHY THE GREEKS WERE FAILURES" (19–21, 24). In the third and last section, "SECRET ARCANE AND HITHERTO UNPUBLISHED PRIVATE NOTES TO *MINOR MORALIA,*" he presents love as an alternative with reference to Buddhism and its *sangha* or community of monks and lay people that make up the Buddha's followers: "The community, the *sangha,* 'society'—an order to love; we must love more persons places and things with deeper and more various feelings than we know at present" (1–3).

Whalen's most outspoken anti-Greek statement appears in his long poem, *Scenes of Life at the Capital,* written from Japan during the Vietnam War. Whalen's diatribe against Western civilization includes the Greeks with a reference to Plato's *Symposium* on the philosophy of love:

22. Aristotle's text presents the idea that conduct should be directed to the good, and in his introduction to this text, Ostwald notes that, for Aristotle, "the mean which is virtue is not arithmetical. . . . Accordingly, the mean, and with it virtue, is not one fixed point. . . . It is a median which is fixed absolutely only in that it lies between the extremes of excess and deficiency. . . ." (Aristotle 1962, xxiv). Whalen may have been influenced here by Pound's discussion of the *Nicomachean Ethics* in the concluding chapters of *Culture* (1938) where Pound is also critical of Aristotle.

If Socrates and Plato and Diotima
And all the rest of the folks at that party
Had simply eaten lots of food and wine and dope
And spent the entire weekend in bed together
Perhaps Western Civilization
Wouldn't have been such a failure?

Rooty-toot, Plato's Original Institute
(Whalen 2007, 87–93)

In this last line, the slang phrase, *rooty-toot,* rhyming with *institute* furthers the put-down of Plato, the implication being that Plato's ideas are as simplistic as Whalen's rhyme.

Despite these somewhat harsh critiques, and the fact that classical allusions diminish in Whalen's poetry after the late 1960s with his stay in Kyoto and subsequent immersion in Buddhism, Whalen strove to keep alive Western cultural and literary traditions in his poetry, as indicated by such poems as "Treading More Water." His long poems can be seen as documents or texts containing the history of the age, including the Greek and Latin authors he knew so well and recalling Pound's famous definition from *ABC of Reading* regarding the epic as a poem containing history. His initial embrace of the classics was also part of his Reed experience in the mid-twentieth century. Although Whalen's use of classical texts may be considered at times to be superficial, elitist, or appropriative, ultimately his many clever and sophisticated classical allusions and wide ranging knowledge affirm his claim to be a teacher of future generations.

More significantly his use of the classical demonstrates his interest in juxtaposing and combining Western and Eastern philosophical traditions and kinds of language to create his New Paideuma, a project that enables Whalen to think through his responses to important texts and ideas of both West and East. In addition, rather than replacing one tradition with another, Whalen's juxtapositions create a tension and attention to differences and similarities. Whalen discusses his attitude in this regard and what is behind his desire to create a new inclusive Paideuma for the mid-twentieth century in an interview of November 1965, an NET Outtake Series from *USA: Poetry* produced by KQED, San Francisco. In this interview, he considers his poetry as part of a longer historical tradition, what he calls Western civilization. Toward the end of the interview he reiterates his interest in history, specifically mentioning the importance of the Greek classics and his desire to break down barriers between Eastern and Western thinking. The interview ends with Whalen's idea that Western civilization has kinks that need hammering out, and the hammers come from India and China. Whalen and his New Paideuma will be the hammerer.

Bibliography

Allen, Donald., ed. 1960. *The New American Poetry.* New York: Grove Press.

Aristotle. 1962. *Nicomachean Ethics.* Trans. Martin Ostwald. Indianapolis, IN: Bobbs-Merrill.

Auden, W. H., ed. 1948. *The Portable Greek Reader.* New York: Viking Press.

Burnet, John. 1957. *Early Greek Philosophy.* Cleveland, OH: World Publishing Company.

Davidson, Michael. 1989. *The San Francisco Renaissance.* Cambridge: Cambridge University Press.

Duncan, Robert. 1985. "The Truth and Life of Myth." In *Fictive Certainties: Essays by Robert Duncan,* 1–59. New York: New Directions.

Falk, Jane. 2007. "Philip Whalen." In *Encyclopedia of Beat Literature,* edited by Kurt Hemmer, 345–47. New York: Facts on File.

Landor, Walter Savage. 1964. *Poems.* London: Centaur Press.

Maud, Ralph. 1996. *Charles Olson's Reading: A Bibliography.* Carbondale: Southern Illinois University Press.

Olson, Charles. 1967. *Human Universe and Other Essays.* Ed. Donald Allen. New York: Grove Press.

———. 1970. *The Special View of History.* Ed. Ann Charters. Berkeley: Oyez Press.

Page, Denys L. 1959. *History and the Homeric Iliad.* Berkeley: University of California Press.

Pound, Ezra. 1934. *ABC of Reading.* Norfolk, CT: New Directions.

———. 1938. *Culture.* Norfolk, CT: New Directions.

Reed College. 1946. "Syllabus: Humanities 11A and 12A." Special Collections, Eric V. Hauser Memorial Library, Reed College, Portland, Oregon.

Rostovtzeff, Michael. 1930. *A History of the Ancient World.* 2 vols. Trans. J. D. Duff. Oxford: Clarendon Press.

Snyder, Gary, Lew Welch, and Philip Whalen. 1977. *On Bread and Poetry.* Ed. Donald Allen. Bolinas, CA: Grey Fox Press.

Von Hallberg, Robert. 1978. *Charles Olson: The Scholar's Art.* Cambridge, MA: Harvard University Press.

Whalen, Philip. 1957. Letter to Gary Snyder, 10 June 1957. Gary Snyder Papers, D 50, Special Collections, University of California, Davis, and courtesy of the Estate of Philip Whalen.

———. 1958. Letter to Charles Olson, 28 June 1958. Box 219, Charles Olson Research Collection, Archives and Special Collections at the Thomas J. Dodd Research Center, University of Connecticut Libraries and courtesy of the Estate of Philip Whalen.

———. 1962. Letter to Gary Snyder, 31 March 1962. Gary Snyder Papers, D 50, Special Collections, University of California, Davis, and courtesy of the Estate of Philip Whalen.

———. 1965. "Philip Whalen: November 10, 1965." *NET Outtake Series.* Poetry. San Francisco: KQED. 11 Nov. 1965.

———. 1968. Letter to Joanne Kyger, 19 Sept. 1968. (Photocopy) Anne Waldman Papers, University of Michigan Library (Special Collections Library) and courtesy of the Estate of Philip Whalen.

———. 1978. "Tiger Whiskers: Interview with Anne Waldman." In *Off the Wall*, edited by Donald Allen, 5–37. Bolinas, CA: Four Seasons.

———. 1994. "Philip Whalen Zen Interview." In *Disembodied Poetics: Annals of the Jack Kerouac School*, edited by Anne Waldman and Andrew Schelling, 224–37. Albuquerque: University of New Mexico Press.

———. 2007. *The Collected Poems of Philip Whalen*. Ed. Michael Rothenberg. Lebanon, NH: Wesleyan Poetry Series.

CHAPTER 11

Troubling Classical and Buddhist Traditions in Diane di Prima's *Loba*

NANCY M. GRACE
AND TONY TRIGILIO

Introduction: Practices and Lineages

In the syncretic visionary long poem *Loba*, Diane di Prima, the most prominent female writer associated with the Beat literary movement, addresses the underlying principle of her poetics through an epigraph attributed to the depth psychologist Carl Jung: "What myth are you living[?]" (1967, 125). Used to invoke the confluence of revisionary spiritual poetics with a concern for material time and history, the question summons *Loba*'s desire to merge the oppositional impulses of historicity and vision through a recovery and restructuring of mythic materials within the context of her long-standing Buddhist practices. While di Prima draws upon many mythological traditions in *Loba*, Greco-Roman narratives function prominently throughout the poem cycle, and, in fact, conclude it in such a way as to imply the centrality of these stories to her own identity as a female Buddhist poet of the modern age.

Loba features 205 short poems divided into fifteen parts, which are themselves divided between two books, the first published in 1978, the second added in 1998. The author's note to *Loba* identifies the series as a "work in progress" with di Prima "reserve[ing] the right to juggle, re-arrange, and osterize . . . in future editions. As the Loba wishes, as the Goddess dictates." As a long poem, *Loba* functions much like seminal Western epics, such as Homer's *Iliad* and *Odyssey*, as well as their modernist descendants, such as T. S. Eliot's *The Waste Land*, Ezra Pound's *The Cantos*, Charles Olson's *Maxi-*

mus poems, William Carlos Williams's *Paterson*, and H.D.'s *Helen in Egypt.* Pound—a major influence on di Prima's poetics—called the genre a "tale of the tribe" or a story encompassing an entire culture's values and history. This definition aptly suits not only the subject matter of *Loba* but also di Prima's persistent representation of the Beat/Digger/Hippie familia as a tribe, a repudiation of both the post–World War II nuclear family and the nation-state.

The syncretic impulse permeating *Loba* has long centered di Prima as a writer and a woman. Born on August 6, 1934, into an Italian, middle-class family in Brooklyn, she has spent her adult life as an autodidact, reading widely across authors, genres, geographies, and historical periods. To know di Prima—and to better understand the classical/Beat/Buddhist maneuvers in *Loba*—is also to know that she, like many of her Beat compatriots, refuses to suffer separations between her life as an artist and her other lives, including those of mother, wife, teacher, daughter, spiritualist, political activist, and now in her ninth decade, a body dying from Parkinson's disease. Deeply cognizant that all poets are products of syncretic processes, she believes that "the one influenced casts a selective light on the influencer. Creates or re-creates," as she writes in *R. D.'s H.D.*, "the Daemon or Genius or Star under which s/he is working by seeing and highlighting those aspects which speak to her/him. No two poets have ever been 'influenced' by the same Dante, or the same Shakespeare" (di Prima 2011, 1). The poetics of influence, then, works dialectically as poets draw upon those who have come before but also sculpt readers' visions of those very precursors through the artist's aesthetic appropriation of them. Defying the trope that Western art comes from "a broken, an incomplete, tradition" to which we remain blind, di Prima credits Western poets with the practice of recognizing "a precision of lineage" and frequently addressing it in their art/lives (2). The poem as she perceives it "stands at a juncture of planes—of whatever lineages have become manifest at a given point" (3). With respect to *Loba* and di Prima's work in general, this statement means that she adapts particular lineages, such as Greco-Roman mythologies, not as a scholar to explicate or historicize them but rather for the purposes of her own work as an artist.

In this light, several features distinguish *Loba* as a poem of multivalent lineage, one that by its very nature asks us to reenvision the texts and authors about which it coalesces. For instance, John Keats has remained one of di Prima's most consistent muses since she first read his poetry in high school, affirming for her the supremacy of poetry over philosophy and the "holiness of the heart's affections and the truth of the imagination" (di Prima 1978, x). After leaving Swarthmore College, which she briefly attended in the early 1950s, to live and write in New York's Lower East Side, di Prima has gravitated toward an eclectic mix of classical, medieval, and modern texts, among them the poetry of Ezra Pound and Allen Ginsberg. Of particular importance, as she noted in her journal for October 1956, have been Greco-Roman authors including Euclid, Ptolemy, Plato, Aristotle, Aeschylus, and Sophocles. From the first two, she intended to learn mathematics; from the others, language (Special Collections, University of Louisville).

Di Prima has also spoken directly about the way her writing processes grew out of early twentieth-century radical art movements. In a 1989 interview with Tony Moffeit, she explained that "all those European elements that we'd been cut off from during the war, late Surrealism . . . were all there. You'd see [for example] *Blood of a Poet* six times, eight times" (Moffeit 2004, 98). She credits Dadaism, in particular, with promoting her reliance on "nonrandom randomness," realized as "looking at the wall and letting the images arise and following any image only as far as it went, not trying to make sense out of it, not trying to complete the sentence and holding on to whatever next image arose" (99). These processes remain di Prima's primary form of writing, influenced as well by Jack Kerouac's theory of spontaneous composition, John Cage's aesthetics, and Jimmy Waring's choreography (103). Eventually di Prima developed deep interests in Eastern religious and spiritual traditions, leading her to study Zen and Tibetan Buddhism focused on the impermanence and nonduality of all phenomena; when she moved to San Francisco in 1967, she sat Zazen with Shunryu Suzuki (90). To this day, she remains a Buddhist, expanding her interests to include the magical practices of Tantric Buddhism. Di Prima has also had a long-standing interest in the Hermetic tradition of alchemy, which can be traced back to Hermeticism as an ancient spiritual, philosophical, and magical tradition named for the God Hermês Trismegistos (Greek, "Thrice-Greatest Hermes"), a Greco-Egyptian form of the Egyptian god of wisdom and magic, Thoth.

With respect to the project of this essay, while di Prima's earliest works reveal little of the classical materials that dominate *Loba,* her developing attention to collecting fables (*Various Fables from Various Places,* 1960), translating Latin texts (*Seven Poems from the Middle Latin,* 1965), and incorporating characters from classical myths and histories into her surreal/absurdist plays (e.g., King Minos in *Rain Fur,* 1959) presaged her modernist/Beat/Buddhist philosophy, grounding material reality in paradigms of mythic narratives, blending cross-cultural texts and traditions to serve transcendental and physical epistemologies. Of all her works, *Loba* pulsates most vibrantly across these poles.

Like many contemporary long poems, *Loba* requires that readers disentangle multiple voices and personas, multiple streams of consciousness, and a tapestry of allusions. These project fragmented, recursive "consciousness[es]" (to borrow a term from Ezra Pound) into the poem's historical era rather than constructing a singular persona at the center of the poem. In other words, di Prima is not manipulating the language, history, and reception of a particular classical author as Ed Sanders did with Sappho for Lower East Side purposes (see Skerl in this volume); nor is she using the Greco-Roman traditions as a model of aesthetic expression, as Ginsberg did in "Malest Cornifici tuo Catullo" (see Pfaff in this volume); nor is she writing her own anthology of classical texts as did Rexroth (see Nesbit in this volume). Instead, di Prima's vision of multiple historical eras impregnated with heterogeneous consciousnesses expands Western religious, political, and aesthetic traditions with a countercultural sensibility and a characteristically Beat fusion of West and East. In particular, her manipulations of classical narratives serve to restage female identity as subject rather than object through an emphasis on the female body thriving in its outsider relationship to masculinized religious cultures.

More specifically, *Loba*'s seemingly ever-changing names for the Goddess—Native American (e.g., *Loba,* Canyon Lady, Spider-Woman), conventional Christian (e.g., Eve), Gnostic (e.g., Eve, Sophia), Buddhist (e.g., Tara, Prajna), Hindu (e.g., Kali), Middle Eastern (e.g., Ishtar), and Greco/Roman (e.g., Athena, Persephone, Calypso, Aphrodite)—place the poem within the realm of *feminist* revisionist mythmaking. This process, explained by Alicia Ostriker in her seminal essay "Thieves of Language," exposes a woman's need to steal male-centered language in order to create and communicate her own perspectives: "Whenever a poet employs a figure or story previously accepted and defined by a culture," Ostriker states, "the poet is using myth, and the potential is always present that the use will be revisionist: that is, the figure or tale will be appropriated for altered ends . . . ultimately making cultural change possible" (Ostriker 1982, 72). In this project, di Prima joins writers such as Anne Sexton, A. S. Byatt, Adrienne Rich, Angela Carter, and especially H.D.

Feminist literary approaches to revisionist mythmaking differ widely. Some choose to reshape individual narratives or traditions with feminist form and content while keeping the masculinist form intact or at least partially visible—as say Sexton does in *Transformations* or as Joanne Kyger, a Beat-associated writer, does with her long poem *The Tapestry and the Web,* a revision of Homer's *Odyssey.* Others, and *Loba* belongs in this group, use mythic materials to create a bricolage, that is a structure, much like a mosaic, built from a seemingly endless cache of many different fragments that unmask the poem's intertextual construction. While flaunting the essentialism of influence and lineage, di Prima deconstructs and rearranges these materials to such an extent that the emerging artifice seems to erase, at least in part, the discrete historical and patriarchal pedestals upon which many of the formative narratives stand, rendering the poem an ahistorical space suitable for female emancipation.

Revisionist approaches such as these have served women (and other) writers well, but they are also subject to the critique that reliance upon myth leads only to a superficial escape from its ideological constraints, that revisionist mythmaking is at its core a charlatan's trick passing off as new the garb of the old, a "fancy-dress version of tradition" (Deane 1992, xxxix).[1] Understandably, readers in this camp may read *Loba* as transparent cross-dressing, the putting on of others' identities to hide what cannot be hidden and thus a failed effort to effect genuine transformation. However, *Loba*'s mythic materialities align themselves more closely to Judith Butler's concept of the drag queen whose outlier performances lay bare gendered identity as a cultural construction created through behavioral and stylistic repetition, under which no essential identity exists.

In drag parody, *Loba*'s appropriation of Carl Jung's query about myth and the lived experience ironically—and sardonically—promises to disrupt notions of gendered identities reified through myth and to replace them with the equally troubled starting point for thinking through contemporary Buddhism, especially for women, that is, the shared empirical focus of all Buddhisms: the primacy of body, speech, and mind in understanding sacred experience as that which *evades* the essentializing impulse of subject-object distinctions, such as those between self-other, history-vision, and, of vital importance in *Loba*, the distinction between male and female. This journey, one grounded in what we have termed "the Greco-Roman Thread," is, in turn, the basis for a truly feminist experience of the Buddhist path to enlightenment, a novel revisioning of classical (and other) traditions.

The Muse(s)

Like many epic poems, *Loba* opens with an invocation to a muse, which reflects a more broadly incantatory tendency throughout the poem rooted in

1. Cf. Marx's observation in *The Eighteenth Brumaire of Louis Bonaparte*: "The tradition of all the generations of the dead weighs like a nightmare on the brain of the living. And just when they seem involved in revolutionizing themselves and things, in creating something that has never before existed, it is precisely in such periods of revolutionary crisis that *they conjure up the spirits of the past to their service and borrow names, battle cries and costumes from them in order to act out the new scene of world history in this time-honoured disguise and this borrowed language*" (1963, 15, emphasis added).

the realm of magic and reflecting a classical precedent evocative, as critic Dale Smith notes, of female voices, particularly that of "Sappho, who appealed also to Aphrodite with simple, earnest direction" (Smith 2010). That connection, however, is so opaque that unless one seeks it intentionally, it remains invisible, especially since *Loba*'s invocation explicitly undermines the very forms of which Smith speaks. First, the invocation is titled "Ave,"[2] from the hail or hello addressed to the Virgin Mary ("Ave Maria"), a gesture that partially replaces the classical foundation of female mythology with a female-centered version of Christian mythology, rendering the classical Muse a muted, palimpsistic figure. Furthermore, di Prima's invocation is addressed neither explicitly to the Virgin Mary nor implicitly to Calliope, the classical muse of epic poetry, but rather to the speaker's "lost moon sisters," fittingly, Beat figures wandering Bleeker and Fillmore streets, mid-twentieth-century souls relegated to the margins of patriarchal, capitalist culture ([1978] 1998, 3).[3]

Bridging the East (Bleeker) and West (Fillmore) Coasts of the United States, these visionary sisters assume more ancient forms of female materiality, withstanding male dominance and violence through the female ability to give birth, while ecstatically expressing androgynous power through acts of masculine physical prowess. In the mythic night of visionary encounters, the speaker calls out to them, and in the echoes of her voice, they morph into the earth upon which she walks, the skins of the tents they inhabit, and the evening star itself. The speaker comes to realize that her "moon sisters" comprise the very nourishment of her body and the very vehicle of her transcendence. Eventually, they aggregate into the "she" who is herself ("I am always you / I must become you" [di Prima (1978) 1998, 6]). The supplicant's apostrophic "O" announcing the invocation becomes in the poem's conclusion a polyphonic, polycultural chant to an out-of-body source for all that is true as well as all that is false: "om star mother ma om / maya ma ah" combines the primal, mantric sound "om" with "star" and "mother," both symbols in many traditions of primordial life, with "maya," the Buddhist term for illusion, and the Sanskrit symbol "ah" (6). In form and content, di Prima's address to the Muse recognizes the power of ancient forms of poetry and spiritual beings, while situating her invocation in a liminal world between the soma and the noumena, a space populated with both the geometric and the surreal, the true and the false, thus allowing the singer to express herself as a physical individual in human time and an all-encompassing force outside of time. This poem, as do many in *Loba*, also suggests that names—be they "Calliope," "Mary," or the

2. Di Prima has said that "Ave" (1971) was the first of the *Loba* poems (Moffeit 2004, 93).

3. All references to *Loba* refer to page numbers in di Prima [1978] 1998.

all-inclusive "she"—cannot be decisively frozen in historical time, nor can the particulars of historical time be altogether evaded or superseded.

Continuing "Ave's" project of troubling form, di Prima introduces a *second* opening address later in the sequence: "DREAM: The Loba Reveals Herself" appears in part 4 of book 1. Its placement, approximately one-fifth of the way into the collection, suggests that the unfolding of consciousness in *Loba* is recursive rather than linear. The invocation forecasts as well that the language of the poem, set in breath-determined fragments in the Projectivist tradition of Charles Olson, will also follow a recursive path. Most importantly for the purposes of this essay, the second address connects the classical and Christian allusions with another muse, the she-wolf Loba for whom the cycle is titled.

Di Prima has stated that the idea for the *Loba* poems emerged from a dream in which she and her children are hunted by a she-wolf. As the dream unfolds, it becomes clear that the she-wolf is both hunter and comrade, both destroyer and muse. The she-wolf recalls a prominent figure in classical legend, the *lupa* that suckles the twins Romulus and Remus, thus saving their lives so that Rome can be founded, but also the less well-known she-wolf of Native American lore, who travels through the desert, gathering the bones of dead wolves, assembling them into full skeletons, and then singing them back to life—at which point they gallop off toward the horizon where they morph into free human females.

"DREAM," unlike "Ave," is not directed to a set of muses but appeals indirectly to a "she" who materializes as the Loba and inspires a language that resists linear, paternal structures of religious power through the use of linguistic fragmentation and the counterforce of Projectivist line trajectories. The Loba mantra that emerges is a spell-like utterance, partly name, "Loba," and partly the drumming sound of the she-wolf's footfalls. In this way, *Loba* develops a textual body that inhabits conventionally gendered social codes in order to empty them of their social force: it is both stereotypically feminine-coded (in its evasion of linearity) and masculine-coded (in its privileging of force). This focus on the concrete experience of visionary consciousness in language may seem at odds with the conventional understanding of the visionary poem as privileging transcendence over immanence. But di Prima's simultaneous emphasis on the primacy of mythic vision and on tactile cause-and-effect relationships in the world suggests an historical urgency that incorporates, rather than opposes, transcendental idealism.

The speaker of "DREAM" is not passive prey, nor was di Prima herself in the dream that triggered this poem. Rather, the categories of hunter/hunted are transposed in a context of maternal protection in which motherhood emerges as that which is alternately nurturing and feral. The Loba "came to hunt, but I did not / stay to be hunted," the speaker asserts: "Instead / wd be gone again. silent / children in tow" (di Prima [1978] 1998, 67). The Loba eventually becomes a "kind watchdog I cd / leave the children with. / Mother & sister. / Myself" (68). Di Prima's real dream and the poem "DREAM" echo alike the Loba myth about the panentheistic link between wolf and woman, both of whom hold the power of resurrection through song. The speaker becomes at once the caretaker of the beast (the Loba) and the Loba herself, a manifestation of masculine fierceness within a feminine nurturing framework and a mother goddess.

Di Prima reenvisions the historical status of women in Western religious traditions as inextricable from their everyday lived experience. The Loba is "eternally in labor," and this experience is the "Materia"—the materials, coded as mother or "mater"—of living in the historical present. In doing so, she challenges what Foucault has termed the persistence of "biopower," the total control of body and gesture in late capitalism, which she relocates in a religious sphere that must be resisted, especially by women, from whom contemporary religious practices still too often demand submergence rather than spiritual seeking. Whether in the economic or the religious realm, the body is held in check by systems of control—in *Loba,* the essentialism of the sacred word—that afford no opportunities for debate and counter-discourse. Di Prima's raveling and unraveling of these systems of religious-based control is crucial to the unfolding of the poem's counter-discourse of female/feminist visions, encapsulated in the initial invocations to different yet identical muses.

The Greco-Roman Thread

Central to this unraveling is a persistent pattern of allusions to and revisions of Greco-Roman mythic characters and narratives. The poems that focus on classical materials, approximately ten percent of the whole, constitute a subcycle within *Loba* in which the poets/speakers/singers create visionary analogues for the muses to whom the two invocations above are addressed. Woven amongst these are sections devoted to a panoply of goddesses and female heroes from across other cultural traditions, as we have noted above. Stitched throughout are surreal, visionary images of wolves, dogs, horses, snakes, and owls, which situate Greco-Roman mythology within a vexing (con)fusion of history and transcendence. Many of the individual parts within the two books and some of the poems themselves are preceded with epigraphs, such as the Carl Jung interrogatory; several of these epigraphs are attributed to an "Imaginary Jungian Scholar" who at times serves as foil for the speaker's message, at other times as a spokesperson for the speakers' perspectives. All of these elements are combined with frequent allusions to both human consciousness and narrative as labyrinthian, web- and maze-like tapestries.

Granted, *Loba* itself reads like a maze, with multiple entrances and exits and a confusing mix of interconnecting pathways, some of them actual dead ends. Nonetheless, there exists a distinct line of Greco-Roman allusions, that is, the Greco-Roman Thread, that not insignificantly, as we will demonstrate, concludes di Prima's 1998 structuring of the cycle. The Thread is introduced in the epigraph to part 3, a line from Ovid's *Fasti* (6.102) implicitly describing Cardea, the goddess of the door hinge: "Her power is to open what is shut / Shut what is open" (39). In other words, the epigraph implies that di Prima, through the Greco-Roman Thread in addition to other mythological components, reveals and conceals knowledge of poetry itself and the essence of all mutable forms.

In the remainder of this section, we present a brief analysis of the *major* allusions in the Thread, ending with a more lengthy discussion of the constellation of Persephone figures who dominate the finale, laying the foundation for our concluding exploration of *Loba*'s Buddhist turn. Themes expressed in the thread include, but are not limited to, birth and death, androgyny, erasure of female and male power, queering gender, female relationships, and the Buddhist concept of nothingness (no-thingness of the universe). They also, we note—*and cannot emphasize enough*—do not move in any particular linear progression but appear and disappear as twinkling lights in a flat night sky, akin to di Prima's definition of poetry itself. Since *Loba* is such a complex and nonlinear poem, to help a reader navigate this terrain, we introduce each element of the Thread with the names of particular poems and the pages on which these figures appear.

1. Goddess (untitled, book 1, part 3, 54)—The first direct reference to figures from classical mythology is a simple eighteen-line list poem presenting in paragraph form the names of many goddesses and historical female figures from across global cultures. Several from Greco-Roman cultures, including Circe, Ariadne, Hera, Aphrodite, and Artemis, appear in the poem.

2. *Nemo* ("FOUR POETS SPEAK OF HER," book 1, part 4, 63–64)—"Nemo" in Latin means "no one" and thus is *not* at all a mythological figure but an allusion to the absence of human or divine character—and to the eternal mystery. Nemo is juxtaposed with "she": "she was, herself, the dweller in the shrine / Nemo & elsewhere & her priest it was who walked / sword in his hand" (63). Through enjambment, "Nemo" fills linguistic and historical

space as both the name of the shrine of the goddess and the name of the Loba herself, she who sends forth her male servant, a warrior priest named "He-Who-Must-Die." "No One" is all things and all powerful—or "no-thingness," the nothingness of Buddhist traditions that negates gendered and all other dualities. The poem continues with four disembodied and unnamed poets who recount the transition from matriarchy to patriarchy, the last of which obtusely ends with the narrative of the Fisher King. In this scenario, the goddess still exists but now only "RULES OVER THOSE / WHO HAVE PASSED OUT OF HISTORY" (64). In other words, she, Nemo, rules over Nemo, the "no ones" who no longer exist. Female power, which once controlled earth, is now merely a subordinated element in an endearing and enduring masculine myth, her essence converted into a stylized object of desire and domination: a jeweled cup described as a ghostly "memory of the goddess in her glory" (64). Her erasure, however, is neither permanent nor absolute, as the poem concludes with a fifth voice that grounds the poem in a realistic tableau, setting forth the condition upon which the myth of female disempowerment is predicated:

> Was it sake cups or wine they
> passed around? Hashish, tequila, bourbon, opium?
> Talk rose & fell, & stopped. Lightbulbs grew dim
> in the cold light of dawn. A Chinese scroll:
> four poets /
>   nodding out
> (64)

This distinctly contemporary and informal voice—it too disembodied and unnamed—might well be that of the Loba herself, who in whatever guise she chooses remains a firm presence in the world, *a counter to the poets' drug-induced narrative,* an historical reminder of who also lives on "in the cold light of dawn." But even this coded refutation of the poets carries within it the validation it seeks to destroy, since in keeping with di Prima's own use of magical thinking to produce her poetry, the poets' use of mind-altering substances links them to the authority of a transcendent space. Nemo and the fifth anonymous poet, then, are one and the same, the symbolic omphalos that generates all.

3. *Aries* ("Loba as Eve," book 1, part 4, 69–75)—This third allusion, almost as oblique as that of "Nemo," appears in the "Loba as Eve" section, a series of five poems based on the short apocryphal Gnostic "Gospel of Eve." The fourth poem in the subseries, titled with a line from that gospel, "& from

wherever thou willst thou gatherest me," (74), begins *in medias res*: "steel, from the belly of *Aries*" (emphasis ours). Refusing clarification, the poem creates reader uncertainty as to whether *Aries* refers to the destructive Greek god of war (a near homonym, *Ares*), or to the golden-fleeced ram sought by Jason and the Argonauts, or to the first sign of the Zodiac. The poem suggests all three, as the speaker (female, male, both, beyond?) lets loose an overwhelming tirade of military and animalistic images, daring the "Thou" (male, female, both, beyond?) to suckle at her tits, "crucify [him] like a beetle on yr desk," and "drink [her] blood" from a vein in its leg. In retribution, the speaker, ultimately transgendered, transforms into a horse and then into a snake who has the power to predict "Thou's" future. In a final declaration comprising the last two stanzas, the speaker explains to "Thou" that this brutal oracular power (e.g., giving "Thou" "apples out of season" and engaging with the darkness) drives "Thou" to love and seek the other, in other words, to transgress patriarchal law.

4. Epigraph to book 1, part 5, 77—"He who listens to her fearing for the safety of the city which is within him should be on guard against her seductions" is from book 10 of Plato's *Republic* and warns against the fallacious nature of poetry, gendered as "she." In the context of *Loba,* the epigraph affirms the potency of women's voices to destroy those who attempt to enslave them, while ironically underscoring the necessity for all men to learn to listen to the wisdom of women's songs.

5. *Helen* (untitled, book 1, part 5, 79–80, 92)—Immediately following Plato's warning against the evils of poetry and women, di Prima introduces two untitled poems that connect Aries with gendered/sexualized transgressions through the image of the apple. Helen, of course, is associated with the apple of discord, which led to her abduction by Paris under Aphrodite's sponsorship and, ultimately, to the Trojan War. These poems we designate "The Bridge of Helen," since (1) they foreground Helen of Troy, the half-mortal and half-divine beauty born to Leda after her rape by Zeus in the guise of a swan, and (2) they directly link the preceding elements of the Thread with the beginning of the Persephone cycle, which concludes *Loba.*

The first Helen poem presents Helen as witch, specter, and woman—an "unholy trinity" repeatedly walking back and forth along the top of a wall in the company of Hecate. It is not clear what the wall separates, but the presence of Hecate—the goddess of magic, the moon, and the night—situates the wall as a liminal zone of transgression. From this place apart, the hybrid Helen births the world and its human inhabitants as "bloody dawn" and an "infant in [Helen's] silver robe" (80), respectively. Just as di Prima transgenders Aries, she does the same with Helen, since Helen stands as a parthenogenetic vessel that needs no fertilization, and her "infant," identified as neither male nor female, apparently replicates its parent.

The second half of the "Bridge" mentions Helen only once—and this time as a *negative*: The goddess "is not Helen," not the half divine/half human symbol of beauty, lust, and betrayal. Instead, the goddess is Lilith—called "Interface" (92), an explicit allusion to the myth that before God created Eve he created the twins Adam and Lilith, who were joined at the back. As one of the myths of Lilith goes, when she failed to acquire equality with Adam she broke free of him—hence her popularity today as a symbol of female autonomy. Di Prima's revision keeps Lilith attached but as an equal, although often invisible, like "flying moon in the clouds / on all the foggy coastlines of the earth" (92), a living presence, akin to skin or air, binding the human and all other bodily and natural worlds as a single whole. Although brief, and thus easily overlooked, the Helen poems significantly advance the themes of female power, bodily and metaphysically; the conflation of disparate mythic traditions; a critique of the stereotypes of feminine beauty, passivity, and feminine dishonesty; the fallacy of the self-other/virgin-whore dichotomy; and, most significantly, sisterhood as well as the mother-daughter relationship in a liminal space.

6. *Apollo* ("Loba, to Apollo, At the Fountain of Healing" and "Reprise," book 1, part 8, 147–48, 150–52, respectively)—While female forms dominate *Loba*, the god Apollo emerges as the object of female truth-telling. In both Apollo poems, the *Loba*—despite her historic identity as wolf, an animal sacred to Apollo—castigates the god of music and intellect, refusing to ignore the brutality to which Apollo has subjected her. In "Loba, to Apollo," accusatory interrogatives describe the dark side of masculine glory:

> were we not killed, out of jealousy, run thru
> w/ a black lance, every moon?
> . . . .
> was I not sold & sold & my daughters broken?
> . . . .
> can you laugh, father
> can you deny
> mouthfuls of blackened blood
> I spit out
> each morning
> to sing?
>
> (147–48)

Lines such as these recount thousands of years of experiences that have set women against their own bodies and denied them their own histories. The speaker, claiming the right to use and overpower the language of the fathers, confronts this excruciatingly real abjection. The poem implies that Apollo cannot refute the tragedy of female history through myth, but through his silence—a privilege that comes with the patriarchal voice, which the patriarch can turn on and off at will—he refuses to acknowledge and accept it. In the face of his silence, Loba generates her own "fountain of healing," using her intellect to "slough off this pain" of her body, end the commonality of woman's "rage," and recreate herself as a unique being. In turn, the next poem, "Reprise," presents similar images and concludes with renewed anger as Loba refuses to give up her animalistic fury and her human voice, declaring that her healing will come about only as she drinks from an ancient well filled with "the black water / Apollo / abhors" (151).

Whether or not di Prima intended this, both Apollo poems can be read as counters to Keats's *Hyperion,* in which Apollo's knowledge of suffering (through conventional male-centered narratives of "names, deeds, gray legends, dire events, rebellions, / Majesties, sovran voice, agonies") transforms him into a god, and thus the true poet (Bush 1963, 125). As a pair, the poems force a reader to consider the possibility that masculinist myths of culture, language, reason, and immortality—as well as aesthetics—are acts *not* of knowledge but of ignorance and ego, repeatedly performed on the back of female silence, subjugation, and invisibility. "Loba, to Apollo" uses the pain of the female body to reveal Apollo's true self and then refuses to allow such bodily pain to create Woman as a category, negating the essentialist trap of apotheosizing Woman as Nature in opposition to culture (i.e., male intellect). "Reprise" returns Loba to the underworld, the land of death and darkness, a transparent representation of passive Nature, but also the realm of Hades, where Apollo's light of intellect has no power. In presenting Apollo as a false god whose focus on intellect as opposed to imagination must be resisted, "Reprise" subtly evokes the Titans who, in a myth retold in Keats's *Hyperion,* are defeated and replaced by Apollo as sun god; here they are resurrected as a female who through dream and poetry defeats him, replacing him with a very different kind of light.

7. Persephone ("PERSEPHONE," book 1, part 5, 94; "Loba as Kore in the Labyrinth of her Beauty," book 2, part 9, 165–66; "THE LOBA PRIESTESS AS BAG LADY UTTERS RAGGED WARNINGS," book 2, part 10, 194–95; "HERMETIC ASTRONOMY," book 2, part 13, 255–59; "POINT OF RIPENING: Lughnasa," book 2, part 16, 305–7; "REPORT TO APHRODITE [Evening], book 2, part 16, 308–10; "ARIADNE AS STARMAKER," book 2, part

16, 312–13; "PERSEPHONE: Reprise," book 2, part 16, 314)—Some may find it surprising that *Loba* concludes with Persephone, since Penelope seems a more likely iconic figure to dominate a text so tapestry-like in nature. Medusa, the snake-haired Gorgon monster of ancient lore and Hélène Cixous's icon of *feminine écriture*, could also function to close the collection—and she does make a cameo appearance in the poem,[4] since much of *Loba* validates female anger and the necessity to write the female self. But for all the Penelopean cunning and patience, and for all the Medusa-like transgression and rage, *Loba*'s Greco-Roman Thread pays them little attention. In fact, the thread repudiates marital fidelity and the honoring of a dead patriarch; neither is it solely a reclamation and transformation of the female grotesque nor a manifesto for female language. Opening like a widening gyre to encompass Aphrodite, Ariadne, Demeter, Athena, and Psyche, this concluding thread serves as a constellation revolving around the more liminal, plastic, and troubling figure of Persephone.

The Persephone cycle is foreshadowed a number of times, beginning with the initial classical allusion to Ovid's characterization of the goddess Cardea. Cardea is not named in the epigraph, nor in a poem in that same section bearing Ovid's lines as its title. By identifying no specific female, mortal or divine, the poem reinforces a cloaked presence envisioned through alchemical symbology of air, water, wind, and fire, as well as allusions that function as a veiled homage to Persephone. Her home is the labyrinthian underworld, a place rimmed with "ice-cut walls" but filled with a "dark fire" that "does not consume" (43). The "she" carries torches to light her way, an allusion perhaps to Hecate who in some versions of the Persephone myth assists Demeter in her search for Persephone and then remains in Hades as Persephone's companion. The speaker also reveals the female's power as that which "raise[s] / the pale green grass of spring" (44). Whether allusions to Persephone who births life in the spring, Hecate her sister in the icy-hot of hell, or both, the "she" invoked is a voiceless presence with the power to conceal and reveal, to open and shut—in other words, the representation of oppositional forces that can both underwrite and undermine biopower.

Persephone herself speaks in the poem "PERSEPHONE" in part 4 of book 1, claiming the language of the masters at a point presumably long after Hades has stolen her from Earth and her mother Demeter. One of the more direct and less fragmented of the entire *Loba* collection, the poem lays out with elegant simplicity the plot points of the traditional myth: Persephone's

4. In *Loba*, see "Medusa Gazebo," which depicts a Latina woman about to commit suicide; the speaker wishes to, but does not, discourage her from going "too near the edge" (271).

ambivalent relationship with Hades, who fell in love with her and abducted her; Persephone being tricked by Hades into eating the pomegranate seeds, which condemns her to spend at least three months of each year with him in the underworld; and Persephone's connection to winter and spring. But it does *not* include Persephone's relationship with her mother or Hades's rape of Persephone. Instead, an epigraph to the poem, attributed to an "Imaginary Jungian Scholar" who serves as foil, diverts the story from the abduction and rape as well as from Demeter's angry and persistent search for her daughter. In turn, the Scholar envisions Persephone in love with Hades, weeping in the spring as she walks over the barren ground "reliv[ing] her winter sojourn" (94); ironically, it is her tears of sadness, the saline source of life, that bring the natural world back to life.

The poem depicts a more ambivalent Persephone, who plaintively asks, "And must I return again to that long hell?" as she descends the icy staircase, but whose love for Hades calls her back home to the underworld (94). In combination, the epigraph and Persephone's lyric reify the image of a young woman in a relationship with a man she loves. She clearly has no mother, which might imply that she has successfully separated herself from that most powerful of symbols, both personally and universally, thus adhering to the heteronormative sexual binary. But she also appears sorrowful and without self worth: Powers greater than her own, including those of the man she loves, have constructed her life. Like Helen/Lilith, she acts as an interface, only *without* agency, linking life and death in an eternal cycle, with the natural world as the space in which she wonders helpless and alone.

"PERSEPHONE" repeats many of the discourses presented throughout the Greco-Roman Thread, but through avoidance, absence, and negation, the poem calls particular attention to the mother-daughter relationship, drawing upon Jungian archetypes and the concept of the collective unconscious. As with many of the archetypes evident in *Loba,* the Mother can have either a positive or negative impact on the daughter. When positive, the force of the mother guides the daughter to accept her feminine being and her maternal role, generally manifested as qualities of nurturing, caring, wisdom, and the spiritual, all themes evident throughout *Loba.* When negative, the mother is often associated with the dark, secret, chthonic, and poisonous—again, themes that dominate *Loba.* In actual as well as imaginary mother-daughter relationships, according to Jungian theory, when the mother archetype acts as a negative, the daughter becomes a wounded individual who has to fight through the complex in order to achieve a balanced, or individuated, sense of self. Not surprisingly, as feminist psychoanalyst Julia Kristeva notes, this process can be extremely difficult, since the female must participate to some degree as Woman within the symbolic order of the collective unconscious but must *not* give in to the masculinist constructs of femininity (Moi 1991, 65), which relegate the female to zones such as nature and space, in opposition to the masculine power of culture and time. Many fail to achieve individuation, becoming suicidal or depressed, as we see in "PERSEPHONE," a poem, one can argue, *not* about successful escape from an all-consuming mother, but about a daughter who without a mother becomes entangled in an unhealthy heterosexual relationship. This struggle in multiple iterations demarcates the Persephone cycle as it moves toward its completion.

"Loba as Kore in the Labyrinth of her Beauty" (165–72 in book 2) features the mother-daughter relationship, now with an emphasis on its primacy, unbreakable by even gods as powerful as Zeus and Hades. This bond is affirmed in another epigraph, again spoken by The Imaginary Jungian Scholar, but this time in philosophical harmony with the poem's speaker:

> The myth of mothers and daughters is not a
> myth of overthrowing (as in myths of the son
> & the father) . . . but one of loss & recovery.
> For there are realms & realms, in which the
> daughter rises to self-knowing, to equal status
> with the mother—& in the feminine
> universe, while some of the realms may be
> distant—"removed"—none is out of
> bounds.
> (165)

In this set of five short lyrics, di Prima sets Kore/Persephone in a *labyrinth* of beauty where she moves back in time to become the ancient Egyptian goddess Nuit, who presides over a tangled maze of openings and dead ends, a female world of power that the man-made history of Nemo attempts to erase. The journey is one of darkness and dim remembrance, eventually leading to the light of primordial stars—the darkest and most frightful of secrets contained in the masculinist concept of the Mother archetype—are birthed from an eternal labyrinth that erases masculine primacy.

Eventually, however, the forces of history and the myth of an afterlife—represented by "the wolf Anubis," the Greek name for the ancient Egyptian god of the underworld and eternal life—become reified ("frozen," according to the speaker) as Western Time and the Finite, a space in which Kore/Persephone's beauty—a simulacrum of primordial female power—erodes. Despite the decline here of female beauty (earlier celebrated as consubstantial with the beginnings of the universe itself), "Loba as Kore" points out that monist myths of a gendered binary built upon primordial supremacy must be questioned in real time, in and by history itself. *Loba* demands the queering of all binaries based on the often-invisible inferiority of one out of the two, in this respect embracing Keatsian negative capabilities, daring the reader to both accept and spurn concepts such as female beauty and primordial Woman.

A sorority of female goddesses next appears in "THE LOBA PRIESTESS AS BAG LADY UTTERS RAGGED WARNINGS," with Demeter, Persephone's mother, assuming equal status with Aphrodite and Artemis, all representing beauty, women, and fertility in various guises. They are accompanied by Ishtar, the Babylonian goddess of fertility; Isis, the Egyptian goddess of beauty, motherhood, and the dead; Asher, from Judaic mythology, the great female teller of truths; and Mother Mamaki, mother of the primordial Buddha in Tibetan Buddhism. As bag lady, the Loba channels her Beat sisters from the opening "Ave" of the cycle to warn an unnamed and ungendered "you" to respect the ancient narratives of these goddesses, who as robed priestesses—not naked objects to be bought, sold, or toyed with—encompass the firestorm (or "tzuname") of "the eternal feminine" (194).

"HERMETIC ASTRONOMY" picks up the Demeter theme once again, but this time positioning her as a denizen of Hades and darkness. In a cryptic mélange of alchemical symbols and folksongs,

> Demeter
>   is ash   is
> ashes
>   Isis
>   all   fall
> (255)

Subtly, the breath-shaped lines echo the folk song "Ring around the Rosie," which at least in contemporary folklore is connected with the medieval plague, sending Demeter into death where she becomes hell itself: "DEMETER is Hades translated / Sekmet. Kali" (258). In other words, hell is both where female power (Sekmet and Kali) resides and the female herself. Female potency is named as "winter earth / & / Kore / green," in other words, the creative life cycle itself (259).

The quest for authentic female creativity takes on its most autobiographical guise in "Point of Ripening: Lughnasa." The speaker, who eschews Persephone's underworld in favor of a liminal space in which "there is no myth" to guide her life story, is transmogrified into a grotesque hybrid: an older (and "ample" [305]) female, a "middle-aged / Hermes" with "large breasts" but no wings—not insignificantly, a poet forging a new trail in the light of the stars. Di Prima's poems up to this point have through images of birth and creation implicitly connected light in its many manifestations to the Loba as an artist, as we saw in the two earlier diatribes aimed at Apollo, but this poem links light specifically to poetry to situate the ur-generative principle squarely within language as art wielded by human energies, even those of a middle-aged genderqueer. This move reflects the equation of poetry and light as one of di Prima's major aesthetic principles. As she stated in a lecture given at Naropa in 1975,

> The actual stuff that poetry is made out of is light. There are poems where the light actually comes *through* the page, the same way that it comes through the canvas in certain Flemish paintings, so you're not seeing light reflected *off* the painting, but light that comes *through*, and I don't know the tricks that make this happen. But I know they're there and you can really tell when it's happening and when it's not. So I've been trying to figure out what makes it happen. And I think it's not very different from the light of meditation. So that I'm beginning to suspect that what makes it happen is the way the sound moves in you, moving your spirit in a certain way to produce a certain effect which is like the effect of light. (di Prima 1978, 13)

She further develops this identification of light with bodily sensation by paraphrasing Cornelius Agrippa, who in *Nature and Occult Philosophy* (1651) speaks to the effects of singing on the body: "Your spirit as a person singing or chanting or reading aloud enters the ear and mingles in the body of the hearer, with his spirit, and so moves and changes the body's humors and dispositions" (di Prima 1978, 13). Di Prima concludes that the artist, in fact all of us, is "nothing but a physical instrument," and the effect—be it light or something else—occurs out of changes in that body.

Empiricists and pragmatists of all kinds may scoff at such Hermetic declarations, arguing that they disconnect art from the intellect, thus rendering art historically, politically, and personally useless. However, di Prima's attention to the consubstantial nature of the imagination, the body, and the physical context in which they reside can be credited with three significant accomplishments. First, it replaces religiosity with poetry as the modern source of spirituality—not an uncommon belief and one that di Prima as well as other Beat writers inherited from romanticism and modernism as neo-romanticism. Secondly, and importantly in the Beat context, it rebuffs the belief that art and life are separate. Poetry as Light, the ur-force of Life, renders Poetry that same ur-force, meaning that the artist—The Poet—cannot live without art and that all Life is Art (see Moffeit 2004, 88). Thirdly, with respect to di Prima's Buddhist and hermetic practices, the focus on light suggests a quest for release from the tyranny of the illusion of the ego.

These concepts pervade all of di Prima's work, and "Point," in particular, leaves the Loba with no script to follow, no category in which to fit oneself, wondering if there can be a myth for anyone such as herself in the modern world. Her life has been marked by unsuccessful efforts to find such a myth, as the next poem, "Report to Aphrodite (Evening)" reveals: service to Aphrodite, Buddha, Amor, Eros, the Rose, Mars, and Adonis have failed her, leaving her with only the inadequate and short-lived narrative of drowning in the passions of heterosexism (310).

The final poems of *Loba* explicitly speak to Jung's question: What myth are you living? And while the answer(s) remains shrouded in a visionary haze characteristic of spiritual epics and much of di Prima's wild, surrealistic poetics in general (see Libby 2002), the Greco-Roman Thread concludes with a plausible response that underscores the ephemeral nature of both myth and history.

"Ariadne As Starmaker," the penultimate poem, continues the theme of a female transitioning from the moisture of earth and darkness to the expanse of galactic space and light, thereby also signaling the way out of the labyrinth of female existence, of human history, and of the long poem itself. The configuration of the labyrinth, an escape from death, and the light correspond most directly to the story of Ariadne giving a thread to Theseus so he could find his way back out of the deadly Minotaur's labyrinth. In some versions, she marries and is then abandoned by Theseus; in others Dionysus marries her, Artemis kills her, Ariadne takes her own life, or Dionysus places the crown he gave her in the stars, thus making her immortal. Di Prima's vision of Ariadne incorporates this last trope [stars (light) equal immortality], while also rendering Ariadne as a hybrid Penelope who with patience and wiliness weaves time into eternity. The opening stanza cryptically announces this transmutation through doubling and grafting:

> she draws me w/ a thread across the beams
> & shuttles of her making
>   static web
> in which we swim
>   patterned ephemerides

unchanged
            exploding instance
terrible freedom
                  in which the speeding quasar
& the camel
             alike are still
in motion
(312)

Water and sky are inseparable, as one swims through beams of light. The physical and the abstract are also one, as one swims through numerical tables showing the position of celestial bodies in human time. The life of an earthly creature and the life of a galactic mass are one, the paradox of static movement, as the camel and quasar are both still and still turning—a subtle allusion created by di Prima's line break to the iconic line "At the still point of the turning world" from T. S. Eliot's "Burnt Norton." And the creator and the created are also one, as the "she" is also the "me": Ariadne creates the speaker, who becomes part of the pantheon of stars, which in mythic lore is Ariadne herself forming the multidimensional matrix of the universe. The female-to-female connection, the continual birthing of the one who gives birth, as the poem suggests, remains inviolable as light.

It is this theme that concludes *Loba*. "Persephone: Reprise," which functions much like a classical epilogue, returns to the myth of the mother/daughter, life/death cycle. Assuming a vatic voice, the speaker discloses the Loba's fate, which is to live at the interface, or "the fluid boundary of Hades," where life and death continuously meet, where shapes shift eternally, where light and darkness flow eternally into each other, and where the mother and daughter remain forever "me" and "thou" as one, nongendered and egoless (314). This becomes not only the myth that the Loba lives but her history as well, epitomizing di Prima's understanding of the ultimate state of poetic creation and reception: a point where no one has to try to "make sense" but instead comprehends that the uncertainties themselves—the illogical and the imaginary—are the materia of the poem that operates as the crucible of truth, in effect, eradicating the very need to answer Jung's question. *Loba*'s Greco-Roman Thread, then, constitutes one of di Prima's primary strategies to restage the female self as subject rather than object as she "empties," to borrow a term from her Buddhist practices, the female body of the essentialized subordinate figurations assigned to it by sacred and historical fathers.

The Buddhist Turn

As a practicing Buddhist, di Prima characterizes the "historical present" as *samsara,* the everyday world of causes and conditions, "the wheel of the quivering meat conception," as Jack Kerouac called it in *Mexico City Blues,* a world tyrannized by the attachment to the ego through identity. Buddhist practitioners, particularly those in the Mahayana tradition, try to free themselves and others from *samsara* by study of, and meditation on, the nonduality of phenomena. In Buddhist mythos, such a process began when Shakyamuni Buddha, the first Buddha, gave his initial teaching known as the turning of the "wheel of dharma." However, focusing on Buddhist conceptions of identity risks an ahistorical positioning of the feminine outside of the scope of the poem: that is, if identity is essentially beyond the fixities of categorizations of language, then so, too, is gender—a move that potentially relegates women to, at best, an outsider's role within Buddhist "no-self" discourse.

Loba's revisionist myth-making addresses this danger. Thousands of years of masculinized spiritual traditions are interwoven to dramatize the allegedly outcast feminine and redefine her identity as simultaneously fierce, feral, nurturing, and redemptive. The poem implies that the "no-self" of Buddhist nonduality is untenable until the speaking subject actually can claim agency over her sense of "self." Despite the speaker's denial of service to Buddha in "Report to Aphrodite," the transgressions of figures in the Greco-Roman Thread are reimagined as the beginning of the Buddhist path to enlightenment. As the Loba-goddess asserts in the guise of Eve, "The fruit I hold out / spins the dharma wheel" (73).

In Buddhism, the *empty* self is present *in full*: that is, emptiness, or *shunyata,* refers to phenomena that are empty of essentialist identity and full of unmediated, nonhierarchized frames of reference, a belief underwritten by *Loba*'s Greco-Roman Thread and also aligned with di Prima's indebtedness to Keats, whom she understands as trying to achieve what Buddhism calls an "egoless state."[5] This emphasis on fluctuations in the material body of an historicized self are illustrated throughout the poem cycle, but emerge with particular clarity in "The Loba Recovers the Memory of a Mare," a poem that reflects *Loba*'s status as a visionary excursion and a Beat generation internalized pilgrimage, both grounded in the emptied self of the Greco-Roman Thread.

---

5. In her 1987 Naropa lecture, di Prima quotes a letter of Keats's from November 22, 1817, "If a Sparrow come before my Window, I take part in its existence and pick about the gravel." This she interprets as his effort to go "partake[e] in the life of every creature. Really, what he's trying to get at, or describe, seems to be some kind of egoless state" (1978, 13).

The mare "has been hunted / but not w/in recent / memory." The compressed, sparse lines of the opening two stanzas contrast remarkably with the sprawling lines that dominate the rest of the poem, and suggest that the quiet rescue of the uneasy mare is only the beginning of a *noisy* recovery, a loud reassertion of something that once was lost or buried. The poem echoes the form and content of Allen Ginsberg's "Howl," with the repetitive-strophe lines of each stanza anchored anaphorically by the word "who," as in "Howl." But in di Prima's poem, the protagonists are not self-styled "secret heroes"—willing outcasts driven underground by a culture of containment—but instead those whose presence is secretive because they have been submerged. This is not to say that "The Loba Recovers the Memory of a Mare" is of interest primarily because of its connection to the more famous work of Ginsberg or that it should be read as an antagonistic response to "Howl." A review of the biographies of di Prima and Ginsberg demonstrates their deep and lasting friendship through the very last days of Ginsberg's life.[6] More important than the carefully crafted stylistic resemblance to Ginsberg is simply di Prima's effort in this poem to recover a visionary female Beatitude, another point of lineage.

As the poem unfolds, it becomes clear that di Prima's mare has not lived life much differently than her counterparts in Ginsberg's poem. The protagonists, those Beat(en) down themselves, write graffiti in lipstick, contend with "white slavers" in their quest for free love, seek a way to make a living for both themselves and infants they have been consigned by their men to take care of—and in doing so, sometimes have to entrust the care of their babies to gangsters. Di Prima's mare, like the moon sisters of "Ave," is a forgotten woman:

> who walked across America behind gaunt violent yogis
> & died o-d'ing in methadone jail
> scarfing the evidence
> . . . .
> [who] wrote lipstick "save yourself" on tin rail of furnished
>   room bed
> . . . .
>   . . . . on borrowed ceiling
> while friends coughed in the kitchen
> (125, 126)

6. Moreover, in a 2000 reading at Columbia College Chicago, di Prima recited this poem as a tribute to Ginsberg.

The mare is still unmoored as the poem ends: everywhere she looks for tradition, for roots, for foundation, she finds nothing but groundlessness—something akin to *shunyata,* or emptiness—and the best she can assert is a question asking of the reader who the male and female archetypes of their childhood look like:

> oatmeal & grist while the old man
> naked in bed / read Bible / jerked off
> & who was the whore of Babylon in the
> kerosene lamp of yr childhood?
> (126)

"The Loba Recovers the Memory of a Mare" suggests the recovery of a female Beat tradition as it questions the male-centeredness (or male dominance) of this tradition. At the same time, it celebrates a nongendered Beat experience as a sacred outsider's experience, as a life lived on the margins because the life of an insider during the Cold War is for the Beats, of course, a life that stifles the imagination rather than expands it. As in other Beat spiritual quests—"Howl" in particular—the traditions of Asia are invoked, but here reinvigorated as a woman's experience, suggesting that a Beat tradition that has been dominated by men and professes to speak beatifically for the entire world is an outlaw tradition that simply does not go far enough in its outlaw response.

For di Prima's speaker in *Loba,* the female body of her outlaw response is a space of interdependence rather than independence. Like the "fluid boundary of Hades" that she re-imagines as a sacred space in the book's final Persephone poem, the female body "is the province of the co-emergent mother," where mother and daughter—and, by extension, sister and sister—are "fruit within fruit" (314). Within its syncretic religious framework, *Loba* incorporates, significantly, a Tantric Buddhist understanding of the singular body as really *two* bodies: an individual body that, in its tactility, exists in an historical moment, and a sacred body that exists as an individual presence only by virtue of its interdependent relation to other bodies. In this larger, nondualistic figuration, the body is a middle-way between self and no-self, a mode of reciprocity, a pluralistic collection of "participatory capacities" rather than a static entity (Weinstone 2004, 128). Individualism is subsumed into a matrix of expressivist potential "based on the premise that matter, consciousness, and energy are copresent, differing expressions of each other, extant in varying intensities within individual manifestations of creation and without absolute delimitation" (121).

This copresence can be extended to relations between gendered bodies in *Loba*, where the ambisexual union of deities in Hindu and Tantric Buddhist practice is part and parcel of a coemergent gendered space critical to di Prima's reenvisioning of Western and Asian traditions that privilege gods over goddesses. For instance, in "The Loba in Brooklyn," the she-wolf goddess pokes her snout through wrought-iron gates, suggesting that, as a goddess, she is barred from the insider knowledge of the gods. She sees her subordinated position expressed in the sacred language of Buddhist mantras: "Every man a seed syllable / every woman its unfoldment" (246). The Judeo-Christian creation myth is reiterated in the Asian tradition of the mantra, where the sacred seed syllable of mantra speech is male and the expressive language that follows is a second-generation, and decidedly female, embodiment of the word.

In this poem's transgressive reinterpretation of the Book of Job, di Prima's unfolding of seed syllables echoes and affirms Job's protest that God needs humans as much as they need their God, destabilizing the authorizing primacy that would place men above women (and, in this poem, the gods above the goddesses) as part of a naturalized, self-evident order of things: "You yearn toward us / to see / your own," di Prima's Job states (246). From the mouth of a man comes a reminder that categories of "men," "women," "gods," and "goddesses" are coemergent, and one cannot exist as a category of value without the equal presence of the other. Indeed, as the frame of reference, and the trajectory of the poetic line, shift back to the she-wolf goddess, the last vision of this opening section of "The Loba in Brooklyn" is nearly an ambisexual one: "soft feminine face / (the snout) // animal eyes" (246).

This emphasis on Job's lament could suggest, of course, that the poem offers a reading of spirituality in which the gods do not have all the answers—but humans do. However, such a reading simply offers facile reversal of the dualisms that di Prima, as a serious Buddhist practitioner, would rather destabilize as part of the struggle of Buddhist practice—the struggle to experience a nondualistic world within linguistic and conceptual formations that otherwise depend on binary oppositions for making sense of everyday lived experience.

In answering the question "what myth are you living?," *Loba* does not withdraw from the material world into a heaven of the individual imagination. Instead, narrative is uttered from a place that proceeds from the nondualistic space of *shunyata*: a space di Prima dares call "love" in her poem "Deer Leap" (dedicated to one of those visionary influences, Robert Duncan)—a space "where light / twinkles in the gap / between the Law / & ourselves" (197). The Law is not underwritten by the propositional, either/or logic of the fathers. Instead, as in the work of H.D., and in di Prima's own Buddhist practice, this is a poetics that fuses seemingly incompatible immanent and transcendent modes of representation.[7] Sacred experience takes place within this gap, between the Law of fathers, both religious and material patriarchs, and the "fruit within fruit" of sisterhood. The Loba might finally pass through the wrought-iron gate here, and even if the landscape seems to evoke a patriarchal order, this is, nevertheless, a world in which "the Laws are different" (199). In reading *Loba*, one learns that it is not enough to highlight what di Prima has called elsewhere the process of "magickal invocation," nor is it sufficient to posit a materialist counter to this process. Instead, a more useful reading of *Loba* works with both these poles of discourse: the body as a force that is pressed upon by social mechanisms of discipline—the dimensions of religious biopower, foremost—and the effort to use Tantra/magick to portray the body as a series of forces, a multiplicity of vectors, that are imagined as free, albeit temporarily so, from social, religious, and mythological institutions that otherwise would hoard them as a means of control. This is a resolutely heterogeneous and feminist vision, born out of di Prima's purposeful fusion of revisionist mythmaking—including the Greco-Roman, Buddhist spiritual practice, and a Beat outsider's questing.

Bibliography

Bush, Douglas. 1963. *Mythology and the Romantic Tradition in English Poetry.* New York: Norton.

Deane, Seamus. 1992. "Introduction." In James Joyce, *Portrait of the Artist as a Young Man.* New York: Penguin.

di Prima, Diane. 1978. "Light / Keats." In *Talking Poetics from Naropa Institute: Annals of the Jack Kerouac Institute of Disembodied Poetics,* vol. 1, edited by Anne Waldman and Marilyn Webb, 13–37. Boulder, CO: Shambhala Publications.

———. (1978) 1998. *Loba.* New York: Penguin.

———. 1988. *The Mysteries of Vision: Some Notes on H.D.* Santa Barbara, CA: am here books.

———. 2011. *R. D.'s H.D.* New York: City University of New York Graduate Center.

Joyce, James. 2000. "James Clarence Mangan (1902)." In *Occasional, Critical, and Political Writing,* edited by Kevin Barry, 53–61. Oxford: Oxford University Press.

Jung, C. G. 1967. *Symbols of Transformation.* Princeton: Princeton University Press.

Libby, Anthony. 2002. "Diane di Prima: 'Nothing Is Lost; It Shines In Our Eyes.'" In *Girls Who Wore Black: Women Writing the Beat Generation,* edited by Ronna C. Johnson and Nancy M. Grace, 45–68. New Brunswick: Rutgers University Press.

7. Writing of H.D.'s influence on her work, di Prima states, "That quality in her which has most value for me as an artist, especially as a woman artist [is] the willingness to speak of what cannot be proved." At the same time, though, she asserts of H.D.'s work: "*What can be seen* is at stake. And the willingness to report *with precision*" (1988, 7, 9).

Marx, Karl. 1963. *The Eighteenth Brumaire of Louis Bonaparte.* New York: International Publishers.

Moffeit, Tony. 2004. "Pieces of a Song." Interview with Diane di Prima in *Breaking the Rule of Cool: Interviewing and Reading Beat Women Writers,* edited by Nancy M. Grace and Ronna C. Johnson, 83–108. Jackson: University Press of Mississippi.

Moi, Toril, ed. 1991. *The Kristeva Reader.* London: Wiley-Blackwell.

Ostriker, Alicia. 1982. "The Thieves of Language: Women Poets and Revisionist Mythmaking." *Signs* 8.1: 68–90.

Smith, Dale. 2010. "Tracking the Spirit: Diane di Prima's *Loba,*" http://www.bigbridge.org/BB14/2010_diprima/DiPrima_Smith_Tracking.HTM

Weinstone, Ann. 2004. *Avatar Bodies: A Tantra for Posthumanism.* Minneapolis: University of Minnesota Press.

CHAPTER 12

Towards a Post-Beat Poetics

CHARLES OLSON'S LOCALISM AND THE SECOND SOPHISTIC

RICHARD FLETCHER

It is a cliché to call Charles Olson (1910–70) the towering figure in the post-war American poetic tradition.[1] As much as for his sheer physical size (he was 6' 8"), Olson stood out among his contemporary poets and intellectuals for the scope of his vision, not only in his far-reaching pedagogic aims, as the one-time rector of Black Mountain College, nor simply as the author of the Poundian epic *The Maximus Poems* but also in his definition of a new poetics in his groundbreaking essays on literature, history, and culture (Olson 1997b). His central role in Donald Allen's influential anthology *The New American Poetry, 1945–1960* (1999) for example, was not only as a poet but also as a theorist of poetry and culture. Olson came first in this anthology of poetry and poetics, and his own contributions included a larger selection of poetry than any other poet's, as well as two pieces of criticism ("Projective Verse" and "Letter to Elaine Feinstein").

For some, however, Olson's towering presence represented an arrogant and patronizing intellectual pedantry. In a 1968 interview for *The Paris Review* by the poet Ted Berrigan, for example, Jack Kerouac reacts in the following way when asked about the date and place of composition of one of his own works:

1. See Fredman 1993 for an account of Olson's significance, not only for the postwar period of American poetry but also for how he took on the mantle of a combination of Thoreau, Emerson, and Whitman for his own time.

KEROUAC: First part written in Mexico, second part written in . . . Mexico. That's right, Nineteen fifty-five first part, '56 second part. What's the importance about that? I'm not Charles Olson, the great artist!

INTERVIEWER: We're just getting the facts.

KEROUAC: Charles Olson gives you all the dates. You know. Everything about how he found the hound dog on the beach in Gloucester. Found somebody jacking-off on the beach at . . . what do they call it? Vancouver Beach? Dig Dog River? . . . Dogtown. That's what they call it, "Dogtown." Well this is Shit-town on the Merrimack. Lowell is called "Shit-town on the Merrimack." I'm not going to write a poem and insult my town. But if I was six foot six I could write anything, couldn't I? (Berrigan 2005, 72).

Kerouac here accuses Olson of a pedantic (and even sentimental) localism, whereby he records historical minutiae and recounts in intricate detail mundane events of a specific, insignificant place. As we shall see, Olson's localism is far from sentimental, but a more expansive conception of the intimate union of identity, place, and time. In addition to the accusation of localism, Kerouac's gruff dismissal of Olson is part of a larger antagonism between the two authors, specifically in terms of their respective claims to primacy in articulating creative ideals of spontaneity. Olson's 1950 poetic manifesto "Projective Verse" called for a poetics of the breath and a harnessing of the energy of language—"the HEAD, by the way of the EAR, to the SYLLABLE / the HEART, by way of the BREATH, to the LINE" (Olson 1997b, 242). As Daniel Belgrad notes: "The relation of beat poetry to Charles Olson's projective verse reflects the semiautonomous development of a common aesthetic" (Belgrad 1998, 199).

Yet earlier in the same 1968 Berrigan interview, Kerouac dismissed Olson's "Projective Verse" as having no direct influence on his own literary style:

> I formulated the theory of breath as measure, in prose and verse, never mind what Olson, Charles Olson, says, I formulated that theory in 1953 at the request of Burroughs and Ginsberg. Then there's the raciness and freedom and humor of jazz instead of all that dreary analysis. (Berrigan 2005, 66)

In more generous terms, as Allen Ginsberg has noted, Kerouac was writing projective verse according to Olson's terminology. Yet rather than simply not acknowledging a poetic debt, Kerouac's attack on the very idea of analysis becomes part of the characterization of the Beat aesthetic against the academic pedantry of the Black Mountain poets (among others). What is key in the Kerouac-Olson exchange, however, and what will be the main focus of this essay, is how Olson will formulate a "post-Beat" poetics in terms of his expansive conception of localism. Furthermore, at the risk of adding to this accusation of pedantry, this essay considers how Olson's articulations of changes in his poetics in the years following "Projective Verse" rely not only on an engagement with the Beats, but also on a conception of history and ideas of localism that he had discovered in the period of Greek literary activity in the Roman Empire of the first three centuries CE known as the Second Sophistic. This was a period characterized by a sense of nostalgia and belatedness, as Greek writers looked to the literary and intellectual traditions of the classical period (5th–4th centuries BCE) for cultural moorings within the context of a globalizing Roman empire.[2] Greek orators, literary writers, and historians under Roman rule modeled themselves stylistically on the early classical authors, hoping to restore through emulation what they regarded as the transcendent values of the classical era. The "localizing" impulse to which Olson responded in some of these authors, was part of this project of cultural recovery and maintenance, which sought to recover not only basic information about a grand, but ever receding, past, but also the *feel* of that past through the *experience* of encountering particular monuments and topographies that had been left for posterity. Olson's particular interest in this later period of classical antiquity is unusual and, as we will see, illuminating as a way into some idiosyncratic aspects of his own poetics.

While Kerouac evoked Olson's physical stature to attack his localism and dismiss his poetics, he misunderstood the sheer range of vision of this localism and Olson's own role in articulating a post-Beat poetics.[3] In the important letter-essay written in 1959 and included in Allen's 1960 anthology, Olson makes the following—admittedly vatic and confusing—claim about both the Beats and his conception of localism:

> Nothing was *happening* as of the poem itself—ding and zing or something. It was referential to reality. And that a p[iss] poor crawling actuarial "real"—good enough to keep banks and insurance companies, plus mediocre governments etc. But not Poetry's *Truth* like my friends from the American Underground [aka the Beats] cry and spit in the face of "Time."
>
> The Image also has to be taken by a double: that is, if you bisect a parabola you get an enantiomorph (The Hopi say what goes on over there isn't happening here therefore it isn't the same: pure "localism" of space-time, but

2. For a useful account of the Second Sophistic, both its history and the ways in which modern scholars have conceptualized this period, see Whitmarsh 2005.

3. For a fruitful discussion of Olson's localism and the limits of this term to describe his poetic project, see von Hallberg 1978, 57–59.

> such localism can now be called: what you find out for yrself (*'istorin*) keeps all accompanying circumstance. (Olson 1997b, 251)

Olson's reference to the Greek verb *historein*—a complicated word meaning something between "to make inquiry" and "to form a judgment based upon inquiry"—which is so central to his work, was likely grounded in the classical historian Herodotus, who used both the noun *historie* and verb *historein* to refer to his own historical project.[4] Yet by the mid-1950s, Olson saw the writers of the Second Sophistic (Plutarch, Maximus of Tyre, and Pausanias) as demarcating a form of localized historical inquiry which aligned with his own and enabled him to propose a post-Beat poetics in the late 1950s. In what follows, we will revisit several key moments in Olson's articulation of his affinity with the authors of the Second Sophistic and see how it was Pausanias in particular whom he utilized to formulate his conception of localism, both in relation to, and as a means to surpass, key figures of the Beat movement and the central claims of Beat poetics.

The Roots of Olson's Localism

In the spring of 1962, Olson was invited by Wilfred Hamlin, a literature professor at Goddard College, an experimental college in rural Vermont, and a fellow alumnus of Black Mountain college, to deliver a reading of his poetry at Goddard.[5] As Kyle Schlesinger notes in the introduction to his transcription, however, this was not a typical poetry reading. He cites, for example, Olson's opening remarks about his own resistance to and divergences from such traditional readings. When asked if he minded being recorded, Olson replied:

> No. As a matter of fact I'm going to just watch it like a fire—let's sit here and watch that tape [*laughter*]. What happens if it just goes on and I don't say anything? Who knows? See, that's the problem with reading, it gets to be kind of a bore, because it's a performing art, you feel as though you have an audience, and as if you're supposed to do a concert or something. I don't think I believe in verse in this respect at all. As a matter of fact, I know I don't. (Schlesinger 2011, 1)

4. On the semantics of *historie* and its cognate forms, see Bakker 2002.

5. We have the original recording (available on the Slought Foundation Website: https://slought.org/resources/olson_1962_reading) and in two recent transcriptions: Maud 2010 and Schlesinger 2011.

As he continues with his lecture, Olson does much more than read his poetry, instead framing it and commenting on it through a broader discussion of his influences and their impact on his thinking. The poems he reads are from the fifth book of his *Maximus* series, which would eventually be published in 1968 in a volume containing the fourth, fifth, and sixth books. Olson introduces his protagonist Maximus as follows:

> I mean this creature Maximus addresses himself to, to a city, which in the instance is, is Gloucester, which, then in turn, happens to be Massachusetts. That is Gloucester, Massachusetts. I'm not at all under the impression that it is necessarily more to Gloucester, Massachusetts, in any more meaningful sense than the creature is, either me, or whom he originally was intended as, which was a, was Maximus of Tyre, . . . [who] mostly wandered around the Mediterranean world from the center, from the, from the old capital of Tyre, talking about one thing—Homer's *Odyssey*. I don't have much more of an impression of him than that. I've tried to read his [works] and found them not as interesting as I expected. (Schlesinger 2011, 2)

After admitting his limited reading of Maximus, Olson proceeds to articulate what Maximus represents for Olson's own age and how it is that age that interests Olson:

> But he represents to me some sort of a figure, that centers, much more than, much more than the 2nd Century A. D. In fact, as far as I feel it like, he's like the neighbor of the world, and uh, in saying that I'm not being poetic or loose, uh. (ibid.)

After a taste of the earlier, published *Maximus* poems, the reading from the fifth book begins with a poem called *A Later Note on Letter #15*, which is Olson's attempt to elucidate his earlier comments:

> **A Later Note on Letter #15**
>
> In English the poetics became meubles—furniture—
> thereafter (after 1630
>
> & Descartes was the value
>
> until Whitehead, who cleared out the gunk
> by getting the universe in (as against man alone

& *that* concept of history (not Herodotus's
which was a verb, to find out for yourself:

'istorin, which makes any one's acts a finding out for him or her
self, in other words restores the traum: that we act somewhere

at least by seizure, that the objective (example Thucidides [*sic*], or
the latest finest tape-recorder, or any form of record on the spot

—live television or what—is a lie

as against what we know went on, the dream: the dream being
self-satisfaction with Whitehead's important corollary: that no event

is not penetrated, in intersection or collision with, an eternal
event
    The poetics of such a situation
are yet to be found out.

January 15, 1962
(Olson 1983, 249)

Olson here juxtaposes Herodotus and Thucydides (whose name he *does* spell correctly elsewhere!) in terms of what he takes to be their basic differences in historical method, that is Herodotus's "finding out for oneself" and then assessing his sources (*historein*) as opposed to Thucydides as the tape recorder, the live television—in other words the historian as reporter.[6] When he reaches his reading of the sixth poem, with his audience already attuned to this distinction, Olson adds another ancient voice into the mix—one that is closer in time to Maximus of Tyre: Pausanias.

CHARLES OLSON: Now number six is—has actually got a title. It's called "Book Two Chapter 37." And it has nothing whatsoever to do with anything, but if you have the power of recognition or the experience of whom I am imitating, you will know:

I. Beginning at the hill of Middle Street the city
which consists most—

6. On the significance of the work of Alfred North Whitehead for Olson, see von Hallberg 1973–74 and Bram 2004. On the specific issue of Whitehead's influence on Olson's conception of history, see McPheron 1973–74, Bram 2004, 91–110, and Mellors 2012.

CHARLES OLSON: Is there somebody speaking? Did I hear voices? Oh, it's that tape talking back at me. I knew it would object! [*laughter*]

> I. Beginning at the hill of Middle Street the city
> which consists mostly of wharves & houses
> reaches down to the sea. It is bounded
> on the one side by the River Annisquam,
> and on the other by the stream or entrance
> to the inner harbor. In the Fort at this entrance
> are the images of stone and there is another
> place near the river where there is a seated
> wooden image of Demeter. The city's own
> wooden image of the goddess is on a hill
> along the next ridge above Middle Street
> between the two towers of a church called
> the Lady of Good Voyage. There is also a stone image
> of Aphrodite beside the sea. 2. But the
> spot where the river comes into the
> sea is reserved for the special
> Hydra called the Lernean monster,
> the particular worship of the city,
> though it is proven to be recent
> and the particular tablets of Poseidon
> written on copper in the shape of a heart
> prove to be likewise new.

CHARLES OLSON: Anybody recognize who that is, beside myself? No?

UNKNOWN VOICE: Is he a Greek?

CHARLES OLSON: Yeah.

UNKNOWN VOICE: Herodotus?

CHARLES OLSON: Uh no, it's Pausanias. It's Pausanias' *Description of Greece* in the second century AD. Do you know that poem? It's remarkable, it's very, very, very—to me, like twin to Herodotus. He was a, he was a traveller, again like the boys of—like everybody—see like *On the Road,* you know. For, for, for really, like those first two centuries you know, I mean like wow, talk about being knocked out. [Laughter from audience] Nobody was at home! And in fact they did the thing that like anybody does who moves, they found very interesting things, [Laughter from Olson] and Pausanias, I think that Pausanias' *Description of Greece* is one of those—is comparable to "Herodotus," [Snaps fingers twice] I

> think for our minds, I think for our interests, yea. [Three strikes against a matchbox] You know everything has gotten very interesting and very complicated and very intellectual, and very satisfying for inquiry. Honestly, expression has lost ground *rapidly*, and a look, see, is really in business. [Blows out a match] I mean this boy is really a cat. Like Plutarch, ya dig? A contemporary, by the way. Plutarch, again, second century. Crazy, crazy, crazy, crazy record. If the Twentieth-Century has one resemblance, it has four, but it has one, one is the second century. (Schlesinger 2011, 13–14)

Olson here uses the Greek writing of the Roman Empire in the cultural milieu of the second century CE in general and Pausanias in particular (whose text he creatively dubs a poem), not only to build on the differences between the Classical Greek historians Herodotus and Thucydides in terms of historical method but also to characterize the Beat movement, here represented by Kerouac's *On the Road*. The comparison is more than just a celebration of the itinerant figures of the Second Sophistic and the protagonists of Kerouac's road-novel. For both, travel is vital for seeing things for oneself and the road becomes the means to understand layers of history and culture while not getting stuck or hung up on either.

A year later, in the summer of 1963, Olson attended the Vancouver Poetry Conference, along with some fully-fledged Beats—Allen Ginsberg and Philip Whalen, as well as other figures like Robert Creeley and Robert Duncan, less central to the "movement."[7] In one of the discussions, which included Creeley, Duncan, Ginsberg, Whalen, and Olson, the topic was "History" at Creeley's request:

> I would like to center on the question of context . . . because I think the first day we were here the poems were still isolated from quote "actual events" unquote, and I'd like to take it not so much into the whole business of what you can do with a poem, where you can put it or hang it on the wall, but where, what is, "history"? (Maud 2010, 46)

Olson responds to Creeley's request by reading the other piece published in *Yugen* 8 called "Place; & Names" (Olson 1997b, 200–201). This short piece is hard to categorize—it *looks* like a poem, but reads like prose and appears in Olson's *Collected Prose*, and it was not part of the *Maximus* series. Nonetheless, it acts as the theoretical underpinning of the *Maximus* Poem "Book 2,

7. On the idea of a distinct "Beat movement," as opposed to a "generation," see Varner 2012, xi.

chapter 37." In fact, at the end of the discussion, Olson not only reads "Place; & Names" again, but follows it with "Book 2, chapter 37." As with the Goddard reading, it is worth paying attention to how Olson frames his reading here (my emphasis):

> **ROBERT DUNCAN:** Let's read the "Place; & Names" again.
> **ROBERT CREELEY:** Yes, relocate.
> **CHARLES OLSON:** I will. And in light of what we've been talking about, and Robert's statement that *if Allen did what he said he would do it would be like Pausanias,* a curious thing happened. There's a poem which appears in published form as though it was the proof of the proposition. And for the hell of it, as long as I've got the proof in front of me, I'll continue, after rereading it, and read you the poem which is called "Bk ii chapter 37" and is simply a secret statement that it is book two, chapter thirty-seven of Pausanias [Olson then reads "Place; & Names" with a few asides] So, let me end my pitch with a poem, uh? "Bk ii chapter 37." It's from the *Maximus* poems:
>
> 1. Beginning at the hill of
>
> Yeah, I'll just read the numbers. I'm doing it that crazy way. I think it's three numbers; it's really the way Pausanias—I don't know why they used to do that number thing within the text, do you, why the Greeks did that? But they sure did. (Maud 2010, 61)

Unlike the reading at Goddard the previous year, Olson's discussion of this poem and the association between a Beat writer—this time Allen Ginsberg—with a Second Sophistic author—here explicitly Pausanias—is actually preempted by Creeley in his reading of Ginsberg. By tracking back through the conversation, we can see precisely what Creeley and Olson are responding to in Ginsberg.

Earlier Olson had recalled how Ginsberg had previously told him that he wanted to go to Laos because he felt that he was not able to trust the media in their reporting of the ongoing Laotian civil war and the US involvement there as part of the Vietnam War. In a letter to his father at this time, Ginsberg wrote that he was upset by what was going on in Laos and the role of the media in reporting on it:

> I think more and more, it is not possible to get an accurate picture of local conflicts without absorbing *both* Western & Communist versions of history,

> (seriously) and cancelling and checking one against the other. (Ginsberg 2001, 211)

Olson proceeds to take Ginsberg's desire to go to Laos as part of his "look-see" version of history. He characterizes Ginsberg as not wanting to "go see a war," but to merely see: "Is there a war? Was it a war? What is it?" Then, a little later, this idea of the "look-see" is linked to writing poetry. Philip Whalen asks Olson, "Why can't Ginsberg write about the war even if he hadn't taken the trouble to go look at it?" In Maud's transcript, Creeley responds to Whalen's questions by referring—obliquely—to some of Ginsberg's recent poetry (collected that same year as *Reality Sandwiches*) and also to Pausanias's brand of localism:

> These journals [*Reality Sandwiches*] these poems that Allen's now writing are operating on the very same principle as Pausanias' walking down the street and seeing what's there. That's the way they work. (Maud 2010, 51)

This is the claim, quoted above, that Olson is picking up on at the end of the recorded conversation:

> In the light of what we've been talking about, and Robert's statement that if Allen did what he said he would do it would be like Pausanias, a curious thing happened. There's a poem which appears in published form as though it was the proof of the proposition. (58)

It is important to note that while Creeley was characterizing Ginsberg's recent poetry—that collected in *Reality Sandwiches*—Olson is developing an earlier comment about Ginsberg wanting to go to Laos, not to see a war "but just to see: Is there a war? Was it a war? . . . You just want to find out for yourself what really this whole thing amounts to, and the only way you can do it is to go there" (49). This emphasis on Ginsberg as a poet who goes to see places, peoples, and events for himself is present in Ginsberg's own comments in the back-cover blurb of *Reality Sandwiches*:

> Wake-up nightmares in Lower East Side, musings in public library, across the U.S. in dream auto, drunk in old Havana, brooding in Mayan ruins, sex daydreams on the West Coast, airplane vision of Kansas, lonely in a leafy cottage, lunch hour on Berkeley, beer notations on Skid Row, slinking to Mexico, wrote this last night in Paris, back on Times square dreaming of Times Square, bombed in NY again, loony tunes in the dentist chair, scream-

ing at old poets in South America, aethereal zigzag Poesy in blue hotel room in Peru—a wind-up book of dreams, psalms, journal enigmas & nude minutes from 1953 to 1960 poems scattered in fugitive magazines here collected. (Ginsberg 1963, back cover)

With Ginsberg's Pausanian journal-poems in mind, I will return to Vancouver and Olson's own Pausanian poem later in this essay. But first I will offer some general observations about Olson's Greeks and Beats, and then turn to what I believe to be the "source" of Olson's associations between the Beats and Pausanias's localism in a 1959 letter to his friend and editor, Donald Allen, on "post-Beat" poetics for the *New American Poetry* anthology.

Olson's Greeks and Beats

Olson's poetry cannot be reduced to any single "source," not to the philosophy of Whitehead, nor to the poetry of Pound and certainly not to any classical author. In fact, throughout Olson's poetic and intellectual writings, the very notion of the Greek and Roman past as valorized by virtue of its "classicality" is strongly resisted. It is within this general stance of resistance, I would claim, that the Greek literature of the Roman Empire attracted Olson nonetheless. In one of his most celebrated early poems, for example, "The Kingfishers," first published in 1949 and the first poem in Allen's anthology, Olson begins with the celebrated Heraclitean tag: "What does not change / is the will to change." Yet by the poem's third and final section, he writes:

I am no Greek, hath not th'advantage.
And of course, no Roman:
he can take no risk that matters,
the risk of beauty least of all.
Olson (1997a, 92)[8]

---

8. What Olson means by "advantage" here has somewhat perplexed scholars. Maud cites those who see Olson here taking a middle ground between the Greek and Roman—lower than the former, but above the latter—thus implying that there is some kind of "advantage" to the Greek worldview (1998, 105). Davenport, for example, reads Olson as saying that his culture and language give him scant advantage in speaking as he would like, compared to the Greek (1973–74, 258). Maud's own interpretation is the opposite. That there is something lacking in the Greek, as much as in Olson's position, and that both should look "backwards" to Near Eastern texts, elsewhere dubbing himself a "Hittite" and Homer, a "late" European poet. However, more recently Maud admits to changing his mind (2008, 132), agreeing with Davenport and others in seeing "The Kingfishers" as offering "a fairly conventional nod to Greek origins." Maud's mistake, as he puts it, was to read Olson's later work *back onto* "The Kingfishers," espe-

The main reference point for "The Kingfishers" and its companion piece "The Praises" is Plutarch's reading of Heraclitus as quoted by his teacher Ammonius of Athens in Plutarch's dialogue "The E at Delphi," a work in which Plutarch attempted to explain the mysterious inscription of the Greek letter "E" that evidently stood in the Temple of Apollo at Delphi. Olson's approach to the Greeks here is, as we can see, highly mediated. He paraphrases Heraclitus in the first line of "The Kingfishers," but he reveals that his *source* for Heraclitus is Plutarch's dialogue, and specifically the discourse of Ammonius. The Second Sophistic thus becomes a vital "hinge" for Olson—a means of accessing and mediating the earlier archaic and classical Greeks, while keeping a critical distance from a simplistic valorization of their presumed "advantage." This idea of "hinge" is explained in the section of his *Proprioception* called "the hinges (of civilization)" in which Olson describes the second century CE (as it looks back to the first) as an "affective" time:

> *the 2nd AD back to the 1st:*
> an "affective" time, the 2nd
> —as well as brilliant
> early secular: Maximus of Tyre
> Marinus of Tyre
> examples
>
> but like the 17th later
> costly in loss of some—
> thing the 1st, as later the
> 15th & 16th still held, a
> sense of the divine
>
> (gain here is to get a load of Gnosticism
> & Hans Jonas particularly useful).
> (Olson 1997b, 190)

What does Olson mean by this? Here he is again using his reading of Whitehead, who focuses on experience as affective rather than cognitive. (In other words we do not perceive the objects in the world before us and then react emotionally, but the reverse—perception is a matter of being affected bodily.)

---

cially his essay "Human Universe," in which Olson *does* attempt to replace the "Greek system" (Olson 1997b, 153–202). While I would agree with Maud that Olson very much fleshes out this approach in escaping the "Western box" in his subsequent essays and poetry, the role of Plutarch in "The Kingfishers" may offer an early form of this later approach.

In short, Plutarch, Maximus, and Pausanias are heroes for Olson because they enact the precise significance that Pausanias gives to the "E" at Delphi—"know thyself"—not merely in terms of its message and meaning, but as an affective process in which we feel and localize the meaning of the inscription of the "E" in our own time, as if to say "this is your time, too."[9] Furthermore, it was specifically Pausanias and what Olson calls his "careful localism" (in the bibliography to his so-called *Mayan Letters* to Creeley) that enacted this affective process most dramatically.[10] And it was precisely this more careful localism that Olson saw in Pausanias that he invokes in "The Kingfishers" to correct the association Creeley makes between Pausanias and Ginsberg's historical method in Vancouver (that is, the simplistic conception of Pausanias's localism as "walking down the street and seeing what's there").

Before returning to Vancouver, we may note a significant moment earlier in the confrontation between Olson and the Beats, not in terms of history, but of poetics (fields which, in many ways, Olson would not have considered separate). This was a moment in 1959 when the very issue of categorizing and defining poetic movements, and contemporary "poetics," was at stake for Olson. I refer to the letters to his friend and editor, Donald Allen at Grove Press, who was compiling the anthology of the "New American Poetry" with which I began this chapter. The immediate context of this exchange involves a series of events in the years 1958–59.

The publication of Kerouac's *On the Road* and the obscenity trials of Ginsberg's *Howl*—both in 1957—gave the so-called Beat movement a prominence and notoriety. Tom Clark, in his biography of Olson, writes that Olson "could not suppress in himself a powerful hunger for at least some taste of the wide exposure the Beats were now getting" (2000, 276). Clark continues his account by emphasizing the ambivalent attitude Olson showed to the Beats in how he engaged with their work both at a distance and in person. For example, Olson would copy out into his notebook "long passages from Kerouac's *On the Road*—despite his misgivings about the naturalistic dimensions of the book" in letters to Robert Creeley (ibid.). The 1959 Harvard appearance of Ginsberg, Gregory Corso, and Peter Orlovsky led not only to a notorious incident of Olson headbutting Corso but also a poem called "A Maximus Written to Throw Back a Hex on Allen Ginsberg and/or Gregory Corso," which, owing to better relations with Ginsberg, he ended up suppressing. But Clark's recon-

9. See Maud 1998, 35–36.

10. "Pausanias' *Description of Greece*, more valuable than Plutarch, his immediate predecessor, c. 100 A. D., because of its careful localism, and taking what is said as how to find out for oneself" (Olson 1953, 87).

struction, with its focus on Olson's reading (for example, of *On the Road*) and anecdotes like the Harvard affair, misses the very fruitful discussion of the direction of what he dubbed the "post-Beat" poetics carried on in Olson's letters, not only to Donald Allen but also to fellow writer Elaine Feinstein. This discussion of poetics, I would claim, informs Olson's later characterization of the Beats, and especially Ginsberg, in terms of the Second Sophistic in general, and of Pausanias in particular.

In the "Poetics" section of Allen's iconic *The New American Poetry 1945–1960*, published in 1960, Robert Creeley writes that, "Charles Olson is central to any description of literary 'climate' dated 1958" (Allen 1999, 409). Allen's anthology is a major topic of discussion in the letters of Olson and Allen dating April 1958–May 1960. In these exchanges with Allen, Olson debates the book's scope and structure (in September 1959), as well as a conception of "post-Beat" poetics that he had outlined earlier. In a letter dated June 17/18, 1958, after a series of apologies for a slow response to an earlier letter, Olson writes, "Actually, its yr book on poetics which starts me now" (Maud 2003, 42). As we discover later, it seems that Allen had asked Olson if he thought the anthology should have a section dedicated to "Poetics" ("So, throw the POETICS in there, I'd say," [ibid.]). But Olson leads into the poetic discussion by mentioning the copy of John Clellon Holmes's *roman à clef* about the Beats, *GO* (1952), that Allen had sent him:

> It also sets me going on how much it seems to me the generation gets itself into experience by creating its own aetiology (in the face, god help us, of such shit of the society, they have reason to make up situations—I am thinking of all the habits, rather than such pure and old fashioned Hamlet like Trocchi. (ibid.)

Here Olson is referring to the Scottish novelist and honorary Beat, Alexander Trocchi, whose *Cain's Book*, published by Allen's Grove the following year, but presumably read by Olson already, was another *roman à clef*, which he proceeds to contrast with those of Holmes and Jack Kerouac:

> In fact Holmes . . . or Jack for that matter are *happier* in being more arbitrary—cause-wise—than Trocchi, who has to be right. And isn't, poor guy! My god, it's wild how wrong he is. (ibid., emphasis in original)

Olson gets back to the issue of poetics by reflecting on the Beat generation represented by Holmes and Kerouac and how they were

> much more displayed, splayed, searching and whatever—just because, I'm thinking, the whole show is set off from the self-made cause. . . . Wow: i mean is there any better example of setting up the all which follows? Which gets me back to the future of poetics. That is: despite what I say, the fact is, whichever way you take the generation, they lead on to the next thing. (ibid.)

Finally Olson offers his impression as to what the next thing will actually be:

> IMAGE. And PUN (these are the two big problems of post-beat: the real hides in art on those: the image, which *equals* the object (whatever the damned object is) & the noun-rhyme, which *trips* the blast off. (ibid., 43, emphasis in original)

This he summarizes in terms of a trajectory from the "open field" of "Projective Verse" via Beat response to the present issue:

> (1) the open field leads to the narrowest gate
>
> (2) sd gate is where the squeeze beat talks is for real
>
> (3) "poetics," at sd point, is most serious, and if technical, suddenly drops to, almost, like they say, who do our living for us. (ibid., 44)

Olson appears here to be saying that the "post-Beat" poetics is one that rewrites Beat claims to poetic Truth in the form of the IMAGE (one stage removed from reality as in any proximate object to which there is a flow of feeling) and the PUN (the poetic inscription of the IMAGE, which is three stages removed from reality). But what has any of this to do with the Beats, let alone the Second Sophistic? We can see the "move" made in the Allen letter, from the novels that depict the Beat movement of Holmes, Kerouac, and, to a much lesser extent, Trocchi, to this "post-Beat" poetics of image and pun. The same "move" is made in Olson's "Letter to Elaine Feinstein," which Allen would end up including in the anthology. Here is the same vatic passage quoted earlier in this essay (see above, 254):

> Nothing was *happening* as of the poem itself—ding and zing or something. It was referential to reality. And that a p[iss] poor crawling actuarial "real"—good enough to keep banks and insurance companies, plus mediocre governments. But not Poetry's *Truth* like my friends from the American Underground [aka the Beats] cry and spit in the face of "Time."

> The Image also has to be taken by a double: that is, if you bisect a parabola you get an enantiomorph (The Hopi say what goes on over there isn't happening here therefore it isn't the same: pure "localism" of space-time, but such localism can now be called: what you find out for yrself (*'istorin*) keeps all accompanying circumstance. (Olson 1997b, 251)

The complexities of Olson's poetics are worth exploring in themselves, but more relevant for our purposes here is his observation that the Beats represent a pivotal moment in the history of poetry, and that the reference to "pure localism" as keeping "all accompanying circumstance" is not only a gloss contrasting Pausanias to Herodotus but also Olson to the Beats. For Olson, the next step *beyond* the Beats' poetics of "Truth" and their crying and spitting in the face of "Time" must be the punning union of a time and place with an image. In the "Letter to Elaine Feinstein," he will call it "tope/type/trope." The Beat poetics of verbal and emotional spontaneity, mixed with seeing for oneself, finding out for yourself, must first be accompanied by the deeper truth of temporal and spatial "circumstance": that is the real. In addition, language and the proper name are loaded images, not only the personal images of the Beats but also the historical images of ancient time and place.

Pausanias, Olson and Localism

Olson's poem as proof "Book 2, chapter 37," read at the Vancouver Poetry Conference in 1963 to make his point about history, does more than insert his Gloucester into Pausanias's Lerna; it engages with Pausanias's localist project in a way that is close to the role played by Plutarch in "The Kingfishers," which is an interpretive, intermediary role. To demonstrate this point, we may compare Olson's poem with Pausanias's text, which he read in Frazer's translation (2.37):

> 1. Beginning at this mountain, the grove, which consists mostly of plane-trees, reaches down to the sea. It is bounded on the one side by the river Pontinus, and on the other side by another river, called Amymone, after the daughter of Danaus. 2. In the grove are images of Demeter, surnamed Prosymne, and of Dionysus : there is also a small seated image of Demeter. These images 2. are made of stone. In another temple there is a seated wooden image of Saviour Dionysus. There is also a stone image of Aphrodite beside the sea. They say that it was dedicated by the daughters of Danaus, and that Danaus himself made the sanctuary of Athena on the banks of the Pontinus.

> 3. The Lernaean mysteries are said to have been instituted by Philammon. The stories told about the rites are clearly not ancient. Other stories, I am told, purporting to be 3. by Philammon, have been found engraved on a piece of copper fashioned in the shape of a heart. But these stories also have been proved not to be by Philammon. (Frazer 1913, 129)

In both Gloucester and Lerna, there are "recent" or "new" additions to the rituals and site: the worship of the Lernian Mysteries "is proved to be recent" while some tablets of Poseidon "written on copper in the shape of a heart/ prove to be likewise new." In Pausanias, there are stories about the rites—claimed to be by their founder, Philammon, but judged by Pausanias to be "clearly not ancient." Yet, as Pausanias goes on to record in 37.3, other stories engraved on a heart of copper, said to be by Philammon as well, were proven by one Arrhiphon to be of a later date—of Pausanias's day. Arriphron's argument is simply that Philammon lived before the Doric Invasion (which would have introduced the Doric dialect into Greece), while the stories purported to have been written by him are in the Doric dialect.

If we made a pilgrimage to Olson's Gloucester, we would find numerous historical plaques set up there as well, although they are bronze and rectangular, not heart-shaped copper. In fact, Olson wrote a *Maximus* poem about these very plaques (2.174). The crucial point here is that Olson's Pausanian poem, as recited amid the characterisation of Beats—Kerouac in Goddard and Ginsberg in Vancouver—generates its expression of localism—of Lerna and Gloucester—in terms of a "post-Beat" poetics of image and pun. The image is manifested in the way that Pausanias encountering Lerna mirrors Olson (as Maximus) in Gloucester; but the Pun is located in the proper name as found in the plaques—both the specificity or localism of each inscription and their crossing of time and space. These plaques may look old, but they are actually new and set up to act as mediators for the past in the present at the same place. In fact, through the realization that these plaques *are* Pausanias's tablets, and, by extension, Gloucester *is* Lerna, Olson literally enacts his "post-Beat" poetics of image and pun; of tope/type/trope, as place (Lerna/Gloucester), its "attending circumstance" of language (plaques/tablets) and the image generated in the recognition of a localized, yet global, history. Indeed, classical scholars share the vision of Pausanias out of which Olson generated his "post-Beat" poetics, highlighting the "complex articulation of a cultural identity" in his work, with "the local and the global in constant and productive tension," and noting the "juxtaposition of the very distant past with the more recent past," as well as Pausanias's roles "as observer, evaluator and commentator" (Goldhill 2010, 67).

With the example of Pausanias at the forefront of Olson's Second Sophistic, we see Plutarch, and Maximus of Tyre as well, as more than just "sources" or ways for him to escape the "Western box," but as figures through whom to articulate a poetics of localism that is at one and the same time heavily contingent on the Beats but also importantly distinct from them. It is only through the dynamic between Olson and the Beats, especially Ginsberg, in their formulations of poetics and history, that the full force of Olson's engagement with a particularly key moment in classical antiquity (the Second Sophistic) can be understood.

Bibliography

Allen, Donald. 1999. *The New American Poetry, 1945–1960.* Rev. ed. Berkeley: University of California Press.

Bakker, E. J. 2002. "The Making of *History*: Herodotus' Historiês Apodexis." In *Brill's Companion to Herodotus,* edited by Egbert J. Bakker, Irene J. F. de Jong, Hans van Wees Bakker, 3–32. Leiden, Netherlands: Brill.

Belgrad, Daniel. 1998. *The Culture of Spontaneity: Improvisation and the Arts in Postwar America.* Chicago: University of Chicago Press.

Berrigan, Ted. 2005. "The Art of Fiction: Jack Kerouac." In *Conversations with Jack Kerouac,* edited by Kevin J. Hayes, 51–81. Jackson: University of Mississippi Press.

Bram, Shacher. 2004. *Charles Olson and Alfred North Whitehead: An Essay on Poetry.* Lewisburg: Bucknell University Press.

Clark, Tom. 2000. *Charles Olson: The Allegory of a Poet's Life.* Berkeley: North Atlantic Books.

Davenport, Guy. 1973–74. "Scholia and Conjectures for Olson's 'The Kingfishers.'" *boundary 2* 2.1/2: 250–62.

Frazer, J. G. 1913. *Pausanias's Description of Greece,* vol. 1. 2nd ed. London: Macmillan.

Fredman, S. 2009. *The Grounding of American Poetry: Charles Olson and the Emersonian Tradition.* Cambridge: Cambridge University Press.

Ginsberg, Allen. 1963. *Reality Sandwiches.* San Francisco: City Lights Publishers.

Ginsberg, Allen and Louis Ginsberg. 2001. *Family Business: Selected Letters Between a Father and Son.* New York: Bloomsbury.

Goldhill, Simon. 2010. "What Is Local Identity? The Politics of Cultural Mapping." In *Local Knowledge and Microidentities in the Imperial Greek World,* edited by Tim Whitmarsh, 46–68. Cambridge: Cambridge University Press.

Maud, Ralph. 1998. *What Does Not Change: The Significance of Charles Olson's "The Kingfishers."* Cranbury, NJ: Fairleigh Dickinson University Press.

———. 2003. *Poet to Publisher: Charles Olson's Correspondence with Donald Allen.* Vancouver: Talon Books.

———. 2008. *Charles Olson at the Harbor.* Vancouver: Talon Books.

———. 2010. *Muthologos: Charles Olson Lectures and Interviews.* Vancouver: Talon Books.

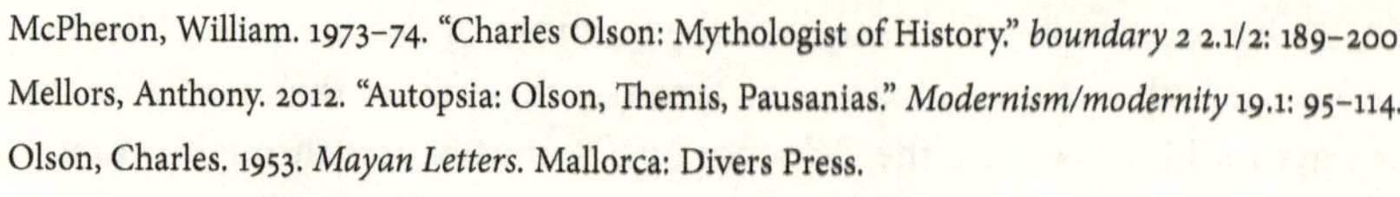

McPheron, William. 1973–74. "Charles Olson: Mythologist of History." *boundary 2* 2.1/2: 189–200.

Mellors, Anthony. 2012. "Autopsia: Olson, Themis, Pausanias." *Modernism/modernity* 19.1: 95–114.

Olson, Charles. 1953. *Mayan Letters*. Mallorca: Divers Press.

———. 1983. *The Maximus Poems*. Ed. George Butterick. Berkeley: University of California Press.

———. 1997a. *Collected Poems*. Ed. George Butterick. Berkeley: University of California Press.

———. 1997b. *Collected Prose*. Ed. Donald Allen and Benjamin Friedlander. Berkeley: University of California Press.

Schlesinger, Kyle. 2011. *Charles Olson at Goddard College, April 12–14, 1962*. Victoria, TX: Cuneiform Press.

Varner, Paul. 2012. *Historical Dictionary of the Beat Movement*. Lanham, MD: Scarecrow Press.

von Hallberg, R. 1973–74. "Olson, Whitehead, and the Objectivists." *boundary 2* 2.1/2: 85–111.

———. 1978. *Charles Olson: The Scholar's Art*. Cambridge, MA: Harvard University Press.

Whitmarsh, T. 2005. *The Second Sophistic*. Oxford: Oxford University Press.

AFTERWORD

"Standing at a Juncture of Planes"

NANCY M. GRACE
AND JENNIE SKERL

The essays in *Hip Sublime: Beat Writers and the Classical Tradition* introduce a critical perspective overlooked by decades of Beat scholarship. While the Beats' debt to romantic, modernist, and American literary traditions, and their exploration of non-Western literatures and cultures, especially Buddhism, have been acknowledged and variously explored by critics, the engagement of Beat writers with the Western classical tradition has been neglected, no doubt because of the dominance of Beat authors' persistent criticism of post–World War II mainstream culture in tandem with their equally persistent rhetoric of eschewing a hegemonic past. This volume seeks to address this rich and sometimes fraught topic, attempting for the first time a sustained, focused exploration of the ways in which Beat writers appropriated, imitated, revised, and recreated Greco-Roman texts and authors as part of their postwar avant-garde project. In essence, *Hip Sublime* exemplifies what the poet Diane di Prima identifies as the ability of Western poets to recognize "a precision of lineage," as they sought to address this lineage in their art and lives. In effect, as di Prima explains in her book on the influence of H.D. (Hilda Doolittle) on Robert Duncan's poetry, the poem "stands at a juncture of planes—of whatever lineages have become manifest at a given point" (2011, 3).

Hip Sublime raises several issues pertinent to Beat Studies as a disciplinary subfield. The most obvious question arising from the particular authors represented in the collection is "who is Beat?" The answer is vexed (it has certainly been repeatedly contested), but suffice it to say that Beats were a loosely affiliated arts community which interacted with the other avant-garde poetry movements after World War II, such as Black Mountain, San Francisco Renaissance, and the New York School. The writers discussed in this volume include those who identified as Beat (Allen Ginsberg, Jack Kerouac, William S. Burroughs, Gregory Corso, Diane di Prima, Philip Whalen, Ed Sanders), those who were associated with Black Mountain College and who interacted with the Beats (Robert Duncan, Robert Creeley, Charles Olson), mentors and supporters from an older generation (Kenneth Rexroth, Olson, Lawrence Ferlinghetti), and one who rejected the label but is seen as allied with the Beats through his public readings and publication history (Charles Bukowski).

The question of who is a Beat is intricately bound to a general aesthetic philosophy associated with the "New American Poetry," a rubric identified by Donald Allen in his groundbreaking 1960 anthology by that name and in the updated and expanded 1982 volume, *The Postmoderns*. All of the authors discussed in this volume, except Bukowski, are included in Allen's two anthologies. Allen and George Butterick's preface to *The Postmoderns* sums up an aesthetic defined as the postwar avant-garde in a poetic line traceable to Pound, Williams, and Olson. Olson's "Projective Verse," published in the 1960 volume, functioned as a manifesto for open, spontaneous form, "composition by field," with immediate perception, breath, and the syllable replacing traditional figures, meter, and verse forms. Allen and Butterick also note that the new American poets, who questioned received literary, political, and sexual values—and sometimes the premises of Western civilization itself—shared an oppositional stance. These writers conceived of themselves, or were perceived by others, as outsiders, including academic outsiders.

While oppositional in many respects, Beat writers were not uniformly anti-intellectual or anti-academic in their craft and their stance. In fact, as *Hip Sublime* subtly suggests, the oppositional aesthetics pursued and propagated by Beat writers was at its most radical, that is, at its root, a modern iteration of a dialectical stance that has for millennia propelled new literary forms and theories, especially through an almost *de rigueur* obligation of younger artists to repudiate their mentors even as they internalized and renovated their works. Many Beat writers, as this volume shows, carefully studied literary history—both through formal education and as autodidacts. One might even say that those who were formally educated (and some at elite institutions—Burroughs at Harvard, Kerouac and Ginsberg at Columbia, Ferlinghetti at the Sorbonne, Snyder and Whalen at Reed College) were also lifelong learners as they pursued their own reading and research, including the classics, to develop their poetic and social resources and their own versions of the classics. In effect, many Beat writers created an alternative academy and therefore a foundation for alternative authority. Philip Whalen's comment on the academy characterizes many of the Beats: "[I] have assumed its function in my own person, and in the strictest sense of the word—*academy*: a walking grove of trees" (Whalen 2007, 153).

All of these writers were individualistic in their response to the classics, which was very much an idiosyncratic process in each case. What they had in common was a post–World War II poetics, not an intellectual approach to the classics. For instance, the most important precursors or models for Beat writers were not the ancient writers but rather modernists who demonstrated how a "modern" could employ the classics as a tool of the avant-garde project. Modernists—especially Joyce, Pound, H.D., and Williams—followed by older contemporaries including Rexroth and Olson, served as important textual mentors for many Beat writers. Joyce's *Ulysses* was an influential model for "the mythical method," and thus the narrative works discussed in this collection—both prose and poetry—use the structure of journey, quest, *katabasis*, and *anabasis* drawn at least in part from classical epics and myths. This strategy characterizes not only the work of Ginsberg, Kerouac, and Burroughs, where this structure is the focus of several essays in the volume, but also Sanders and di Prima. For the poets, Pound and H.D.'s imagism remained powerful, and the *Cantos* were a model for the modern long (or epic) poem. The long poems of midcentury free verse continued to employ a modernist collage of fragments that combined epic and lyric. Thus, the classical genres of epic, lyric, and epigram persisted in avant-garde configurations.

However, for many Beat writers (and other post–World War II writers, as well), T. S. Eliot's "The Waste Land" signaled through its heavy reliance on dozens of cultural and linguistic traditions—including classics such as Ovid's *Metamorphoses*—the return of poetics to the academics, to those, as Terrence Diggory contends, with "the knowledge to translate Eliot's many foreign phrases and explicate his mythical allusions" (Diggory 2014, 60). Eliot, for better or worse, became the scapegoat for Beat rhetoric and practices that sought to approach the classics apart from midcentury "classicism," which promoted a "great books" curriculum as the foundation of mainstream postwar values.

On a broader level, the anti-Eliot trend coincided with the diminution of the Greco-Roman classical curriculum as the foundation of Anglo-American education, a reality that classicists addressed. Recognizing this slippage, for example, the editors of *Arion*, a long-standing classical studies journal published by Boston University, distributed a classics questionnaire to major literary figures in the early 1960s, including luminaries such as Allen Ginsberg, Robert Graves, Marianne Moore, Robert Fitzgerald, Kenneth Burke, Iris Murdoch, John Updike, and René Wellek. The questions posed repeatedly reinforced a need to assess and affirm the role of classical studies post–World War II, as the following three illustrate: "Claims are still made for a living continuity between Graeco-Roman civilization and our own. If these claims are anything more than familiar cultural gestures, at what levels, and in which contexts, can they still valuably be made?"; "How far can the classics live meaningfully within our culture, and our literature, when so few people have a real command of Greek and Latin?"; and "What has been the effect of the *Musée Imaginaire* metaphor by which Greece and Roman are no longer two uniquely privileged, paradeigmatic father cultures, but simply two cultures among many? Liberating, or destructive?" (Anon. 1964, unnumbered foldout sheet attached to back cover). In such a context, Beat writers confronted and were confronted with the paradoxical power of the classicism of the era: a former formidable giant to be both respected and depreciated—a tradition that they, to varying degrees, opposed and yet drew upon as an impetus for their individual attempts to reclaim, rediscover, rewrite, or reject. Michael Pfaff's discussion of Ginsberg and Catullus in this volume provides a trenchant example.

As the *Arion* questionnaire indicates, Beats' classical materials were also mediated by a historical series of translations, allusions, and precedents in English literary traditions, and they themselves are "translators" in their turning to the Greeks and Romans to support an avant-garde aesthetic and a countercultural ethical stance. As this volume demonstrates, to these ends certain Beat authors attempted a careful translation of sense and sometimes meter, while others concentrated on creating free or loose translations. Others engaged in imitations and/or adapted subject matter, paradigms, and attitudes from classical traditions not only to reinterpret the classics but also to support their own postwar values through critique and/or appropriation of the Greco-Roman heritage. One striking and revealing pattern that we see across the essays here is the choice of a classical writer as a precursor, model, guide, and companion: Sappho, Catullus, Pindar, Maximus of Tyre, and Pausanias emerge as especially significant. In each case, the classical author is embedded in the contemporary poet's vision and craft, and refigured as part of the author's countercultural critique. The volume also reveals the persistent relevance of the Greco-Roman legacies, even among those who have not pursued formal academic study of the field. Allusions to gods and goddesses, authors such as Sappho and Homer, along with many others, appear like cultural touchstones used almost instinctually as a lingua franca and are interpreted with equal facility. These essays, then, reveal that Beat engagement with the classics was complex and far from superficial. They grappled with these precursors and how they have been traditionally received. If they didn't reject, they sought to fuse with their outsider perspective.

Not all writers associated with the Beat generation aligned themselves with Greco-Roman traditions, whether implicitly or explicitly: among those who did not were Joyce Johnson, Bonnie Bremser Frazer, LeRoi Jones (Amiri Baraka), and Hettie Jones. We would also be remiss if we did not point out that some of the authors addressed in this volume were not as enamored with that particular lineage as were others. Although Kerouac's early creative efforts, such as *Orpheus Emerged*, rely thematically on the classical figures of Orpheus and Prometheus as models of artistic identity, his Duluoz Legend does little with explicit classical history and myth except through his Joycean language-based experiments and more general quest narratives. In the case of Burroughs, although the quest is present in his early work, he undercuts its authority by avoiding narrative closure, and, in his later experimental fiction, he disrupts all narrative to deconstruct the Western humanist subject. It is worth speculating that certain Beat writers—and here we refer to Ginsberg as a prime example—may have initially turned to classical models as a way to legitimize themselves as literary talents recognizable to those with already established literary credibility, a move that should not be surprising considering the power of mainstream academic curricula, even among members of a counterculture. With respect to Ginsberg, Diana Trilling, in her insightful close reading of his complex personality, suggested that the young poet "wish[ed] to meet the teacher on equal ground," that is, "to propose an alliance between the views of the academic and poet-rebel, the unity of a deep discriminating commitment to literature which must certainly one day wipe out the fortuitous distance between . . . pupil and teacher" (2003, 92). Later in his career, Ginsberg decentered classical allusions in a broader field of cultural traditions drawn from Eastern and other ancient cultures. A similar decentering takes place in the later poetry of Whalen and di Prima, who were drawn to non-Western thought as a corrective to the dominance of the Greco-Roman legacy.

Finally, an intriguing issue raised by this anthology relates to the nature of Beat production as multivalent, logically leading to the question of how to approach the study of Beat texts from a similar perspective. *Hip Sublime* illustrates the way scholars from different fields approach this issue. In this collection, we see in operation translation work, interestingly from two perspectives, that of the Beat artist (e.g., Kenneth Rexroth and Robert Creeley) and that of the literary critic (Gideon Nisbet and Nick Selby, respectively). Close readings focused on textual forms dominate, exemplified by Loni Reynolds's quasi-Proppian structuralist interpretation of William S. Burroughs's narratives. We also see the standard cross-disciplinary practice of literary critics, which is to integrate close readings with attention to composition and cultural histories along with the application of theoretical tools from other disciplines—in this case not only various features of the histories and mythologies of the Greco-Roman periods but also crosscultural religious practices and beliefs, along with feminist philosophies, linguistic methods, and musical corollaries.

Most significantly, however, the collection combines various historical, linguistic, and literary approaches to further our understanding of the intersections between Western avant-garde practice and the cultural legacies of ancient Greece and Rome. It is a challenging process for scholars of both classics and Beat studies, to say the least, but *Hip Sublime* presents a balanced critical approach well suited to illuminating the complexities of Beat generation writing. In total, *Hip Sublime* has taken a crucial first step toward situating Beat artists and aesthetics within a rich literary tradition that, in the end, the writers themselves could never fully escape, even if this was, at times, exactly what they professed to do.

Bibliography

Allen, Donald M., ed. 1960. *The New American Poetry.* New York: Grove Press.

Allen, Donald M., and Butterick, George F., eds. 1982. *The Postmoderns: The New American Poetry Revisited.* New York: Grove.

Anon. 1964. "An Arion Questionnaire: The Classics and the Man of Letters." *Arion* 3.4: 6–100.

Diggory, Terence. 2014. "Why *The New American Poetry* Stays News." In *The New American Poetry Fifty Years Later,* edited by John R. Woznicki, 59–80. Bethlehem, PA: Lehigh University Press.

di Prima, D. 2011. *R. D.'s H.D.* New York: City University of New York Graduate Center.

Whalen, Philip. 2007. *The Collected Poems of Philip Whalen.* Ed. Michael Rothenberg. Lebanon, NH: Wesleyan Poetry Series.

Trilling, Diana, 2003. "The Other Night at Columbia: A Report from the Academy." In *The Beats: A Literary Reference,* edited by Matt Theado, 91–100. New York: Carroll and Graf. First published in *Partisan Review* Spring 1959: 214–30.

CONTRIBUTORS

Stephen Dickey is Senior Lecturer in the UCLA English Department. He teaches various courses in Shakespeare, the English Renaissance, and the Beat generation as well as introductory courses in poetry and drama. From 2002–16, Dickey served on the faculty of the Teaching Shakespeare Institute, a program for high school teachers from across the country, held biennially at the Folger Shakespeare Library in Washington, DC. Recent publications include works on *Romeo and Juliet*, the *Henry IV* plays, and American interest in Shakespeare during the Civil War. In 2016–17, he curated *America's Shakespeare: The Bard Goes West* at the Central Library in Los Angeles.

Jane Falk recently retired as Lecturer in English Composition at the University of Akron. She has written on Beat avant-garde writing practices, on Beats and independent film, and on several Beat writers, including Joanne Kyger, Lew Welch, and Philip Whalen. Publications on Whalen include an appreciation of Whalen's *The Diamond Noodle* (Fish Drum Press, 2005) for *Continuous Flame*, a tribute volume to Whalen, and biographies of Whalen in the *Encyclopedia of Beat Literature* and the *Greenwood Encyclopedia of American Poetry*. In addition, she has published essays on Zen influences on Whalen's poetry in *The Emergence of Buddhist American Literature* (SUNY P, 2009) and on Whalen's writing from Japan in *The Transnational Beat Generation* (Palgrave Macmillan, 2012).

Richard Fletcher is an Associate Professor in the Department of Classics at The Ohio State University. His core research focus is on the intersection of literature and philosophy in ancient Rome, especially the works of the Platonist Apuleius of Madauros. He is the author of *Apuleius' Platonism: the Impersonation of Philosophy* (Cambridge UP, 2014) and is coeditor (with Will Shearin) of *The Oxford Handbook of Roman Philosophy*, forthcoming. He also works on the dynamic between classics and contemporary art through collaborations with artists, curating exhibitions, and writing the blog *Minus Plato* (minusplato.com). He is currently engaged in a multifaceted project about the way ancient sites are appropriated and reactivated by contemporary artists, exhibitions, and institutions.

Christopher Gair is Senior Lecturer in English Literature and Associate Director of the Andrew Hook Centre for American Studies at the University of Glasgow, Scotland. He is the author of *Complicity and Resistance in Jack London's Novels* (Edwin Mellen, 1997), *The American Counterculture* (Edinburgh UP, 2007), and *The Beat Generation* (Oneworld Publications, 2008) and is the editor of *Beyond Boundaries: C. L. R. James and Postnational Studies* (Pluto Press, 2006). He has edited editions of Stephen Crane's *Maggie: A Girl of the Streets* (Penguin Classics, 2000) and Jack London's *South Sea Tales* (Modern Library, 2002). He has published essays in journals, including *Modern Fiction Studies, Journal of American Studies, Western American Literature, Studies in the Novel,* and *Studies in American Literature,* and is founding editor of *Symbiosis: A Journal of Anglo-American Literary and Cultural Relations.* He is coeditor of *Beyond a Boundary at Fifty: New Critical Essays* (Duke UP, 2018).

Nancy M. Grace is Virginia Myers Professor of English at the College of Wooster. Her many publications on writers of the Beat generation include *Girls Who Wore Black: Women Writing the Beat Generation* (Rutgers UP, 2002), *Breaking the Rule of Cool: Interviewing and Reading Beat Women Writers* (U of Mississippi P, 2004), *Jack Kerouac and the Literary Imagination* (Palgrave Macmillan, 2007), and *The Transnational Beat Generation* (Palgrave Macmillan, 2012), which was coedited with Jennie Skerl. She edited *The Beat Review* from 2007–11 and is currently coeditor of *The Journal of Beat Studies,* as well as coeditor of Clemson University Press's new Beat Studies book series (both with Ronna C. Johnson).

Marguerite Johnson is Associate Professor of Ancient History and Classical Languages at the University of Newcastle, New South Wales, Australia. She is an interdisciplinary cultural historian of the ancient Mediterranean and a comparative cultural analyst. She is the coauthor (with Terry Ryan) of *Sexuality in Greek and Roman Society and Literature: A Sourcebook* (Routledge, 2005); coeditor (with Harold Tarrant) of *Alcibiades and the Socratic Lover-Educator* (Bristol Classical Press, 2012); and author of *Sappho* (Bristol Classical Press, 2006), *Boudicca* (Bristol Classical Press, 2012), and *Ovid on Cosmetics: Medicamina Faciei Femineae and Related Texts* (Bloomsbury, 2016).

Victoria Moul is Senior Lecturer in Latin Language and Literature at King's College, London. She works mainly on the relationship between neo-Latin, classical, and English poetry in the early modern period. Additional interests include the theory and practice of poetic translation and the reception and translation of classical lyric in modernist poets. She is the author of *Jonson, Horace and the Classical Tradition* (Cambridge UP, 2010) and editor of *The Cambridge Guide to Neo-Latin Literature* (Cambridge UP, 2017). She has published a large number of chapters and articles on classical, neo-Latin, and English poetry; her next monograph, *The Other Muse: Latin and English Poetry in Britain, 1550–1700,* is forthcoming with Cambridge UP.

Sheila Murnaghan is the Alfred Reginald Allen Memorial Professor of Greek at the University of Pennsylvania. She is the author of *Disguise and Recognition in the Odyssey* (2nd edition, Lexington Press, 2011); the coeditor of *Women and Slaves in Greco-Roman Culture: Differential Equations* (Routledge, 1998) and *Odyssean Identities in Modern Cultures: The Journey Home* (Ohio State UP, 2014); and the coauthor (with Deborah H. Roberts) of *Childhood and the Classics: Britain and America, 1850–1965* (Oxford UP, 2018). She is currently writing a commentary on Sophocles' *Ajax*.

Gideon Nisbet is Reader in Classics at the University of Birmingham. His recent research has combined two main strands: ancient epigram and classical reception. His recent book, *Greek Epigram in Reception: J. A. Symonds, Oscar Wilde, and the Invention of Desire, 1805–1929* (Oxford UP, 2013), studies how translators and popularizers in the later nineteenth century came up with ways of talking about Greek epigram that let them redefine ancient Greece as a social ideal for the present day.

Matthew Pfaff recently completed his PhD at the University of Michigan in Comparative Literature, where he has been a Lecturer in their Great Books Program. His dissertation concerned how American experimental poets after modernism turned to Greek and Latin texts as pretexts to explode the ideal of the classical tradition. He asks why and how "the classical" is a key site for poetic experiments by several generations of poets, including Louis Zukofsky, David Melnick, Allen Ginsberg, Jack Spicer, Charles Bernstein, and Susan Howe.

Loni Reynolds completed a PhD at Roehampton University in 2011 with a dissertation on the place of religion and spirituality in the works of the Beats, focusing particularly on William S. Burroughs, Allen Ginsberg, Jack Kerouac, and Gregory Corso. Recent publications include "'A Humane Yet Dark Tribute to Life': The Eucharist in the Work of Gregory Corso" (*Religion and Literature*, Spring 2016) and "'The Mad Ones' and the 'Geeks': Cognitive and Physical Disability in the Writing of Jack Kerouac and Allen Ginsberg" (*Journal of Literary and Cultural Disability Studies*, 19.2, 2015). Her current research interests include *kenosis*, negative theology, and the literature of the American South; she is also working on various fictional and poetic projects.

Ralph M. Rosen is Vartan Gregorian Professor of the Humanities and Classical Studies at the University of Pennsylvania. He publishes broadly in various areas of Greek and Roman literature, with special interests in comic and satirical literary genres, comparative poetics, ancient aesthetics, and ancient medicine, especially Galen. He is cofounder of the Penn-Leiden Colloquia on Ancient Values and coeditor of five published volumes (Brill) of essays from these events. His most recent book is *Making Mockery: The Poetics of Ancient Satire* (Oxford UP, 2007), and he has recently coedited *Ancient Concepts of the Hippocratic* (Brill, 2016).

Nick Selby is Professor of American Literature in the School of Art, Media, and American Studies at the University of East Anglia. He joined UEA in 2007, having taught previously at Swansea University and Glasgow University. He has a wide range of research interests, with poetry of the twentieth century at their core. As well as focusing on American experimental poetry, avant-gardism, and the issue of what constitutes an American poetics, his current interests also include transatlantic connections in British experimental poetry, ecocriticism, and theories of the ethics and politics of close reading. Nick's *Poetics of Loss in The Cantos of Ezra Pound* was published in 2005 (Mellen Press), and his *American Poetry since 1900* is due to be published by Edinburgh UP in 2018. He has published three other books, on Herman Melville, T. S. Eliot, and Walt Whitman, as well as numerous essays on topics concerned with American literature and culture.

Jennie Skerl retired as Associate Dean of the College of Arts and Sciences at West Chester University. She has published *William S. Burroughs* (Twayne, 1985), *William S. Burroughs at the Front: Critical Reception, 1959–1989* (coedited with Robin Lydenberg, Southern Illinois UP, 1991), *A Tawdry Place of Salvation: The Art of Jane Bowles* (Southern Illinois UP, 1997), *Reconstructing the Beats* (Palgrave Macmillan, 2004), and *The Transnational Beat Generation* (coedited with Nancy Grace, Palgrave Macmillan, 2012). She edited the Winter 2000 special issue of *College Literature* on Teaching Beat Literature and was a major contributor to the *Dictionary of Literary Biography* volume on the Beats (edited by Ann Charters, 1983). Jennie Skerl is a founding board member and former president of the Beat Studies Association.

Tony Trigilio is a Professor in the Department of English and Creative Writing at Columbia College Chicago. He is the author of *Allen Ginsberg's Buddhist Poetics* (Southern Illinois UP, 2nd ed., 2012) and editor of *Elise Cowen: Poems and Fragments* (Ahsahta, 2014). His most recent poetry collections include the book-length poems *Inside the Walls of My Own House* (Blaze VOX [Books], 2016) and *White Noise* (Apostrophe Books, 2013). His critical essays on Beat generation literature have been published in the *Journal of Beat Studies, Reconstructing the Beats* (ed. Jennie Skerl, Palgrave Macmillan, 2004), and *Girls Who Wore Black: Women Writing the Beat Generation* (ed. Ronna C. Johnson and Nancy M. Grace, Rutgers UP, 2002). He coedits *Court Green*, and he is an Associate Editor for *Tupelo Quarterly*. He edited *The Beat Review* from 2011–12. He is a founding member of the Beat Studies Association.

INDEX

Abelard, 189

academia: Beats outsiders to, 272, 275; Bukowski's absence from, 100; Ginsberg's rejection of, 75, 88–90, 92; Philip Whalen's attitude toward, 212. *See also* classicism; colleges and universities; education

Academy, of Plato, 212

Achilles, in the *Odyssey*, 31

Adams, John, 45n9

Adorno, Theodor, 45

adultery: and ethics, 128; poetics of, 12, 116–17, 120, 124, 127–29, 131; as principle of existence, 133, 135; and translation, 118

Aeneas, 11, 21, 59, 71

Aeneid, 16, 32; opening lines of, 42

aesthetics. *See* poetics

Agathias Scholasticus (Greek Anthology), 195

Agrippa, Cornelius, 243

alchemy, 228, 239, 242–43

Alcman, 5, 198

alcohol, 28–29, 31. *See also* drugs; opiates; yagé

Aldington, Richard, 185

alienation: in Burroughs, 58–59, 65, 67; in Joyce, 45–46; in Kerouac, 48–49; in Philip Whalen, 220

Alighieri, Dante, 16–17, 25, 31, 153; *Inferno*, 16, 28–29, 32; influence on Ginsberg, 22; influence on Kerouac, 25–26; as Pilgrim, 11, 28, 149

Allen, Donald, 44, 117, 145, 252, 254, 262, 264, 266, 272

Altieri, Charles, 90

American Dream, 48, 100

Ammianus (Greek Anthology), 196–97

anabasis: in Burroughs, 61, 71; necessary for katabasis, 16, 26, 28, 42–43, 50, 273. *See also* journey, epic; quest

Anabasis (Xenophon), 9, 11, 38–53

Anacreon, 75, 78n9, 85, 202

Anaximander, 197–98

Anchises, 21

Anonyma (Greek Anthology), 194–95, 198–99

Ansen, Alan, 39

Antikleia (*Odyssey*), 21, 60

Antipater of Sidon (Greek Anthology), 191, 202

Aphrodite, 244, 246

Apollo, 179, 237–38, 243, 263; and the lyre, 165

archery. *See* bow

archetypes, use of, 11, 46–47, 49, 240–41, 248. *See also* Jung; myth

Ares, 236

Ariadne, 244

Aries, 235–36

Arion (journal), 74, 273–74

Aristophanes, *Frogs*, 29, 32

Aristotle, 220–22

atomic bomb, 15–16, 17n4, 31, 220; and hell, 34; Moloch as, 23
Auden, W. H., 211, 216
Ausonius (Greek Anthology), 189–90
authority: Beats' rejection of, 39–40, 100; cultural, 76–77
avant-garde: Burroughs as, 3, 55, 57; classics used by, 3, 273; and the Lower East Side, 11–12, 138–45, 148, 150–51; and Sappho, 138–39, 150–52, 155–56. *See also* beatniks; counterculture

Balfour, Ian, 92n20
Banes, Sally, 139n4
Barnstone, Willis, 146
Beat: definition and etymology of, 1–4, 15, 24, 100, 134–35, 142
beatniks, 138–39, 140, 148. *See also* Sanders, Ed
belatedness, cultural, 14, 254
Belgrad, Daniel, 140, 252, 253
biopower, 233, 239, 250
Blackburn, Paul, 116
Black Mountain College (Black Mountain poets), 73n1, 94, 139, 145, 163, 252, 253, 255, 272
Blake, William, 22
Bloom, Leopold (*Ulysses*), 45, 48, 52–53
Bloom, Molly (*Ulysses*), 52–53
bodies: female, 13–14, 231–32, 238, 248; as focus of art, 141; fragmentation of, 68; as limiting, 67; sexualized, 152, 156; and singing, 243; as site of cultural struggle, 143–44. *See also* gender; sexuality
bohemians, 85, 139, 149. *See also* avant-garde; beatniks; counterculture
bookstores: City Lights Bookshop, 99, 143; Peace Eye Bookstore, 143. *See also* publication; readings, public
Bosch, Hieronymus, 17
boundaries, violation of, 140–41, 143
bow, as symbol, 163, 175–77, 179, 218
Bowra, Maurice, 164, 168n12, 171, 198
brotherhood: Beats' quest for, 16, 24, 56, 60, 63, 66; of Catullus and Bukowski, 12, 97, 105–6
Brower, Reuben, 161
Buddhism, 13–14, 77–78, 210–11, 213, 216–18, 222–23, 226, 228, 231, 234–35, 242, 244–45, 246–50, 271
Bukowski, Charles, 2, 12, 97–113, 272; audience for, 103; Catullus imitated by, 97–113; Catullus mocked by, 102–3; Catullus read biographically by, 107–8; employment of, 100; Ginsberg mocked by, 103–4; homophobia of, 109–10; invective used by, 104–5; "the love poems of Catullus," 105–6, 107–8; as outsider, 99–100, 113; "red up and down," 108–9, 111; relations with Beats, 98–99; "to the whore who took my poems," 104–5, 111; "what have I seen?," 100–102; on women, 107–9
Bundy, Elroy, 161
Bunting, Basil, 168n12
burials, 27–28
Burroughs, William S., 2–3, 9–11, 17, 32, 55–71, 99, 139, 143–44, 253, 272–73, 275; as avant-garde, 3, 55, 57; censorship of, 17; death imagery in, 60; as didactic, 70; education of, 57; as experimentalist, 11; *Junky*, 11, 55, 58–60, 68–69; *Naked Lunch*, 11, 17, 31, 55, 59, 67–71; *Queer*, 11, 55, 59, 63, 69, 70; self-mythologizing by, 34–35; style of, 11; *The Yage Letters*, 11, 55, 59, 62–67, 70–71. *See also* Vollmer, Joan
Butterick, George, 272
Bürger, Peter, 140, 141
Byron, George Gordon Lord, 39, 153

Cage, John, 228
Callimachus, 210, 215; as source for Catullus, 119
canons, cultural and literary, 3, 9, 12–13; and the avant-garde, 94n24; Beats' presence in, 2; Catullus' presence in, 74; and censorship, 74; Greek Anthology in, 186; personal, 13. *See also* education; Great Books curriculum
capital, cultural, 74, 78, 89–90. *See also* academia; canons; culture
Cardea (Roman goddess), 234, 239
Carmina Burana, 189, 190
Carroll, Paul, 12, 116
Cassady, Neal, 26n19, 32–33, 53, 87n17, 99–100
Catullus, G. Valerius, 2, 11–12, 274; and Bukowski, 97–113; as Bukowski's com-

rade, 98, 101–3, 106–9; Bukowski's mockery of, 102; *Carmen 6*, 102; *Carmen 11*, 97–98, 102, 111–12; *Carmen 14B*, 97; *Carmen 38*, 70, 81, 93; *Carmen 41*, 102; *Carmen 42*, 105; *Carmen 59*, 102; *Carmen 70*, 116, 119–24; *Carmen 76*, 108; Ginsberg's use of, 73–89, 104, 229, 274; homosociality in, 77, 83; invective used by, 104–5; Juventius poems of, 109–10; as outsider, 12, 112; as queer, 85; and Robert Creeley, 116–36; as Romantic, 80n10; Stoicism rejected by, 117, 126, 135; translation of, 74, 76–78, 98; verse forms of, 83–84

censorship: of Catullus, 93; Fugs' defiance of, 143–44; of the Greek Anthology, 186; of *Naked Lunch*, 17; within classics, 74. *See also* obscenity; sexuality

Cerberus, 29

Chapman, George, 9

Charon, 21–22, 24, 87n17, 103

China, poetry of, 216–17; Kenneth Rexroth's interest in, 184, 193–94. *See also* Eastern culture

Circe, 27

City Lights Bookshop. *See* bookstores; readings, public

Cixous, Hélène, 239

classicism: detached from Greek and Latin, 77; hegemonic, 94; ideology of, 85; institutional, 75, 77, 85, 88–89, 92; oriental, 93. *See also* academia; colleges and universities; education

Clements, Paul, 100, 110–11

Cocteau, Jean, 64

Cocytus, 68

colleges and universities: Columbia, 32, 73n2, 89, 91, 100; Harvard, 4, 32, 264–65, 272; Naropa Institute, 4, 33, 243; New York University, 138, 144; Reed College, 13, 211–12, 223, 272. *See also* academia; education

Collis, Stephen, 163n6

comes: Catullus as, 98, 101, 113; meaning of, 98. *See also* brotherhood; Bukowski; Catullus

community: Buddhist, 222; Burroughs' quest for, 58–59, 64–65, 69–71. *See also* brotherhood

Connell, R. W., 111

consciousness, expansion of, 59, 63–64, 67. *See also* Buddhism; drugs; religion

Coolidge, Clark, 219

Cooney, Seamus, 99

Corso, Gregory, 2–4, 9, 38–39, 56, 264, 272; ambivalent toward antiquity, 6–7; birth of, 4–5; education of, 4, 32–33, 38–39; *Gasoline*, 4; "Greece," 6; *The Happy Birthday of Death*, 5; "Marriage," 5; surrealism of, 3–4

counterculture: Beats as, 118, 126, 274; and Burroughs, 55; and Ginsberg, 75, 88; of the Lower East Side, 156; Robert Creeley as part of, 116; Sappho as part of, 12, 139; and sexuality, 140–41. *See also* avant-garde; beatniks

Creeley, Robert, 2, 12, 116–36, 259–61, 264–65, 272, 275; as Beat, 118; "The Rain," 117, 135–36; "Stomping with Catullus," 116–17, 130; "The Whip," 120, 128, 129–31

crisis, as starting point of epic, 42, 47

culture: of containment, 118, 120; industrial production of, 49–50; popular, 49, 51, 142, 144. *See also* academia; canons; capital, cultural

Cummings, E. E., 15

cup, as image, 163, 172–74, 180, 204

Cupid, 165–66

Dadaism, 10n11, 228

dance, in Pindar and Robert Duncan, 167, 168n13, 171–72, 174–75

Dante. *See* Alighieri, Dante

Davenport, Guy, 262n8

Davidson, Michael, 86n12, n13, 94, 127, 217n14

Davie, Donald, 163n5

Deane, Seamus, 230

death: depictions of, 61–62; drugs identified with, 61–63, 68; in the Greek Anthology, 199–201, 204; in *Loba*, 234, 238, 240, 242, 245; personified, 196–97. *See also* katabasis; mortality

Dedalus, Stephen (*Ulysses*), 41, 45, 51–53

DeJean, Joan, 139

De Loach, Allen, 139

Delphi, 263–64

Demeter, 242

democracy, 7, 73–74

Demos, in Lawrence Ferlinghetti, 7

Descartes, René, 256
dharma, 246
Dickey, Stephen, 10n9, 11, 42n4, 49–50, 61, 69
Diggory, Terence, 140n4, 141, 273
Dionysus, as inspiration for the Fugs, 143
di Prima, Diane, 2, 13–14, 140, 226–50, 271–72, 275; "Ave," 231–32; Buddhism in, 234–35, 242, 244–50; eclecticism of, 228; education of, 227; *Loba*, 226–50; *R. D.'s H.D.*, 227; *The Tapestry and the Web*, 229
Divus, Andreas, 8–9
Dougherty, Sean Thomas, 142, 155
drugs: in Burroughs, 55, 58–59, 61–63, 65–68; identified with death, 61-63, 68; quest for, 61–65
dualism, negated, 237, 249. *See also* Buddhism
Dublin, in *Ulysses*, 46
Duchamp, Marcel, 140
Duluoz. *See* Kerouac, Jack
Duncan, Robert, 2, 13, 160–82, 215, 249, 259, 271; *Bending the Bow*, 177, 179; dance in, 167, 168n13, 174–75; imagery in, 163, 172–73; "Let Him First Drink of the Fountain," 179; *The Opening of the Field*, 160, 163, 170–71; "A Poem Beginning with a Line by Pindar," 160–68, 174–75, 178, 182; poetics of, 169–72, 175; "A Set of Romantic Hymns," 182; spirituality of, 160n2
Dylan, Bob, 100, 203

Eastern culture, as influence on Beats, 12–13, 74, 76, 87, 210–11, 216, 218, 223–24, 229, 248–49, 271, 275. *See also* Buddhism
eclecticism: in Beat poetry and arts, 142, 163; of Diane di Prima, 228, 237; of Ed Sanders, 144; in religion, 149, 154–55
ecstasy: quest for, 142, 152; vatic, 100. *See also* joy
Edmonds, R. G., 56, 57
education: of Allen Ginsberg, 78, 87, 89; Ancient Greek, 39; of the Beats, 1, 32, 104n22, 184–85, 272; in classics, 13, 39–41, 45, 73n2; of Diane di Prima, 227; of Gregory Corso, 4, 38–39; of Jack Kerouac, 32; of Kenneth Rexroth, 184–85; of Philip Whalen, 216; poetry as, 212–13, 223; Xenophon's role in, 40–41, 45. *See also* academia; canons; classicism; colleges and universities; Great Books curriculum; Greek language; Latin; New Paideuma
ego, in Buddhism, 245–46, 248
Eliot, T. S., 32, 160, 226, 245, 273
Emerson, Ralph Waldo, 49
Empedocles, 217
Eos, 214–15
Epicureanism, 132–33, 135
epigrams: in the Greek Anthology, 187, 191; as model for Philip Whalen, 215; origin and types of, 186, 196, 201
epitaphs, as poetic genre, 201–3
Erinna, 198
eros. *See* sexuality
Erskine, John, 73n2
ethics: Greek, 222; and love, 128–29; and poetry, 117, 128, 132, 134
Euripides: as influence on Corso, 7n6; H.D.'s revisions of, 187
Eurocentrism, 76n78. *See also* Eastern culture; orientalism
Eurydice, 35, 59, 61
Eve, 246
everydayness, and poetry, 129–31

Faas, Ekbert, 116
Falk, Jane, 13
Feinstein, Elaine, 252, 265, 266, 267
feminism; in Diane di Prima; and myth, 229, 231; and Sappho, 147. *See also* gender; masculinity; sexuality; women
Ferlinghetti, Lawrence, 4, 7–8, 10, 26, 39, 99, 143, 272
fidelity: marital, 118–19, 122, 124; poetic, 12, 104, 106, 117–19, 122, 124; to self, 127; in translation, 125
film, avant-garde, 142
Fitts, Dudley, 205
Fletcher, Richard, 10, 14
folktales, 56–57. *See also* Propp, Vladimir; quest
formalism, Ginsberg's attitude toward, 77, 89–90, 91n19
Foucault, Michel, 233
Fredman, S., 252n1
Free Speech Movement, 73, 141, 143

freedom: artistic, 2, 10, 75, 132, 141, 151, 166, 182, 252; quest for, 48, 50, 52, 62; social, 40, 152

Frye, Northrop, 46

Fugs, The, 141, 143

Gair, Christopher, 9–10, 11, 120n8, 127

Gaisser, Julia Haig, 98n5, 117, 119, 122n11, 133

Garcia Lorca, Federico, 19, 103

Garland of Meleager, 186, 190, 203. *See also* Greek Anthology

Gates, David, 94n24

gender: and Apollo, 237–38; and Buddhism, 235, 246; construction and refashioning of, 139, 147–48, 152, 156, 241–43, 245; and language, 239–40; in *Loba*, 230, 232, 234, 236–37; and myth, 238, 249; and poetry, 236; and spirituality, 13–14, 246. *See also* feminism; masculinity; sexuality; women

genre, constraints of, 1, 161, 273

ghosts, junkies as, 60–62, 69

Gibbon, Edward, 215

Gilgamesh, 4, 16, 33

Ginsberg, Allen, 1, 2, 3, 10, 11, 12, 17, 32–33, 42n4, 98–100, 102–3, 119, 139, 145, 160n2, 184, 228, 247, 253, 259, 260–61, 264–65, 269, 272–75; "After Reading Kerouac's Manuscript *The Town and the City*," 33–34; ambivalent toward classicism, 75; "Bible," 88; "The Big Beat," 87; "classical silence" of, 88, 92; as countercultural, 88; critical reception of, 89; education of, 78, 87, 89; on formalism, 77, 89–90, 91n19; and Greek love, 39; *Howl*, 11, 17–18, 22–25, 77, 86–89, 92–93, 119, 184, 204, 247, 264; *Indian Journals*, 92–93; "Kaddish," 88; katabasis in, 33–34; "Malest Cornifici tuo Catullo," 77–86, 88–89, 91n19, 92–93, 103–4, 229; mocked by Bukowski, 103–4; multiculturalism of, 75–76; obscenity trial of, 75, 184, 264; "Orient," 88; "oriental classicism" of, 93; "Plutonian Ode," 34; Senate testimony of, 75, 91n19; sexuality of, 75, 78, 86, 102–3; "Siesta in Xbalba," 34; "Stotras to Kali Destroyer of Illusions," 88; "A Supermarket in California," 11, 18–22, 24, 34, 102–3, 104; "White Shroud," 34; "Wichita Vortex Sutra," 90, 93

Gloucester, Massachusetts, 256, 267–68

goddesses, in *Loba*, 229, 234, 242, 249. *See also* gender; religion

Goldberg, Jonathan, 129

Goldhill, Simon, 268

Goya, Francisco, *Cupid and Psyche*, 163, 167

Grace, Nancy M., 2, 10, 13, 51n11, 56–57, 127

Grauerholz, James, 35n43

Graves, Robert, 212

Great Books curriculum, 9, 13, 32, 73, 89, 185, 211, 273. *See also* canons; education

Greece, Beats' visits to, 38–39

Greek-Americans, 38, 40–41

Greek Anthology: compilation and organization of, 186–87, 189–90, 192, 195, 200; death in, 199–201, 204; homophobia in translations of, 193n19; Kenneth Rexroth's translation of, 13, 184–207; reflecting Greece's doom, 201; translation history of, 192–93

Greek language: as impediment to translation, 193; Kenneth Rexroth's knowledge of, 193, 197–98, 202, 207; learning of, 40–41n2, 45, 77–78, 144, 161, 193, 211, 274; in Philip Whalen's poems, 213; Robert Duncan's use of, 163n7, 165. *See also* education; Latin

Greene, Ellen, 138n1

Gruen, John, 139

Guayaquil, 64–65

Gunn, Thom, 161n4, 169–70, 171, 180–81

Hades, 239–41, 245, 248; postwar America as, 25. *See also* Hell; katabasis; Persephone

Hadot, Pierre, 135

hands, as measures and signs, 128–29, 131, 133

Hardwick, Lorna, 138n2, 156

Hardy, Emma and Thomas, 153

Harrison, Jane Ellen, 13, 215, 220n20

Haydon, Benjamin Robert, 45

H.D., 9, 145, 185, 187, 227, 229, 249, 250n7, 261, 273

Hecate, 236, 239

Heidegger, Martin, 129

Helen, 236–37, 240

Hell: and the atom bomb, 34; Beat depictions of, 16–17, 25–27; in *Big Sur*, 26–27; gods of, 15–16; Harrowing of, 16; in *Howl*, 22–25; journeys through, 64; as lived experience, 31. *See also* Hades; katabasis

Heller, Michael, 161
Heraclitus, 179, 217–18, 220, 262–63
Hermes, 33, 43, 165, 179, 228, 243
hermeticism, 243–44. *See also* alchemy
Herodotus, 255–59
heroes: for Beats, 10n9, 15–18, 36; in Burroughs, 55–56, 59–61, 64, 65, 67, 69; defined, 58; epic, 9, 11, 21, 31, 46, 57–58, 61, 64, 69; epitaphs for, 201; female, 233, 247; in Ginsberg, 21, 102–3; in Kerouac, 25, 30–31, 48; literary. *See also* journey, epic; katabasis; quest
Herrigel, Eugen, 218
Hesiod, 5
Hieron of Syracuse, 162, 173
Hill, Walter, 45n9
history: and poetics, 253, 255–56, 264, 269; Philip Whalen on, 219–20
Hoffman, Abbie, 3
Holland, Brad, 193n19
Holmes, John Clellon, 3, 16–18, 265–66
Homer, 39, 41, 62, 210, 274; *Iliad*, 32, 41–42, 176, 219, 226; *Odyssey*, 2, 6n5, 7, 10, 16, 18, 21, 29n28, 31–32, 41–42, 46, 60, 62, 226, 229, 256; Sappho's challenge to, 147, 148; translations of, 8–9
homosexuality. *See* gender; sexuality
Horace (Q. Horatius Flaccus), 181–82
Horvath, Brooke, 152, 155
Hungerford, Amy, 92n21
hunting, imagery of, 232–33, 247

identity: construction of, 74–75, 85, 128; public, 77–78, 80, 86, 91n19, 92–93; queer, 75, 86
images, in Charles Olson's poetics, 266, 268. *See also* painting
imagism, 145, 185, 187–88, 273
immortality: literal, 215, 244–45; through poetry, 171
influence: Beat rejection of, 6n5; indirect, 52–53; and originality, 6; poetics of, 227
invective, Bukowski's use of, 101–2, 104, 106–7; Catullus' use of, 12, 101–2, 105, 110; and gender, 102, 112; and masculinity, 111–12
IT, Beat quest for, 126, 134. *See also* ecstasy; joy

jazz: Beats' affinity for, 253; as countercultural, 120, 121n10; in Robert Creeley's poetry, 120–21, 126–27, 135
Job, Book of, 249
Johnson, Leni, 102n19
Johnson, Marguerite, 12
Johnson, Ronna C., 127
Johnson, Samuel, 212
Jones, Hettie, 139
Jones, Le Roi, 140, 275
Jonson, Ben, 210
journey, epic, 11, 42–44, 66, 273. *See also* anabasis; katabasis; quest
joy, Beat quest for, 23, 48, 50, 135–36. *See also* ecstasy
Joyce, James, 6n5, 9, 11, 38, 42, 44, 51–53, 273; *Ulysses*, 41, 44–46, 51–53
Jung, Carl, 226, 233–34, 240–41, 244–45

Kane, Daniel, 140n4
katabasis, 11, 15–36, 56, 64, 69, 273; in Burroughs, 59–60, 68, 71; different types of, 16, 42, 47, 49; in Ginsberg, 18–24, 33–34; in Homer, 60; in Kerouac, 25–33, 43; and prophecy, 18; therapeutic function of, 17; in Vergil, 68. *See also* anabasis; journey, epic; quests
Keats, John, 8, 154, 227, 238, 242; "On First Looking into Chapman's Homer," 8–9
Kelly, Michael, 193
Kerouac, Jack, 2, 6n5, 9–11, 40, 77, 87, 100, 104, 118, 121n10, 134–35, 139, 142, 194, 204, 228, 246, 252–54, 259, 264–66, 268, 272–73, 275; addressee of "Malest Cornifici Tuo Catullo," 81; *Big Sur*, 18, 25–31, 35–36, 42, 46–53; *Doctor Sax*, 40, 46, 52; education of, 32; katabasis in, 25–33, 43; Legend of Duluoz, 26, 30–31, 39–40, 44–45, 47–53, 275; *Lonesome Traveller*, 42; as Maenad, 35; *Maggie Cassidy*, 40; mental health of, 26; myth in, 55–56; *On the Road*, 10, 30, 42–43, 47–48, 52–53, 57, 118, 126, 134, 258–59, 264–65; *Orpheus Emerged*, 18, 33; "Sea," 50–52; *The Subterraneans*, 11, 18, 26n19, 46; *Vanity of Duluoz*, 41; *Visions of Cody*, 41–42, 46–47
Khayyam, Omar, 41
Kitaj, R. B., 163n7
knowledge, quest for, 69, 216. *See also* education; Greek; Latin

Kristeva, Julia, 240
"Kubla Kahn" (Coleridge), 29–30
Kupferberg, Tuli, 143
Kurosawa, Akira, 11, 18
Kyger, Joanne, 212, 229

labyrinth, 241, 244; *Loba* as, 234, 239
language: American, 43; and expansion of consciousness, 45; and gender, 239–40; informal, 43, 53. *See also* meter; poetics; verse forms
Lardas, John, 76n6
Latin: Bukowski's ignorance of, 98, 104–5; Diane di Prima's use of, 228; Ginsberg's knowledge of, 77, 104; Philip Whalen's use of, 212–14, 216–17; in Rexroth's *Greek Anthology*, 188–90, 203; widespread knowledge of, 211, 274. *See also* colleges; education; Greek language
Laughlin, James, 188
Lerna, 267–68
Lesbia (Catullus), 97, 104, 106, 108
Leslie, Shane, 192
Lethe, 21–22, 87n17, 103
Libby, Anthony, 244
libraries, Bukowski's use of, 98n4. *See also* colleges; education
light, as symbol, 243–45; and birth, 245
Lilith, 237, 240
liminality, 28, 61, 71, 231, 236–37, 242
limits: bodily, 64, 66–67; of the self, 63, 71; transcendence of, 64
localism: of Charles Olson, 14, 255–62; and the creation of meaning, 180, 264; of Pausanias, 261
Loeb Classical Library, 73–74, 85, 202, 206, 213
London, 187
Lothian, Alexander, 192–93
Louys, Pierre, 205
love, in Robert Creeley, 121–22, 126–27
Lowell (Massachusetts), 31–32, 38, 40, 253; compared to Dublin, 44
Lowell, Amy, 145
Lowell, Robert, 15
Lower East Side (New York), 12, 139, 149–51, 227–29, 261
Lucian of Samosata, 212, 219n18. *See also* Second Sophistic
Lucretius (T. Lucretius Caro), 117, 128, 132–35
Luxorius (Roman poet), 189
lyre, as symbol of poetry, 163, 165, 174–76, 179, 218
lyric, history and theory of, 80n10. *See also* poetics

Mackail, John William, 186–87, 188, 190, 192, 193n18, n19, 199, 200, 201–2, 204
Mailer, Norman, 17, 143
Manhattan, 22, 24
Marchand, Suzanne, 76n7
margins: cultural, 12, 75, 78; philology of, 77. *See also* outsiders
Martial, 188, 189, 190, 205, 212, 215
Martinelli, Sheri, 99
Marx, Karl, 230n1
masculinity: in Catullus and Bukowski, 12, 110–11; construction of, 97; and invective, 111–12; and outsider status, 113. *See also* gender; sexuality
Masuzawa, Tomoko, 76n8
mater dolorosa, Sappho as, 149, 154–55
Maud, Ralph, 260, 262n8, 265
Maximianus (Greek Anthology), 189
Maximus of Tyre, 10, 14, 255, 256, 257, 263, 264, 274
McCarthy, Cormac, 45n9
McClure, Michael, 3, 212, 213
McNamee, Gregory, 205–6
Medusa, 239
Melville, Ronald, 135
mental illness, in Kerouac, 47, 52–53
Messerschmidt, James W., 111
meter, 51, 75, 100, 120–21, 126, 145, 272; in Catullus, 12, 38, 81–84; in Ginsberg, 78, 81–84, 89–90; in Robert Creeley, 122–23. *See also* language; poetics; verse forms
Mexico City, 62, 63
Milton, John, 23, 179n22
misogyny: of Bukowski, 111–12; of Catullus, 111–12, 125; of Nietzsche, 130. *See also* gender
modernism, literary, 3, 8, 11, 13, 15, 32, 39–40, 46, 51, 145, 160, 243, 271, 273
Moffeit, Tony, 228, 244
Moi, Toril, 241
Moloch, 23–24

Moore, Marianne, 15
mortality: acceptance of, 22; in Kerouac, 25, 27. *See also* death; katabasis
motherhood, in Diane di Prima, 232–33, 240–41, 245, 248
Moul, Victoria, 13
Murphy, Timothy S., 70
muses, in Diane di Prima, 230–33
mysticism, in Philip Whalen, 215–16. *See also* religion; spirituality
myth: of the American West, 47; of the Beats, 10, 15–16, 18, 22, 25, 31–32, 36, 56, 86, 118; as central for Diane di Prima, 227, 232; classical, 227–28, 233; feminist, 229, 231, 239; and gender, 229, 238–39, 242–43, 249; Ginsberg's creation of, 86; in Gregory Corso, 4–5; in Kerouac, 56–57; as lived experience, 226, 244, 249; Native American, 39; origins of, 215; in Pindar, 162; for the space age, 56, 59

Nadel, Alan, 120n8
Nagy, Gregory, 61n10
nature, humans' relation to, 43, 49, 50–51
nekyia: defined, 18; in Ginsberg, 18, 20, 34; inverted, 20, 34; in the *Odyssey*, 31; in Whitman, 20, 22
Nemo (*Loba*), 234–35, 241
neoteric poets, compared to Beats, 101, 118. *See also* Catullus
Nesbit, 229
New American Poets (*New American Poetry*), 73–75, 77, 94, 117, 132, 145, 252, 262, 264–65, 272
New Orleans, 61–62
New Paideuma (Whalen), 13, 216, 218–20, 223. *See also* academia; education; Greek; knowledge; Latin
New York. *See* Lower East Side; Manhattan
New York School, 139, 272
Nietzsche, Friedrich, 130
Nike, 6
Nisbet, Gideon, 13, 275
Nisetich, Frank, 161, 164, 168, 182
Norris, Frank, 48
nowness, as Beat aesthetic, 1, 6. *See also* spontaneity

obscenity, trials for, 17, 75, 184, 264. *See also* censorship
Odysseus, 11, 21, 28, 31, 59, 71, 213
Olson, Charles, 2, 10, 13, 14, 117n4, 128, 133, 145, 162, 171n16, 212, 220–21, 226–27, 232, 252–69, 272–73; "The Kingfishers," 262–64, 267; "Letter to Elaine Feinstein," 252; *The Maximus Poems*, 226, 252, 256, 259–60, 268; as pedant, 252–53; poetics of, 252; "Projective Verse," 252–54, 266, 272
Olson, Kirby, 4, 33
opiates, 58–59. *See also* alcohol; drugs
orientalism, 3, 75, 76n7. *See also* Eastern culture
Orlovsky, Peter, 77, 264
Orpheus, 11, 33, 59, 61, 64, 178, 275; and Gregory Corso, 4–5; as model for Beats, 33, 35
Ostriker, Alicia, 229
Ostwald, Martin, 222n22
outsiders: Beats as, 272; Bukowski as, 99
Ovid, 60–61, 234, 273; on Sappho, 146

Page, Denys, 13, 219
painting, and poetry, 170, 178. *See also* images
Palatine Anthology, 186
Parker, Douglass, 185
Parker, Holt, 146
Parthenon, 5
patriarchy: Apollo as voice of, 238; opposition to, 12, 147–48, 156, 230, 235–36, 239, 241, 250. *See also* feminism; gender
Pausanias, 14, 255, 257, 258–60, 262, 264, 265, 267–69, 274; localism of, 261. *See also* Second Sophistic
Paz, Octavio, 218n17
pearl tale (Gnostic), 56–57
pedantry, of Charles Olson, 252–54; of Philip Whalen, 212; in translation, 192, 193
Penelope, 59, 239, 244
Perelman, Bob, 93n22
performance, of poetry, 100, 221, 255–56. *See also* readings, public
Persephone, 30, 238–41, 245, 248
Petronius (G. Petronius Arbiter), 190, 205
Pfaff, Michael, 11–12, 104n22, 127, 229, 274

philology, Ginsberg's interest in, 78–79, 85. *See also* Greek; Latin

philosophy: and poetry, 227–28; in Rexroth's Greek Anthology translation, 197–98

Pindar, 13, 75, 274; and Beat poetics, 180; dance in, 167, 168n13; hostility to, 160; imagery and metaphor in, 163, 167–68; imitations of, 181; immortality bestowed by, 171; myth and politics in, 162; *Nemean 5*, 168; *Olympian 1*, 173, 180; *Olympian 2*, 176; *Olympian 7*, 173–74; *Pythian 1*, 161–62, 164; *Pythian 10*, 171; style of, 166–68, 181; translation of, 164–65

Plato, 220–23; on poetry, 236; *Symposium*, 222–23

Plutarch, 222, 255, 259, 263–64, 267, 269. *See also* Second Sophistic

poethics. *See* poetics, and ethics

poetics: of adultery, 127–29; of Allen Ginsberg, 75–77, 79, 83, 85–86, 92–94; Beat, 80, 117, 121, 131–32; of Charles Olson, 252, 265–66; countercultural, 127; of Diane di Prima, 226; and ethics, 117, 128, 132, 134; and history, 264, 269; of influence, 227; modernist, 160; post-Beat, 254–55, 265–66, 268; of Robert Creeley, 129; of Robert Duncan, 169–72, 175, 179; Sapphic, 144; spiritualist, 226. *See also* language; meter; verse forms

politics: Beats' engagement with, 3, 7, 9, 87–88, 92n21, 139–43, 148–49, 155, 160, 162–63, 180, 227, 243, 272; classics used in service of, 45n9; in Pindar and Robert Duncan, 160, 162–63

Pound, Ezra, 7–8, 145, 160, 162, 163n7, 166, 180, 185, 212, 214, 216, 223, 226, 228, 229, 252, 262, 272, 273

Presocratics, 197–98, 217, 220. *See also* Anaximander; Heraclitus

Priapus, 111–13

projective verse, 252–53

Projectivism, 232

Propp, Vladimir, 56–57, 58n7, 61, 65n14, 67, 275

prostitution, in Bukowski and Catullus, 101, 104–5, 106–7

Psyche, 165

publication, of poetry, 99, 140, 143. *See also* bookstores; readings, public

puns: in Charles Olson's poetics, 266, 268; in *Howl*, 23n12; in Kerouac, 52; in Philip Whalen, 213

quest: as Beat principle, 134–35; in Burroughs, 55–71; by heroes, 10–11, 58, 71; for joy, 134; by readers, 69–71; spiritual, 248. *See also* journey, epic; katabasis

Quinn, Kenneth, 119, 121

Rabelais, François, 41

Race, William, 164n9

readings, public, 118–19, 204–5, 255–57, 265, 267; 6 Gallery Poetry reading, 118, 184, 204, 210; Vancouver Poetry Conference, 259–60, 262, 264, 267

Reininger, Gustave, 39n1

religion: and gender, 13–14; innovative, 142, 149, 154, 156, 229; as inspiration for poetry, 182; syncretic, 149, 154–55, 248

Retallack, Joan, 132–33

Rexroth, Kenneth, 2, 13, 184–207, 210, 215, 216n13, 229, 272–73, 275; approach to translation, 191–92, 194; education of, 184–85; facts and truth in, 190–91; knowledge of Greek, 197–98, 202, 207; as modernist, 3; *The Phoenix and the Tortoise*, 185, 188–89, 206; as Rheinhold Cacoethes, 184n1, 204. *See also* Greek Anthology

Reynolds, Loni, 9–10, 11, 275

Reynolds, Margaret, 147

rhyme, Robert Creeley's use of, 121–24, 126. *See also* meter; verse forms

rhythm, Robert Creeley's use of, 116, 118–19, 120, 122–24, 125, 126–27, 128, 130, 133, 136. *See also* meter; verse forms

Rice, Wallace, 187, 188, 192, 194, 199

Richlin, Amy, 111

rites of passage, 28, 61. *See also* journey, epic; quest

Romanticism, as influence on Beats, 2, 32, 39, 75–76, 92n20, 144–45, 243, 271

Rome, in the Greek Anthology, 188–89

Rood, Tim, 40–41n2, 41n3, 45

Roshi, Richard Baker, 213

Rostovtzeff, Michael, 211

Ruffell, Ian, 202n28

sacrifice, human, 23, 27, 35

Sakall, Geraldine, 185
Sampas, Sebastian, 38, 39
samsara, 246
Sanders, Ed, 2–3, 12, 138–56, 229, 272; eclecticism of, 144; *Fuck You/A Magazine of the Arts,* 141, 143; *Poem from Jail,* 142; role in the avant-garde, 142–43; "Sappho on East Seventh," 12, 144–45, 148–54; *Tales of Beatnik Glory,* 12, 138–39, 144, 147–48
San Francisco, 43, 47–48, 81, 83, 104, 118, 196, 214, 220, 231
San Francisco Renaissance, 73n1, 94, 145, 210, 272
sangha, 222. *See also* Buddhism
Sappho, 12, 138–56, 193, 229, 231, 274; associated with the Virgin Mary, 146, 149, 154–55; biographies of, 107–8, 152; constructions of, 138–39, 145–46, 156; eros in, 153; as exemplum, 138–39; as goddess, 149–50; as icon, 147; as lesbian, 146–47; as *mater dolorosa,* 149, 154–55; modernist imitations of, 145; as muse, 148, 149; as myth, 156; *Poem 1,* 149; *Poem 16,* 147–48; *Poem 118,* 149; in Rexroth's Greek Anthology, 190; as teacher, 146, 149–54; translation of, 144, 150–51
Schelling, Andrew, 212
Schjeldal, Peter, 140
Schlesinger, Kyle, 255, 259
Schumacher, Michael, 77, 78, 91n19
Scylla and Charybdis, 213
sea: as goal, 42; and modernity, 50–51; as monster, 48; as mother, 41, 46, 48, 51; as nature, 49; as symbol, 43, 49; and transcendence, 48; in *Ulysses,* 41, 46; as utopian promise, 43–44
Second Sophistic, 14, 254–55, 259–60, 263, 265, 269
Selby, Nick, 12, 275
self: limitations of, 71; as prison, 63
Sexton, Anne, 229
sexuality: Bukowski's attitudes toward, 109–10; in Burroughs, 53, 55, 59–60, 63, 68–70; in Catullus, 74, 85; construction of, 92; and counterculture, 141; as creative force, 152–53; and death, 69; freedom concerning, 94, 152; of Ginsberg, 75, 78, 86; Greek, 39; in the Greek Anthology, 193n19, 199; and invective, 109–11; Kenneth Rexroth's attitude toward, 196, 199; as liberating, 156; plants associated with, 151–52; Sappho as teacher of, 151–52; women's control of, 147. *See also* gender
shunyata, 246, 248, 249. *See also* Buddhism
Simonides, 81, 190, 202
Simplicius (Greek Anthology), 197–98
sincerity: in Catullus, 81; in Ginsberg, 76–77, 79–81, 84–85
Skerl, Jennie, 2, 10, 12, 55n1, 56, 69–70, 229
Skinner, Marilyn B., 112, 113
Smith, Dale, 231
Smith, Evans, 32
Snyder, Gary, 3, 134, 160n2, 210, 211, 216
Socrates, 220, 223
Solomon, Carl, 24
Sounes, Howard, 99
Spengler, Oswald, 75
spirituality: of Diane di Prima, 226; and gender, 246; in Kerouac, 43; and light, 243; of poetry, 243
spontaneity, as Beat value, 51, 53, 94, 118–19, 123, 126–27, 131–32, 160n2, 192, 195, 228, 272
Starr, Chester, 205
Stein, Gertrude, 41, 219
Steinmayer, Otto, 206
Stephenson, Gregory, 25n18
Stoicism, rejected by Catullus, 117, 126, 135
Strange Case of Dr. Jekyll and Mr. Hyde, The, 27
stream of consciousness, in Joyce and Kerouac, 46–47, 53
Stull, W. L., 55, 61, 63n12, 69
Styx, 21
subways, as site of katabasis, 23–24, 60
Sukenick, Ronald, 139, 143
Sulpicius Lupercus Servasius Jr. (Greek Anthology), 202–3
Sumerians, 221
surrealism, 3–4, 228
swerves, of atoms, 132–33
Symonds, John Addington, 198, 199
symposium: epigrams concerning, 191, 196, 199, 204; in Pindar, 174

Tacitus, P. Cornelius, 5–6

Talman, Ellen, 163n7
Tatum, W. Jeffrey, 113
Teiresias, Walt Whitman as, 18–19, 22
Tennyson, Alfred Lord, 29n28
Tesla, Nikola, 219
theft, in Bukowski and Catullus, 104–5
Thompson, George, 216
Thoreau, Henry David, 39, 49
Thoth, 165, 228
Thucydides, 257, 259
Thymocles (Greek Anthology), 203
Tithonus, 214–15
Toohey, Peter, 57–58
transcendence: in Diane di Prima, 231, 235, 250; quest for, 59–60, 63–69, 71; and the sea, 48
translation: adaptive, 192–93; of Catullus, 12, 79, 82–84, 116–19; compared to jazz, 118; fidelity in, 120–21, 125, 127; by H.D., 187; of Homer, 8–9; impressionistic, 193; Kenneth Rexroth's approach to, 191–92, 194, 205–6; of Pindar, 164–65; of Sappho, 144, 150–51; secondhand, 202; theories of, 79, 187, 191–92, 194, 273–75
travel, writing on, 10, 14, 24, 66, 258–62. *See also* journey, epic; katabasis; quest
Trell, Bluma, 138, 150n20
Trigilio, Tony, 13
Trilling, Diana, 275
Trocchi, Alexander, 265, 266
Tymnes (Greek Anthology), 190, 203
Tytell, John, 48

unconscious: classical, 42, 51; folktales as, 57
underworld: in the *Aeneid,* 61; Greek, 18, 21; in Ovid, 61; suburbs as, 9; types of, 17, 24, 42, 56, 60. *See also* katabasis; journey, epic; quest
Updike, John, 26n19
utopia, fantasies of, 50, 141–42

Vandiver, Elizabeth, 187n8
Van Gennep, Arnold, 28
Van Ghent, Dorothy, 10, 15–16, 17, 18, 22, 24, 25, 31, 32, 36, 56, 57, 58, 63
vatic voice, of poets, 100, 198, 245, 254–55
Vergil, 30–31, 60, 61, 149, 153; katabasis in, 68. *See also* Aeneas; *Aeneid*
verse forms, 5–6, 83–84, 89–90, 121, 247, 272. *See also* language; meter; poetics
Virgin Mary, 146, 149, 154–55, 231
Vollmer, Joan, 34–35, 46

Wagner Literary Magazine, 15
Waldman, Anne, 212, 219
Warhol, Andy, 142
Waring, Jimmy, 228
Warriors, The, 45n9
water, imagery of, 122, 133–36, 173–74
Watten, Barrett, 92n21
weariness, of the Beats, 134
weaving, as symbol of poetry, 175–76
Webb, Jon, 99
Webb, Louise, 99
Weinreich, Regina, 126
Weinstone, Ann, 248
Welch, Lew, 210, 211
West, American: as destination, 118, 134; mythology of, 47–48
Western culture: critique of, 220, 222–24, 227; and Eastern culture, 13, 92. *See also* education; Great Books; Greek; Latin
Whalen, Philip, 2, 13, 41, 210–24, 259, 261, 272–73, 275; education of, 211; "The Education Continues Along," 219; "Gradus ad Parnassum," 214; "The Greeks," 221; "Minor Moralia," 221–22; "Since You Ask Me," 211–12; "The Slop Barrel: Slices of the Paideuma for All Sentient Beings," 211; "Sourdough Mountain Lookout," 217; "To My Muse," 214–15. *See also* New Paideuma
Whigham, Peter, 112
Whiston, Paul, 100
Whitehead, Alfred North, 218n16, 256–57, 262, 263
Whitman, 9, 11, 39, 49, 103, 162; "Crossing Brooklyn Ferry," 19–22; as Ginsberg's hero, 34, 103; as Teiresias, 18–19, 22
Williams, William Carlos, 15, 17, 25, 145, 162, 166, 180, 181, 227, 272, 273
Wilson, Edmund, 15
Winkler, John J., 151n23
Wiseman, T. P., 112, 119n7
Wizard of Oz, The, 49
Wolfe, Thomas, 41n3, 42

wolves, as symbols, 232–33, 241, 249
women: among the Beats, 2; Bukowski's encounters with, 107–9; Catullus' invective toward, 102; as signs, 130. *See also* gender
Woolf, Virginia, 187
Wordsworth, William, 4
Worman, Nancy, 107n25
Wray, David, 80n10, 98n5
Wrighton, John, 133n20

Xenophon. *See* Anabasis

yagé, 62–67, 71. *See also* alcohol; drugs

Zen Buddhism. *See* Buddhism
Zeus, 7, 241
Zonas (Greek Anthology), 190, 204
Zukofsky, Louis, 93n22; as translator, 73n2, 80n10

CLASSICAL MEMORIES/MODERN IDENTITIES

Paul Allen Miller and Richard H. Armstrong, Series Editors

Classical antiquity has bequeathed a body of values and a "cultural koine" that later Western cultures have appropriated and adapted as their own. However, the transmission of ancient culture was and remains a malleable and contested process. This series explores how the classical world has been variously interpreted, transformed, and appropriated to forge a usable past and a livable present. Books published in this series detail both the positive and negative aspects of classical reception and take an expansive view of the topic. Thus it includes works that examine the function of translations, adaptations, invocations, and classical scholarship in personal, cultural, national, sexual, and racial formations.

Hip Sublime: Beat Writers and the Classical Tradition
EDITED BY SHEILA MURNAGHAN AND RALPH M. ROSEN

Ancient Sex: New Essays
EDITED BY RUBY BLONDELL AND KIRK ORMAND

Odyssean Identities in Modern Cultures: The Journey Home
EDITED BY HUNTER GARDNER AND SHEILA MURNAGHAN

Virginia Woolf, Jane Ellen Harrison, and the Spirit of Modernist Classicism
JEAN MILLS

Humanism and Classical Crisis: Anxiety, Intertexts, and the Miltonic Memory
JACOB BLEVINS

Tragic Effects: Ethics and Tragedy in the Age of Translation
THERESE AUGST

Reflections of Romanity: Discourses of Subjectivity in Imperial Rome
RICHARD ALSTON AND EFROSSINI SPENTZOU

Philology and Its Histories
EDITED BY SEAN GURD

Postmodern Spiritual Practices: The Construction of the Subject and the Reception of Plato in Lacan, Derrida, and Foucault
PAUL ALLEN MILLER